COLLECTION
DEVELOPMENT

COLLECTION DEVELOPMENT

The Selection
of Materials
for Libraries

William A. Katz
State University of New York at Albany

HOLT, RINEHART AND WINSTON
*New York   Chicago   San Francisco   Atlanta   Dallas
Montreal   Toronto*

Library of Congress Cataloging in Publication Data

Katz, William A
    Collection development.

    Includes index.
    1. Collection development (Libraries). 2. Book
selection. 3. Acquisition of non-book materials.
I. Title.
Z689.K32   025.2   79–19861

ISBN 0–03–050266–7

0 1 2 3 4 5 038 9 8 7 6 5 4 3 2

For Eric and Ilse Moon

PREFACE

THIS BOOK introduces the reader to the basic principles of collection development for the library. At the same time, the book will assist the librarian by suggesting specific aids and steps that can expedite the selection of materials.

At one time *selection* meant little more than a discussion of books, with a nod in the direction of periodicals. Now, even in the smallest, most remote library, selection implies casting a wider net. Today's library has not only books and magazines but is also likely to have or have access to recordings, films, microform, and a dozen or so other nonprint media. This is particularly true for special libraries and school media-center libraries, where much attention is given to finding the best ways of presenting information, regardless of format.

Selection, and the need for an overall view of what a library is and should be, is a major concern of all libraries. Among the conditions that make carefully planned selection an absolute necessity for survival are: declining budgets, expanding numbers of materials, lack of space, adoption of automation and computers, a new reliance on networks. Thus collection development must be mastered by the professional librarian.

It is impossible to divide theory from practice, a working philosophy of service from actual selection. This book is therefore concerned with both the philosophy and the practical aspects of selection, collection development, and collection analysis.

No single type of library is the focus. The method is to work from the general aspects of selection to the particular and, where useful, to demonstrate how a selection policy or action differs from one type of library to another. School, public, academic (including university, college, and two-year institutions), and, to a lesser extent, special libraries are considered. It is impossible to spell out particulars for each type of library, and while there are considerable differences in the operations of each, enough remains common ground for one to use this approach without undue emphasis on, or lack of attention to, any single type of library.

Several aspects of this book should be noted: (1) No effort is made to trace the problems of selection for particular subject fields. Subject study in depth is the province of specialized courses in library schools. Once such experts as Helen Haines could skillfully balance the general with the subject specialty in a single text, but that day is past. (2) Some attention has been given to acquisitions, and there are brief sections on ordering materials. Nevertheless, this is not the real purpose of this book, and the day-to-day activities of an acquisitions section or department are better handled elsewhere; there are one or two fine textbooks limited to acquisition alone. (3) Major forms are considered, but with varying emphasis. For example, full chapters are devoted to books and periodicals, but other forms (from microform to reports) are treated in shorter sections. Detailed discussion of the selection of government documents has been avoided because this is a separate study. Reference work is not included because I have considered this elsewhere.

No book of this length can be entirely satisfactory in scope to all readers, particularly to instructors who have favorite areas and topics that may have been only lightly examined here. But, to keep any book to a manageable length and still maintain balance, some areas must be severely cut or eliminated. Nevertheless, I believe this volume fairly covers most areas of interest in the field of collection development.

. . .

I am grateful to a number of people—and books. Among the latter I would place five titles in particular: Mary Carter, Wally Bonk, and Rose Magrill, *Building Library Collections*; Helen Haines, *Living with Books*; Stephen Ford, *The Acquisition of Library Materials*; Les Asheim, *The Humanities and the Library*; and Robert Broadus, *Selecting Materials for Libraries*. I believe there is limited duplication between my treatment and that found in these titles. Among the people I am grateful to are the following, who read the manuscript and made constructive suggestions: Fay M. Blake, University of California, Berkeley; Ron Blazek, Florida State University, Tallahassee; Robert Broadus, University of North Carolina, Chapel Hill; Arthur Curley, Detroit Public Library; James K. Foyle, University of Denver; Elizabeth Futas, Emory University, Atlanta; Richard Gardner, University of California, Los Angeles.

A special word for Eric Moon and Lawrence Clark Powell; both did much to inspire me.

W.A.K.

CONTENTS

FINAL ⑦ *Ordering Books*   155

8 *Periodicals*   178

Part One

SELECTION: INTRODUCTION

I

The Philosophy of Selection

Selection of materials for a library is an exciting challenge. It requires sagacity, adroitness, and attention to people's needs for everything from books and periodicals to films and recordings. It is a curiously rewarding professional assignment, and while no one is ever completely satisfied with the results, it is rarely dull.

The librarian who chooses material for individuals is a media czar whose income may be less than that of the television mogul but whose range of choice is more impressive. Also, selection is fun in that, if nothing else, it gives the librarian a first chance to examine most books, magazines, recordings, and films—a bonus that is one of the secret joys of being in selection.

Among the attributes you need to select materials is a substantial tolerance for work and an extremely flexible attitude about people's perception of their needs. You are in a position to enliven and enrich the lives of the people you serve, and, in some cases, to assist them in their daily effort simply to survive. This is a serious responsibility that requires an equally consistent knowledge of books, films, periodicals, and other forms of communication. You must be able to say what is best—and why and for whom.

This also requires some affection for people. It is not possible to select a book solely on the basis that it is "good," without a concept of potential readers. You must understand not only why people come into your library but also why they do not. Further, it is imperative to know both what people do or do not find in the library and to what uses they put the information, the recording, the magazine. In other words: Is the library and the materials you have selected for it really of importance to people?

The focal point of selection is the book or the film or whatever the users of your library require, but there are related questions of budget, space, reaching nonreaders, and scores of other constraints that modify and govern the selection process.

It is possible and advisable to take a dispassionate view of selection. Still, on occasion a strong feeling should be generated by the notion of selecting materials for your fellows. One can make too much of the spirit of selection, but commitment to the importance of the whole process is crucial. Few tasks so nicely combine the intellectual with the emotional, action with visible advance in improvement of both yourself and those for whom you are selecting materials.

This is not to suggest there is a consensus about the precise attributes of the ideal selector, bibliographer, acquisitions librarian—or whatever term is used to describe the person who selects for the library. While one may take an overall view of selection, there is going to be some disagreement about emphasis.

Professionalism and Selection

Those who work in library selection fall roughly into one of two camps. One group, strongly involved with books and other print materials, resists any effort to make a science of selection. For them selection is an almost intuitive process whereby the expert knows what is best for the community served. True, they do follow some rules, but on the whole they are likely to shrug off complicated formulas for collection development and selection.

At the other extreme are the "library scientists" who endeavor to objectify the whole selection process. This group's argument is that, given enough data, a model can be constructed whereby selection may be predetermined. Obviously it is not that simple, and the selector as artist would term it another effort to quantify what is essentially a human process.

Actually, most librarians take a stand somewhere in between—leaning, to be sure, toward the artist in the process. (Primarily this is due less to any hostility toward science than to failure to decipher the complicated formulas for selection put forth by the scientists.) In this book we recognize that both approaches have much to offer.

The whole concept of professionalism is tested on the selection battle line. The professional can claim to be the person in a position to evaluate and monitor the needs of the public served. As one librarian put it:

Who but a librarian with previous training and experience can to an extent anticipate what is likely to be required and select a basic stock at the required level and degree of comprehensiveness which can be expanded as user demand dictates?[1]

Selection and Type of Library

While different types of library have developed to meet different needs, there is a consensus that public, academic, school, and special libraries are all concerned with acquisition, organization, and provision of efficient access to materials. It is quite possible to concentrate on the problems of a public

[1] Ella McNeill, "Book Selection Policy," *Assistant Librarian, March* 1978, p. 30.

library while pointing the way to solution of similar problems in other kinds of library.

Over a lifetime, people use a number of libraries. Almost everyone comes in contact with public and school libraries, and through cooperative schemes users may draw on resources of academic and special libraries. The inter-reliance of various types of library is illustrated in adult independent learning programs. While adults will use libraries in colleges and universities, they may go beyond the traditional campus boundaries. In New York state in 1977, for example, a graduation ceremony was held in a public library for eight students who had completed their degree programs after three years of study entirely at that library.

FINANCIAL PROBLEMS

The single most important problem confronting all libraries going into the 1980s is lack of funds. Allocations required to meet traditional needs are being cut, and there is less and less available for experimental and new programs. Even fairly well-off libraries have had to consider measures to reduce expenditures to keep up with inflation.

Nationally it is estimated that about $2.4 billion was spent for all libraries in the United States in 1977. The National Inventory of Library Needs, an objective national survey, indicates $8.7 billion now needed. While most of this should be spent on school libraries, academic libraries require at least another $621 million a year.

Library Journal now has a regular column on library finance, and it is dismal reading. Almost everywhere budgets are being cut, or at least not being increased to meet the problem of inflation; this is true for all types and sizes of library. In 1978–1979, for example, some $2 million was cut from the Philadelphia Free Library's budget. In New Jersey there is a 5 percent cap on annual municipal budget growth, while California has sought to cut many library budgets.

At the same time the cost of books and periodicals has increased from 80 to as much as 200 percent over the past ten years. And even where appropriations have grown, inflation has cut into the book budgets. For example, in Boston the book budget has been cut from $1.1 million in 1976 to $796,000 in 1978–1979.

All of this means substantial changes in selection policies. It has also resulted in the development of a new semiscientific accounting approach to selection and acquisitions known variously as book collection development procedures, collection evaluation, collection building, and acquisition rate models. (Many of these procedures are considered in Chapter 3.) No matter what it is called, the selection process has now become an almost desperate method of simply trying to stretch the budget, to save the library. There are no pat solutions, although almost everyone is agreed that there are three basic roads to salvation: (1) Federal funding, which is becoming more and more important; the 1979 White House Conference on Libraries was concerned primarily with the pros and cons of government aid to libraries. (2) Interdependence, networks, interlibrary loan, automation, and the like are seen as likely ways for libraries to cooperate in the selection and purchase of materials. (3) Cutting services, staff, hours, and the materials budget.

There are many other suggested solutions, but all agree that libraries are embarked on a period of change, entering a time in which traditional methods of materials selection require constant re-evaluation. Some think of this in terms of scientific management and models, others see an even more technical approach, while most librarians are convinced that creative service, even against terrible financial odds, will in the end not only save but also improve library service.

PROFILE OF AMERICAN LIBRARIES

There are many ways to view American libraries, but as "haves" and the "have-nots" is at least a beginning.

There are an estimated 9360 public libraries in the United States, but only 619 have book funds over $50,000; 6000 have no more than $1000 to $5000 to spend annually.[2] Sixty representative public libraries in 1977 had materials budgets ranging from over $2 million to a low of $5000.[3] (Precise surveys are difficult because libraries with truly low budgets are not likely to respond.)

Of 2500 college and university libraries, only 992 have materials budgets over $25,000, although for the 100 or so large research libraries the allocations exceed $1 million.[4] There are no satisfactory data for the 107,000 elementary and secondary school libraries and media centers (only 74,600 include libraries).

The vast financial gulf means two basic, sometimes quite different approaches to selection. The "haves" are vitally concerned with the glut of materials. The librarian's responsibility here is to separate out the gold from the garbage, not to preserve everything. (We will return to this problem later.)

The "have-nots" are not involved with the "information explosion" or the "exponential increase in the volume and complexity of the record of human experience" (to quote the public library guidelines). Librarians in under-

[2] Data from the "Mailing Lists" section of the 1979 R. R. Bowker Catalog, which breaks down libraries by size of budget, and from the National Center for Education Statistics, quoted in John P. Dessauer, Library Acquisitions: A Look into the Future (New York: Book Industry Study Group, 1976), p. 8.

[3] Elizabeth Futas, Library Acquisition Policies and Procedures (Phoenix, Ariz.: Oryx Press, 1977), p. xxvii.

[4] "Rankings of Research Libraries at Universities, 1977–78," The Chronicle of Higher Education, February 20, 1979, p. 4. This lists some 95 libraries in order of volumes in the library, volumes added, current serials, and spending for materials. Top-ranking Harvard spent more than $3.5 million in 1977–1978, while Kent State University, near the bottom, spent slightly over half a million dollars.

financed libraries are concerned with finding enough money to buy essential items, in determining what is better and best, not with an information overload.

The problem of the "haves" and the "have-nots" is complicated by inflation and rising prices of materials. For example, between 1970 and 1976 library expenditures for 75 large research libraries increased 63 percent while expenditures for costly serials exactly doubled. The result is that the allocation for books for the 75 libraries dropped by 1.3 percent for that period.[5] Similar difficulties are faced by all libraries.

Numerous solutions have been suggested. These range from vast federal and state funding to increased and sophisticated interlibrary loan of materials through related bibliographic networks to automation and streamlining of services. None is likely to be the entire answer, although potential solutions do point up the necessity for careful local, state, regional, and national planning.

In terms of selection, this planning should first be in the development of a collection policy (discussed in detail later in this chapter). This implies that the librarian has an overall view of selection goals, how much effort and funding must be allocated for certain materials, the ever-present problem of user access to those materials, the constraints of budget, personnel, building size, and all the rest.

PUBLIC LIBRARIES

Diversity is the key word to describe the more than 9000 public libraries in America. They serve many different audiences, reflect needs of almost every conceivable socioeconomic and political group. Selection priorities differ from library to library. Some librarians believe that "the public libraries are in serious trouble" because they have not yet caught up with the needs of their communities. Here the plea is for "new forms of communication" and the renewal of the traditional conviction that "every person" deserves free access to libraries.[6] In this view, the selection policy should consider materials of value to "all current and potential individuals and groups in society."[7] Not all public librarians agree with this assessment and contend that more emphasis should be placed on existing audiences, not on potential audiences.

Still, regardless of the audience envisioned, there is some consensus that the public library should furnish all types of

information on such social concerns as laws, services, and public policy; on such life needs as health and housing, food and transportation, employment and welfare assistance; on such human problems as aging, the family, sex, work, politics, love,

---

[5] "The Money Problem," *AB Bookman's Weekly*, December 4, 1978, p. 3454.
[6] Paraphrased from "A Mission Statement for Public Libraries," *American Libraries*, December 1977, pp. 616–617.
[7] Ibid., p. 618.

and leisure; on such issues as will permit the meshing of American society and culture amicably and benefically with others in the world.[8]

Fay M. Blake puts it another way:

Before we can approach the subject of access, maybe we need to devote our collective minds to the problem of what kind of information most people need access to. . . . All people need information, but the kinds of information most people need is different in form and content from that required and made available by the educated elite for its own use. . . .[9]

Materials being selected may have to be re-examined, if everyone is to be served (or, more precisely, those who now make up the heart of many large urban centers); the materials needs of the traditional middle-class and student user should also be re-examined. An example of this is to be found in a resolution:

WHEREAS many materials relevant and valuable to minorities, women, poor people, and the incarcerated are produced by the ethnic, feminist, and alternative press; BE IT RESOLVED that libraries make it a firm and continuing policy to secure a wide representation of such materials, and BE IT FURTHER RESOLVED that these materials should be regularly and prominently displayed so that library users realize they are available.[10]

Most public librarians do believe in library equity: every individual should have equal opportunity for the best public library service available. In this regard the action of the Connecticut State Library's Department of Planning and Research is typical. At a December 1978 meeting the group gave priority to expanded "use of all types of communication technologies" to assure adequate library service. This, in turn, means particular attention to selection of materials.[11]

SCHOOL LIBRARY MEDIA CENTERS

A school library by any other name remains a library, yet there are important differences between traditional elementary and secondary school libraries and school media centers. Terminology is not the substantive difference, although a cursory reading of the literature gives the impression that terms are important.[12]

[8] David Kaser, "Toward a Conceptual Foundation for a National Information Policy," *Wilson Library Bulletin*, March 1978, p. 546.

[9] "Let My People Know—Acess to Information in a Postindustrial Society," *Wilson Library Bulletin*, January 1978, pp. 396–397.

[10] Resolution passed by the Minnesota Governor's Pre-White House Conference on Library and Information Services, Minneapolis, September 12, 1978.

[11] "White House Preconferences," *Library Journal*, February 15, 1979, p. 453.

[12] There are at least a dozen names for what used to be called simply the school library. Among the favored: school library media center, school media center, media center, multimedia library, library media center, resource learning center, school learning resource center, instructional materials center, audiovisual center.

"Media" is frequently used in any description of the library, as is "resources," since today's library includes much more than print (books and periodicals) and may put as much effort into selection of nonprint materials as of books. Veteran children's librarian Augusta Baker explains what happened:

Eager to show that they were not made in the outworn image of card-stamping, book-guarding librarians which was ingrained in the hearts and minds of so many school board members, principals, parents, and teachers, school librarians decided in the [1960s] that they would be known henceforth as *media specialists*, presiding over media in a media center—instead of a library. There were good and compelling political and financial reasons for this: money was available for "media" and there was a need to dramatize the programs as innovative and entirely different from what had gone before under the name of the library.[13]

Today *media* is the key word for change, the banner that flies high and proudly over the school library, although there is much more to change than the inclusion of different types of educational materials in the library. The "concept of a true media center differs from that of a traditional library in six dimensions: program, personnel, facilities, collections, administration and financial support."[14]

The crucial difference is the involvement of the school media librarian not only with selection of materials, but also with various aspects of the total educational scene. This in turn means expanded service, personnel, facilities, and collections.

One may distance oneself from all of this progress and ask is it really all needed, and, essentially, has the library changed that much? Yes, say more and more critics.

So long as teaching and learning was restricted to two-by-four concepts of education (the information contained between the two covers of the textbook and the four walls of the classroom) the school library was required to serve in no other way. . . . [Now] the function of the library must change from study hall–book dispersal center to a learning laboratory . . . from the sporadic use of media to the planned and purposeful integration of library resources and service with the ongoing teaching and learning enterprise.[15]

Objectives for the average school media library today are sure to include these major tasks: (1) Help to establish the library as an integral part of the

[13] Foreword to *School and Public Library Media Programs* (Syracuse, N.Y.: Gaylord, 1977), p. 13.

[14] Betty Martin and Ben Carson, *The Principal's Handbook of the School Library Media Center* (Syracuse, NY.: Gaylord Professional Publications, 1978), p. 20. The reader who does not understand the difference between the media center and the traditional library should check the outline summary on pages 26–27, which shows differences between the two in considerable detail.

[15] Ruth Ann Davies, *The School Library Media Center* (2nd ed.; New York: R. R. Bowker, 1974). This concept is hardly foreign to the "college learning resources programs" and to many public libraries with community and independent learning programs. It is more concentrated in school libraries.

total educational system. (2) Provide training and instruction in the use of the library by both students and teachers. (3) Involve teachers and students with books and other materials in the library, particularly as they relate to development of meaningful curriculum and life styles. (4) Provide for a continual evaluation of materials to aid in the educational process. There are other objectives and other approaches, but these four embrace the major goals of most libraries today.

Reduced to selection of materials, the essential differences between the new media center and the old school library are: (1) In the old system the bulk of the material was books and periodicals; in the new there are extensive collections of films, recordings, videotapes, realia, and other nonprint materials. (2) The traditional library did offer films and recordings, but only in small numbers. The media center has access to both in greater quantity and better quality. (3) The librarian tried to do almost everything, from acting as a study-hall guard to filling orders for books. The media expert tends to have a larger staff, often with subject experts available.

Another difference between the old and the new is the emphasis on centralization of selection and distribution of materials.[16]

There are two types of school media library. The first is the individual library, with its own staff and selection practices. It may have several branches or serve several schools, but it is essentially a single-school service. The second major type is the school district media center. Here a single center feeds materials and ideas to a score or even 200 or more schools, many of which have their own libraries but rely on the district center for leadership and, to a great extent, selection of materials.[17]

This situation exists in public and even academic libraries as well; many public libraries belong to systems such as those in the Los Angeles County area, and cooperative selection is usual for academic libraries with multiple branches or multiple campuses.

While the variations of administrative organization profoundly affect the day-by-day operation of selection, too much can be made of this when one turns to the more universal themes that run through selection principles. These are much the same, no matter how the library is organized.

ACADEMIC LIBRARIES

There are 2700 colleges and universities, of which 1500 are four-year institutions. Of the 1500, at least 750 have student bodies of fewer than 1000, are privately controlled, and have limited funds. Evan Farber, a librarian at

---

[16] Differences between the school and other types of library is more than a matter of selection of materials. For a good workaday view see A. Carolyn Rice, "The Tyranny of the Bells," *Library Journal*, March 15, 1978, pp. 618–620.

[17] For a detailed study of the district school library see John T. Gillespie, *A Model School District Media Program: Montgomery County as a Case Study* (Chicago: American Library Association, 1977).

the Earlham College Library in Richmond, Indiana, draws a good comparison between the large and small academic institution:

I'll use the annual listing compiled at Bowdoin College, a listing of statistics for forty-one colleges that might be described as "selective"—institutions such as Amherst, Davidson, Earlham, Lafayette, Sewanee, Vassar, and Williams, most of them with between one and two thousand students. . . . The size of the professional staffs averaged 8.8 with a total staff of 22, and their average total expenditure for books, periodicals and binding was $151,000. Now, compare these figures with Princeton University Library which, at the end of 1974 . . . has a professional staff of 294, and spent about 1.6 million dollars on acquisitions and binding. Thus, when comparing Princeton Unversity Library with even the more affluent college libraries, it has . . . ten times the professional staff, thirteen times the total staff, and spends more than ten times as much on acquisitions and binding.[18]

The basic difference between the college and the university library is: (1) In the college library acquisitions are geared more to the student body than to the needs of research scholars found in larger institutions, and (2) the smaller school tends to purchase materials that are timely, relevant, and quickly accessible. The larger institution may buy all of these items but is likely to put more emphasis (and money) on retrospective scholarly materials and highly specialized current journals and reports.[19]

The academic library enjoys the same homogeneous audience as the school library and does not encounter the drastic educational differences faced by public libraries. The age group is about the same in all academic libraries; public libraries must serve a wide range. Possibly the greatest single difference is in emphasis. The average public library must select a wide variety of materials, with special concern for popular approaches to information and entertainment.

TWO-YEAR-COLLEGE LIBRARIES

The two-year community or junior college is a distinctive unit in the academic-library circle. It is unique in that: (1) The student population is varied in age and experience. Most community colleges offer both beginning academic and vocational courses for young and older individuals. This means a diverse set of programs not likely to be found in many academic libraries. (2) The librarian must be closer to the school media librarian in abilities because there is a great emphasis upon educational media. Junior-college librarians should be able to assist teachers and administrators with planning curriculum, aiding in instructional development and in turn asking for advice on selection. (3) The selection skills required here include a solid acquaintance with the various media and the tools employed for selection.

[18] "The Administration and Use of Microform Serials in College Libraries," *Microform Review*, March-April 1978, p. 81.

[19] O. B. Hardison, "The Ivory Tower in the Arena: Research Libraries and Public Outreach," *Wilson Library Bulletin*, January 1979, pp. 384–391. A good overview of research libraries and how they differ from other types of academic and college libraries.

SPECIAL LIBRARIES

There are almost as many types of special libraries as definitions of the term. The R. R. Bowker Company mailing list includes 12,670 special libraries—2544 business and corporation; 3497 technical; 2082 social and behavioral science; 1347 agriculture, botany, fisheries, food, forest; 861 art; 738 historical; 447 music; 1164 law; 2489 medical. And one might add about 1400 governmental and armed forces libraries. A suitable definition of a special library is one "maintained by an individual, corporation, association, government agency or any other group for the collection, organization, and dissemination of information and primarily devoted to a special subject and offering specialized service to a specialized clientele."[20] Here selection tends to rely heavily on current materials, particularly periodicals, reports, government documents, and reference books.

The "specialized clientele" requires equally specialized materials, usually to support research programs. Many special libraries simply grow, operate without a defined philosophy or clear written goals, and are established on a formal basis only when informal arrangements fail.[21] The librarians fairly often report to administrators who may not even use the library, but there are no common patterns.

The actual selection process depends on whether the library has a separate budget or is within a department out of whose money the library is funded. Given a separate budget, the librarian, usually with the help of users, makes decisions about what is purchased.

The special library is usually part of a much larger unit, often another library.[22] It is common to speak of special collections (special libraries) within academic libraries. For example, rare book rooms, map collections, even government documents may be considered special collections.

Selection Objectives and Goals

The ultimate goal of any library is to provide the right book for the right reader at the right time. This is an ancient library creed, and if you substitute "information" or "film" or whatever for "book," it is as true today as it was many years ago. The St. Louis Public Library is right when it points out:

---

[20] Leonard M. Harrod, *The Librarian's Glossary of Terms Used in Librarianship and the Book Crafts and Reference Book* (London: André Deutsch, 1971), pp. 603–604.

[21] Among 200 Canadian special libraries investigated only eight had written acquisition policies (*Research Collections in Canadian Libraries, II Special Studies*, 1974).

[22] For example, in a Texas survey of state agency libraries it was found 51 libraries "receive their funds from their parent agency's biennial appropriation rather than directly from the Legislature. . . . The libraries were almost entirely dependent on a parent agency" (Mary C. Grattan, "Collection Development in State Agency Libraries," *Special Libraries*, February 1977, p. 69).

"The distinctive advantage of what the library can offer over those sources of information contemporary people can provide for themselves is richness of resources and trained expertise in their use."[23]

The "richness of resources" is possible if materials are carefully selected for basic goals:

1. *To meet obligations of teaching programs, research, and adult education.* This obligation is a top priority in school and academic libraries, less so in public libraries, although there is now a concerted effort by many of them to sponsor literacy training and adult education, often in conjunction with local school systems.

2. *To meet the information needs of the community.* This is a somewhat broader objective that takes in everything from materials, to answering queries on how to install a fireplace, to an analysis of nuclear submarine capacities in wartime.

3. *To meet the social needs of the community.* This includes 1 and 2, but is a net cast even farther because selection considers materials of value to everyone, from the individual seeking help in organizing a community club to a group that wants to establish a storefront medical or legal clinic.

4. *To meet the cultural and spiritual needs of the community.* This traditionally has been the goal of many libraries. Culture is understandably a less-than-easy objective to define, and most libraries are satisfied not to try. The goal is a type of catchall for what does not fit in the other categories, although in many ways it may be the most important goal of the library.

5. *To meet the recreational needs of the community.* Traditionally this has received low priority in theory, but in practice has often governed selection, particularly in small to medium-sized public and some school libraries. Today recreation and relaxation are at least seen as legitimate activities for libraries and the librarian need no longer apologize for directing selection effort toward recreational materials. Enjoyment and relaxation may be the two most important elements added to the structure of library policy in the last quarter of the twentieth century. Keith Harrison notes:

There is in our profession a horrible resistance to providing materials whose sole purpose is unashamed pleasure. . . . If we accept that librarians in the community have a definite social responsibility to lighten everyday human experience, then it seems fairly obvious that through our materials we should be trying to amuse and entertain as much as anything else.[24]

PRIORITIES

There is general agreement that the library is a multipurpose agency, but less on priorities. Within the context of the type of library you are selecting materials for, how would you rank the preceding five objectives? And do you have one or two of your own to add?

[23] Futas, op. cit., p. 88.
[24] "Community Stock," *Assistant Librarian*, March 1978, p. 34.

If this question is presented to a group of librarians, there will be many answers. The public librarian might add that the most important objective is missing—the goal of removing barriers that now keep a majority of Americans out of libraries. Make access the key objective. Set up the library and the collection so it will have something for everyone, from every age, economic, and educational group.

The school media librarian might counter that the real objective of the school media center is to help shape the educational process. This requires careful selection of materials based upon an understanding of curriculum needs and the objectives of a particular school. Equally, it necessitates knowledge of changes in educational patterns and discovering materials to satisfy new approaches to teaching.

Academic librarians might say that the goals do not give sufficient weight to the instructional objectives of the modern library. Although the academic library "continues as in the past to serve as the repository for the printed information needed by its patrons, its resources have now been extended to embrace new forms of recorded information, and its proper purpose has been enlarged through changes in the scope of the curriculum and by new concepts of instruction."[25]

USERS AND NONUSERS

Only a relatively select group of people (which ranges from the scholar and technologist to the businessperson and student) use the library with any regularity. Libraries are a natural part of their working and recreational life patterns. But how about nonusers?

There are two points of view regarding how to get more people to use the library. One, which is as negative as it is in debt to Thomas Hobbes, sees the task as hopeless; cultural, economic, and educational background will insure library use by one group, discourage use by another group. Here the Hobson's choice is no choice at all since is felt that education level virtually dictates who will or will not use the library, and the librarian simply serves those who are inclined to enter.

A less skeptical, more widely held view is that there are methods and means to encourage library use. Certainly they do not always succeed and often the librarian will feel like a cousin to Sisyphus, but at least there is always the chance that the methods will introduce a library nonuser to the joys of the library. If one agrees that people should be encouraged to use the library, and given that encouragement will turn their collective backs on the skeptic, there are numerous methods for coaxing people to use the library. Among the tried:

(1.) Select materials (books and periodicals, films and records) of interest to the people you are trying to draw to the library. This implies an under-

25 Standards for College Libraries, *College & Research Libraries News*, October 1975, p. 278.

standing of the needs of the individual and the community, discussed in Chapter 2.

2. Once the materials are available, let the individuals who normally don't use a library know the library has something for them. This is done in numerous ways. Today the so-called storefront or information and referral system is popular: the librarian goes out to the public with materials to aid that public in its everyday needs, whether they be how to cope with car payments or how to find relaxation in a magazine article or book. This requires publicity, advertising, public relations, or whatever you wish to call the art of drawing people to what you have to offer.

3. Wherever the materials are located, the librarian helping people must have a natural empathy with people of all types and from all educational and social backgrounds. Fear of the librarian (that is, of the unexpected, of the bureaucrat) keeps the majority of library nonusers out of the library. It is imperative that the nonuser understand the librarian has a sincere desire to be helpful. The physical aspects of the library (whether a giant building or a small storefront) must be attractive and inviting, easily accessible, easily understood in terms of where to find what is needed.

4. At the primary, secondary, and academic level special effort must be made to make the library a useful as well as a relaxed place. Traditional techniques range from teaching students how to find information for themselves to offering lectures, films, and slide-tape programs in special subject areas or supplying information staff at handy places throughout the library. Actually, several studies find that the best way to get reluctant users to the library is through the teacher who uses the library and expects the students to follow. This requires that the librarian work first with the teachers and next with the students instead of the other way about.

5. The library should work with related social agencies and educational institutions to serve them with advice, if not always the materials themselves. This can be a sensitive situation, but the librarian who has an understanding of literacy programs, adult education, personal improvement classes, and the like can often be of help to both students and instructors—and in so doing attract both to the library.

6. Whether serving the disadvantaged, labor groups, minorities, the aging, members of literacy programs, or the recreational and cultural needs of the average middle-class library nonuser, the librarian must make a personal effort to generate a feeling of real interest, of good will, and—to be sure—compentence and interest in the individual. This is more than being pleasant in the library; it implies going out into the community—both during and after working hours—and trying to be of assistance to all who need help. This may sound like a combination saint and knight without horse, but in the final analysis it seems the best approach to drawing nonusers to the benefits of the library.

Beyond the general are a great number of specific methods of drawing people to the library, of eliminating the frustration factor. The literature is filled with these ideas. For example, one study suggested that men can be appealed to by materials on home improvement, sports, and business. Women can be attracted to the library with a good collection of handicraft, cooking, child-care, and general recreational materials.

The trick is to let people know these materials are available. This can be done through brochures passed out in Welcome Wagon calls and by television and radio public-service spots.

All of the suggestions also require several other things: having what is required by nonusers or moderate users, making it readily available by having the library open at the right hours, and having involved and interested librarians on duty. The library has to be easy to reach, easy to use, and quick to discover the needs of people, often before they really know their own needs. All of this is too often more ideal than real, but there is no reason the librarian should not make an honest effort—despite discouragement and lack of financial support—to reach the people who need the library most.

Issues in Selection Philosophy

Librarians speak of a philosophy of selection on many levels. A major concern may be attitudes about censorship (see Chapter 14) or in charting a general course for what is selected or not selected. At another level the librarian's viewpoint or philosophy may shape what type of service is offered. For example, one librarian may firmly believe in trying to reach as many people as possible while another may concentrate on in-depth service to existing users.

Since most selection decisions are not controversial and are influenced by known needs of users and budget constraints, the librarian's philosophy of service and selection is not likely to be a major daily issue. Still, it is imperative and, possibly more important, to appreciate the viewpoint of other librarians.

At the risk of oversimplification, let's label the different selection philosophies liberal, traditional, and pluralistic, although the problem with such labels may be demonstrated by a national poll. According to this survey, 43 percent of the American public served by libraries contends it is conservative. Only 30 percent consider themselves liberal, with 10 percent in the middle and 17 percent with no opinion.[26] But while Americans call themselves conservative they consistently vote Democrats into office and support liberal legislation. Closely questioned, most Americans seem to be pluralistic, nearer the center of the political spectrum than either liberal or conservative.[27]

[26] Gallup Poll reported in the Albany (N.Y.) *Times-Union*, September 17, 1978, p. A18.

[27] Adam Clymer, "Conservatives Share Liberal View," *The New York Times*, January 22, 1978, pp. 1, 30.

This confusion is to acknowledge the difficulty of semantics and to recognize that an important task in setting library goals is to arrive at a common understanding of terms employed. Failure to do so will mean the day-to-day work in the library will have little or nothing to do with the statements of an institution's philosophy.

Perhaps the last word on the problem should be an illustration of why materials selection is thought by some to be an art form: "Until we have a total, unassailable theory of human personality, I do not see how we can have a totally satisfactory theory of [selection], universally applicable as, say, we understand the law of gravity to be."[28] No, but the librarian must keep trying to find that theory.

THE LIBERAL VIEWPOINT

Much of the library literature and general social commentary today emphasizes the idea of change, and in that context can be considered liberal. National guidelines call for: (1) Widening of service patterns to include as many people as possible, not simply the middle classes and their children; (2) need to revise attitudes about print and nonprint materials, with a swing toward the latter; (3) concern about the importance of education and information; (4) a belief in activism rather than passivity, both in selection and dissemination of information; and (5) a watchful trust in technology, cooperation, and managerial skills to bring all things to all people.

Here the librarian as social activist believes in transformation of service and the idea that "the library can actively bring every person . . . into effective contact with the human record."[29] In a public library this attitude will be reflected in many ways, although in terms of selection there will be a particular effort to choose materials people want and, at the same time, materials most people do not even know exist but that will be useful and rewarding. For example, the liberal will be quick to purchase books requested by users but will also make a strong effort to select only the best and most useful of other books the user may turn to at a later date. As one librarian put it: "Of course, people should find what they want, but they should also find things they never expected."

School and academic librarians will be consistent in trying to reach non-users (both students and faculty), push programs in the use of the library, join with teachers and administrators in planning the total educational program with the library as an integral part, rely on all types of materials to meet these goals and try for larger units of library service. Those in special and government libraries will have a modified view, although they will carry out programs and activities to make the library increasingly important to its self-selected users.

[28] Daniel Gore, "Things Your Boss Never Told You . . . ," *Library Journal,* April 1, 1977, p. 767. Gore is speaking of management, but selection fits just as well.
[29] "A Mission Statement for Public Libraries," *American Libraries,* December 1977, pp. 616–617.

THE TRADITIONAL VIEWPOINT

Traditionalists turn the activist or liberal service coat inside out.[30] They believe that the solution to library difficulties is to stop the breathless charging here and there at the public's red banner of indifference or be destroyed by the public. Here the argument is that "continuity, not change, is the most striking feature of American values today."[31]

Conservatives argue that to demand equality of opportunity is fine as a social standard, but realistically it is rarely practicable. Encouraging people to come to the library (no matter how enthusiastically it is done) still will not confer equal opportunity, particularly on a group that has been discriminated against for centuries.

The economic argument is often heard in this context. The library rarely has enough money or staff to serve those who now use the library. Extending service to nonusers will simply diminish service to users—who are then likely to join the nonusers. And who really is this nonlibrary public? Does the librarian actually know who is being served and not served, or is this based on mass hysteria about service to the poor and minority groups?

The traditionalist view of selection of materials takes exception to purchasing materials simply because they are demanded by the public. Many, although far from all, traditionalists object to the purchase of popular, best-selling fiction and nonfiction. They may take an equally strong stand against purchase of books they believe harmful to the community.

THE PLURALIST VIEWPOINT

Most librarians, like the public they serve, tend to borrow from both the traditional and the liberal viewpoints. Here the rationale is that there are more than two types of reality, and to opt for either one or the other is to defeat the purpose of the library, which is to serve, equally, all groups in society. In this sense, the middle-ground point of view may be called pluralistic since it borrows from both liberal and traditional, adds a dash of common sense and experience, and comes up with a selection policy as wide in scope as it is generous in purpose.

Actually, few librarians are absolutely consistent; they move from one position to another, often in keeping with the selection discussion rather than with any long-range overview of the library and its goals. Philosophical compartments are fine in a textbook, but should only be taken as relative

---

[30] The literature is filled with passionate intellectual arguments for what is essentially a return to traditional library service. The best, certainly one of the most carefully considered, is Pauline Wilson, *A Community Elite and the Public Library* (New York: Greenwood, 1977).

[31] Everett C. Ladd, "Traditional Values Regnant," *Public Opinion*, March-April 1978, p. 45.

methods of evaluating what is going on in a library. Unfortunately, in selection librarians, like many other people, tend to take the less adventurous path and really don't care what it is called. This fact is supported by surveys, which indicate many librarians favor rather than fight self-censorship in the library (see Chapter 14).

Still, the primary test of a philosophy is simply whether it works. If it does, it can be put to work in the development of a selection policy for the library.

Collection Development Policy Statement

Many libraries today have formal selection policy statements (often referred to as collection development policies). These are prepared for numerous reasons, but generally a statement is considered desirable because it:
REASONS FOR HAVING A FORMAL SELECTION POLICY:
(a) enables selectors to work with greater consistency toward defined goals, thus shaping stronger collections and using limited funds more wisely; (b) informs users, administrators, trustees and others as to the scope and nature of existing collections, and the plans for continuing development of resources; (c) provides information which will assist in the budgetary allocation process.[32]

The policy statement is an effort to bring order, logic, and common sense to bear on selection and evaluation viewpoints—which, as the preceding sections indicate, are far from settled or universally acceptable.

In some libraries [writes Elizabeth Futas] the policy statement is a theoretical document which stresses the intellectual reasoning used to select materials for inclusion in the collection. For others, it is a practical explanation of fiscal, community and space limitations which control the purchasing of items.[33]

There are other reasons for a written statement. The policy will:

1. Assist in establishing methods of reviewing materials before purchase.

2. Help in determining the best method of acquisition—directly from the publisher or through a jobber, for example.

3. Offer some help against censorship by a clear statement of the type of materials to be purchased and indication that the policy has the support of the ruling body of the library.

4. Help in long-range budget planning by stating priorities and outlining growth and development goals.

5. Assist in planning with other libraries such cooperative programs as interlibrary loans and networks.

6. Offer suggestions for what types of materials are to be weeded, stored, or discarded.

---

[32] "Guidelines for the Formulation of Collection Development Policies," *Library Resources and Technical Services*, Winter 1977, p. 41. For several articles on the practical aspects of preparing a selection policy see *Library Resources and Technical Services*, Winter 1979, especially Charles Osburn's article. See, too, frequent articles on the subject by the expert of experts, Elizabeth Futas, in various issues of *Collection Building*.

[33] Op. cit., p. ix.

The policy statement helps the librarian exert general control over selection. A statement will "help determine the types of materials acceptable to the collection, thus controlling the growth rate."[34] And, not least important:

FINAL REASON for ~~accountability~~ WRITTEN POLICY:

While a written policy might seem unnecessary to many, the issue of accountability to the public is the real core of the issue. Whether a library has 10,000 books or 10 books, the items were bought with public funds—whether they were bought outright, or paid for indirectly, in terms of time and labor required to request, sort, and process every item received. The public, then, has the right to expect libraries to have definite and responsible reasons for acquiring and maintaining a collection of library items and for keeping the collection in peak condition to allow for maximum use.[35]

WHO PREPARES THE STATEMENT?

Responsibility for the policy statement rests with the librarian, although in larger libraries this may be shifted to subject bibliographers, the acquisition department, and others involved with aspects of selection and acquisition of materials.

Ideally, everyone who uses the library should be involved in the preparation of the policy. This means drawing in faculty and teachers, board members, administrators, and others. Involvement of people other than librarians "is essential to ensure that the policies support present programs. It also serves a publicity function in drawing the attention of the . . . community to the transition from comprehensiveness to a [selection process]."[36]

POLICY FORMULATION – *what to include*

Once the reason for the statement is clarified, the next question is what to include. Here the librarian will find four sources of particular value:

1. "Guidelines for the Formulation of Collection Development Policies," *Library Resources and Technical Services*, Winter 1977. Prepared by an American Library Association Committee, the guidelines trace step by step what is required for a complete statement.

2. Elizabeth Futas, *Library Acquisition Policies and Procedures* (Phoenix, Ariz.: Oryx Press, 1977). A well-organized, carefully chosen selection of representative policy statements from academic and public libraries in the United States and Canada. Within its 400 pages are examples suitable for modification and use in your own library policy statement.

3. National standards and guidelines for various types of libraries. The standards point up basic points concerning both qualitative and quantitative considerations for selection.

---

34 Mary C. Grattan, op. cit., p. 72.

35 Ibid., p. 73.

36 Barbara Rice, "The Development of Working Collections in University Libraries," *College and Research Libraries*, July 1977, p. 311.

4. C. B. Osburn, "Planning for a University Library Policy on Collection Development," *International Library Review*, April 1977, pp. 209–223. Beginning on page 219 there is a good suggested work plan with a step-by-step analysis of how to write a policy statement. Osburn outlines the basic elements, including: (1) Introduction with definitions, operations covered by the policy, the philosophy and goals of the library, and how the policy is to be used. (2) Subject statements for each subject area, including criteria for selection. (3) Kinds of materials to be collected or rejected. (4) Table of contents and good index.

POINT BY POINT – how to write a policy statement

Statements differ in specifics, but most have several things in common. They all tend to begin with a brief description of the objectives, philosophy, and purpose of the library. This should be followed by a brief description of the community served. Beyond that, you should include the following:

1. A specific statement indicating who is legally responsible for the operation of the library and who has been given authority for selection of materials (by titles or positions).

2. Method of selection as well as limitations of budget, community served, different age groups of user, and similar information.

    a. Guidelines and criteria used to select materials.

    b. List of reviews or types of reviews checked to determine what is to be purchased.

3. Problem situations, carefully listed. These may range from types of materials excluded (textbooks to law books) to how many copies of a single title should be purchased, rules about binding, and policy for replacement of lost materials.

4. An indication of how the collection is to be built in terms of specific subject fields and what fields are to be emphasized. For each subject category, the "Guidelines for the Formulation of Collection Development Policies" recommends an analysis in these terms:

a. Levels of collection intensity
    —existing strength of collection
    —actual current level of collection activity
    —desirable level of collecting to meet program needs
b. Language
c. Chronological period covered
d. Geographic areas collected
e. Forms of material collected (excluded)
f. Who is responsible for selection[37]

5. Statements on foreign-language materials, increasingly being limited because of lack of accessibility by most people. (The exception: foreign-

[37] P. 44.

language materials for Spanish-speaking peoples or others in an area served by a library.)

6. Definitions. At one time "materials" meant little more than books and periodicals, but now no library can ignore other forms of communication. The media are spelled out in the selection policy statement with a note about what is or is not to be purchased, and sometimes about the relative importance of the materials to the total collection. Among such special collections might be newspapers, microform, manuscripts, government publications, maps, audiovisual materials, and data tapes.[38]

7. A statement about handling of gifts.

8. Something about interlibrary loan policy; an increasing number of libraries include network statements as well. There may be a paragraph on how the library coordinates its purchases with those of other libraries and what is done "to select and deselect in conformity with regional needs and resources."[39]

9. Clarification of weeding or discarding practice.

10. Statements regarding intellectual freedom. These find their way into the general selection statement, but many libraries also append basic American Library Association codes in support of intellectual freedom, such as The Library Bill of Rights, freedom to read statements, and similar documents.[40]

PROBLEMS

There are problems with even the best statement: It may not reflect the day-by-day reality of procedures used in the library. It may be so ideal as to be something to admire from afar, but not to use; months may go into the construction a statement that will be filed away and rarely used. (One might nevertheless argue that in thinking through and writing the statement the library staff was forced to think about both general goals and daily activities and that perhaps this process helped to improve things in the library.)

One answer to this problem is to review the document periodically, something called for in most statements (although a college- and university-library survey found that about half of the librarians rarely or never review the statement once it is written, and public libraries are even more indefinite about reviewing policies).[41]

Sometimes an overly anxious administrator forces a policy statement on the library, with the result that the librarians do their best to ignore both its construction and its ultimate implementation. Nevertheless, the biggest

---

[38] "Guidelines," p. 45.

[39] Ibid., p. 44.

[40] *The Library Bill of Rights* (Chicago: American Library Association, 1948, amended 1961 and 1967). *The School Library Bill of Rights for School Library Media Center Programs* (Chicago: American Library Association, 1969). *The Student's Right to Read* (Urbana, Ill.: National Council of Teachers of English, 1972).

[41] Futas, op. cit., pp. xxvi, xxxiv.

single problem is that in small and medium-sized libraries, many librarians can't see any reason for a policy. The library is too small, or they don't have the time, or (more likely) they simply don't believe a written policy statement is necessary. The result is that from a third to half or more of college, university, and public libraries have no formal policy of materials selection.

No one is ever totally satisfied with a policy statement, but if collection development is to proceed, such a statement is necessary. As one librarian put it: "All documents that include guidelines, statistics, definitions and principles are boring. They are necessary."[42]

[42] Mary Eble, "School Library Standards," *Catholic Library World*, February 1977, p. 295.

2

The Public and Selection

THE LIBRARY has little importance in the lives of many people. Quantitative use of the library never has been impressive, although librarians agree this may be because we know so little about the real needs of people. Actually, most Americans do think fondly of the library, much as they do of a museum. Numerous studies indicate that even those who do not use a library like to think it is available for family members, for their children, or for their community.

Librarians are fond of counting how many people check out how many books, and the standard circulation record is as much a part of the history of libraries as Melvin Dewey. This simplistic attitude may be rapidly disappearing. As librarians become more sophisticated about themselves and their public, they are longer satisfied merely to quantify. The real questions have become: Why does someone use or not use the library? Did the person find anything of use in the library? If the individual did not come to the library, was it for lack of need or lack of knowledge about what the library has to offer? Conversely, does the librarian really know what kinds of information and materials people need and for what purposes?

In this chapter we examine those questions and some of the methods of finding answers. But first, let's look at the "average" library user.

The Average User

A librarian asked to describe the average individual user normally calls up the image of a member of the American middle class: white, with average or better-than-average income, high school- or college-educated, married, a homeowner, with interests documented each week in *Reader's Digest* and *Time*. The children and young adults a library serves most often come to the school media center or the public or academic library out of the middle-class American home. The much-maligned American middle-class individual is likely to remain the prime user of any type of library.[1]

It is the middle-class family that purchases books—and in increasing numbers. Individual sales "will increase even faster during the next five years, and . . . could well reach three-fourths of all book sales by the mid-1980s."[2] Sales of books to individuals are impressive, and would indicate that reading is far from finished. They may account, too, in a small way for the decrease of borrowers in some libraries. Many people now buy rather than borrow: "When [one library user] realized he was spending carfare to withdraw a book from the library and another $1 to return it, he decided it was just as cheap to buy a book."[3]

The fact that the middle-class American is most likely to remain a library user tells the librarian very little about the rest of the existing or potential library audience. For that we must turn to community analysis.

Community Analysis

The task of determining a library's real and potential users is known as community analysis or community study.[4] The basic questions are: What do we know about the community? and What do we know about how the

---

[1] The middle class will be the prime users of most libraries because there are more of them, and the ranks are increasing. According to the Bureau of the Census, about 65 percent of the work force is middle-class—that is, in white-collar jobs. Many among the 33 percent in manual work are middle-class in terms of income and, to a lesser degree, education and interests. These percentages have dramatically changed since the beginning of the century, when only 28 percent were middle-class, 37 percent in farm work (the figure is now about 3 percent), and 36 percent in manual work.

[2] *Publishers Weekly*, October 9, 1978, p. 47. Libraries are expected to retain about the same level of book purchases over the next five years, despite concern engendered by budget cuts. Libraries now account for about 8.5 percent of publishers' sales, while schools account for 14.8 percent (which would include textbooks). Individuals account for 66.6 percent—expected to rise to 77.1 percent by 1982.

[3] *Publishers Weekly*, April 17, 1978, p. 21.

[4] Titles useful for an understanding of community analysis include the January 1976 issue of *Library Trends*, which is devoted to "Community Analysis and Libraries" and concludes with an annotated bibliography. Methodologies are suggested in almost any work by Lowell Martin and in F. W. Lancaster's *The Measurement and Evaluation of Library Services* (Washington, D.C.: Information Resources Press, 1977). Dated but still useful is *Studying the Community* (Chicago: American Library Association, 1960). Dorothy Turick's *Community Information Services in Libraries: LJ Special Report No. 5* (New York: R. R. Bowker, 1977) has a section on community analysis; in a sense the whole excellent report is concerned with the subject. See also the February 1975 *Illinois Libraries*, which reports on public libraries and community analysis.

Young adults are the subject of *Look, Listen, Explain: Developing Community Library Services for Young Adults* (Chicago: American Library Association, 1975), but the methodology of discovering youth groups can be applied to other categories. Specific techniques in the analysis of community characteristics have also been developed by Roger Greer, formerly of the Community Research Analysis Institute, Graduate School

community does or does not use the library? Related queries include: (1) How do existing library users compare with the larger group of nonusers? (2) Do groups within the community have special information needs that the library can meet? (3) Is library use increasing or decreasing? (4) How does the population served compare in type and number to population served by other public agencies? (5) How long does it take the library to respond to the needs of minorities, the disadvantaged, the elderly, and is that response adequate? There are, of course, scores of other questions a community study may answer as well.

Community analysis documents what may have only been librarians' impressions about the library community. The importance of the process is generally recognized, and a survey of 97 public libraries and 39 state library agencies found that the majority think the library can become an integral part of the population served by "(1) continuous or periodic study of the community, (2) participation of librarians in the life of the community, (3) correlation of library programs with those of other community organizations." While the surveyor admits "the data in no way identify norms for public libraries," the study does indicate most librarians are "sensitive to community need."[5]

Anyone seriously concerned with community analysis, or who simply wants to have a better idea of how it operates and the results to expect, should check several good examples. One of the more current is Ray L. Carpenter's report "of North Carolina socioeconomic characteristics, media use, and life styles" as related to libraries.[6] The classic national model is Bernard Berelson's *The Library's Public* (New York: Columbia University Press, 1949). Narrower in scope, controversial, and informative is a market survey (conducted by an advertising firm) that included a query about library users and nonusers. This was reported in *American Libraries* and is available in more detail from the University of Illinois.[7]

---

of Librarianship, University of Denver. The Institute issues a number of aids and publications for community analysis studies.

The International City Managers Association published *How Effective Are Your Community Services?* (1977), which lists techniques of value in community analysis. Ernest R. Deprospo, et al., *Performance Measures for Public Libraries* (Chicago: American Library Association, 1973), although dated, is of much use, and Deprospo and Ellen Altman's *Data Gathering and Instructional Manual for Performance Measures in Public Libraries* (Chicago: Celadon Press, 1976) is a valuable guide. A short collection of papers gives a solid overview of the subject: Allan F. Hersfield and Morrell D. Bone (eds.), *Approaches to Measuring Library Effectiveness* (Syracuse, N.Y.: School of Library Science, 1972).

[5] Margaret E. Monroe, "Community Development as a Mode of Community Analysis," *Library Trends*, January 1976, p. 501.

[6] "The Public Library Patron," *Library Journal*, February 1, 1979, pp. 347–355. See also Timothy Hays, et al., "The Patron and the Public," *Library Journal*, September 15, 1977, pp. 1813–1818, which deals with the Piedmont area of North Carolina, and note the readings at the end of both articles.

[7] Michael Madden, "Marketing Survey Spinoff: Library User/Nonuser Lifestyles," *American Libraries*, February 1979, p. 81. (Reported in full in "Lifestyles of Library Users and Nonusers," *Occasional Paper No. 137* [Champaign: University of Illinois

A limited example is suggested by Parker and Paisley's study of ten community characteristics (from education to total population size) that serve to predict what types of reading will be the most popular in a community with some or all of the characteristics.[8]

The Seattle Public Library launched a community analysis in order better to translate the library's philosophy of service into action. The study made it possible to convert impressions into facts and showed that librarians need to prove that the library is helpful and make its services visible.[9]

BEYOND THE PUBLIC LIBRARY (Community Analysis)

Most of the literature concerning community analysis focuses on the public library, primarily because its audiences are so diverse. In this section primary attention is on the public library, although most of the methods suggested are applicable to other types of library. School, academic, and special libraries must also periodically take a careful look at the public served or not served.

Community analysis may have other functions, too. For example, in an academic library:

community analysis enters in the construction of the acquisitions budget. Past records of expenditures, special research or instructional programs, the size of enrollments in the various disciplines, and other similar considerations form a large part of the decision to budget a given amount for a subject area. . . . Much the same kind of [analysis] can come from formulation of policy statements on collection development. . . . Library staffs are making distinct efforts to relate collecting priorities more closely to the academic program and research activities on the local campus.[10]

In a school media center, when a decision to spend more (or less) this year than last for films is required, some type of community analysis is necessary to see if the decision is in keeping with the needs of the teachers and the students. For any type of library, a sampling of community opinion is desirable when more than a minor change in collection patterns or services is contemplated, or when joining a network, consortium, or other cooperative organization is likely to alter collection habits. The community analysis is also a way of letting people who use the library know what the library is about.

Graduate School of Library Science, 1978].) For an analysis of the marketing survey and community analysis see Morris E. Massey, "Market Analysis and Audience Research for Libraries," *Library Trends*, January 1976, pp. 473–481.

[8] Edwin B. Parker and William J. Paisley, "Predicting Library Circulation from Community Characteristics," *The Public Opinion Quarterly*, Spring 1965, pp. 39–53.

[9] Susan F. Tait, "Community Analysis," *School Library Journal*, February 1978, p. 42.

[10] James F. Govan, "Community Analysis in an Academic Environment," *Library Trends*, January 1976, pp. 542–543.

BASIC CONSIDERATIONS

There are many ways to develop and carry through a community analysis, but all must answer one central question: How can we develop a method for analyzing the population that will give us the information necessary for modification of service—and, of course, selection policies?

Edwin Olson properly observes that three basic characteristics affect users' library-use patterns: "(1) psychological factors—the values, attitudes, perceptions about formal information service facilities and the people who work in them; (2) effectiveness of available services—the depth or quality of the services provided; and (3) characteristics of the user and his environment, the personal characteristics of the user and the formal information resources . . . available to him."[11] While all studies consider some of the psychological factors (usually through interviews, questionnaires, and observation), concentration is on the latter two clusters, the services and the general characteristics of the users. Librarians rightfully tend to shy away from any close psychological profile of the community because few are qualified to make judgments in this area.

Several elements are standard for the average study: (1) The librarian must know the library goals and objectives as related to what he or she hopes to learn from the study. (2) There must be a clear designation of responsibility for the study. (3) Data should be as current as possible, collected from all existing reports, studies, census data, and the like. (4) Procedures must be developed to check the statistical data against the actual needs of the community; interviews and questionnaires are usually employed. (5) A final report with an indication of action to be taken must be prepared.

GOALS

The most important aspect of the community study (or any evaluation of library services and selection) is a statement of objectives. The goals should be clear, as specific as possible, and measurable in some way. In other words, librarians must say what they hope to accomplish, how they plan to go about it, and how they are going to evaluate the results.

Given a collection development policy (see Chapter 1), the librarian has

[11] "User Population Characteristics Related to Library Utilization," in I. B. Hoadley (ed.), *Quantitative Methods of Librarianship* (Westport, Conn.: Greenwood Press, 1972), p. 109. This is a useful guide, as is Altman's *Data Gathering and Instructional Manual*, which gives detailed instructions on data collection and, equally important, methods of presenting and analyzing the results.

A Community Analysis Checklist will be useful for giving an idea of what is involved in data gathering and can be found in the appendix (pp. 139–149) to Helen Lyman's *Literacy and the Nation's Libraries* (Chicago: American Library Association, 1977). An easy-to-understand explanation of what to watch for in statistical data and other sources of information will be found in Jeffrey Katzer, et al., *Evaluating Information* (Reading, Mass.: Addison-Wesley, 1978), which is particularly strong in pointing out methods of detecting misleading data.

a beginning point. The policy-statement goals should be evaluated by others in the community, particularly those who will assist in the patterning of the study.

If the community has been involved with the drawing up of the collection development policy, the goals are understood by at least the leaders. Where these leaders have not been consulted, the librarian should: (1) Call for those directly involved with the administration of the library to examine the goals. This would be the library board in a public library, the school board in a school, the faculty advisory group in an academic library, and so on. Everyone should be asked to suggest revisions, deletions, or additions. (2) In a school library the goals should be distributed to all teachers or, at a minimum, to department, section, area heads and supervisors—again with an invitation for comments. (3) The same procedure might be followed in an academic library. (4) Some public libraries have found it useful to hold minor town meetings to discuss the library and its goals. Where this is not practical, the public librarian should attempt to bring the goals to the attention of the public through newspapers, radio, and bulletin boards throughout the library. Provision should be made for the users to have a way of making suggestions, possibly simply the old-fashioned suggestion box. There are other ways of involving the community in the goals, but these are at least a beginning.

WHO CONDUCTS THE STUDY?

Even the most limited community analysis requires time, people, and money. In the early stages full support must be received from administrators, trustees, library-faculty board, or other governing bodies, and it is useful to present plans and results to the officials who first approved the study as the analysis proceeds.

Whenever possible the analysis should be planned and executed by the librarians involved. A librarian best understands the problems peculiar to the library and is in a better position than outsiders to evaluate present and future services. At the same time, a sophisticated analysis requires specialized skills. Professional consultants or advisers from various state, educational, and related agencies can assist. Names may be obtained from the American Library Asociation, from the state library, and from other libraries of about the same size and type where studies have been made in the past.

Community analysis is an ongoing concern of many individuals and groups, and the librarian will do well to consult other community agencies. Involving related disciplines and organizations in the study will do much to broaden the scope of library effectiveness. Such things as the role of community centers in the area will have a direct bearing on the study.

Periodic meetings should be held between librarians, representatives of other organizations and agencies, and people who use the library. The meetings may be workshops or committee get-togethers or simply talking over a cup of coffee.

In school and academic libraries it is ideal to have a committee composed of teachers, students, librarians, and others involved with the library (alumni, parents) to define goals, implement procedures, and be on the alert for community changes that may or should affect the library. The larger the library, the more the committees should include subject bibliographers, media specialists, and general library experts who can discuss collection building and evaluation with knowledgeable faculty members.

Data Gathering

Once the goals and questions of the community analysis are determined and the planning group and primary organizers are named, the time has come for the collection of data. This entails gathering information about the community from documents, reports, government studies, and so on. The printed material will be balanced by questionnaires, interviews, and observation. Essentially, the librarian will be looking for information on the number of people in the library area, economic levels, educational levels, religious affiliations, population growth or decline, minority groups, age, and a host of other facts about the community.

The library itself (or larger or specialized libraries in the region) is the best source for much of the data, something that may not be obvious, particularly when one considers certain overlapping categories of knowledge. Among the more significant related categories: (1) Social and industrial psychology data about the immediate community. (2) Sociology, which "offers a valuable body of knowledge and methodologies that are indispensable to an understanding of the library's publics, of its consumers, of the behavior of the market for library services, and of the demographic and other social changes that affect the library's mission."[12] (3) Works on systems analysis, community economics, and public finance and political science.

Of the various types of existing data the librarian can tap, that available from the Bureau of the Census is likely to be the most useful. The Bureau's statistical studies, maps, and other material are normally a part of the library's existing collection or are in the local depository library. The reports can be traced through the *Bureau of the Census Catalog*, the *Monthly Catalog*, the *American Statistical Index*, and the *Index to Selected 1970 Census Reports*.

Before using census data the librarian should determine the scope of the geographic boundaries of the service areas. In a small community this may mean no more than the town boundaries, but in an urban situation the boundaries may include the whole of the city or simply a single branch or central library service area. Specific boundaries must be established or the study will become tangled in misunderstanding. How do you establish those lines? The most useful single method is to employ the readily available by census maps.

---

[12] William R. Monat, "Role of the Social and Behavioral Sciences," *Library Trends*, January 1976, pp. 585ff.

The Bureau of the Census produces various types of maps among them:
(1) Outline maps, useful to show geographic boundaries, may be obtained
for counties or specific areas within an urban center. These may be broken
down by county subdivisions, central business districts, retail centers, and
so on, and (2) display maps, which give the various geographic distributions
of social, economic, and other data within the outline maps.

Most librarians will be working with SMSA (standard metropolitan
statistical area) maps. These cover a county or group of counties that
contains at least one city having 50,000 or more inhabitants, with the name
of the central city used as a means of identification.

Census tracts are the most familiar and certainly most valuable means for
pinpointing specific characteristics of the urban community served by the
library. The tracts are designed to show about 5000 or less population, most
of whom share common characteristics of income, living conditions, and so
on. For example, an urban center may be divided into scores or even
hundreds of census and block tracts which tend to indicate such things as
the center of the richest and poorest sections of the community, the industrial areas, and concentrations of minority groups. A combination of the
various tracts will soon establish a profile of the community in which the
library is located and its probable physical bounds of service. Within the
physical bounds the tracts and blocks will give the most detailed amount of
information available on the community.

A typical use of census data was made at the Detroit Public Library.
Demographic information was provided for a service area within 1.5 miles
of each branch library (a standard distance, which may vary half a mile one
way or the other, but rarely any more or less). Various workshops included
librarians, involved community members, and personnel from other agencies:

The library pinpointed the locations of each branch library and books were prepared for each branch showing all statistical information from the census figures
for the service area of that branch. In this way a study of the ethnic characteristics of each neighborhood was begun, detailing the percentage of children and
their age groupings, the educational levels, etc. . . . [From the data and discussions]
gradually information about the population became more clear.[13]

As in most community analysis, the data pointed to action: "It was also
clear from these workshops and other contacts with city agencies that there
was no decentralized information and referral service available in the
city. . . . At this point, the theoretical vehicle for the revitalization of
the branch libraries was attained."[14]

There are numerous other sources of community data, including (1)
reports and studies made by local, county, regional, and state governments,
normally part of the same government documents collection that supplies
the census studies; (2) state education agencies, university schools of educa-

---

[13] Robert Croneberger and Carolyn Luck, "Analyzing Community Human Information
Needs: A Case Study," *Library Trends*, January 1976, p. 517.
[14] Ibid.

tion, even local school districts, which will have data on current and projected enrollment in elementary school through university; and (3) statistics gathered by the U.S. Office of Education, particularly those regarding libraries from the National Center for Educational Statistics. All of this, including the census material, may be analyzed by local banks, industrial firms, businesses, or chambers of commerce, who may be interested in supplying the library with nonconfidential material about the community.

LIBRARY IN-HOUSE DATA COLLECTING

Once the community at large is analyzed (or at the same time), the librarian should be working on in-house studies to indicate who now uses the library and for what purpose, the degree of satisfaction, and similar information. Useful models may be readily located by searching *Library Literature* or consulting with state library agencies, special organizations, or library schools that have files of library surveys and use studies.

Libraries have traditionally employed user statistics to show library activities quantitatively. These range from basic circulation figures to much more sophisticated studies of age groups, occupations, and reader interests. Almost all libraries maintain figures reflecting circulation, normally tabulated and presented in annual reports (a solid retrospective source of information about the library). Often, too, individual departments maintain statistical data that can be useful. A reference section, for example, may tally types and numbers of queries as well as source material found (or not found). Such data will give an indication of patterns of library use and effectiveness.

In determining who is using the library one might simply check to see how many times certain types of books, recordings, or films circulated. One could then check the written card against the registration files and find, for example, that the particular type of book was favored by teenagers who lived in relatively middle-class neighborhoods. Variations on this method, such as matching gross circulation with who is using the material, is a much-valued way of evaluation.

Thanks to computerized circulation records and registration files, it is now possible to find this type of information not only more quickly and accurately but also with considerably more sophistication. A quick check, for example, will tell the librarian what segments of the collection are heavily used (in the sense they are checked out), titles that should be duplicated because of heavy use, or areas where materials might be cut back, and loan periods.

Analysis of records is not simple, particularly in a medium-sized to large library. If you do not have statistical training, at least find out how much information is necessary to qualify the work as an objective sampling—and, of course, determine how to sample the records objectively. Typically one may take every fifth or tenth or twentieth record, depending upon the overall size of the file. Time limitations may allow no more than one hour of one day a week for a given period.

This is only a brief overview of the kinds of data available, both from and about the community at large, and from and about the library itself. The type and amount of data, as well as the order of collecting, will depend upon the goals established for a study. Each library has its own needs.

BEYOND THE DATA

Gathering objective data is the first step in community analysis, but it is equally important to weigh the data with what some call a "feeling" for the community. As summarized by Minzey and LeTarte,

Good community assessment must recognize that the communities share certain beliefs and values and mutually hold certain aspirations, concerns and community goals. To ignore the subjective "feeling" aspect of a community when attempting to assess it, parallels an attempt by a medical student to establish the basic determinant of life by studying only a cadaver. Human beings are more than a combination of factual data; and communities, because they are composed of humans, require more than an overview of easily collectable facts if meaningful assessment is to occur.

To appraise or diagnose a community by utilizing information beyond what is normally collected, to determine to what extent goals of the community are being achieved, and to determine what might be done to further the attainment of these goals, requires a response to a variety of questions, such as:

1. Is there a set of common understandings, goals, beliefs, and values held by the community?
2. Is there unity within the community that allows it to function at an acceptable level?
3. Is there a tendency for large sub-groups to develop with opposing purposes, causing conflict and tension within the community?
4. Are the institutions within the community (churches, schools, government agencies, etc.) viewed as positive community forces or as burdens to the taxpayer?
5. Do people have an opportunity to confront their problems as a group and solve them?
6. Do barriers exist that reduce opportunities for people to become actively engaged in working for social change, community change and institutional change?[15]

Simple data collection does not answer questions of this type. They require various approaches, from observation to questionnaires and interviews. Where the latter are employed, it is wise to begin with community leaders, activists from organizations and agencies, businesspeople, and anyone else who may have a sixth sense about the community.

QUESTIONNAIRES AND INTERVIEWS

There are many articles on the construction and use of the questionnaire and the interview, but the librarian who is unfamiliar with either process

[15] Jack D. Minzey and Clyde LeTarte, *Community Education: From Program to Process* (Midland, Mich.: Pendell Publishing Co., 1972), pp. 66–67.

should turn to library schools, social research centers, and the like for assistance.[16] Advice on methodology is particularly necessary when the librarian is dealing with library nonusers, who are likely to be less than familiar with even basic concepts of library service.

Questions and interviews should be kept relatively short (ten minutes or less) and should be tested on a few people (including librarians) before the actual study is launched. As with the overall community study, the librarian must know precisely the purpose of the question and whether or not the information is really needed. Questions should be direct and specific, and with nonusers it is useful to preface either the written or oral remarks with a brief explanation of the study—if only to insure the suspicious that you are not a salesperson.

OBSERVATION

An observant individual can often learn more about the community than the best-structured formalized system of data gathering. One need only stand by the card catalog to ascertain who uses it. Observing for an hour or two each day in the periodical section will reveal more about what titles are popular than the most thorough circulation records.

A variation on static observation is the community walk. The librarian should walk through the charted areas to discover something about the real flavor of the area, how people actually live, not how they live according to statistics. And, in addition to the subjective feeling about the area (which can be later checked by more objective data), the librarian who walks learns much about other serving community services—where people go for recreation, for social assistance, for business, for shopping, and so on.

I particularly like the walkabout step because it is feasible even if the library is not committed to a full-scale community analysis. . . . The benefits . . . are many. One is acquiring a better idea of how to handle publicity . . . or where to post flyers and posters. . . . Also you might get additional program ideas . . . as your knowledge of the area increases.[17]

The so-called community walk is now a legitimate device for community analysis and is certainly a suitable way of double-checking the gathered data.

[16] Sybilla A. Cook's "The Delphi Connection" (*Wilson Library Bulletin*, May 1978, pp. 703–706) is a lucid discussion of one type of questionnaire-interview technique; see also the short references at the end of the article. A good, more general approach is suggested by Elizabeth W. Matthews, "Describing the Descriptive Survey or Communications by Questionnaire," *Illinois Libraries*, March 1978, pp. 255–259; again, note the references. See the "Questionnaire for User-Rating of Library Services" at the conclusion of Steven Chwe's "A Model Instrument for User-Rating of Library Service," *California Librarian*, May 1978, pp. 51–55. Another good source is M. G. F. Beeler, et al., *Measuring the Quality of Library Service: A Handbook* (Metuchen, N.J.: Scarecrow Press, 1974). Questionnaires appear in library surveys; *The Library Listens*, a 1973 survey by the Delaware Library Association, includes in the appendix the "Questionnaire Used in Delaware Library Survey."

[17] Tait, op. cit.

In the Detroit Public Library study librarians were asked to take community walks in order to:

(1) Advertise the services of the library, describing not only the new information and referral services, but all other services of the system; and (2) to discover in human terms "who was out there, what were the needs and wants of the community, what were the existing services, and how we could best link the resources of the library to existing agencies and groups and transform the branch libraries into the neighborhood information centers we wanted them to be.[18]

As a method of both alerting the community to the presence of the library and learning more about the community, the walks are extremely rewarding. The Detroit methodology is suitable for other places: at least two people normally went on the walk, to check each other's impressions, and each branch was given about six months for the initial walk, after which another began. This procedure keeps the librarians aware of changes.

THE REPORT

The final report usually appears in offset form, complete with maps, charts, and tables. The last draft should be prepared by someone who is familiar with writing, has a sense of style, and can avoid jargon. Form is nevertheless secondary to how the information is employed. As many people as possible should be involved with the interpretation and implementation of the results, and the people who planned the initial study should be given an opportunity to evaluate the findings. It is one thing to discover there are not enough periodicals in the library, quite another to decide whether the demand can be best met by periodicals, books, films, slides, or something else.

Nonuser and Nonreader

Only 20 to 30 percent of the adult American public (as an undifferentiated whole) goes into a library. Among young people the figure is closer to 50 or 60 percent.[19] The familiar picture of the sporadically used public library emerges. People know where it is, but if they have used it, it was quite a while ago. It is still too closely linked in the adult mind with public-school education and marginal entertainment.[20]

Another concern is the apparent falling away even of readers. Poet and critic Joel Oppenheimer well summarizes what many people now think about reading:

[18] Croneberger and Luck, op. cit., p. 518.

[19] A Gallup Poll found that "one in five Americans indicated they made use of the library for information" (Lyle Eberhart, "A Closer Look: A Gallup Survey of American Adults . . . ," *American Libraries*, April 1976, p. 207).

[20] Timothy Hays, et al., "The Patron is Not the Public," *Library Journal*, September 15, 1977, p. 1815.

I . . . know nobody's reading. Don't give me any tests or polls, or market research —just come with me to City College or St. Andrew's Presbyterian College in North Carolina or the College of the Atlantic in Maine. I've taught in all three places in the last three years. There are bright students and dumb students in each of them, and none of them know what a book is. Oh, they dutifully get whatever is listed as a course requirement, and they are capable of spelling out the words page by page, but the idea of reading a non-required book—or of keeping a required one after the course is over—seems not only alien to them, but ridiculous.[21]

Oppenheimer makes an even more telling observation about the faithful readers who, "subsumed in the onslaught of TV, movies, records, the kids, and facts," hardly read any more. "The era when I'd devour a book a day is long gone."[22]

Several 1978 studies seem to contradict traditional surveys of library users, not to mention the sense of such critics as Oppenheimer that people no longer read very much. Only one year after its surveyors found few using the libraries, Gallup came up with an opposite figure: 51 percent of adult Americans had visited a public library in the past year. Not only that, 59 percent of the Americans sampled had read a book in the preceding month. According to another study, nearly half the American public never reads a book, and close to 40 percent of the population over the age of sixteen read only newspapers or magazines.[23]

inconsistency in studies to determine how many adults read and use the library

The problem with these surveys, and certainly with individual feelings about the state of reading and use of libraries, is summarized by a book-company executive:

why

[Such surveys tend to be] filled with flaws, including internal inconsistencies and conclusions that do not jibe with industry figures on the number of books sold. We have just about given up on this kind of research because we couldn't figure out how to make people tell the truth. They have a sense of guilt that makes them join a book club. They think it will impose a discipline on them and they will read more books. Thinking they ought to read, they say they do, but don't.[24]

ETHNIC GROUPS

There is no satisfactory definition or term for ethnic groups or minorities. For library purposes (borrowing from the summary in the *ALA Yearbook*) the groups, in alphabetical order, include: American Indians, Asian Americans, Black Americans, Hispanic Americans, Italian Americans, Jewish Americans, Polish Americans—and any other ethnic group found in your library area. Within each of these groups there are wide varieties of educa-

---

[21] "All Booked Up," *The Village Voice* (New York City), October 2, 1978, p. 14.
[22] Ibid.
[23] These surveys are summarized by the editor of *American Libraries* in "Naked Came the Reader, Or a Tale of Three Surveys," *American Libraries*, December 1978, pp. 639–640. One, the Gallup report of 1978, is available from the American Library Association.
[24] "Experts Suggest Action, Cite Problems," *Publishers Weekly*, November 6, 1978, p. 17.

tional, social, political, and economic sophistication. But for the moment, and only as an example, consider how library materials selection would be modified for the foreign-born Hispanics:

1. Many are young, under twenty-five, but likely to have dropped out of school. Some have reading skills; most are likely to be classified as close to functionally illiterate.

2. Most live in clusters in urban centers, probably in poverty.

3. Many may have tried the library once or twice (particularly the school library) and given up for lack of any cultural reinforcement. More drastic reasons for not using the library range from lack of materials in Spanish to absence of bilingual librarians.

In such circumstances, several basic considerations must enter the selection of materials: for minority groups in the community

1. First and most important, service should be given because the groups deserve the service. The library should be condescending neither in materials selected nor in assistance given.

2. The standard formats (from books and records to microfilm and pamphlets), should stress materials in Spanish and in English. The materials must emphasize information and referral content that will help users in everyday survival as well as in mastery of a second language and the cultural aspects of America. (In no case is English or American culture to be presented as superior or the second language as inferior.)

3. Variations exist within the groups, and bilingual materials must meet these differences. For example, not all Spanish-speaking people are from the same country, the same cultural background, or the same economic situation.

4. Sometimes new, traditionally nonacceptable forms should be purchased because these will make the user feel at home in the library. "Items such as novels in picture forms and children's literature in comic book formats are very widely read in Latin America but are considered unacceptable by some libraries."[25]

5. Levels of reading competence vary widely, not only in terms of literacy but also in familiarity with English and other printed languages. Materials should accommodate the various levels; again, rules must be broken and basic textbooks (otherwise not acceptable in many libraries) should be considered.

ILLITERATES

The library should do everything in its power to fight functional illiteracy. Anyone who believes this to be idealistic, or thinks it should be left to others, should consider what it means to be illiterate:

Linguistic refugees in a society where reading is taken as much for granted as the ability to tell time lead an existence fraught with loneliness and bewilderment.

[25] Yolanda Cuesta and Patricia Tarin, "Guidelines for Library Service to the Spanish-Speaking," *Library Journal*, July 1978, p. 1355.

Theirs is a private anguish laden with self-doubt, resentment, anger and shame. In constant fear of ridicule and rejection, they say they feel as if they never belong.

Many say they feel "cheated," robbed of an opportunity to make something more of their lives. Others say that the inability to read is a form of paralysis. . . . Unable to utilize calendars, date books, telephone directories, street maps and other mnemonic devices, those who cannot read commit enormous detail to memory.

"It is almost like the blind man who has to be more aware of smells and taste," said a 32-year-old security officer. "You have to watch everything. You have to remember everything. I might not be able to read a street sign, but I know every single house on that street."

To the illiterate there are few aspects of travel, employment or correspondence that escape their handicap. A messenger, for example, is sometimes unable to deliver a package because he cannot decipher the address.[26]

Experts disagree widely over the definition of illiteracy and interpretation of its causes and cures; some even prefer to call courses in literacy "adult new reader" programs. There is no consensus as to how many adults (over fourteen years of age) are totally or functionally illiterate, but the combined figure may be from as low as 6 percent to as high as 30 or even 50 percent, depending upon what is meant by illiteracy.[27] The higher figures are probably much closer to the truth if one measures reading skills in terms of ease of writing, understanding basic written material, and filling out forms.[28]

The same experts disagree about how to solve the problem, but legislatures and boards of education in 33 states have adopted minimum-competency standards for their schools. And a 1977 survey of U.S. companies found that at least 10,000 employers had begun running remedial education programs in basic subjects for their workers—an obvious place for library involvement.

Recognition of the serious problem of illiteracy has been given by the top level of government: in September 1978 there was a White House-sponsored International Literacy Day Conference. After the talks and the papers it became apparent that many publishers are as concerned with the need to eliminate illiteracy as to publish new books on the subject.[29]

The perennial problem in selecting materials for adult groups with low reading abilities (because of illiteracy, cultural shock, poor education) is to find high-interest, low-vocabulary books. Librarians who believe this prob-

---

[26] Dena Kleiman, "For the Illiterate, A Daily Frustration," *The New York Times*, April 30, 1978, section 12, p. 1.

[27] John B. Carroll (ed.), *Toward a Literate Society: The Report of the Committee on Reading of the National Academy of Education* (New York: McGraw-Hill, 1975).

[28] Much the same is true in Canada, England, and western European countries, in all of which the degree of functional illiteracy is quite high. See Mary Flanagan and Cheryl Moore, "Materials for Adult Basic Reading," *Ontario Library Review*, December 1977, p. 280, and Raymond Astbury, "New Adult Readers and the Public Library in the United Kingdom," *UNESCO Bulletin for Libraries*, January-February 1977, pp. 26–34.

[29] "The First R," *Publishers Weekly*, September 25, 1978, p. 47. For a library-related study of illiteracy and a program for its cure, see Helen Lyman, *Literacy and the Nation's Libraries* (Chicago: American Library Association, 1977).

lem is restricted to public libraries and some school libraries will discover it is now universal. A community-college librarian notes: "Many of the titles found in the traditional sources are too difficult for a great number of our students."[30]

This question has never been satisfactorily resolved, and from time to time there are such stop-gap suggestions as:

The High Interest/Low Reading Level Information Packet, prepared for YASD's 1978 preconference program "Dispelling the High-Low Blues," might help. . . . In addition to Patsy Perritt's bibliography, "Sources of Materials for Poor Readers," it reprints the Eastern Massachusetts Regional Library System's graded "Easy Reads for Teens" and articles on evaluation criteria. The packet is available for $1.50 prepaid from the UASD Office, ALA, 50 E. Huron St., Chicago, IL 60611.

Ruth Rausen, Assistant Coordinator of Young Adult Services at the New York Public Library, believes many of the titles in NYPL's 8-page annual pamphlet, "Easy-to-Read Books for Teenagers," might interest adults. The 1978 edition can be ordered for 25 cents from the Office of Young Adult Services, NYPL, 5th Ave. at 42nd St., New York, NY 10018.[31]

Two elements in the selection of high-interest, low-reading-level materials:
1. They must be books that are adult in content, yet provide reading and instruction at a level compatible with the individual's reading abilities. Beyond that one must consider the format (not too juvenile), the style of writing (not condescending), and relationship to the individual's background (Spanish-speaking people have needs that differ from those of native-born American Indians).
2. One must find bibliographies, lists, and the like for selection. In the past few years there have been a number of these issued, if only by libraries with literacy programs. A good beginning, for example, is the list of readings in Flanagan and Moore's "Materials for Adult Basic Reading," which deals with Canadian programs.[32]

The best single attack on the problem is offered by Helen Lyman in her *Reading and the Adult New Reader* (Chicago: American Library Association, 1977), in which primary concern is with how to evaluate and locate materials for adults. For current materials, *Booklist* publishes an Adult Basic Education column on the fifteenth of January, April, July, and October.

There are, then, many existing and potential audiences for library services and, in turn, need for new approaches to materials selection. Community analysis will help librarians find those who need library assistance, but the librarian must have a firm understanding of library *uses* as well as library *users*. As Mary Jo Lynch put it: "We need to know a lot more about library uses before we can decide what role the educational, cultural and recreational

---

[30] Rina Krasney, in Action Exchange, *American Libraries*, October 1978, p. 516.
[31] Ibid.
[32] Pp. 282–285, a good, annotated listing that concludes with a basic bibliography; note also the outline guide to selection criteria and the list of publishers.

functions of the public library for adults . . . will play in establishing the public library at the center of the life of a community."[33]

One major effort to make the library a center of community use is demonstrated by information and referral services (I&R). For the most part I&R is directed to other than the traditional middle-class audience so familiar to many libraries. I&R is, in fact, a result of community analysis—which demonstrates the need of various other audiences for service.

Information and Referral Services – Public Outreach Program

(incorporates a liberal view) for non users

Sometimes known as "community information service," this is a public-library outreach program.[34] Rather than asking who library users are, I&R is an effort to put the library to use, to work for many who never considered using a library. Among services usually provided:

(1.) Current information and data of a practical nature on aspects of life likely to require information, particularly for those who have problems. The librarian supplies answers or refers the user to places answers can be found to questions about health, consumer problems, social services, housing, job training, adult education, and recreation.

(2.) A file of organizations, institutions, and individuals in the community to whom the librarian may refer someone for additional assistance and information.[35]

The referral aspects of the service, whereby the librarian puts the user in touch with agencies or individuals for help with a problem, is the added dimension. In a real sense, the librarian has become a counselor, an aggressive assistant for people who need help. For public libraries this concept is becoming more of an accepted pattern than an exception.

There are numerous examples of I&R service. One is the New York Public Library Directory of Community Services, issued in 1979. Compiled by staff

[33] "Educational, Cultural and Recreational Services of the Public Library for Adults," *The Library Quarterly*, October 1978, p. 186.

[34] I&R is the topic of numerous books, articles, and reports. See William Katz, *Introduction to Reference Work* (New York: McGraw-Hill, 1978), vol. 2, pp. 19–26, for a discussion of I&R and for readings. An excellent overview is offered by Clara S. Jones in her *Public Library and Information and Referral Service* (Syracuse, N.Y.: Gaylord, 1978).

A survey of relatively current I&R activities will be found in Dorothy Turick's "Community Information Services in Libraries," *LJ Special Report No. 5* (New York: R. R. Bowker, 1977). The broader implications of I&R are discussed by Guy Garrison in "The Changing Role of the Public Library as an Information Agency," *Suid-Afrikaanse Biblioteke*, July 1978, pp. 11–18.

[35] Della L. Giblon, "Backtalk," *RQ*, Winter 1977, pp. 167–170. Giblon explains how a "people index" is compiled and used to direct library patrons to people who can assist them or give information. See also what is virtually an outline of services likely to be offered by I&R in Catherine McKinnon, "Developing an Information Service," *Ontario Library Review*, September 1978, pp. 210–215.

members in 82 branches, it is a bilingual (Spanish and English) guide to 2000 various agencies:

The listings cover every imaginable need, and are supplemented in each branch with other directories, and with staff librarians well-versed in the neighborhoods they serve. . . . From the Memphis/Shelby County Public Library . . . comes an equally excellent *Directory of Human Services.* . . . [This is updated by a newsletter.] The library's files also contain triple the information in the *Directory*, and [the library manual] is a model for libraries developing I&R services, rich in the most intimate detail of dealing with other agences, specific patron problems, and personalities.[36]

Another example is the Detroit Public Library; deploring the loss of circulation of books (in 1958 1 million, in 1977 about 2 million), it turned to TIP (The Information Place). TIP is an information and referral service for both regular library users and those who rarely or never go to the library. It is typical of services in almost all major urban centers today, and, to a lesser degree, in public libraries in smaller communities.[37]

This philosophy also should be represented in school libraries. The concerns of young people, particularly at the junior high and high school level, need to be answered in part by the librarian. This means purchase of materials that answer real questions these people have—from films on skin care to books on sexual and emotional development. Equally important, as more than one librarian has observed, is the necessity of actively listening to and helping the individual:

The concern of young adult librarians is to provide information that realistically meets the needs of young patrons, to establish a trusting relationship, to create an environment of accessibility and satisfaction. . . . The only real question is often not whether the young adult librarian should act as counselor, but whether the counseling is effective or ineffective.[38]

Doing more than passing out a book or a nonprint source of information is a recommended practice as much for public librarians as for school librarians. First, however, it requires a head-on analysis of your own capabilities and sympathies and a recognition in purchase of materials that some should be grounded in the everyday concerns of people.

[36] John Berry, "I&R in Libraries, Alive & Well," *Library Journal*, February 1, 1979, p. 331.

[37] Critics of the Detroit program and similar ones point out that the process drains money away from books and other materials. For example, in 1977 Detroit spent 8.1 percent of its budget for materials, considerably less than the national average. One critic said: "Twenty years from now, people in Detroit are likely to find a shortage of books." To which the Detroit library director replies: "A library that provides books on auto repair or home improvement and directs people to services has a much more meaningful information system than one that simply buys books to strengthen its esoteric literature collection" (John Camper, "Libraries Today Give You Hot Tips, Not Cold Facts," Albany [N.Y.] *Times-Union*, September 17, 1978, p. E6). Clara S. Jones, op. cit., includes a lengthy section on Detroit's TIP program on pp. 167–224.

[38] Sara Fine, "The Librarian as Youth Counselor," *Drexel Library Quarterly*, January 1978, pp. 42–43.

I&R AND MATERIALS SELECTION

rather: Information is less likely to be in traditional book form than available as (1) a current file constructed and updated by the librarian through community contracts, (2) local directories of individuals and organizations (which may be a combination of books and library files), and (3) more traditional selected periodicals, articles, government documents, newspapers, and the like.[39]

Paralleling the development of I&R centers in libraries is a tendency toward new emphasis on information and less on traditional activities. This view is summarized by Guy Garrison, who—tallying the drop in use of large urban public libraries—concludes there is need for further efforts to reach nonlibrary users: the disadvantaged, adults with learning problems, minorities. He sees "compelling reasons . . . to hold the provision of information as the primary goal and to see other goals—book provision, educational and cultural activities, recreation—as subsidiary."[40]

The view fits in nicely with I&R but seems a bit one-sided, if not premature. It is certainly worth considering and is given here as an example of one of scores of would-be solutions to the apparent lack of interest in many public libraries. Were it accepted, there would be a drastic change in selection policies, at least in terms of emphasis.

Several points should be made briefly here about what I&R has to do with the type of materials selected.

1. There will be an emphasis on current reports, pamphlets, and ephemera gathered from local, state, regional, and federal agencies and organizations. Little of this is ever indexed or reviewed, so the librarian must be constantly on the lookout for what is available—by close contact with the various issuing agencies. The librarian will also be watching for films, recordings, slides, and other materials issued by the same organizations that can be used in I&R services.

2. Librarians will probably solve the problem of currency of data by doing most of the collecting themselves and, in a sense, become publishers and distributors.

3. There will be a constant interest in "street" materials, from easy-to-understand books and pamphlets on the law and medicine to drugs and sex. A good key to this type of material will be found in the alternative press publications, many of which are listed and annotated in the author's *Magazines for Libraries* (3rd ed.; New York: R. R. Bowker, 1978).

---

[39] There are nevertheless an increasing number of reference books directed specifically to information and referral services, such as *The New York Women's Yellow Pages: Original Source Book for Women* (New York: St. Martin's, 1978), an annotated directory of 11 categories of sources of use to women. Similar directories now exist in other major cities.

[40] Op. cit., p. 17.

4. The librarian will be always on the alert for more standard books, periodicals, films, slides, and so forth, found in standard sources discussed throughout this book. In addition, effort will be made to purchase foreign-language and bilingual materials of direct use to the people served in I&R centers.

THE FUTURE OF I&R

Not all librarians are sold on the idea of I&R, and it would be an error to think there is a consensus. An annual news report for 1978 (*Library Journal*, January 15, 1979, p. 156) noted that lack of funding, lack of staff, and lack even of public support has forced many librarians to reconsider the traditional outreach philosophy and has in fact resulted in a temporary abandonment of the nonuser. The new call in 1979 was for "more serious attention [labeled "inreach" by some] to the needs of people who actually use and support the libraries." TRADITIONAL VIEWPOINT

At least one public library is nevertheless increasing outreach programs because "libraries will be needed more than ever by more people because things are going to get worse and not better for most." Furthermore, the pragmatists believe that the only way libraries will retain government backing is by proving they serve a large segment of the population, not simply the middle class.

If bets were to be taken, the odds would be with a developing I&R service: in 1977 more than 800 librarians had joined the Alliance of Information and Referral Services, a new organization devoted solely to I&R. Furthermore, standards are now available from the same organization. And as Miles Martin put it: "It seems clear that I&R centers are numerous, that public libraries are increasing their services in the area and that changes in both library and social work education will be made to meet the need for trained I&R specialists."[41]

[41] "Information and Referral Centers," *ALA Yearbook* (Chicago: American Library Association, 1978), p. 148.

3
Collection Development

No LIBRARY operates completely by itself today; each depends on regional, state, national, and international libraries and networks. This interaction is reflected in formal and informal agreements among libraries, and a whole literature has developed around the subject. We will therefore examine briefly the subject of library cooperation and how it influences collection development in the individual library.

Library Cooperation {how it influences collection dev. in the indiv. library}

NETWORKS

The *National Inventory of Library Needs* (1977) is an overview of American library needs that calls for both local and national networks of library service.[1] Out of this study has developed renewed interest in the activities of the National Commission on Libraries and Information Science, which sponsored the inventory. The commission has examined such things as the role of the Library of Congress in an emerging national network and (more important perhaps) how existing local library networks would fit into the master plan. This in turn has led to wide discussion of the implication of networks—everything from who finances and governs such organizations to the role of private industry in information.

Networking is a complicated affair that does not lend itself to easy explanation, but the commission suggests a workable definition:

Two or more libraries and/or other organizations engaged in a common problem of information exchange, through communications, for some functional purpose.

[1] *National Inventory of Library Needs* (Washington, D.C.: Government Printing Office, 1977). The report has been discussed widely; see Ralph Blasingame, "Son of Inventory," *Library Journal*, June 1, 1978, pp. 1144–1146, and Edwin Castagna, "Will the National Inventory Lead from the Slough of Despond to the Celestial City?," *American Libraries*, October 1977, pp. 491–492.

A network usually consists of a formal arrangement whereby materials, information, and services provided by a variety of types of libraries and/or other organizations are made available to all potential users. (Libraries may be in different jurisdictions but agree to serve one another on the same basis as each serves its own constituents. Computers and telecommunications may be among the tools used for facilitating communications among them.)[2]

In terms of selection of materials, networks are important because they can develop sophisticated bibliographic methods of organizing, storing, and retrieving information to assist in interlibrary loan, and almost instant checks on who has what (and, therefore help answer the question: Need we purchase?). Although more than 2000 libraries now have some such services through OCLC, BALLOTS, and similar channels (see below), the system itself is still in its infancy and the majority of libraries remain outside the network. Or as Al Trezza, head of the National Commission, put it: *still new*

In spite of the seeming omnipresence of computerized bibliographic services, it is well to recognize that only a small portion of the library community is being reached. Mostly restricted to academic libraries, these services have hardly made a dent in public and special libraries. Moreover, the products offered are surprisingly unrefined and, for the most part, oriented narrowly toward cataloging support and reference services.[3]

Technology will one day link most of the nation's libraries by online machine-readable data bases and give book selectors at one library immediate information about the selection decisions of librarians at another. This quicker access will make it possible to discover quickly who has what and much easier to decide whether, for example, to buy an extremely expensive, esoteric encyclopedia. The same knowledge may make it easier to persuade users, who now insist the library have all major books and journals, that libraries can share resources without harmful effects on the users' research activities. This realization might make it possible to change thinking about the necessity of having giant collections in every large library. The dramatic impact for smaller libraries is that the world of information will be immediately available, at least in theory, and not dependent almost entirely upon what is in the library itself or the region. (Of course, it is one thing to locate book X, another to have it delivered, but even that bottleneck may be solved in time.)

The major national systems beyond the activities of the National Commission on Libraries and Information Science include:

1. OCLC By far the largest of the online bibliographic services, OCLC has more than 2000 computer terminals in over 1500 of the nation's libraries.

---

[2] Quoted by Bernard Franckowiak in "Network Data Bases . . . ," *School Media Quarterly*, Fall 1977, pp. 15–16.

[3] "Networks," *ALA Yearbook* (Chicago: American Library Association, 1978), p. 202. This offers a solid picture for 1977. For a total overview see William Katz, *Introduction to Reference Work* (3rd ed.; New York: McGraw-Hill, 1978), vol. 2, chap. 7, "Networks."

Originally a channel for Library of Congress cataloging, it now includes cataloging data from member libraries and has expanded its services in many directions. A six-year plan that began operation in 1977 will carry OCLC into acquisitions as a source of information on interlibrary loans as well as selection of materials—periodicals, maps, and so on.

2. **BALLOTS** (at this writing the name was to be changed) Stanford's network is a strong challenge to OCLC and a competitor not only for West Coast libraries but also for those in the East. (It services the Research Libraries Group, made up of Yale, the New York Public Library, Columbia, and Stanford.) It offers many of the same services as OCLC, but is competitive pricewise and is ahead of OCLC in efforts to search records by subject (OCLC in early 1979 offered only a title-author search pattern.) Its membership level of about 200 is in keeping with the goals of the system, which sees itself as primarily serving the needs of large research libraries plus those of smaller libraries in the Western states. The goals shift with administrators, and there is a current debate on how national the system should be.

3. **WLN**   The Washington (State) Library Network, an effort to offer complete automated services from cataloging and circulation controls to reference searches and interlibrary loan, is moving toward interstate activities and has expanded to Alaska, Idaho, and Oregon.

In addition to these national and regional systems, there are a number of regional and local operations: CLASS (California Library Authority for Systems and Services), MINITEX (Minnesota Interlibrary Telecommunications Exchange), MIDLNET (Midwest Regional Library Network), and several others. Most provide union catalogs and online bibliographic searches, and in general augment and improve upon the national network operations.

Each of these systems often goes its own way, and the need for more cooperation is becoming obvious. In fact, one service of the National Commission is to work out an operational plan whereby there will be networks within networks, thus assuring local control and local speed of delivery of materials while enjoying the benefits of national searches.

Not everyone favors the network system, or at least its implications. Some librarians, and certainly many users, say that nothing can be better than local access to resources. If one has to wait for delivery of magazine Y or book P, the wait may not be the promised day or so, but weeks or even months. It is one thing to plan a central storehouse, a central library, quite another effectively to find and deliver what is needed by the individual at the local level. There are numerous other objections; for example, private industry opposes a proposed national periodicals center because it is seen as a virtual monopoly on document delivery—delivery now carried out to a limited extent by private firms (such as the Institute for Scientific Information, which provides articles from items included in its own indexes).

Networks will not solve all problems in any event. Consider the difficulties of combining school and public library collections, a cooperative or network scheme suggested by some communities with economic problems (there are now six such systems in operation in Colorado). This has certain economic advantages but parallel service drawbacks. In reporting on this scheme, two librarians pinpoint the essential problem with any cooperative or network plan, local or international:

Much depends upon individual circumstances and personalities involved. A strong commitment and a cooperative spirit are necessary to make the project a success. Each community must examine its own resources and situation carefully to determine whether cooperation is the best means of satisfying its particular needs.[4]

Despite the problems, no librarian today can even begin a discussion of selection without taking into account present and future network and co-operative programs. If, as will be shown, a portion of most library collections is little used, one solution would be to centralize the less-used materials for recall by not one but several or thousands of libraries. This in turn requires sophisticated planning—or, as Allan Kent put it:

. . . resource-sharing alternatives to local purchases must . . . be explored. One of the consequences of this exploration could be decisions to acquire fewer materials locally, and to depend, for access, on resource-sharing networks. But the typical resource-sharing network uses only a general policy statement regarding how to divide the burden of acquisitions among member libraries. The acquisitions person cannot apply this policy well when faced with a specific purchase decision in the gray area. This uncertainty can only be relieved by specific knowledge of what resource-sharing partners are buying and what they hold.[5]

CENTRAL STORAGE

While discussion of a national periodicals center went on, at the close of the 1970s the best example, and a model for central storage of materials, was the Center for Research Libraries. Founded in 1949 by ten Midwestern university libraries, the center had expanded to almost 100 members throughout the United States by the late 1970s. Its purpose is multiple, although it primarily acts as a storage base for little-used materials of member libraries

[4] Cindy McClure and Linda Raybould, "Pros and Cons for School/Public Libraries," *Colorado Libraries*, March 1978, p. 71. There is already an overwhelming amount of material on networks and cooperation, but to get a good idea of what is going on at the practical level, see R. D. Galloway, "Library Cooperation at the Grass Roots . . . ," *Journal of Academic Librarianship*, January 1979, pp. 430–433. A larger view is suggested by Henrietta Avram's "Toward a Nationwide Library Network," *Journal of Library Automation*, December 1978, pp. 285–298; for an annual summary of network activity see "Networks" in the *ALA Yearbook* (Chicago: American Library Association, since 1976). Books are being published on the subject, among them *Multitype Library Cooperation* (New York: R. R. Bowker, 1977).

[5] "Crystal Gazing into the Future," *Journal of Library Automation*, December 1978, p. 333. For numerous articles see Allen Kent (ed.), *Resource Sharing in Libraries* (New York: Marcel Dekker, 1974) and *Library Resource Sharing* (New York: Marcel Dekker, 1977), both compilations of articles from conference proceedings.

and provides direct access to all science and social science journals (except in medicine and history) published since 1970; for this the center includes access to the British Library Lending Division. The primary advantage of the center to members is that of journal provision and fast access to relatively little-used materials the libraries otherwise might have to purchase:

[It] serves as an insurance policy. We do not justify our annual membership fee in the center by the number of items we borrow every year but by the fact that our membership gives us access—if and when we need it—to several million research items which might otherwise not be available.[6]

INTERLIBRARY LOAN

An essential element of any cooperative or network library program is effective interlibrary loan. Almost all libraries offer this service, employ a standard form, and follow rules set forth in the American Library Association National Interlibrary Loan Code (scheduled for discussion and revision in 1979) and in the generally more permissive state, regional, or local codes modeled on the national one. Samples of many local forms can be had on request from the American Library Association, which keeps an extensive file.

Library loan service is found at the local level where two or three libraries have cooperative service arrangements to borrow materials from one another. From there it moves to the state, to the region, then becomes national and even international. The UAP (Universal Availability of Publications) international organization says that "every published document, whenever and wherever published, should be available to anyone who wants it more or less when he wants it."[7]

It does not require experience or much thought to see that if such a system is to operate there has to be considerable coordination of selection activities among librarians. Improvement and sophistication of selection are necessary, as is coordination, not only between the large national and research libraries but also between the smaller local units that may be tied to those libraries through a formal or informal network.

What this suggests is the need for an increased number of local, national, and international union lists and bibliographies in a machine-readable data banks. Given rapid access to records of what is available in library X, the librarian in library Y will be in a better position to decide whether or not to buy an item.

As already noted, the best-known central storage of bibliographic records in the United States today is in OCLC and Stanford University's BALLOTS system. More than 2000 libraries are linked to one or both of these services,

[6] Richard De Gennaro, "Copyright, Resource Sharing, and Hard Times . . . ," *American Libraries*, September 1977, p. 434.

[7] Maurice Line, "Universal Availability of Publications," *Library Association Record*, November 1978, p. 570.

which are complex but offer more than four million records that may be called up for viewing on a CRT (television screen) by any of the member libraries. The records consist primarily of the catalog cards produced by the Library of Congress and by the members of the system. The result is a massive union catalog showing who has what. Originally limited to books, it now includes periodicals and is being expanded to include other materials.

Since locations are given for the materials in the OCLC and BALLOTS systems, the librarian may use them as an interlibrary-loan device. This has already been done informally, and a regular procedure is to be worked out whereby the whole transaction—from locating the material to ordering it from the other library—can be done at the same terminal. The promise of OCLC and BALLOTS and related networks for selection and acquisitions is so great as to drastically change the whole of collection development policies in even the smallest libraries. Meanwhile, anyone who follows network growth recognizes that we are on the border of a new country with much promise.[8]

Once the average librarian is able to sit down at a terminal and have the almost-instant location of any item flashed on a screen or printed out, it will be considerably easier to find materials not in the local library. At the least, the librarian will no longer have to search standard printed bibliographies (if they are available) for that information.

But there is a drawback: the system does not now include a method of assuring rapid delivery of materials. It is one thing to locate book X quickly, quite another to deliver it to the user. In fact, the technological developments in the rapid access to who has what has a dark side. Some of the large research libraries, from which most interlibrary loan materials are drawn, have begun to charge fees for interlibrary loans. The hoped-for solution is that once all or the majority of the nation's libraries are connected, interlibrary loans from smaller libraries will be more feasible and that the librarian will not have to turn automatically to the large library for needed materials. Some librarians nevertheless think the trend will continue to be more and more reliance on the holdings of larger libraries. The results are likely to be disastrous as more libraries take to borrowing not only esoteric materials but also books that may still be readily available.

Whatever the reason, this trend will continue as an increasing number of libraries become OCLC members, as more and more records are inputted [*sic*] into the data base, and as this borrowing/lending practice achieves an unofficial sanction through widespread usage. . . . A difficult situation is thus presented for libraries since the borrowing of in-print books imposes a serious burden upon the loaning library. Often that library's patrons have an equally pressing need for the same

---

[8] OCLC and BALLOTS are favored topics of library writers, and much has been produced about both systems. A clear explanation will be found in *American Libraries*, January 1977, pp. 21–28. For additional information, see Kalus Musmann, "The Southern California Experience with OCLC and BALLOTS," *California Librarian*, April 1978, pp. 28–39, and "OCLC in all Kinds of Libraries," a series of articles in the November–December 1978 *Wisconsin Library Bulletin*.

materials, although strict enforcement of the interlibrary loan code would curtail the borrowing of in-print books to some extent. However, universal enforcement of the code is nearly impossible. Many libraries would continue to request in-print books, and libraries would continue to loan them. Further, all libraries are sympathetic to the commonly shared, much-discussed predicament of rapidly escalating book prices in a time of leaner and leaner library budgets, yet another stimulus for the sharp rise in interlibrary requests for in-print books.

Certain parallels to the ongoing, unsettled furor over the new copyright law, PL 94–553, were revealed by this situation. The borrowing and lending of in-print books undoubtedly deprives publishers of income as a growing number of libraries resort to borrowing, rather than purchasing, in-print books, a trend confirmed by this study. In a real sense, this practice violates the "fair use" concept applied to periodical photocopying, and a reaction to it is inevitable. Implementation of the OCLC interlibrary loan subsystem, with its capacity to simplify an interlibrary loan transaction to a completely automated operation, will increase this in-print borrowing substantially.[9]

This is only one of the issues that link interlibrary loan to materials selection. There are many others, such as what materials shall not be borrowed (rare books, genealogical items, bound periodicals, some dissertations, and so on). Still, of most importance is the question of who is going to pay for what. It is one thing to establish a national network, quite another to expect larger libraries in that network to carry the cost of purchasing materials to be used in smaller libraries.

Some confusion comes from a misconception of what the interlibrary loan may or may not be able to do for libraries. It is expensive, particularly for the larger research public or state libraries, which serve as the lenders of most of the materials required by the medium-sized and small libraries. It does not mean sharing so much as it often does a larger library carrying the financial burden of a smaller library.

The current confusion in interlibrary loan policies is one example of our attempt to exploit a mechanism designed for the sharing of abundance in an environment of scarcity and increased demand. . . . Columbia University . . . is a net lender, lending as many as 20,000 volumes annually while borrowing only 2000 volumes with a resulting institutional subsidy of $75,000 a year. Under these circumstances —shared by other large research libraries—an important question needs an answer: "Can we afford to maintain the professional stance of free access to information for all citizens when adherence to that very principle is slowly eroding the quality of our distinctive research collections?"[10]

Large research libraries, and even the large public and state libraries, may soon no longer be in a position to fill the materials gap of the smaller libraries through interlibrary loan. Needed is a reassessment of the whole process and of how it is to be financed. This in turn calls for a much larger view

[9] Ronald Rayman, "OCLC and Interlibrary Loan," *RQ*, Fall 1978, p. 55.
[10] John Cole, "News in the Library World," *Library of Congress Information Bulletin*, May 5, 1978, pp. 294–295.

of interlibrary loan and its implications. It requires a national—even an international—overview of what it means to lend materials, particularly from a large, rich library to a small, poor one. Who, for example, is going to finance the national interlibrary loan network? Who is going to decide what library should buy what types of material, not simply at the level of 100 or 200 research libraries but at the level of thousands of public and school libraries? Should, in fact, anyone or any group be in a position to tell (or even suggest) to smaller libraries what to buy or not to buy because of existing or potential interlibrary loan procedures?

COPYRIGHT

Ronald Rayman's reference to the "furor over the new copyright law" has to do with the 1977 law. This law affects interlibrary loan and other cooperative schemes between libraries in determining "fair use." The law limits the number of times a library may copy something out of a book or journal, send a copy of that material to another library, or put that material on reserve. It prohibits "systematic copying," which has been interpreted to mean more than five articles a year from the last five years of a periodical title. Actually, this may have little to do with selection since it will not usually be necessary to buy additional copies of magazines or books simply because of copyright.

The University of Pennsylvania found that the number of articles requested was minimal. For the period from mid-1976 to mid-1977, "Articles were requested from 247 different journal titles. Of these 173, or 70 percent of the journals, had requests for only one article. Five had five requests, two had six requests, and one had seven requests."[11]

The University of Pennsylvania experience is supported by the much larger British Lending Library Division. A 1976 survey found that "the average copies per article was 1.24; only 2 percent of the titles were copied more than once."[12]

This is not to dismiss the importance of copyright in the scheme of regional and national networks. It promises to be a major headache, at least in the opening stages of closer cooperation between libraries, and when and if a national periodical center is established. The fair-use debate will continue for years to come, as will court cases, conferences, revisions—and scores of conflicts among publishers, authors, and librarians.[13]

[11] De Gennaro, op. cit., p. 431.

[12] "Copyright and the Libraries," *Publishers Weekly*, August 9, 1976, p. 35.

[13] Much continues to be written about copyright and libraries. A good summary is *Copyright Handbook* (New York: R. R. Bowker, 1978). See, too, the 26-page "Reproduction of Copyrighted Works by Educators and Librarians" available from the Copyright Office, Washington, D.C. (1978), one of the clearest explanations available of the law.

The Question of Size

Today the damper is on large collection efforts. Recognition that there are ways of assuring rapid access to materials other than building miles of library shelves in each community has taken hold.[14] The information explosion, too, has done much to check the drive to larger collections.

THE INFORMATION EXPLOSION

The statistical estimate of the information explosion differs from survey to survey, but all agree on one point: There is too much material available for even the most energetic expert to handle in a hundred lifetimes of constant reading, viewing, and listening. Visit the local newsstand. How many of the magazines there have you read or are likely to read? Which ones are best for your purposes? You can make a rough estimate by the title and by thumbing through one or two, but this becomes tiresome as well as time-consuming. Or wander into any bookstore. How many of the titles, even those only in paperback, do you know? How can you select what you need?

This emphasizes the problem when information growth is measured as follows: (1) The amount of raw information available (in any form) doubles about every ten to 15 years. (2) Some 500,000 books are published throughout the world each year, more than 100,000 of them in English; *Books in Print* alone lists some 500,000 titles. (3) There are 65,000 to 100,000 periodicals available at any given time, but the numbers double when you are concerned with all titles published since the seventeenth century. (4) Nontheatrical (primarily educational) films produced in 1977 in the United States alone totaled 14,390, and the basic index to such films lists more than 110,000.

(margin, handwritten) Statistics on the information explosion

DEFUSING THE INFORMATION BOMB

How are libraries to cope with this mass of information? The first way is self-evident:

[14] This is not to suggest all librarians have given up the notion of size as equivalent to quality. Many, for example, quote R. R. Downs, who found a close relationship between the number of doctoral degrees awarded and the size of the collection ("Doctoral Programs and Library Resources," *College and Research Libraries*, 1966, pp. 123ff). Other reports find the relation between size of collection and doctorates minimal and the teaching faculty more important; see, for example, M. S. Subbarao, "The Place of Library Resources in Doctoral Programs," *College and Research Libraries*, September 1968, p. 424. There is truth in both findings.

Even enthusiasts of growth, however, have come to recognize that there is a point of deceleration in development. See, for example, a study of giant libraries: Steven Leach, "The Growth Rates of Major Academic Libraries: Rider and Purdue Reviewed," *College and Research Libraries*, November 1976, pp. 531–542.

The traditional emphasis on developing large local research collections must be shifted towards developing excellent local working collections and truly effective means of gaining access to needed research materials wherever they may be.[15]

Different libraries have different definitions of a working collection—sometimes referred to as a circulating collection because most of the material is used regularly. However, one approach to a definition is to study how individuals handle the information explosion, how they build their own working approach to too much information. The average person solves the problem of too much material by ignoring almost all of it—the rejection or turn-your-back technique. Instead of trying to cope with mountains of information, these individuals choose only the mountain's core.

BOOK USE

As will be documented in this section, it is generally accepted that the average library user relies on only a small number of books. Given this assumption, and discounting for the moment the value of a library as a source of in-depth information ranging over years and centuries, one may draw several conclusions about daily library use: (1) Fifty to 60 percent of the library collection is not used. (2) The 50 to 40 percent of the collection that *is* used seems to satisfy about 99 percent of the users. (3) Approximately 10 percent of the titles in a library subject area meet the needs of 90 percent of the users in that area. (4) In science and technology (less so in social sciences and often not even applicable in the humanities), concentration is on materials published within the past year or two. If the library eliminates material five or ten years old, it will do little harm to current scientific research.

While the figures will decrease or increase with size and type of library, in all but the smallest collections actual use is relatively the same. Many of the materials are used rarely, if at all. These conclusions are borne out by many studies. Among the most recent:

1. University of Pittsburgh Approximately 40 percent of the titles ordered in 1969 did not circulate; 56 percent had not circulated more than twice by mid-1976. "It is evident that any given book purchased [in 1969] had only three chances in five of ever being borrowed. When a book did not circulate within the first two years of ownership, the chances of it ever being borrowed were reduced to less than one in five. And when a book did not circulate within the first six years of ownership, the prospects of it ever being borrowed were reduced to less than one chance in 50."[16]

[15] Richard De Gennaro, "Austerity, Technology, and Resource Sharing . . . ," *Library Journal*, May 1975, p. 917.

[16] Thomas J. Galvin, "Use of the University Library Collection," *Library Journal*, November 15, 1977, pp. 2318–2319. This is documented in detail in Allen Kent, et al., *The Pittsburgh Library Use Study* (New York: Marcel Dekker, 1979). See also the

Journals used bore out the findings: 11.4 percent of the total physics journals subscribed to accounted for 70 percent of use; and in life sciences, of the 507 journals owned only 21.5 percent were used.

2. Small community college Using a modification of the circulation technique employed in the Pitt study, Harold J. Ettelt found much the same correlations for a collection of about 20,000 volumes (against some three million at Pitt). In a circulation sampling of 15 months' activity for one out of every 18 books: (1) Less than 50 percent of the books circulated. (2) The "older the book, the less likely to circulate up to five years old, after which date its use seems to stabilize."[17] (3) A small number of books are used frequently, a large number are used seldom, and many are not used at all.

The most surprising finding was that even in a quite young collection [founded in 1969], the age of a book matters greatly. . . . The dropoff in use once the books are two years old is marked, and then once the books get five years old, the decrease in use stops.[18]

3. University of Chicago In a detailed analysis of the collection to determine what might be removed from the shelves and stored without disrupting service, Fussler and Simon found much the same pattern as Pitt. They tried to ascertain with what frequency a book might be used in a large research library; using circulation records of a given sample of books and journals, they discovered the almost-obvious: the more a book was used in the past the more it is likely to be used in the future, and the amount of use tends to decrease with the age of the book.[19] Furthermore, a good percentage of the books are never or rarely circulated.

4. Academic collections Trueswell found in the late 1960s that about 60 percent of the typical academic collection is not used and that the best indication of future use of a book is past use—or nonuse. Based on this, he believes a core collection could be built to satisfy about 99 percent of need through elimination of 60 to 75 percent of the average research library's holdings (the unused material should be removed to a limited-access area).[20]

---

following in *Library Journal*, primarily reactions to the Galvin article: "Pitt and the Pendulum," an editorial in the same issue (p. 2295); Richard De Gennaro, "The Changing Fortunes of Research Libraries . . . ," February 1, 1978, (pp. 320–321); and "Letters," April 15, 1978.

[17] "Book Use at a Small (Very) Community College Library," *Library Journal*, November 15, 1978, p. 2315. (The college is Columbia-Greene Community College in Hudson, New York.)

[18] Ibid.

[19] H. H. Fussler and J. L. Simon, *Patterns in the Use of Books in Large Research Libraries* (Chicago: University of Chicago Press, 1969). See also F. W. Lancaster, *The Measurement and Evaluation of Library Services* (Washington, D.C.: Information Resources Press, 1977), pp. 180–192, for numerous other examples.

[20] Richard L. Trueswell, "Some Behavioral Patterns of Library Users," *Wilson Library Bulletin*, January 1969. See also *Library Journal*, August 1977, p. 1564.

PERIODICAL USE

Much the same use pattern holds for periodicals. One study found that out of 248 journals in a science subject field only about eight will be highly read and therefore the source of most information. Another 40 will give moderate added bits of information, while 200 would be low in information. "It is clear that had [the user] wished to find a further batch of relevant papers, consultation of no fewer than 1000 extra journals would be necessary."[21] Frequent studies find that a small group of journals account for the bulk of materials cited in articles, books, and reports. Much the same is true of books, where a selected group of publishers issues the majority of titles in a given subject field. For example, one study of social science literature found that "half the cited books were accounted for by only 12.6 percent of the publishers" in the field.[22]

SIGNIFICANCE OF THE FINDINGS

If on an average only 12 to 15 percent or less of journals published are read by the majority of people concerned and if only 40 to 60 percent of the book collection is used, it seems obvious that:

1. The average library might cut back its subscriptions by 80 percent and its book collection by 40 to 60 percent and still serve 99 percent of the people using the library.

2. If the library can more than halve its materials budget, it has worked its way out of the inflation–high-cost-of-everything budget bag. Or, as the author of the Pitt study put it: "Can research libraries continue to afford to purchase material that is not likely to be used?"[23]

3. Libraries would be economically more secure if they shared little-used materials (through local cooperation, storage, interlibrary loan) rather than purchased them outright. Here, of course, there is still the question of cost: it may sometimes actually cost more to set up an organization from which the library can borrow than simply to buy the materials.

THE PROBLEM

All these studies and data make it seem logical for a librarian to cut the size of the book collection by about half and judiciously do the same with

---

[21] Wilfred Ashworth, "The Information Explosion," *Library Association Record*, April 1974, p. 67.

[22] James C. Baughman, "Toward a Structural Approach to Collection Development," *College and Research Libraries*, May 1977, p. 248.

[23] Galvin, op. cit., p. 2320. Criticism has been leveled at the Pitt study by some librarians, who think it is another way of justifying budget cuts in materials. A more objective view is taken by the editor of *Library Journal*, John Berry, who notes that the Pitt study is a step toward developing "new and better ways to measure library use and determine its costs" (*Library Journal*, November 15, 1977, p. 2295).

annual selection of other materials. Few librarians do so because of two basic questions: Which half of the collection do I eliminate? and Which half do I keep and continue to purchase for? And a third problem: the specter of censorship. Cut out some materials for economic reasons and the person who wants them may cry "Censored!"

Still another applicable question concerns access. If the card catalog were easier to use, if the classification system were easier to follow, if there were signs around the library to help people find individual sections and books, would more of the collection be used? If there were more staff to assist, would even more materials be used?

These and other factors are so confusing that some librarians would just as soon avoid the whole problem of collection development. They find support in those who question quantitative studies. For example, Melvin Voigt challenges the validity of evaluating who uses what on the basis of circulation figures alone. He estimates that 70 to 90 percent of the materials used are not brought to the checkout point.[24] In other words, the titles not circulated may actually be read or consulted.

Beyond the numbers are the real questions, applicable to all libraries. What, one should ask, is the reason this book fails to circulate or is not consulted? Turning to a critique of a basically quantitative survey (the Pitt study), one critic observed:

The report says that a study of book materials purchased in 1969 indicates that only 56 percent of the books actually circulated. So what? Where are the answers to "why"? Were the other 44 percent inherently valueless? What are the differences between the items used and those not used? Can something be discovered about the differences which will benefit future acquisition decisions: If not, then the study is useless. Pitt could cut its book budget in half and then buy the wrong half of the books. Perhaps a study of library users is needed. Maybe Pitt students and faculty read only half as much as an intelligent acquisitions librarian expects them to read.[25]

[24] "Scholars Need Sources" letter, *American Libraries*, November 1977, p. 533. This view is challenged by several studies in which a correlation was found between lack of circulation of a title and lack of use in the library itself: "The number of in-library uses that are recorded seem to be very closely associated with numbers of issues." At the same time this report, like others, admits that "the number of books being consulted is approximately twenty times as high as those receiving recorded in-library use" (C. Harris, "A Comparison of Issues and In-library Use of Books," *Aslib Proceedings*, March 1977, pp. 125–126). The Pitt study also took this into consideration and, "on the basis of extensive 30-day samples of in-library use," decided that "74 percent of the titles used in-house had also circulated externally. . . . This suggests that external circulation data can be utilized with a high level of confidence to measure total book use" (Galvin, op. cit., p. 2318). As Harris and others have found, the real answer is that no one is sure, and much more work must be done on circulation and use studies before in-house and circulation figures can be matched.

[25] Betty-Carol Sellen, "Collection Development and the College Library," *Collection Building*, vol. 1, no. 1 (1978), p. 22.

Another rationale for a larger-than-used collection will be evident to any reader with a personal book collection. Only a few of the titles are used regularly, but it is a comfort to know the others (less used, or not used at all) are at hand. A golden test of this subjective feeling is to get rid of one of the less- or never-used books. The next day—or next week—you will have a great, sudden need for the title.

Among reference librarians there is a debate concerning the validity of the statement "The larger the collection, both of reference works and of nonfiction, the more likely the librarian is to find a suitable answer." This presupposes immediate access to materials and is a strong argument for a library to build its own collection, relying only in a minimum way on resources of other libraries. Various studies seem to support the suspicion that a book in hand is worth a dozen in the network:

Within the context of this study [of public libraries], strong indicators of reference performance were found to be related to the size of the reference collection. . . . The major research hypothesis, which predicted that the greater the number of volumes in a library's reference collection the greater percentage of reference questions that the library's reference staff would be able to answer correctly, was supported by the findings of this study.[26]

An argument against simply chopping away half the collection is put forward by Voigt:

Those librarians who rationalize their unwillingness to fight for the research collections by using the argument that a high-circulation collection will do just as well are doing both the scholars and the institutions a major disservice. The end result will be the impossibility of carrying out effective scholarly research on those campuses, particularly if no other extensive research collections are easily available in the immediate area.[27]

Still, this hardly eliminates the need to examine collection development policies—particularly in the majority of American libraries, where research is not a major consideration.

If this were a simple-minded, single-occupation, single-purpose society, most libraries could simply follow the basic individual-rejection, turn-your-back method of selection. As it is, even the highly defined special library must cater to more than one audience, although there must be an optimum size even for a pluralistic audience. Many attempts have been made to work out at least a minimum collection. Most librarians begin the quest for an answer with standards and guidelines developed by the American Library Association.

[26] Ronald Powell, "An Investigation of the Relationship between Quantifiable Reference Service Variables and Reference Performance in Public Libraries," *The Library Quarterly*, January 1978, p. 13.
[27] Op. cit.

Standards and Guidelines

Various types of library have national standards and guidelines. These vary in detail and length but do offer interested librarians an overview of the current philosophy and goals of that type of library and, in some cases, specific quantitative data on materials to be selected and acquired.

The standards for public, school, and academic libraries may be defined as

the criteria by which . . . library services may be measured and assessed. They are determined by professional librarians in order to attain and maintain the objectives they have set themselves. Standards may be interpreted variously as the pattern of an ideal, a model procedure, a measure for appraisal, a stimulus for future development and improvement, and as an instrument to assist decision and action not only by librarians themselves, but by laymen concerned indirectly with the institution.[28]

THE VALUE OF STANDARDS

Just how useful are the standards?

The ultimate answer depends on the individual library and how the standards are applied, whether as a self-evaluative guide or a way of encouraging more community support, or both. No one is entirely satisfied. Studies indicate the standards are "a useful tool for providing basic theory, furnishing a set of objectives, and stimulating research in evaluation of performance."[29] And, certainly, they can be used to give shape and substance to any library's selection and acquisition policy statement.

Differences of opinion, witnessed by the length and detail of the various standards, occur primarily about whether or not it is possible (or even advisable) to try to propose a single set of quantitative criteria for all libraries.

There is more to standards and guidelines than theory. Librarians asked to justify budgets are better able to do so when they can demonstrate quantitative standards. This presupposes that the standards give detailed criteria against which local authorities can measure and evaluate their library. But the standards tend to be too general, or are not standards at all in the sense that the figures given for collection size are minimal, designed more to frighten than to encourage.

Writing about the new public library standards, the editor of the *Library Journal* commended the stand on social issues but observed that the state-

28 Robert H. Rohlf and Gary M. Shird, "Applying Standards for Public Library Evaluation," *Catholic Library World*, February 1977, p. 270.
29 Alice S. Clark and Rita Hirschman, "Using the 'Guidelines' . . . ," *College and Research Libraries*, September 1975, p. 364.

ment "gives little ammunition to convince governing authorities to finance the urgently needed changes."[30]

This, of course, is the problem not only with nationally promulgated guidelines and standards, but even with those at the local level. It is one thing to have an ambitious written policy statement, another to gain the local financial support necessary to make it possible to carry out some of the programs envisioned by the statement.

Size and Standards

Existing standards and guidelines have various approaches to numbers. School libraries give definite figures, although public libraries now avoid quantitative measurements. Academic libraries are strong on quantitative measures; special libraries make no effort in this direction, primarily because they are too diversified. Looking at the standards one will find the following guidelines for printed materials (nonprint materials and standards are discussed on pages 232–238).

PUBLIC LIBRARIES

The Mission Statement for Public Libraries concluded that it was "no longer appropriate . . . to propose a single set of standards which would be valid for all public libraries."[31] The result is little direct guidance for quantitative evaluation of a collection. Some agree and others disagree with this attitude; for beginners it is useful to go back to the 1966 standards for a public library system (*not* an individual library). Here it was established that a system serving 150,000 to one million people should have available:

1. Books: At least 100,000 nonfiction titles, and "a comprehensive collection of older as well as current fiction."

2. Periodicals: At least one currently published periodical title . . . for each 250 people.[32]

SCHOOL-LIBRARY MEDIA CENTERS

The school-library guidelines focus more on the user than in the past: "The central concern is the quality of the educational experience for the learner."[33] (Chapter 6 of the guidelines is devoted to 25 pages of exhaustive qualitative and quantitative statements concerning selection policies, pro-

[30] John Berry, "A Mission Statement for Public Libraries," *Library Journal*, December 1, 1977, p. 2379.

[31] *American Libraries*, December 1977, p. 615.

[32] *Minimum Standards for Public Library Systems* (Chicago: American Library Association, 1966), pp. 42, 43. The emphasis is on systems, not individual instructions.

[33] *Media Programs: District and School* (Chicago: American Library Association, 1975), p. 105.

cedures, and evaluation, with the proper admonition that each district should develop its own media selection policy.)

Quantitatively, the standards call for a total of at least 20,000 items in the media collection, broken down into major areas:

1. Books: 8000 to 12,000 volumes, or 16 to 24 per user, with access to 60,000 titles needed to insure satisfaction to 90 percent of initial requests.

2. Periodicals and newspapers: 50 to 175 titles.

3. Pamphlets: No way to measure numbers; type and quantity vary according to program needs.

COLLEGE LIBRARIES

Approved in 1975 by the Association of College and Research Libraries, the Standards for College Libraries clearly state the need for codifing objectives of the library.

The college library shall develop an explicit statement of its objectives in accord with goals and purposes of the college. . . . The statement of library objectives shall be reviewed periodically, and revised as needed.[34]

There then follows a formula for the collection prefaced by a statement that the college is to supply materials for "educational, inspirational, and recreational purposes":[35]

1. Books: The exact amount of print material is to be determined by a formula that calls for a basic collection of 85,000 volumes, with an added 3000 to 6000 titles per masters field and an allowance of 25,000 more volumes per doctoral field. After that the school is to have 100 volumes per FTE (full-time equivalent) faculty member and 15 volumes per FTE student.[36]

2. Periodicals: There is no quantitative recommendation for periodical holdings because "institutional needs vary so widely . . . but in general it is good practice for a library to own any title . . . needed more than six times per year.[37] Reflecting a common attitude of the 1970s, the standards also note that "the goal of college library collection development should be quality rather than quantity. . . . No easily applicable criteria have been developed . . . for measuring quality in library collections."[38]

Carried a step further, the guidelines suggest methods of grading a library by its holdings:

[34] "Standards for College Libraries," *College Research Libraries News*, October 1975, p. 278. See also Guidelines for Branch Libraries in Colleges and Universities.

[35] Ibid.

[36] The Canadian standards (*Guide to Canadian University Library Standards* [Toronto: Canadian Association of College and University Libraries, 1965, pp. 40ff]) call for 100,000 volumes minimum with 75 volumes per full-time equivalent student.

[37] "Standards for College Libraries," p. 290.

[38] Ibid.

Libraries which can provide promptly 100 percent as many volumes or volume equivalents as are called for in this formula shall, in the matter of quantity, be graded A. From 80 to 99 percent shall be graded B; from 65–79 percent shall be graded C; and from 50 to 64 percent shall be graded D.[39]

TWO-YEAR JUNIOR COLLEGE LIBRARIES

The standards for two-year colleges, approved in 1972, lack the specific formulas for collection development found in the college standards. This is intentional; the guidelines were an effort to move away from quantitative criteria to more general descriptions of what should and should not be in a collection.[40]

Individual colleges and regions have more specific formulas. For example, Illinois recommends in its Quantitative Standards for Illinois Community College Learning Resource Centers:

1. Books: At least 20,000—or 20 titles per full-time student.
2. Periodicals: A minimum of 300 titles.

An appendix lists 1975 community college statistics showing a high of 72,000 volumes (750 periodicals) in one college and a low of 8000 (260 periodicals) in another.[41]

SPECIAL LIBRARIES

There are no widespread standards for special libraries because of the wide diversification of type, size, and the like. Individual special libraries nevertheless tend to establish basic quantitative goals. In addition to standards developed by library associations, regional accrediting associations for academic libraries have standards for libraries, as do other professional associations; there are nearly 40 specialized accreditation groups. George S. Bonn lists portions of several of the accreditation standards.[42] School and academic libraries, in particular, should familiarize themselves with standards applicable to their libraries.

The basic accrediting agencies include everything from the Middle States Association of Colleges and Secondary Schools to the Western Association of Schools and Colleges. There are six of these regional associations, which periodically examine institutions—including library service.

The standards range from "complete permissiveness to almost complete restrictiveness as to numbers of volumes and specific titles of books and journals, with the only common denominator being adequate support of

[39] Ibid., p. 279.

[40] "Guidelines for Two-Year College Learning Resources Programs," *College and Research Libraries News*, December 1972, pp. 305–315. The guidelines are designed to "provide criteria for information, self study, and planning, not to establish minimal [or accreditation] standards" (p. 306).

[41] *Illinois Libraries*, February 1977, p. 120.

[42] "Evaluation of a Collection," *Library Trends*, January 1974, pp. 285–290.

the educational program."[43] Librarians should be sure what standards are applicable to their situation, particularly those that are requirements (in some states, for instance, there is dual certification of school library media specialists, which requires they be certified as both librarians and teachers).

Turning from the standards back to the various surveys of collection development, the same question remains: How big is too big? How does the librarian evaluate the maximum and minimum size for a given type of library and collection? Some tentative answers will be found, of course, in both the standards and the studies, but beyond these we must consider the scale by which collections are generally measured quantitatively.

Collection Levels

There are four primary levels of collecting intensity, defined more in terms of type of library than of budget or philosophy:

1. The *comprehensive level* is the aim of such large national collections as the Library of Congress and the National Library of Medicine. Much the same is true for large or specialized university and research libraries such as those of Harvard and Yale. Here, of course, "comprehensive" does not mean "all," and even the national libraries have certain limits to types of material collected. Comprehensive, however, may mean "almost all" in certain subject areas; the Library of Congress, for example, aims at building a collection of various materials that accurately reflects most aspects of American life and culture.

2. The *extensive or research level* is a form of the comprehensive, limited by certain factors such as time, country, language, and the like. Here, for example, the library may collect material on American culture from Europe but not from China. This usually means a library of more than the magic million volumes.

3. The *selective or study or working level*, the one familiar to most librarians, is an effort selectively to choose the important materials for the audience served. This may cover a wide range of subject areas and leave few gaps in the Library of Congress or Dewey classifications on the shelves. Certain areas and forms (from law to manuscripts) will not be considered. This will be a collection of roughly 200,000 volumes.

4. The *demand level* is generally limited to what users request that, for one reason or another, has not been previously needed in the collection. Users should have an active voice in the other three collection levels, but there are many who participate only when a particular title is desired. Demand must be measured by many factors (discussed elsewhere), although this level of collection development is one of the more important. Size here ranges from 50,000 to 200,000 volumes.

[43] Ibid., p. 290.

FORMULAS

Over the years there have been numerous efforts to arrive at mathematical formulas to assist the librarian in ascertaining the maximum-minimum size of a collection. For example, Verner Clapp and R. T. Jordan in 1965 devised a scheme to measure minimum size and proposed a formula to judge the adequacy of an academic collection.[44] This was followed by modifications and, of course, other studies such as those of Melvin Voigt.[45]

Examples of current objective methods of evaluating maximum-minimum size of collections can be found in many of the articles in *Collection Management*, although many of them are more theoretical than practical.[46] Another constant source of models is the *Journal of the American Society for Information Science*.

The basic formula approach to collection development presents certain problems:

There are still areas where quantitative methods are not widely accepted. In some cases the literature presenting the methods is not intelligible to all librarians; in other cases, the proposed approaches are based on inadequate data or involved a very simplified analysis of the problem. In addition, there are those who distrust the seemingly precise results obtained from manipulation of basic figures subjectively assigned. In some of the operations research applications, models are based on assumptions which cannot be verified by librarians in their day-to-day experiences with library users.[47]

The fact remains that some kind of quantitative measurement of a collection's size and effectiveness is necessary. Those who select materials may not be directly responsible for collection of such data, but they certainly

[44] "Quantitative Criteria for Adequacy of Academic Library Collections," *College and Research Libraries*, 1965, pp. 371–380. The authors list variables that must be considered in evaluating size, claim 42,000 volumes is a minimum for undergraduate collections, and would add 60 (rather than the standards' 100) volumes per full-time equivalent faculty member.

There is a vast literature of material on acquisition models and related collection evaluation. Several typical but outstanding recent examples (all with extensive footnotes and bibliographies to lead the reader to other studies) include Paul H. Mosher, "Collection Evaluation in Research Libraries . . . ," *Library Resources and Technical Services*, Winter 1979, pp. 16–32, and George A. Hodowanec, "An Acquisition Rate Model for Academic Libraries," *College and Research Libraries*, November 1978, pp. 439–447. See, too, related articles in this issue; Charles B. Wenger, et al., "Monograph Evaluation for Acquisitions in a Large Research Library," *Journal of the American Society for Information Science*, March 1979, pp. 88–92, and Joy K. Moll, "Bibliometrics in Library Collection Management . . . ," *Collection Management*, Fall 1978, pp. 195–198. (Actually, the whole issue makes several points that may be useful to beginners in the field.)

[45] "Acquisition Rates in University Libraries," *College and Research Libraries*, 1975, pp. 263–271.

[46] For a clear explanation of several formulas, see F. W. Lancaster, *The Measurement and Evaluation of Library Services* (New York: Academic Press, 1978), pp. 165–172.

[47] Rose M. Magrill and Mona East, "Collection Development in Large University Libraries," in *Advances in Librarianship* (New York: Academic Press, 1978), vol. 8, p. 39.

should see that means exist to make necessary quantitative figures available when necessary. Meanwhile, there are numerous less complicated (some would say simplistic) methods of judging the size of a collection. Among the favored:

1. Devise a formula for subject-area size. One expert has determined that 2000 to 10,000 titles is a minimum requirement for almost total coverage of a single subject area. "And of these perhaps 10 percent or less represent the truly active material in the field, the current important new works of wide interest, plus the backlist of basic and core works."[48] There are approximately 60 basic subject areas of interest to a library. Using the above figures, one multiplies 6 times 10,000 and has a collection of 600,000 volumes. However, if one accepts the 10-percent formula, it is possible to refigure and come up with a core collection of major titles of only 60,000 volumes—or considerably less, if a base figure is 2000 rather than 10,000.

2. A sometimes more satisfactory method is to compare the size of collections of similar libraries in your area. This can be done either informally or by formal questionnaires and interviews. The procedure assumes library X is good—or that a group of libraries has competent selection policies. This assumes, too, that libraries can be compared, which is not easy. More than one effort has been stopped by the failure of librarians to agree on such basics as what is counted or not counted; is it the total number of volumes or the total number of unique titles, or the total number of in-print materials (including books and periodicals), or . . . ?[49]

3. You may check the size of the collection against other similar libraries by using the *American Library Directory* (New York: R. R. Bowker, since 1923; biennial), which gives statistical data on library holdings, often including how much is spent.

4. Where necessary you may call for a formal survey, although this is expensive and hardly worth the effort unless you are trying to impress or pressure officials charged with budget control.

5. Published surveys of other libraries of the same size and type often give raw data. The surveys may be found through *Library Literature* and other indexes; if you are near a large library school, the school will probably have a number of these readily available.

THE PROBLEM

"How large?" is a question that simply cannot be answered across the national board for libraries. The guidelines, and formulas worked out by individuals and institutions, are useful but hardly universally applicable.

[48] Paul Doebler, "Special Interest Marketing," *Publishers Weekly*, May 31, 1976, p. 138.
[49] The question presupposes that the librarian knows how much material is in the library, the result of an inventory, not an easy thing as the library increases in size. (Even the necessary inventory steps are complicated enough: see Marianne Goldstein and Joseph Sedransk, "Using a Sample Technique to Describe Characteristics of a Collection," *College and Research Libraries*, May 1977, pp. 195–202.)

There are too many variables—from interlibrary loan programs, through changes in curriculum and direction of a library, to the effectiveness of librarians. This leads George S. Bonn, among others, to admit that quantitative measurement is of limited use and that the need is for "stress on quality and on user needs rather than on quantity . . . as the basic factor in building a collection and evaluating it."[50]

Budget and Selection

Budget is a inevitably major factor in any discussion of collection development. While actual budgetary practices are normally relegated to others than those who select materials, at least some rudimentary understanding of budget is necessary. There are two primary variables: How much of the total budget is allocated to materials? and How is the materials budget divided?

ALLOCATION OF TOTAL FUNDS

The total library budget is divided in many ways, but in general about 60 percent of each dollar goes to salaries and another 25 to 30 percent is designated for materials—although these figures may shift from 50 to 70 percent for salaries and to 20 to 45 percent for materials.

Precise relationships of materials budgets to the total budget are difficult because of wide variations. Elizabeth Futas found the "overwhelming number of public libraries spend between 11 percent to 24 percent of their budgets on materials." The majority of academic libraries show wider swings, the materials budget ranging from 15 to 50 percent of the total. There is apparently no correlation between the size of a library and the percentages allocated for materials.[51] A 1978 report on college and university libraries found expenditures for staff to account for 60.6 percent of the budget, with 16.3 percent for periodicals and books and 10.9 percent for periodicals.[52]

DIVISION OF THE MATERIALS BUDGET

Once the materials budget is determined, librarians have various ways of dividing the funds by subject, form, or area. For example, one library may divide the budget so 20 to 25 percent goes for the purchase of materials in the humanities, 10 to 15 percent in the sciences, 25 to 30 percent in the social sciences, and 25 to 40 percent for general recreation and reference. Another approach, particularly among academic libraries, is to apportion the funds among departments.

[50] "Evaluation of the Collection," *Library Trends*, January 1974, p. 296.
[51] *Library Acquisition Policies and Procedures* (Phoenix, Ariz.: Oryx Press, 1977), pp. xxvii, xx.
[52] "Book Buying Down . . . ," *Library Journal*, March 1, 1978, p. 499.

When one turns to breakdown by format or types of materials, once more only generalizations are possible. The public library is likely to spend from 60 to 90 percent of the materials budget for books, with another 6 to 24 percent going to periodicals. Other materials, including audiovisual, may account for 4 to 14 percent of the budget. Academic libraries tend to spend about 50 percent of the budget for books and from 20 to 40 percent for periodicals, the rest going for other media. Special libraries, with a particular dependence on recent materials, may spend 90 percent or more on periodicals and serials. School libraries divide the budget with 50 percent or so going to books, another 30 to 40 percent for nonprint materials, and less than 10 percent for periodicals.

These figures are so relative as to be virtually meaningless except in the most general way. They indicate the necessity for a librarian who is about to explain how a budget is allocated to do so by instinct and by what other libraries in the area of the same type and size are doing. National figures or even a consensus on various types of budgeting systems is difficult to isolate. An explanation of this problem is suggested in a debate between a librarian and an economist. The latter bemoans the lack of statistical data available from libraries; the former counters that libraries (including their budgets) fail to lend themselves to measurement because "their books reflect the amazing diversity of human perception. . . . This diversity makes library measurement complicated and somewhat uncertain."[53]

All that can be said with certainty about budget allocation is that there is no single satisfactory formula for every library. The futility of such a formula is nicely explained in one criticism:

Develop an elaborate mathematical formula based on some or all of [several] subjective methods, announce that the formula is an objective method of allocating funds, and tell those who complain of the results that they simply cannot grasp complex, abstract formulations."[54]

[53] David W. Heron, "More on the Production and Distribution of Knowledge in the United States," *AAUP Bulletin*, November 1977, p. 289.

[54] Peter Spyers-Duran and Daniel Gore, *Approval plans* . . . (Westport, Conn.: Greenwood Press, 1974), p. 29, outlines numerous budget-allocation methods and manages to find fault with them all.

4
Collection Analysis

THERE ARE NO definitive methods of determining the size of a collection and size does not indicate the usefulness of the collection for the user, so selection must come into play. The librarian becomes the mediator, the gatekeeper between the flood of information and user needs. The idea is hardly new. This is precisely the role played by indexing and abstracting services, bibliographies, newsletters, magazines, and the like. *Fortune* magazine, for example, justifies its existence by assuming the role of mediator between the individual and the "avalanche of business information." In a full-page advertisement, the magazine explains:

Business news is coming from all directions. There are more specialized trade publications. More and more bigger newspaper sections. More business news on the front page. . . . All this, plus a glut of company-generated reports, analyses, and forecasts. It's a business information explosion, and no one has time to absorb it all. Let alone sort out and then pull together the things that are useful, reliable and essential. . . . Our editors sort, sift and select only what's useful. . . .[1]

The role of the professional librarian is similarly to dig through the mountain of information and "sort out and then pull together the things that are useful," and to sort and sift is the purpose of materials selection. Whether in a school, public, special, or academic library the librarian must understand precisely what to add, what to delete. The rules of this game are spelled out throughout this book, particularly in the next section. Several generalizations may nevertheless be made here about how selection is carried out.

Core Literature

Each discipline, each subject field, has its own core literature. One important part of a subject expert's education is to learn what basic journals to consult, what basic channels of information to trust. The librarian must learn these

---

[1] *The New York Times*, November 7, 1978, p. 83.

sources in all their variety and forms. They may come as books and periodicals or as films, recordings, reports, government documents, pamphlets, or other media.

One comfort is that while the core changes shape and direction from year to year, the changes are not drastic. With attention to a subject area, the librarian will be able to keep up with new development.

CORE MODIFICATIONS

Modifications to the core collection are obviously necessary. The first need is to show concern with current developments; this in turn requires a thorough knowledge of review media. The second need is the ability to weed out what is not needed and the parallel ability to make a decision about replacing or not replacing the discarded item. Third, the librarian should judiciously accept the core, the standard reviews, weed as necessary, but always be on the lookout for the unusual, materials that will meet the needs of those who may not conform to the core concept.

The librarian must not only conserve the traditional approaches to selection but also explore new territory. Some people rely on the librarian to introduce them to developments in a field, to new imaginative ideas and literature: they expect the librarian to keep them one step ahead of the competition. In a more sophisticated and important way, the librarian is looked to as the guide to the future, the one daring enough to take chances with books, periodicals, films, and other materials.

Hal.

THE SUBJECT EXPERT

Appreciation of a core and how to modify the core collection assumes that the librarian has a command of one or several areas. This means, equally, an appreciation of the needs of users—children or faculty or administrators or businesspeople, or anyone who might benefit from the library. It means, too, a complete understanding of the materials available and what is useful, reliable, and essential.

SUBJECT DEVELOPMENT

Great attention should be given to the interrelation of subject areas. This is specially true in academic and school libraries where, for example, courses are being reorganized along new multidisciplinary lines.[2] Subject relationships concern all librarians, but selection people particularly must realize these relationships.

[2] James C. Baughman, "Toward a Structural Approach to Collection Development," *College and Research Libraries*, May 1977, pp. 241–248. The author analyzes and suggests methods of collection development based upon the structure of subjects.

Any library system, whether by size or Dewey, enacts a formalized vision of how the world is put together, of what are the optimal sight-lines between the human mind and phenomenological totality.[3]

Subject considerations are basic to the selection process. For example: The humanities require far more books than periodicals; the sciences require more periodicals than books; the social sciences may require a balance of both; and all the disciplines rely on other materials, from films to recordings. Any policy that advocates selection or withdrawal at a standard across-the-library rate will raise difficulty.

As anyone who has actually tried to allocate a budget by subject knows, each subject area is only as good as those who use and demand materials. One year the humanities may have a stronger teaching faculty than the sciences and demand more materials. Five years later the newly revived science section discovers it has lost five years of valuable materials—and so on. Collection development must take into consideration all of these subject variables.

Exploiting the Available

Once improved selection is instituted, "a second major way in which the effects of the information explosion can profitably be parried is by improved exploitation of available stocks."[4] Use of what is available may be increased by:

1. More guidance by librarians, assisting people to find specific bits of information as well as books, journals, films, recordings, and the like. This may be both in terms of information and referral or the old-fashioned, still-applicable readers' advisory service.

2. Better use of all materials, not simply periodicals and books. For example, the librarian should make an effort to educate instructors as to alternatives. Students do not have to use a single book—why not try several periodical articles, other titles, or perhaps material more readily available in microform or on audio cassettes?

LOAN PERIODS

Shorten the loan period of much-used materials. In one university the loan period was reduced to one week and the per capita circulation doubled.[5]

The natural question remains: How do you identify "much-used materials"? This was done at the aforementioned university by checking all

[3] George Steiner, *On Difficulty and Other Essays* (New York: Oxford University Press, 1978), p. 200.

[4] Wilfred Ashworth, "The Information Explosion," *Library Association Record*, April 1974, p. 66.

[5] Daniel Gore, "Let Them Eat Cake," *Library Journal*, January 15, 1975.

the volumes in the library. Where machine-readable circulation records are available and the information is part of the record, the process of isolating perhaps 10 percent of the heaviest-used part of the collection is relatively easy. (If isolating much-used material is a problem, a simple solution is to shorten the loan period on all titles.)

THE GORE FORMULA

In his continuing quest to make what is available in the library useful by first purchasing what is used rather than what is supposed to be used, Daniel Gore has arrived at a formula: (1) *Holding rate*: The percentage of all books your patron wants to read that are held by the library. (2) *Availability rate*: The percentage of wanted books held by the library that are available on the shelves when your patron wants them. (3) *Performance rate*: The product of holding rate times availability rate, or the percentage of all books (both those you own and those you don't) immediately accessible to patrons when they want them.[6] This type of approach is hardly scientific, although it seems at least to indicate failures and successes in how well the library serves users.

The performance rate is another way of measuring user satisfaction. One method to jump that rate from a miserable 40 or 50 percent to close to 100 is to consider purchase of multiple copies of much-used materials.

MULTIPLE COPIES

Explaining policies of multiple copies to faculty members, one writer fairly summarizes an old attitude—shared by librarians in other types of libraries:

Historically, it would be fair to say that large research libraries' acquisition policies have in general discouraged the purchase of multiple copies of the same title. The acquisition of a new title has almost always been favored over an additional copy of a title already held. Also, replacement of lost volumes has been, in many libraries, a slow and cumbersome procedure. Adding to the difficulties of the uninitiated user has been the curious assumption on the part of many academic and research libraries that university faculty and students are, or ought to be, able to cope with library-use problems unassisted. Until recently there has been little attempt to go beyond providing traditional basic reference service so as to truly "open" large collections to the vast majority of academic users.[7]

In a university library it was found that, of a total of 200,000 circulating titles, only about 40,000 different titles circulated at least once in the course

---

[6] "The Mischief in Measurement," *Library Journal*, May 1, 1978, pp. 933–934.

[7] John Smith, "Research Libraries in Transition," *AAUP Bulletin*, May 1978, p. 80.

of a year, and "of those 40,000 the computer analysis indicated that 3257 titles needed more than one copy to assure a 95 percent availability rate."[8]

In addition to multiple copies, the library must provide a constant watch on what is needed, what is missing from the stacks, and so on. Conscientious stack maintenance is of major importance, because one misshelved book may undo the best efforts in multiplication.

Multiple copies are not the only approach to improving the success rate of users in finding what they need. Improved binding procedures, checks on lost items, methods of rapidly replacing mutilated and stolen copies would all considerably reduce frustration.

There are as many formulas to determine the number of added copies of a book to be purchased as there are books but some of the more common approaches include the following (actual figures will increase or decrease depending upon the size of the library and the extent of demand):

1. Best sellers: Six to 12 for the initial order with two copies purchased for every eight requests.

2. Replacements: Usually only one copy unless it is a particularly popular work; in that case use the formula for best sellers.

3. Classics or outstanding modern works: Purchase as many copies as necessary to keep a representative collection of the author's best works on the shelves.

4. Heavy student use: As one college put it, "Multiple copies should be requested only when . . . numerous students are . . . required to read with a limited time . . . substantial portions of a book which is . . . too expensive for the students to buy individually."[9]

How much money should one spend on duplicates? This is really a two-part question. Ongoing selection of materials should be enough to satisfy the needs of readers and eliminate long waiting lists for titles, even best sellers. Gore says that in one college "We found that by spending three percent of our annual operating budget on multiple copies we had cut the frustration rate by a third in just one year."[10]

Multiple copies are a problem for a single library but can be a sore subject where there are branches or divisions that each want the same book, the same film, or duplicates of other media. This calls for systematic plan-

---

[8] Gore, "Let Them Eat Cake." Actually, the library found that it had duplicates of most titles, based on the librarian's active selection policy. Only 570 of the 3257 needed more copies.

[9] Hartwick College Library. Elizabeth Futas, *Library Acquisition Policies and Procedures* (Phoenix, Ariz.: Oryx Press, 1977), p. 321. The statement goes on: "Of course, a very high price also militates against the purchase of multiple copies; on the other hand assurance that the book will be used for many years counts in favor. As a rule we should start with the smallest possible number of copies and add others only as the demand, measured by circulation, justifies them." South Georgia College concludes that "When the demand for more than three copies of a given title for class-related assignments becomes evident, this title should be considered as a textbook adoption" (Ibid., p. 322).

[10] Daniel Gore, "Things Your Boss Never Told You . . . ," *Library Journal*, April 1, 1977, p. 1.

ning, usually with an efficient central collection that makes it possible to move needed materials to a given spot without delay. For example, within a large school, public, or academic library system it is more expedient to buy one or possibly two films. If a proper booking method is established (and publicized and functional), delivery can be arranged so that there is no undue delay or frustration. The key word here is *delivery*.

Weeding and Collection Development[11]

Commenting on changes in collection development, Jesse Shera observed:

I'm sure that for every situation there is an optimum size for the library, we do not know what the optimum size is and when I say this we all agree, but what are we doing about it? We keep on buying more books, there is safety in numbers. There is always the fear of the librarian that somebody is going to come to the library some day and not find the book he wants and we're going to be embarrassed. This is all very well and I applaud it for the spirit that is behind it even though I criticize the mental processes by which it is achieved. I think the day is going to come when the problem for the librarian will not be book acquisition but book elimination. This is a far more difficult job because it is always easy once you get a book to keep it—oh it is there, it's not doing any harm, let it stay, it's difficult to say this stuff is no longer valid. Let's get rid of it.[12]

Oddly enough, the reluctance to discard is less true for nonprint materials. Mildred Nickel rightly observes: "Many people will readily throw away a mutilated filmstrip, yet tend to feel guilty about discarding a book."[13] This section concentrates on weeding of books and periodicals, but almost all the rules are equally applicable to nonprint materials—and weeding of nonprint items is just as serious a matter as weeding of printed items.

The major reason for weeding, at least from an objective viewpoint, is to check the glut of materials being distributed. An ability to divide the noise from the music, the trivia and the timely from the useful and the lasting is the responsibility of the professional librarian. The importance of weeding has been elevated to a tenet in the public-library standards:

Perhaps for the first time in history, barriers to the human record exist not so much in a scarcity of materials as in a glut. . . . [There is] a growing mass of trivial and redundant material which threatens to engulf the information seeker. . . . Decisions are, and must be, made to erase portions of the record deemed insignificant, irrelevant, and unrepresentative.[14]

[11] Stanley J. Slote, *Weeding Library Collections* (Littleton, Colo.: Libraries Unlimited, 1975), is the best book on the subject. See also "Weeding in Academic and Research Libraries: An Annotated Bibliography," by Barbara Rice, in *Collection Management*, Spring 1978, pp. 65–72.

[12] "The Upside Down Library," *Utah Libraries*, Spring 1978, p. 11.

[13] *Steps to Service* (Chicago: American Library Association, 1975), p. 74.

[14] "A Mission Statement for Public Libraries," *American Libraries*, December 1977, pp. 616–617.

The librarian must be able to evaluate what is "insignificant," "irrelevant," and "unrepresentative" not in general but for the library audience being served.

The day of book elimination is at hand, at least for librarians desperately trying to make space for growing collections of new materials, and it is a central concern for all librarians involved with collection development. Weeding is one of the best techniques available to insure the long-range usefulness of any collection.

Weeding and selection are twins; it is difficult to imagine one without the other. Both keep the collection functional and current. Without weeding the collection would be choked with useless materials.

Weeding raises numerous problems, not the least of which is to convince some librarians that it is necessary. It can be a complex, nervewracking business, and the result is often inaction:

The complicated nature of the . . . decision and the number of variables to be analyzed, as well as the special nature of a research collection . . . probably explains why few large university libraries have found the staff time to undertake extensive weeding and storage problems, except under pressure.[15]

No matter what the size or type of library, there is more to weeding than the decision to pull something off the shelf. Next the librarian must remove the shelf-list cards and the catalog cards, and update other records. This alone is enough to give pause in libraries where there is a limited budget or limited personnel.[16]

Weeding Procedures

Discarding of books and other materials takes two distinctive forms. The first and most familiar is the actual weeding of materials from the library collection. These are later destroyed or sold but are no longer part of the collection. This is the process likely to be followed in most small to medium-sized libraries where the primary purpose of weeding is to provide necessary space for new materials and to keep the collection current.

The second approach is limited to larger research libraries. Here discarding or weeding is really a synonym for storage. Rarely is the pulled material sold or destroyed; it is simply moved to a cheaper-to-operate storage center, which may be part of the library system or in a collective. Good examples of the latter are the Center for Research Libraries and the New England Deposit Library. The thinking behind this type of weeding is that everything

[15] Rose M. Magrill and Mona East, "Collection Developing in Large University Libraries," in *Advances in Librarianship* (New York: Academic Press, 1978), vol. 8, p. 30.
[16] G. Edward Evans, "Limits to Growth, or the Need to Weed," *California Librarian,* April 1977. This perceptive article lists numerous other excuses for not weeding—from lack of time and putting it off to fear of making a mistake and reluctance to throw a book away (see pp. 13–15).

may be useful at one time or another, and one role of the large research library is to preserve materials, even those that are little used.

Most studies are concerned primarily with the economics and the strategy of weeding at the large research-library level. To date there has been no entirely successful formula (although all have certain basic approaches) helpful to all librarians in determining what to weed.[17]

THE SELF-RENEWING LIBRARY

Weeding is the other side of selection, and one is as necessary as the other. This can be demonstrated by the concept of the self-renewing library.[18]

Here, as in most situations, a limit is imposed on the size of the collection. This limit is maintained by a definite rate of acquisition and a simliar definite rate of withdrawal of materials. The concept is based on the idea of maintaining stocks at a certain level to reduce the need for extra space. Withdrawn materials are housed locally, easily retrieved within 24 hours—or where demand is great, simply returned to the library. Conversely, if after five years the material is unused it will be withdrawn to a national store, in this case the British Library Lending Division.

This type of procedure is now used, if less formally, in most large regional, county, and school library systems, where a central headquarters staff (aided by the local librarian) selectively weeds and adds to a more-or-less basic collection. In fact, many of the more complicated weeding-storage schemes are little more than extensions of practical, certainly more direct methods employed by librarians in smaller libraries for generations.

Even on a small scale, weeding aids selection. Librarians who go over the shelves book by book, periodical by periodical (or, for that matter, film by film and record by record) are more likely to have a sense of what is being used or not used in the library than those who do not. This in turn reveals much about collection development that can be translated into selection.

THE PRACTICAL APPROACH

Turning from large research libraries to the average small to medium-sized public, college, school, or special library, what methods for weeding are

[17] F. W. Lancaster, *The Measurement and Evaluation of Library Services* (Washington, D.C.: Information Resources Press, 1977), pp. 180–197. A clear explanation of the Fussler-Simon project also dedicated to a scientific approach to weeding, primarily in large libraries. See also almost any issue of *Collection Management*, which usually has one or more articles on weeding and storage of materials, complete with somewhat complicated formulas, such as Colin R. Taylor, "A Practical Solution to Weeding University Library Periodicals Collections" (Fall-Winter 1976–1977), pp. 27–46.

[18] P. Havard-Williams and Anne Gilman, "The Self-Renewing Library," *International Library Review* (1978), 10, pp. 51–58. There are problems: what do you do with gifts, special collections, etc., when their number throws off the balance of the regular selection-weeding process?

most commonly applied?[19] Again, there is no single rule, but in general librarians tend to follow fairly well-established patterns.

In other than large public libraries, an effort is made to turn over most of the collection every five to ten years. A special library, where emphasis is on currency and probably periodicals and reports, may carry on a much more stringent weeding process. Here it is not unusual to have a turnover rate of from two to five years. Weeding intensifies with the size of the library. The smaller the space, the more intensive the discarding. College and school libraries may follow the five-to-ten-year public-library pattern, although with more caution since some materials are more or less permanently tied to curriculum and do not change drastically.

Obviously, in every library there is a core of titles that meets both demand and the basic educational-entertainment-informational standards expected of a library. The core, however, may be quite small and, in any case, should never become static.

Weeding tends to be more stringent in public libraries, where current and popular reading rather than reference and research is emphasized. Another aspect of this process concerns information and referral systems in the public library. Here currency of data is of the utmost importance. Weeding of outdated directories, law books, medical works, and other reference materials is an almost daily preoccupation that, of course, carries over to the formal files of local material.

WEEDING RULES

There are some general weeding rules, all of which can be broken and none of which should be followed without question. Still, in most libraries guidelines for weeding follow a pattern:

1. Last date of circulation If the material has not been used in ten years (or less, depending on the type of library), it is weeded. (Conversely, where the material is being used constantly it should be kept in good condition, possibly duplicated.) Some libraries weed if the material has not been circulated more than twice in the past one, two, or three years.

2. Physical condition If the condition is bad, the item is weeded, although a decision must be made whether to replace.

3. Timeliness This is one of the most frequent criteria. Reference may be to: (a) Out-of-date materials, particularly in the sciences and technology. A rule of thumb is to weed almost anything more than three to five years

---

[19] For data on the practical approach see Slote, op. cit.; Mary McDonald, "Weeding the Collection," *Library Development* (British Columbia), March 1975, pp. 1–4; and Evelyn D. Reagan, "An Interim Solution to an Overcrowded Academic Library," *California Librarian*, April 1977, pp. 44–49.

of age. (b) Materials no longer in demand or that do not support the curriculum or current community programs. (c) Older editions no longer used. (d) Dated textbooks, where they are part of the collection.

There is a catch to this process. How do you know the old edition is not valuable? The new edition may have deleted materials of considerable interest to historians or social scientists; how do you know? Unless it is explained in the introduction or preface or by a reviewer, you must laboriously check the new against the old—and few librarians have the time. The result: "I am often baffled about what to do and usually resolve the problem by retaining too much, for fear of destroying potentially important information."[20]

4. Reliability Viewpoints change and must be reflected in the collection. Yesterday's reliable explanation may no longer be useful, particularly if there are scores of titles that support the outdated view.

5. Language Where changes in the community or the teaching program or the activity of the library have outstripped books in foreign languages, they should be discarded. Also, translations of works into languages other than English should be checked periodically.

6. Ephemera Certain subject areas, from inspirational tomes to how to make a million dollars, go out of fashion and use. This type of fad literature should be weeded, particularly when it is found that a title no longer circulates, is no longer timely, or the information seems unreliable.

7. Duplicates Where there are many duplicates and none seems to be circulating or used, all but a single copy is discarded. At a later date (one to two years) the single copy should be reconsidered for weeding.

8. Subject areas and material types Many libraries develop systems whereby rough rules are established for the weeding of types of reference works (from dictionaries to encyclopedias), types of material, and subject areas. For example, a library may discard sermons, prayers, and meditations with regularity in religion, and weed out equally outdated law codes and texts in law. Most libraries develop their own methods to meet their own special needs.

WHAT NOT TO WEED

The other side of the weeding coin is what not to discard. This will vary from situation to situation, but these factors generally govern:

[20] Jeremy W. Sayles, "Letters," *RQ*, Spring 1978, p. 284. This detailed letter indicates clearly the problem and one suggested solution to reviewers and publishers.

1. Research value   In a research library it is important not to weed material with research potential. This is particularly true in the humanities and the social sciences, where a title may flunk almost all the tests for retention and still be valuable.

2. Out of print   Where a title is out of print and there is even the least likelihood it may be of use, it should be retained.

3. Local   Most local history, humanities, and social science materials should be retained, no matter what their condition or lack of use.

4. Balance   When the weeding of a title is going to throw off the balance of materials in a subject area, careful thought should be given to the decision. For example, title X may be the only one available in population studies, although it is dated and in poor condition.

5. Rare items   No librarian will discard a Gutenberg Bible, and care must be given to weeding valuable material, no matter how little used.

6. Listing   If the material is listed in a standard current core bibliography (*Children's Catalog, Books for College Libraries*, etc.), it may be retained. The librarian should not follow lists blindly, but they can be a help when a difficult decision has to be made about replacement.

Fiction presents certain problems because much popular fiction is not listed in "best" lists. Where it is in heavy use it should be replaced. Even when a novel is not being used and is not on a core list, it should be carefully examined—writers have a way of coming back into fashion, as do their topics. More stringent rules are applicable for young adult and children's fiction, which, except the classics, should be removed if not circulated for one to three years or where the material is dated.

Once it is determined an item should not be removed from the collection, if it is mutilated the librarian must decide whether it would be less expensive to repair or rebind or to replace with a new copy or new edition. The choice may not be possible because the book is no longer available to the extent that it is not listed in *Books in Print*. If the copies are beyond repair, the librarian should seek to replace them with copies from out-of-print dealers.

PERIODICALS

The weeding of periodicals has other problems: (1) It is costly to start up and cancel a periodical subscription, and most cancellations must be made at the end of the subscription period. (2) Librarians are naturally reluctant to cancel a subscription when they suspect it may be reinstated in a few years. What's to be done about acquiring all those missing issues? There is no easy answer, since most publishers do not keep back copies.

(Microform is one answer, but it has its own disadvantages.) (3) The library with a long run of a serial ends up with a nice historical set, but no current materials, when that serial is canceled. In effect the investment of years is as dead as the next issue of the periodical. (4) A decision has to be made when to cut back on the serials budget, which usually involves planning that some librarians are reluctant to do. It is much simpler, for example, not to buy a single book, record, or film than to have to think about the consequences of not buying or killing an ongoing subscription to a magazine that comes in multiple copies.

The problems are the same for all libraries, but they increase in intensity with the size of the periodical collection. One may cut back or judiciously stop ordering new titles where only about 140 to 300 periodicals or continuations are taken, but when the number jumps to 6000 to 30,000, the problem intensifies. That is why most of the literature on this subject centers around the difficulties of weeding in larger research libraries. The question of how much and what to weed is worked out with some rather fascinating formulas, although essentially they all come down to: (1) If the serial has not been used over the past ten years: cancel. (2) If the serial is readily available on interlibrary loan and is rarely used: cancel. (3) If the titles are not found in standard lists or indexes or abstracting services, and are old enough to have been so treated: cancel. (4) If experts in a subject area report the serial is of little value: cancel.

There are numerous other rules to assist in weeding periodicals in both large and smaller libraries. They inevitably fail, at least from a purely quantitative formula point of view, and even comparative studies are of limited value. "Aside from a very small common core of periodicals there exists a situation in which the peculiarities [in the good sense] of teaching faculty and librarians contribute to the diversity of a collection so there is little commonality between collections and no comparability, therefore there is not help here."[21] This applies equally to public libraries.

The weeding of periodicals comes down to the problem to be faced with the weeding of any materials: Who uses it, and if it is taken out of the collection will it be missed? To answer that question intelligently the librarian must know the public using the library. And, as already indicated, since only a small part of the collection is likely to be used actively, the librarian should try to isolate the active titles from those rarely or never used. Much help here can come from the public. This requires particular attention to bringing the community involved into the decision making. Ask and ask again before a periodical is canceled.[22]

[21] David Perkins, "Periodical Weeding, or Weed it and Reap," *California Librarian*, April 1977, p. 35. Perkins explains how weeding is handled in his library; this in itself will be useful for many librarians in smaller college libraries.

[22] The amount of material on weeding of periodicals in library literature is impressive. See, for example, Jeffrey Broude, "Journal Deselection in an Academic Environment . . . ," *The Serials Librarian*, Winter 1978, pp. 147–165. Bronde's bibliography cites the pertinent articles in this area.

PROBLEMS

Aside from determining what has been circulated or not and the easy observation of what is worn or dated, most of the rules for weeding are subjective and qualitative. They assume the librarian has a solid working knowledge of the subject fields in which the discarding operation is to take place. More important, the librarian must know who uses the materials, how they are used, and why they are not used.

Many libraries try to solve this problem by having double or even triple checks. The librarian in a school library, for example, may weed and then present the list of not-to-be replaced materials to the teachers and administrators for comment, suggestions, and even disagreement. The same procedure may be followed in an academic library, possibly limiting the proposed weeding lists to subject experts on the faculty. Public libraries often have several librarians decide.

Gifts and Exchanges

A parallel aspect of weeding concerns gifts and exchanges.[23] Often, for example, the library will exchange items or give away materials to another library. The exchange of materials may be formalized by means of a special section in the library or simply by a routine procedure closely connected with selection and weeding decisions. But whether material is received as a gift or by exchange, the golden rule is to apply the same standards of selection that one applies to purchased materials.

GIFTS

Gifts are a welcome addition to any library as long as they are given with "no strings attached." Most libraries insist on such a provision before a gift is accepted; a typical library policy reads: "Gifts of books and other materials are accepted but without commitments as to final disposition and with the understanding that they are not necessarily to be added to the collection. The same criteria used for the selection of all other materials will be used in evaluating gift materials."[24]

Sometimes the donor requests that the titles be separated from the regular collection, even to the point of assuring a special section for the contribution. Unless the circumstances are highly unusual—such as the gift of an

---

[23] Gifts and exchanges are primarily a function of the acquisitions department in many libraries. Stephen Ford devotes a chapter to the process in his *The Acquisition of Library Materials* (2nd ed.; Chicago: American Library Association, 1978).

[24] Rolling Prairie Library. Futas, op. cit., p. 353.

extremely valuable collection in a subject area or by a single author—the library will not agree to the separate treatment.[25]

Finally, gifts must be limited to what the library can use. Clocks and stuffed horses and similar objects are not appropriate for a library, and it is normal to refer the would-be donor of such items to a local museum.

The concern about gifts is based to a great extent on cost. Gifts ultimately are not free; once the item is accepted by the library it must be cataloged, processed, and housed. To keep such expenses to a minimum, the librarian must insist on tight control. Lack of control can result in a collection "composed of unsolicited items arriving in the mail and of donations from agency staff members. . . . Lack of a firm policy for dealing with unsolicited items puts the library into the position of being a passive depository for cast-off books, magazines, pamphlets, and the like."[26]

GIFT VALUES

Some donors are generous for income tax purposes; depending on current Internal Revenue Service rulings, the donation may be tax-deductible. The librarian should rarely set a value on books or other gifts, but is free to indicate how many were given. Value is too nebulous, and even experienced book dealers hesitate to evaluate the worth of a collection unless paid for their service. A librarian could end up in tax court explaining how the appraisal was determined.[27]

Of course there are ways the friendly librarian may at least indicate the value of an item without committing the library. The most direct method is to refer the potential giver to a standard list of book prices such as

[25] Unwanted gifts can be a distinct problem for a librarian. See Larry N. Osborne, "Hassling Memorials," *Library Journal*, March 15, 1978, pp. 621–622, and letters regarding the articles in the same journal, September 1, 1978, p. 1546.

[26] Mary C. Grattan, "Collection Development in Texas State Agency Libraries," *Special Libraries*, February 1977, p. 72.

[27] The Internal Revenue Service may or may not accept the library's evaluation, and the donor should be told as much by the librarian. The usual practice, and one to be encouraged, is to suggest the donor get a disinterested professional, normally a local bookdealer, to appraise the gift. For a small number of titles the librarian may suggest that an evaluation of $7 to $8 each is probably in line with IRS rules, although *probably* has to be stressed. Professional appraisers usually charge a fee, which may run from $25 up, depending upon the value of the gifts.

It is not out of order for the librarian to volunteer to look at a collection that cannot conveniently be brought to the library—say, more than 30 to 40 books. The librarian can suggest the relative value of the gift, informally and not for tax purposes.

For additional information, see "Statement of Appraisal of Gifts" adopted by the Association of College and Research Libraries in 1973 (*College and Research Libraries News*, March, 1973). As James Weaver discovered ("Gift Appraisal Practices in NAPCU Libraries," *PNLA Quarterly*, Fall 1978, pp. 3–5), little has been written on the subject of gifts and appraisal. Weaver's survey of Northwest Association of Private Colleges and Universities libraries showed that "One-half of the libraries [out of 22 replies] appraise gift materials so that the donors can have records for income tax purposes." The size of the library has little or nothing to do with the policy.

American Book Prices Current or *Bookman's Price Index*. For new titles, reference to *Books in Print* will do, and the donor can look up the books and arrive at a conclusion about their relative value.

Aside from need and the quality of the would-be gifts, the librarian should consider whether or not the books might be used for sale. Many libraries have annual or semiannual book sales and encourage donations for this purpose. Larger libraries are likely to handle unwanted gifts by a more formalized exchange program of titles with other libraries.

EXCHANGES

Exchange of materials between libraries serves a number of purposes: First and foremost, it is to obtain materials otherwise difficult to purchase or unavailable by any other means. This is particularly true of some foreign government documents, periodicals, and so on that are sent to libraries only on an exchange basis. Second and much less important, the exchange system offers a way for the library to get rid of unwanted duplicates and gifts. Third, exchange promotes good will among libraries, especially at the international level. Except for informal exchanges of materials between libraries in a community or region, however, most of the major exchange programs are limited to large national, special, and research libraries.

Exchange of materials was greatly curbed in the 1970s. The cost of such programs in librarians' time and red tape alone sometimes fails to justify what is gained by exchange of serials and books from other institutions. Also, the library may not have much to exchange because otherwise free material is now sold. Still, a 1970s study found that 57 percent of the responding academic libraries have more than 1000 exchange agreements with other libraries.[28]

Gifts tend to be more important, at least quantitatively, in larger libraries. For example, in one 1970s study of large research libraries it was found that 61 percent of responding librarians reported receiving between 3000 and 26,000 items annually.[29] The historical importance of gifts in the building of library collections is well known, and some special collections within larger libraries are now maintained almost exclusively on gift funding.

SALE OF DISCARDS

Not all materials are stored or exchanged with other libraries. Some must be discarded, not simply destroyed. This leaves the librarian in the position literally of becoming a salesperson.

[28] *Gifts and Exchange Function in ARL Libraries* (Washington, D.C.: Association of Research Libraries, 1976). The report notes that most important exchange agreements are with foreign institutions, and libraries sometimes purchase materials in order to continue the exchange. For an example of how an exchange program may be established see Harriet Carter, "Setting up an Exchange Operation in the Small Special Library," *Library Resources and Technical Services*, Fall 1978, pp. 380–385.

[29] *Gifts and Exchange Functions in ARL Libraries* (Washington, D.C.: Association of Research Libraries, 1976).

Sometimes overlooked, the sale of materials is an important aspect of weeding, particularly of materials that are still useful, although not to the library. Generally where there is a question of how to dispose of (not destroy or store) materials, the librarian should consult legal authorities to see if the materials may be sold (in some areas law prohibits this) and, if sale is possible, consult with local dealers or those able to handle purchase. Some libraries, too, may simply want to sell the books directly to the public—a common feature of annual open houses. It is also wise to ask the advice of other librarians in the area who may well want the materials or who can suggest other avenues of sale.

Understanding of the collections of regional and national librarians is important—is at least one copy of what you propose to discard in a local or national collection for use at some later date? Any material that is purely local (particularly pamphlets and ephemera) or anything more than 50 years old, or any items about which there is any question regarding use or value should first be cleared with the larger libraries in the region. An item may appear shabby and of little use but prove to be a unique copy.

One fear all librarians should have is that, in the process of discarding materials, they will dispose of a valuable book, periodical, record, film, or other item. This has sometimes happened, and dealers even today make a practice of raiding small libraries by offering "new" copies for old, sometimes even rare first editions. Antiquarian bookmen's catalogs and records of book auctions are made up of books that at one time were considered no longer of use. Many that now command high prices are frequently described as "ex-library"; that is, they were discarded and carefully stamped (too often on the title page) as being discharged from some library.

The chances of discarding, storing, or selling a valuable item are actually small when the librarian has any understanding of books and other materials. However, when in doubt as to the value of an item, the librarian should always check with a subject expert or with such useful bibliographies as *American Book Prices Current*.[30]

Theft and Inventory

A certain amount of gratuitous weeding is carried on regularly by people who walk into the library and walk out with material they failed to check out. This is a case of simple theft, no matter if the intention may be to return what was taken one day.

Theft takes a tremendous toll each year. Estimates vary, but theft results in about 20 percent of the loss of current, new books from all types of libraries each year and about an equal percentage of reference books and expensive art, science, and similar materials.

[30] Martin Erlich, "Pruning the Groves of Libraro," *Wilson Library Bulletin*, September 1975, pp. 55–58. An excellent article on the subject that ends with a 30-point criterion for *not* discarding books; must reading for anyone involved in weeding.

One gauge of the volume of the loss is that if only 1 percent of the holdings of American libraries was taken each year the replacement cost would be some $268 million.[31] (Elaborate security systems are now in operation but hardly keep off professional thieves—who, for example, in 1977 managed to steal some 500 volumes of reference works from a subject collection at Harvard.)

Aside from loss of individual books, and even records and films as well as microform, the hardest-hit section of the library is the periodical room. As much as one-third of the periodical collection can be stolen or damaged annually. Here impatient users tear or cut out what is wanted. The loss is obvious to almost anyone who has tried to find an article. At one time or another the wanted item simply turns up missing.

And there are those who dutifully check out material but do not return it on time—or at all. Individual libraries lose thousands of dollars from non-returns each year.

INVENTORY

What does inventory have to do with weeding and selection? Everything, in that it is not enough to simply weed a title without first checking to see whether other similar titles are available. This may be the case when one scans the shelf list, but where theft (or loss due to other reasons, from misshelving to faulty records) has taken place, one can never be sure. Obviously, too, selection comes into play when a vital title is missing and must be replaced, often with a substitute. It is essential, particularly in critical areas of user need and interest, to double-check again what is actually in the library (or in circulation) before an item is discarded.

Ideally, the library should have an inventory of its holdings every few years. While this is feasible in smaller collections, where it can be done almost by simple observation, it is a major headache in larger libraries. However, just as there are security steps the librarian can take to check theft, so are there methods of random sampling to check the library inventory.[32]

A step-by-step inventory approach for school media libraries is suggested by Mildred L. Nickel,[33] and there are even more detailed explanations in most basic school library manuals. Many of these are applicable to smaller libraries of all types.

There are numerous methods of checking theft in the library; the most

[31] "Book Theft," *New Jersey Libraries*, January 1977, pp. 12–13.
[32] One approach is suggested by J. W. Griffith in "Library Thefts: A Problem That Won't Go Away," *American Libraries*, April 1978, pp. 224–227, which includes a good bibliography on the subject of security and inventory sampling. See also P. Niland and W. H. Kurth, "Estimating Lost Volumes in a University Library Collection," *College and Research Libraries*, 1976, pp. 128–136 (the method is applicable to other types of libraries).
[33] *Steps to Service* (Chicago: American Library Association, 1975), pp. 75–77.

common is to mark all items. Given a library mark on the verso of the first leaf of the opening text, the book's resale value is minimal.

"The Marking of Books and Manuscripts" is carefully explained in the proposed guidelines of the Rare Books and Manuscripts Section of the American Library Association. For details see the March 5, 1979, issue of *AB Bookman's Weekly*.

Aside from marking of books, the next most common procedure, which usually parallels the identification procedure, is the security measure.

SECURITY SYSTEMS

A rule-of-thumb approach to security installations is suggested by one librarian:

Should you invest in a system? At today's prices, book losses ranging from 450 to 500 volmes per year and more would appear to justify the installation of a detection system. At a 475-volume loss level, the most economical model should pay for itself in around three years and after that should produce a substantial savings. Losses of 600-plus a year will more than justify the installation of a moderately priced detection system. Estimates include the cost of sensitizing at 20 cents per each item, installation charges, maintenance contracts, and the purchase price of the system spread over three years of operation.[44]

CONSERVATION

Another aspect of loss is conservation of materials. As a result of inferior paper—and equally poor storage—many books deteriorate over a number of years. Figures vary, but roughly about 40 percent of the books published between 1900 and 1939 will have become almost unusable by the mid-1980s, and another 50 percent will reach the same condition in the early part of the twenty-first century. Acidity in paper, which literally eats it away, is the major cause.

Thanks to microform, it is at least possible to preserve content, and many libraries have adopted other procedures as well. The literature has numerous articles on this serious problem.[35]

Collection Analysis and Evaluation

The purpose of collection analysis and evaluation, among other things, is to determine the quality of the collection. Quality may be measured in numerous ways, although in terms of libraries it is essentially a double-edged analysis: Intrinsically how good is each individual item, whether it be a

---

[34] Griffith, op. cit., p. 226.

[35] A good nontechnical, practical article worth consideration by even smaller libraries is P. W. Darling, "A Local Preservation Program: Where to Start," *Library Journal*, 1976, pp. 2346–2347.

periodical, a book, or a recording? and How good is that item for the particular needs of the audiences served? The first is somewhat easier to
answer. The second presupposes a thorough knowledge of how people use
the collection.

The evaluation of a library and its collection falls essentially into two
parts. First, one must evaluate the collection itself in terms of numbers,
quality, currency, and the like. Second—and some would say even more
important—the collection should be judged on how well it serves the needs
of the community.

Bonn points out that numerous techniques are available for evaluation.
Several methods are likely to be used:

[There are] five reasonably distinct methods for evaluating library collections plus
one or two others that do not quite fit into any of the five: (1) compiling statistics
on holdings, use, expenditures; (2) checking lists, catalogs, bibliographies; (3)
obtaining opinions from regular users; (4) examining the collection directly; and
(5) applying standards (using various of the foregoing methods), plus testing the
library's document delivery capability.[36]

TALKING TO THE USER

Despite the uncertainty of it all, those are the basic steps one may pursue
in the quality evaluation a collection. Space permits consideration here of
only a few of the more basic steps.[37] It is assumed that the librarian understands the public served and the public sought. The librarian knows the
philosophy, objectives, and service policies of the library. This is the point
of departure for any useful analysis of the collection itself.

Interviews, questionnaires, and observation are methods of ascertaining
how well the goals of the library are being met; the librarian needs some
relatively objective measurement of how well John and Jane Doe like (or
dislike) types of materials available. More likely than not these three methods
are going to be more subjective than sociologists and evaluators would like,
but at least they give the librarian some measure of user satisfaction. More
important, they may indicate steps to be taken to improve ongoing selection
policies.

COMPARATIVES

How do I look next to you? That is the heart of the comparative method
of quality evaluation, and it is extensively employed by librarians in several
ways:

[36] George S. Bonn, "Evaluation of the Collection," *Library Trends*, January 1974, p. 267.
[37] Much of this chapter has been concerned with evaluation of collections, but for
specific methods see the Bonn article (which includes a solid bibliography of 138 items
plus general background reading). This remains one of the best summary articles available, but for further information see other articles in the same issue of *Library Trends*
and F. W. Lancaster, *The Measurement and Evaluation of Library Services* (Washington, D.C.: Information Resources Press, 1977), Chapters 3 and 5.

1. Comparison of specific parts of the collection or random samplings of the total against basic lists, bibliographies, "best books," and so on. If a majority of titles in the lists selected are in the library, the collection is likely to be at least minimally suitable.

For example, how good is the reference collection? One may take the standard count of titles, then go to the more useful sampling against a basic list. Here the librarian might use *Guide to Reference Books* (9th ed.; Chicago: American Library Association, 1976). By statistically set random choice of titles the librarian simply checks what is in the *Guide* against the collection. A high "hit" percentage would indicate a good reference collection. Other works—from *Fiction Catalog* to Carl White's *Sources of Information in the Social Sciences* (2nd ed.; Chicago: American Library Association, 1973)—might be used for evaluating other parts of the collection.

2. A favorite approach, too, is compiling of a "basic" list of sources or even thousands of titles. This then can be checked title by title against the collection. Much the same approach is applicable to other materials, and can be employed wherever a master list (in print or made up by the surveyor) is available for the materials to be checked, from periodicals to slides.

3. While lists are primarily used to check retrospective standing collections, it is possible to use the same approach for current selection. Here one would compile a list of new books reviewed, say, in *Choice* and thought useful for a college library. How many of the titles reviewed over the past six months (or year) are in the library or on order? A similar method may be used by employing other review media or checking through *Book Review Digest*'s monthly listing. The obvious variable here would be a list to suit the selection needs of the library being evaluated.

4. Reviews are another useful avenue to evaluation. Here the librarian takes all the library holdings in a given subject area and checks them against retrospective lists and book reviews. If the majority of titles appear on the lists, the collection is sound. If the majority of titles are neither reviewed nor on the lists, their relevance is questionable.

PROBLEMS

The list approach has built-in problems. For large libraries the lists are rarely sophisticated enough to include esoteric materials that separate the fine library from the average. For smaller libraries, even the most basic of published lists may be too specialized. What is good for a dozen libraries may not be applicable for your library. Lists are also rapidly dated. Several critics point out that the very lists sometimes used to evaluate a collection are the ones originally used to build the collection. What one finds from using them is worth nothing.

The single greatest problem with lists is that there are no totally satisfactory lists for all libraries, all times, all situations. Even the lists made up by the librarian evaluating the collection are likely to suffer from individual bias or ignorance.

EXPERTS AND CONSULTANTS

The comparative method may be used in another, less formal way. Here the librarian calls upon experts to evaluate the collections.

Expert advice is useful because someone who knows a subject area well need only spot-check the catalog or the shelves to say how good the library is in that area. Students, the general public, and even nonusers who have an interest in other areas may be used in much the same way. The opinion is admittedly subjective, but it tends to reflect the feelings of those who use the library. And it has the bonus, as more than one librarian has observed, of involving people with the library. Along the way they often make suggestions useful for other than collection development.

Consultants are another source of expert advice, for a fee. Lists of these are available from different places, including the American Library Association and the Special Libraries Association.[38]

It has been said that any good bookperson who walks into a secondhand or antiquarian bookstore can almost sense whether the collection is of value. The expert knows that much about books.

Much the same should happen when an experienced librarian walks into a library. With a little care one soon can judge the worth of the library. This hardly takes more than a few minutes—a glance at the subjects one knows in the card catalog, a cursory check of indexes, a cruise through a section of the stacks, a hard look at the periodicals. This method, of course, is so subjective as to frighten the statistician out of his calculator. It is hardly recommended for serious study of a library, but it is worth considering.

Add to the brief observation several days, weeks, or months of working in that same library and the librarian who cannot answer the question "How good is this library?" is either blind to the public served or to the whole purpose of the library collection.

Given a little experience, time, intelligence, and imagination, the good librarian can tell you more about the general worth of a library than even the most profound and detailed survey.

[38] Beginning in 1978 the Council on Library Resources and the Association of Research Libraries began training more than 100 librarians to give smaller and medium-sized academic libraries administrative assistance as well as to serve as consultants in collection development (*Library Journal*, September 15, 1978, p. 1685).

5
The Selection Process

WHEN THE LIBRARIAN is familiar with the philosophy and goals of the library, understands its audience, and has moved toward a rational collection development, it is time to consider the actual selection of materials.

There are many guidelines for selection, but the rule for all libraries should be to select materials for *individual need*. National surveys and check lists and reviews are valuable, but the librarian must always be careful not to use national assumptions for local selection. For example, it is assumed that in an average library fiction is more likely to circulate than mathematics books. As a guiding national hypothesis this is fine: the librarian normally would buy more novels than mathematics books. But hypotheses are not always valid. For example: "We intuitively knew the math students didn't use the library much; yet math books circulated about as heavily as fiction and more heavily than American history."[1] This finding at a small community college considerably modifies the national assumption.

At the same time, even local assumptions should be tested, particularly as audiences have a habit of changing. At large urban public libraries, for example, it was too slowly realized that the needs of the current inner-city population were not the same as the needs of those in the suburbs.

---

[1] Harold J. Ettelt, "Book Use at a Small (Very) Community College Library," *Library Journal*, November 15, 1978, p. 2315. See also "Who Reads Books and Why . . . ," *Publishers Weekly*, November 6, 1978, pp. 16–18; October 23, 1978, p. 18, the report of a national survey undertaken by a professional opinion firm for the American Book Industry Group. The small community college diverged from national guidelines in other ways. For example, whereas the 1978 survey reported that fiction was the most popular reading material (which checks out in most public and school libraries), in the college survey, fiction made up only 34 percent of the total circulation.

Evaluation and Selection

Two key words are used in the selection process: evaluation and selection. They are different in an important way.

Evaluation is judging the intrinsic merits of materials.

Selection is determining whether the materials meet the needs of the individual users.

Librarians must "first distinguish between evaluation and selection, knowing that even those materials rated highly on their evaluation scales might not always be appropriately selected for a particular collection."[2] To put it the other way, the library often does select material of questionable value because it will bring considerable pleasure to readers. For example, though most of the late Faith Baldwin's novels would fail objective evaluative tests, most librarians selected the novels because they are of a type eagerly read by millions of less than discriminating people. Such best-selling titles as *Gnomes* or *Dynasty* might not be evaluatively acceptable, but they were widely selected because they were best sellers.

When discussing the relative merits of a controversial work for library purchase, it is important to keep the two principles separate. Both the intrinsic qualities—evaluation—and the potential use of the item by users—selection—must be judged differently. Ideally, evaluation and selection do not conflict; actually, they usually do not.

POINTS OF VIEW

Evaluation and selection assume different weights in decision making. The precise emphasis put on one or the other depends on the librarian's viewpoint.

The *traditionalist* will insist on judging a work primarily on its intrinsic merits. If it fails, it is not selected. The traditionalist sees the function of the library as a preserver of materials, a bastion for objective information and culture in the community.

The *liberal* modifies such thought processes and supports the library selection policy on the basis of popularity. Unless most material is likely to be used, it is not purchased. Emphasis is on today, not tomorrow. Intrinsic quality is important but must give way almost every time to popularity. The liberal believes in the traditional core collections of classics, in all fields, and will certainly continue to purchase superior titles likely to have a limited readership. The liberal nevertheless differs from the traditionalist in that potential popularity is a major consideration in selection. In an extreme case, for example, the liberal will purchase gothic romances, nurse stories, and the

[2] Kay E. Vandergrift, "Are We Selecting for a Generation of Skeptics?," *School Library Journal*, February 1977, p. 41. This article draws many solid distinctions between evaluation and selection in the library.

like while the traditionalist will dismiss most of the genre for total lack of quality.

Most librarians stand between the two. *Pluralists* judiciously weight the selection and evaluative factors, try to keep each in balance. The library is more than a museum. It is also more than a drugstore paperback rack. It must represent both the currently popular and the standard classics, both the best and—where demand is evident—some of the intrinsically worse.[3]

Of these three viewpoints, the last is the most difficult in that no one is entirely satisfied, but it is the most viable and is the one recommended here.

An example of the three viewpoints in operation may be useful. Here is a review of a novel:

Beardwood, Roger. *Innocent Employments*. Doubleday. 1978. A challenge is issued. Four financial experts turn international business into a game. The one who makes the most money in six months wins the game and takes one-fourth of the others' profits. Each one has a different specialty and operates from a different European capital. Beardwood tells us much more than we need to know—about scenery, cities, residences, restaurants, stocks, commodities, and foreign currencies, and the plot is not original or lively enough to justify the effort of wading through the extraneous material to find it. An optional purchase.—Jack Oakley, Dearborn Dept. of Libs., Mich.[4]

Based on the review, the traditionalist (primarily concerned with quality) would dismiss the novel. The liberal (more involved with audience needs) would purchase it because the library is operating in a community where there are readers unable to cope with difficult materials or readers who like this type of novel. The pluralist might dismiss the novel outright if there were others of its type in the library (and a small audience for such work) but would consider it where a shortage of such books existed. Of course, this is purely hypothetical; local conditions might dictate different courses for all three. It is nevertheless a pattern of decision making familiar enough to experienced librarians.

Guidelines for Print Materials

The best guide to selection and evaluation of print materials (books, periodicals, pamphlets, and the like) is the experience and knowledge of the librarian. It is not unusual for a subject expert or someone working in allied subject areas to be able to accept or reject a title simply on the basis of the publisher, the author, or, more likely, an informed and intuitive sense about the value of the work for the library. Even so, there are some relatively objective methods of evaluating print material.

What follows is an outline of the steps the experienced librarian is likely

[3] *Best* and *worse* are used here in a general sense and in the way material is likely to be evaluated in standard reviews.

[4] *Library Journal*, November 15, 1978, p. 2348.

to take in evaluating the intrinsic merits of a book. Most emphasis is on evaluation, although this can't be separated from selection—how the book meets the need of the community served. While emphasis here is on the book, the same guidelines are applicable for most print materials (and, for that matter, many nonprint items).

EVALUATION CRITERIA

Among criteria the librarian should use to evaluate the intrinsic merits of a book are the ten following guidelines:

1. Purpose, scope, and audience

The *purpose* is usually clear from the title, the table of contents, the index, or the jacket blurb in which the publisher tries to summarize what the book is about. *Memoirs* by Richard Nixon has the clear purpose of setting forth the author's personal story and viewpoints. It will be an extraordinary reader who accepts the story in total, but there is no question as to the purpose of the book—or, for that matter, the scope and the audience.

The *scope* can readily be ascertained from the contents and publisher's description. It is "from his earliest recollections to the moment . . . he leaves the White House."

The *audience*: "This is a book written not for scholars and historians but rather for individual readers."[5] This means any adult with an interest in Richard Nixon and the presidency.

Once the purpose, audience, and scope are determined, it is easy enough to see how close the purpose of the library (selection) matches the purpose of the book; how near the audience who uses the library matches the audience seen by the writer; and whether the scope is unique or interesting enough to warrant inclusion in the collection.

Of course with the Nixon volume, as with any book by a well-known writer or celebrity, the primary question concerns the audience. Is this a title my readers are likely to request? Inevitably the answer is yes, and, all things being equal, the librarian tends to order the title without much more thought.

Purpose, scope, and audience are constantly open to interpretation and modification. The publisher and writer may have had one audience in mind, whereas in reality the library sees another audience as well. The library audience may be young adults, people with reading problems, ethnic groups, or others. Nevertheless, purpose, scope, and audience are the major considerations that modify other objective guidelines.

2. Difficulty

The librarian has certain broad methods of measuring difficulty of the reading matter, which is closely related to audience. First is the obvious

---

[5] The quotes are from an advertisement by the publisher, Grosset & Dunlap (*Publishers Weekly*, March 13, 1978, p. 1)

tipoff by the publisher, who clearly issues books for children, young adults, and adults. In the latter category, it is customary for the publisher to indicate relative difficulty by the title. For example, *Bishop and Chapter: The Governance of the Bishopric of Speyer to 1552* is clearly written and well researched, but it is not *The Soap Opera Book*. Beyond the title, publishers themselves are an indication of difficulty; university presses issue one type of work for better-educated readers while most supermarket-paperback publishers issue quite a different type of book.

Popular, scholarly, and *technical* are the three key words to keep in mind when evaluating the difficulty of a book for a particular audience. The obvious flaw in this is that one person's "popular" book may appear "technical," even "scholarly," to another. Quick ways to judge difficulty include: announcements from the publisher, a knowledge of types of books issued by a publisher, familiarity with the author or with the subject matter, or a tip given by the title—all these factors help the librarian determine the relative difficulty of the book. Finally, when in doubt, wait for a review and look at the book yourself.

3. Authority, honesty, and credibility of author and publisher

If the librarian knows the author is an authority in his or her field of nonfiction or fiction, the tendency is to purchase the book—all other aspects of purpose, scope, and audience being met.[6] Neither librarian nor the majority of readers have to agree with the writer, but it should be understood that the author does have an honest, creditable point of view, no matter how foreign that attitude may be to your own. For example, when the former director of the Central Intelligence Agency, William Colby, writes an inside story of the agency, you may accept or reject his version, but it is, so far as anyone knows, an honest and authoritative look at the CIA. You may not like mysteries, but you realize that almost anything by William Hallahan, such as *Catch Me, Kill Me*, is acceptable to mystery buffs. When the author is not known or there is a question about the approach, it is always better to look at the book yourself as well as wait for reviews.

Much the same can be said about the publisher. Harper & Row; Harcourt Brace Jovanovich; Houghton Mifflin; and Holt, Rinehart and Winston—to draw only from the "H" publishers among some 6000 in America alone—are known for their high standards. None has published or is likely to publish a title of really questionable quality, although all have published and will publish books that are less than well received by critics and librarians or by readers—or by both groups.

Beyond generalizations about the authority, quality, and standards of a publisher, matters begin to thicken. The real selector soon begins to learn

[6] The Baltimore County Public Library, for example, has a list of adult authors who are "identifiably popular and are regularly purchased by a majority of branches. . . . Being listed does not mean that each and every author or title will be bought automatically." But it is suggested that most often the title is purchased (Futas, op. cit., p. 286).

not only what publisher is likely to meet library requirements but also, more important, which ones publish what type of books. For example, Warner Books is known for its hard-hitting adventure-romance paperbacks, often manufactured to order for the publisher. These may or may not be acceptable, just as titles from Lyle Stuart tend to be sensational and worth double-checking. Both, of course, have issued and will issue titles every library will want, but they require a hard second look. Viking issues outstanding fiction, Knopf concentrates on books that require a better-than-average education to enjoy, and Time-Life Books give nonfiction topics rather brief, popular treatment, enhanced by beautiful formats and illustrations.

Knowledge about authors and publishers comes only from talking to other librarians and reading books. However, it will help if you regularly read book reviews (who is writing what and who is publishing the better writers), publishers' blurbs, advertisements, and the like. It is essential to read the publishers' trade magazine, *Publishers Weekly*, regularly.

4. Subject matter

Let's say there is a constant call in your library for books on popular economics and travel guides. When you find books advertised, listed, and reviewed in these two subject areas you tend to pause, to double-check purpose, scope, and audience to see whether or not they fit. If you think the book passable, even if it fails one or two lesser objective and subjective tests of evaluation, you buy it primarily for the subject matter. For example, you know Rand McNally is a creditable publisher, and you know from experience and user requests that their *Mobil Travel Guides* are much used. You see from a publisher's advertisement that there are some new editions in this series. The series covers your area or an area in which there is considerable interest. Given the importance of the subject, knowledge of the publisher, and the series—you buy. When Leonard Silk, an editor of *The New York Times*, writes a book called *Economics in Plain English*, you purchase because the subject matter is important to your library and Silk has first-rate credentials.

Of course there are times when even the most often requested subject matter is so badly done in a book that you don't order, or if you do order by mistake, you pull it from the shelves.

5. Comparison

How does the work compare in scope, purpose, and audience with other works in the library collection? This is more difficult to answer than the first tests, but it is of major importance. Will the material really add something to the collection or simply duplicate what is there?

The majority of standard library review sources fail to compare titles with other titles in the field. (An exception is *Choice*, and sometimes *Library Journal*.) Fortunately, the longer, although later, reviews that appear in subject and scholarly journals generally do a fairly good job of comparison.

Theoretically, comparison should be important, but in a practical world where librarians are not computers and do forget things from time to time, duplication of material in various books is more the rule than the exception. A certain amount of duplication (even of titles) is actually good policy, but ideally the librarian will avoid useless duplication as much as possible.

Another theoretical aspect of this question concerns library networks. If the library can draw freely on the resources of another library, should it duplicate the other library's holdings? That question has not been resolved, although libraries within easy distance of one another should not duplicate holdings. (In highly esoteric areas they even tend to split things up: "I'll collect books on Finnish firemaking and you limit yourself to titles in Polish about nineteenth-century carriages.) Cooperative acquisition, discussed by Stephen Ford in *The Acquisition of Library Materials* (Chicago: American Library Association, 1973, pp. 81–91) is based on this principle of sharing less-used materials.

Other librarians point out that duplication of materials, even in libraries relatively close to one another, is desirable. Audiences have different reactions to different types of libraries: An adult might hesitate to go to a school library to find a book not in the public library a block or so away; a college student might not look for a title in the public library. As one critic points out, the argument that duplication of titles is wrong in libraries within easy distance of one another assumes homogeneity of user status and institutional purposes, overlooks motivational complexities, and leads to such ideas as that a single library can serve the local college, schools, and the general community.

One justification for a degree of duplication is a reflection of one of the dangers of the interlibrary loan syndrome for books: too often the larger libraries dismiss the smaller ones. In fact, the standard interlibrary-loan codes usually do not permit a smaller library to borrow an in-print title from a larger library. While this is modified by local practice, the idea persists. The odd notion is that only scholars and researchers frequent large libraries, and that housewives, children, totem-pole collectors, and little old men in worn tennis shoes go to smaller libraries. This stereotype of purpose and audience is so widespread as to often pop up in written selection policy statements; one college, for example, observes that "The collection shall include titles for the serious adult readers and rely on the public library for materials of a lighter nature."[7]

6. Timeliness

Some types of book, particularly the classics in both fiction and nonfiction, are literally timeless. Most—well over 95 percent of any collection—date rapidly. This is evident in numerous studies, which show conclusively that a book is most heavily read during its first one or two years on the shelves, and then there is a dramatic dropoff until the number of times the book is

---

[7] Ibid., p. 314.

examined goes down to once or twice a year to point zero in four to five years. Exceptions there are, of course, but timeliness is a factor that must be considered in a number of ways:

a. Some libraries refuse to buy titles that are more than five years old—again, classics being an exception. The date can easily be checked on the title page or on the copyright page (the verso of the title page). Older titles are selected only when nothing comparable has been published recently. Other libraries go so far as to make it policy that no title more than two years old is to be added unless it meets a very specific need. This mechanical approach to selection by date is highly questionable and one that should be avoided—no matter what misguided librarians may say. More important are the subject matter, purpose, scope, and audience.

b. Justification for not purchasing an older book can be shown, to be sure, when the subject is no longer of interest to the library audience. Books that give detailed information on the repair of iceboxes are not a good item. Books on scientific, technical, and to a lesser extent social and political issues of the day tend to date quickly. Novels seem to have a longer life, although best sellers do go out of date rapidly.

c. Most important in terms of timeliness is the new edition. When a book is a success, it is often brought out again in three or five years, updated and sometimes partially rewritten. Be sure to check on a new edition to see if there is new material, if it truly is "new," and if it is timely. This can be done quickly by comparing a few current facts in the earlier edition with the new edition.

7. Format

Is the type legible, the covers likely to withstand repeated use, the photographs current? The format requirement is applicable to a novel as well as to nonfiction, particularly in terms of binding and typography.

The greatest difficulty librarians have with format is the binding. They all tend to be attractive, but too many are less than durable. Illustrations play a major role in certain types of book, from the lavish art volume through the travel piece to children's work. Where they are the center of interest, they should be carefully checked for accuracy of reproduction (especially color register and faithfulness) and their positioning in the book.

8. Price

Cost should not be a factor in itself, but it is a major consideration when the price of a book—or any other library material—is far beyond the average. For example, the average art book retails for $25 to $50. If the library is considering an art book that costs $300 to $500 or more, pause certainly must be given to consider whether potential use justifies the expense.[8]

---

[8] In many libraries it is a policy that books and other materials costing over a certain amount must be approved for purchase by the director.

The Texas State Technical Institute Library goes a step further with its policy that materials costing over $50 will be "selected with specific assurance that they will be used . . . expensive material will be justified not by the provision that it will remain in the building, but by the anticipated use it will receive."[9]

9. Curriculum support

In college, university, and school libraries one valid, relatively objective test of a book or other materials is the question: Does this support the teaching program? A related query: Does this support the research programs of the college? Beyond both of these criteria may come the question: Does this support anticipated or possible future programs of the school? The last query, however, seems less appropriate as most schools cease to expand programs.

10. Demand

Where there is a request for a book, in most cases the title should be purchased. The question of demand is discussed elsewhere (see page 104).

DISAGREEMENT

Most of the ten preceding points are objective: they can be measured and ascertained without difficulty or disagreement. Once, for example, it is determined that a book is authoritative, timely, and for the age group intended, it may be purchased to support the curriculum or the expected demand. One may argue about the interpretation of "curriculum" and "demand," but not the objective value of the book.

But what happens when librarians can't agree about the intrinsic merits of a book? There are times many of the previously enumerated points of evaluation simply don't operate, at least so far as a final decision is concerned. One may agree that the format, the price, the subject matter, and the authority of the book are passable but still not like it. Why? This side of psychoanalysis, the answer is what criticism is all about—and criticism sometimes defies objective criteria.

It is not enough to say "I don't like it" or "I do like it" unless, of course, you are in complete charge and there is no one to disagree—a situation that may happen too often in some libraries. Given the need to justify acceptance or rejection of a title on its instrinsic merits, the librarian should:

1. Go back over the ten objective points to see if any errors in fact have been made about the title.

2. Allow yourself and your group time. Where possible, return to reviews. Read as much as you can about the specific book, author, and subject.

3. Try to justify to yourself why you like or dislike the book. If possible,

put it in writing. Is your reaction rational, based on legitimate criticism, or is it too personal? Do you really object to the book, or the subject, or the language, or the . . . ? Try to be specific about what you do or don't like with page and line number. (This of course assumes that the librarian has taken the time to read the book, or at least to look closely at the contents). To argue solely on the basis of reviews, publisher, author, title, and the like is pointless.

Once a negative decision has been made, the decision should be filed, with the reasons for rejection. Then the librarian should be open to a change of mind, particularly if there is demand for the title. Unless it is a highly unusual situation, demand should override the librarian's negative decision.

Instant Acceptance and Rejection

Certain types of titles are accepted almost automatically by libraries:[10]

1. Reprints and new editions of classics that are already part of the library or accepted in other libraries and often listed in bibliographies, lists of "best" books, and similar indexes. Selection of so-called classics is simple in that these basic works "have acquired a firm reputation and . . . are designated as classical because they are models of good taste, have contributed to the adoption of the canons of good writing and, uniting the useful and the agreeable, are a source of pure joy."[11] However, small libraries, any library with inadequate funds, and those staffed primarily by liberals will subject classics to the same scrutiny as all other titles.

2. Books from series the library has long considered important to the collection, such as Rivers of America, Fielding travel guides, and the like.[12]

3. Picture books for adults where the emphasis is on the photographs, drawings, and diagrams, and there is little or no text to evaluate. (Obviously, the rules about audience, price, format, subject matter, and so forth hold, but this is usually easy to tell.)

4. Certain basic research or reference titles that, because of subject matter, author, and publisher, can be ordered safely without actually seeing the book.

[10] Library size plays a large part in automatic acceptance and instant rejection. The larger the library budget, the less likely that material is automatically rejected or accepted —at least in theory. In practice, despite the number of people who may have to approve the decision, there is a generally understood code that does govern acceptance and rejection.

[11] Rinaldo Lunati, *Book Selection: Principles and Procedures* (Metuchen, N.J.: Scarecrow Press, 1975), p. 5. This European study is particularly useful for its concise historical background of selection and practical suggestions.

[12] Don Lanier, "The Library and Series Books," *The Southeastern Librarian*, Fall 1978, pp. 169–171. Lanier defines a series as "A group of books published under a series title and usually in uniform format and design."

INSTANT REJECTION

Considering that more than 800 titles are published each week, it would help to have a method of instant rejection. As Peter Andrews says,

Traditional methods such as skimming or speed-reading are of little value. . . . Even a moment spent reading a book you don't want to is a moment lost forever. . . . Bad books must be fought at the water's edge; at the very bookstore shelf itself. The reader must learn to master the art of Instant Rejection (I.R.).[13]

Andrews then explains the art form of instant rejection, and in so doing suggests certain methods that are of use to librarians. Before turning to his individualized approach, let us note some fairly universal rules for library I.R. Most libraries today reject:

1. Books, pamphlets, periodicals, and other materials from vanity presses.

2. Textbooks in most fields. In some cases, however, there may be nothing quite as comprehensive as a good textbook, and the library will then purchase.

3. Titles in foreign languages not likely to be used by the community. However, if the library is in a Spanish-speaking neighborhood an equal effort will be made to accept almost automatically passable books in Spanish that relate to the interests and needs of the Spanish-speaking community.

4. Titles in certain subject areas in which the library audience has no interest, or where a library in the immediate area (or part of the network) collects extensively.

Equally impressive are the rules set down by the inventor of I.R., Peter Andrews, who explains a system that includes under "Do Not Read":

—Any book entitled *Notes On.* . . .
—Any book by someone who has personally known Henry Kissinger, Judy Garland, the Kennedys, or Hugh Hefner.
—Any book that promises to raise your consciousness or lower your weight.
—Any book that "reads like a veritable 'Who's Who' of show business."
—Any book by an author who has inherited the mantle of either Damon Runyon or Macaulay.
—Any book illustrated by tarot cards or signs of the zodiac.
—Any compilation of the wit and wisdom of anyone.
—Any book by an author over 30 who has his or her picture taken wearing jeans.
—Any book on philosophy by a manual laborer or any book on manual labor by a philosopher.
—Any book on the funny things kids do.
—Any book set in a tumultuous period of America's history. Indeed, any book that is described as tumultuous anywhere.
—Any book that quotes either Robert Frost or James Joyce in the title.
—Any book of fairy tales for adults.
—Any book that promises to fill every moment of every day of your life.

[13] "Surviving the Title Glut . . . ," *Bookswest*, April 1977, p. 11.

—Any novel set in a plane, bus, train, ship, or any other conveyance where people from all walks of life meet and share one climactic moment.

—Any novel of a mighty family whose compelling story is told amid the holocaust of world war.

Although the list is long, be sure to keep plenty of blank paper handy, because new categories are being added every day. And don't worry about what you might be missing. There are still plenty of great books around.[14]

Fiction

Selection of fiction for the library illustrates various points about evaluation raised in this chapter.

The traditionalist has no difficulty in separating out the extremes in fiction (or nonfiction). Given traditional rules of measurement, the librarian can say with certainty that Saul Bellow's latest novel is likely to be somewhat more acceptable than a historical romance of Rosemary Rogers. Furthermore, this librarian would buy Bellow and reject Rogers on the intrinsic quality of the work.

The liberal would prefer Rogers to, say, John Hawkes because she has more than 3 million copies in print, compared to several thousand for Hawkes. (The liberal will nevertheless have no trouble with Bellow, whose many novels now regularly make the best-seller lists and for that reason are acceptable.)

Between choosing or rejecting on the intrinsic quality of the novel (the traditionalist) or the demand for the novel (the liberal) stands the pluralist, who would say one should judiciously weigh both positions and, where feasible, purchase both the good-to-excellent titles and the popular titles. The acquisitions line might be drawn, for example, only at the highly esoteric literary title at one extreme and the frighteningly bad, little-read title at the other.

For the sake of debate one may grant that the angels are smiling on the pluralist, but even this librarian needs some guidelines. Between the obviously excellent, highly regarded, and much-reviewed novel and the equally best-selling romance is the mass of fiction, which realizes neither distinction. In this middle group are most of the 3500 to 4000 novels published each year in paperback and hardback. The amount of fiction published annually is usually at least two to one over such other popular categories as religion, biography, political science, and even children's books.[15] Novels account for from 50 or 60 to even 70 percent or more of the books circulated in the average public, school, and even smaller college library.

It is true that librarians (at least those who subscribe to the pluralistic

[14] Ibid., p. 12. The list given here is somewhat shorter than in the original publication.
[15] "Updated Book Trade Statistics—1977," *Publishers Weekly*, August 21, 1978, p. 22. This survey of 1977 publishing shows there were 3836 novels published. The only subject with more titles was sociology, with 6993.

notion of selection) often automatically buy novels by certain publishers, by certain authors, even in certain subject areas. Still, this hardly solves the problem of the vast number of novels that require some consideration in terms of value judgments.

To make a wise decision as to what to buy or reject (again granted the pluralistic viewpoint), one should carefully weigh the demand for certain types of fiction with the intrinsic quality or lack of quality of that fiction. This is to say once again that evaluation and selection must be separated, considered, and then brought together for a final decision.

INTRINSIC MEASUREMENTS

In dealing with the intrinsic qualities of a novel it is customary to set out a check list. The librarian then theoretically reads the novel (or a review), examines the check list, and makes a decision. A typical set of rules for evaluating the novel might include:

1. Is it true to life? Sensational? Exaggerated? Distorted?
2. Has it vitality and consistency in character depiction? Valid psychology? Insight into human nature?
3. Is the plot original? Hackneyed? Probable? Simple? Involved?
4. Is dramatic interest sustained?
5. Does it stimulate? Provoke thought? Satisfy? Inspire? Amuse?[16]

One suspects that a novel lacking all of these qualities (pornography or a polemical tract aside) simply would not be published. The problem is that most novels, no matter how bad or how good, fail or pass on some of these points.

A more sophisticated approach is suggested by literary critics. Cleanth Brooks and Robert Penn Warren, for example, would have the reader judge a novel as a failure if written by a "dogmatist":

The *dogmatist*, who is author, paints a world of black and white, a world in which right and wrong, truth and falsehood, are clear with statutory distinctness, a world of villain and hero. The *artist*, who is author, paints a world in which there is, in the beginning, neither black nor white, neither right nor wrong which can be defined with absolute certainty. The certainty can only come in terms of the process, and must be *earned*. . . . The artist realizes that, if the opponent—"villain" or "idea"—is a straw man, the conflict will lack interest.[17]

The difficulty with this approach is the supposition that all people at all times read, or want to read, only the "best" of fiction. Such is hardly the

---

[16] To a literary critic such as George Steiner or the late Lionel Trilling this would seem ridiculous. Still, one can admit that while none of these questions is applicable in evaluating the "new novel" (Sarraute, Pinget, or Robbe-Grillet, for example), they are at least mnemonic devices for popular fiction.

[17] Cleanth Brooks and Robert Penn Warren, *The Scope of Fiction* (New York: Appleton-Century-Crofts, 1960), p. xiii. As the title of this well-known book indicates, the comments are about fiction, but they are also applicable to nonfiction.

case. Even the most avid elitist will sometimes find pleasure in a well-written mystery or adventure story.

ACCESSIBILITY AND PLEASURE

The essential difference between one type of novel and another, all things being equal, is the degree of accessibility and pleasure. To read a serious, carefully written novel by a dedicated and skilled writer usually takes a commitment, if only of attention. Conversely, the well-written novel with no message but pleasure is usually highly accessible and all one needs to enjoy the work is relaxation.

A first rule of accessibility and the novel should be that the work bring pleasure. "Pleasure is by no means an infallible critical guide, but it is the least fallible."[18] If a novel is written to be popular it should meet not only the rule of accessibility and pleasure, but should have built in:

1. A narrative element that is easy to follow and holds the reader's attention. Speaking of *Ragtime*, the author summarizes his intent:

I've always wanted my work to be accessible. Literature, after all, is for people, not some secret society. It probably seems so accessible this time because I was very deliberately concentrating on the narrative element. I wanted to recover that really marvellous tool for a novelist, the sense of motion. Two or three hundred years ago it was much more common—Defoe had it, Cervantes, more recently Edgar Allan Poe. You have to make sacrifices for it, of course.[19]

2. A clear unobtrusive style. The style should not be so bad as to make the reader aware of the writer's lack of skill or so overt to make the reader pause and consider it. One critic terms this the "plain style," which always gets right to the point. More has been written about style than almost any other aspect of writing, yet there is really no satisfactory definition. All that can be said with certainty is: "Style and content are indissoluble . . . the strongly individual style of each important writer is an organic aspect of his work and never something merely 'decorative.' "[20]

The content or message of a novel is in itself not enough to govern rejection or acceptance. The mere presence in a novel "of an idea which is held to be important in itself on ethical, religious, philosophical, sociological or other grounds, does not necessarily indicate anything about the importance [of the novel]. One might almost as well commend a [novel] for exemplifying good grammatical usage."[21]

Much of the mistrust of fiction rests with the development of the novel itself. Today we have the anti-hero, which runs counter to many people's

[18] W. H. Auden, *The Dyer's Hand* (New York: Random House, 1962), p. 5.

[19] John Sutherland, "The Selling of *Ragtime* . . . ," *The New Review*, June-July 1977, p. 4.

[20] Susan Sontag, *Against Interpretation* (New York: Farrar, Shaus & Giroux, 1966), p. 15.

[21] Brooks and Warren, op. cit., p. xii.

notion of the moral, upstanding American; language that is not delicate; actions, particularly sex in and out of bed, graphically described; and style and language that not only lack simplicity and bourgeois notions of decency, but simply can't be understood.

So, if one moves from standard lists on how to select fiction to literary critics to authors, the problem remains. The librarian is still presented with criteria that may or may not be acceptable—or even understandable.

The problem with check lists against which to evaluate fiction (no matter how broad or how subtle) is that if a trained librarian needs such a list, he or she should not be evaluating fiction. One of the marks of the professional librarian, as noted time and time again, is training that allows an informed opinion. And an informed opinion about fiction comes only after considerable education, reading, and conscious evaluation. This is not to say that librarians who have had the same courses, read the same novels, and even come from the same cultural background are likely to agree more than 50 percent of the time on what is intrinsically good or bad within a given area of fiction. They will, however, be able to do two important things: intellectually justify acceptance or rejection of a particular novel and be able dispassionately to separate selection from evaluation.

SELECTION MEASUREMENTS

Much of the difficulty in fiction selection comes from failure to separate novels of a certain genre or form. Not all fiction is the same, nor can it be evaluated in the same fashion. It is unfair, as well as unjustified, to expect in an average gothic novel the literary qualities one might expect from a work of fiction in *The New Yorker*. At the same time, one should not judge efforts of the avant garde, no matter what the banner flown, in the same way one would read a story in *The New Yorker*.

One has certain minimal expectations from all these approaches to fiction, but to judge a novel by Renata Adler the same way you would evaluate the work of Virginia Holt is to do both a wrong—and certainly to build a strange if not wonderful book collection.

VARIOUS FORMS

Specific novels and authors aside, the library is faced with the problem of form.

The problem is evident to any mystery fan. Granted that the library should buy the form, how can you readily tell the bad from the better and the best? Should the library buy all the novels of Andrew Garve and Ellery Queen? How do they compare, after all, with Agatha Christie or Patricia Highsmith? "Well, let's get them all. Fine, but there is a limited budget and they do fill up a lot of valuable space. Well, how about eliminating most of Garve's work? I suppose that might work, except the mayor [or principal or college president or library board member] is a Garve fan."

According to [one] poll, 53 percent of all college graduates are avid readers of mystery stories. Another independent survey, taken earlier in 1977, came up with the information that the average mystery buff reads three books a week. . . . A personal poll of the PW [*Publishers Weekly*] editorial staff clinches it. Surrounded by every conceivable variety of book . . . 13 of us are authentic, diehard mystery buffs. One is "sometimes"; three are "nevers."[22]

Much the same results might be found when one asks about the popularity of science fiction, gothics, romances, and so on. Audiences for these forms cross all educational and even interest lines. Given this consideration, it is difficult if not impossible to decide who is likely to read what based on such things as education, age, and experience alone.

The art of selection is to be able to separate the various forms of novels—and then (and only then) evaluate their intrinsic quality within each category. Once this is done, the librarian must decide (although never in a purely quantitative way) how many titles from each category should be purchased that week, that month, that year.

POLICY STATEMENTS

Librarians concerned with the difficulties of fiction selection usually have something to say about novels in their policy statements.[23] These statements are of value to us here in that they demonstrate a wide variety of viewpoints and attitudes about fiction—and by implication about selection of other materials. Most should spark discussion. They are presented here at random without comment:

The importance of the novel as a medium for recording and molding public opinion and changing attitudes is recognized. The sound treatment of significant social and personal problems or of racial and religious questions through novels can contribute much to the betterment of human relations. Therefore, novels of serious purpose are purchased in preference to many titles of light fiction and adventure. . . . Since an attempt is made to satisfy a public varying greatly in education and social background and taste, competent, pleasing and successful novels in varied categories are also chosen. . . . [The library excludes novels that are] weak, cheap and sentimental writing as well as the intentionally sensational, morbid or erotic. [P. 20, Public Library]

Every library on a limited budget must of necessity employ a policy of selectivity in acquisitions. Books may be limited on the basis of cost, demand and availability in other libraries. Books wrtten in a sensational, inflammatory manner or tending to stir class or race hatred, and those offensive to good taste or contrary to moral or ethical standards, call for positive exclusion. However honest works which present an honest picture of a problem or side of life are not necessarily excluded because of coarse language or frankness in certain passages. [P. 195, Public Library]

[22] "The Eternal World of Mystery and Suspense," *Publishers Weekly*, March 13, 1978, p. 45.

[23] Elizabeth Futas, op. cit. The quotes are from this book.

The broad range of fiction poses a special problem in book selection, and a seriou attempt is made to supply titles representing the entire spectrum. . . . It is realistic to note that when a book, however disturbing, is written by a recognized author published by a reputable publisher, and reviewed favorably and widely in nationa and international journals by competent reviewers, this library will not set itsel up as a censor by invoking single items of its book selection policy to keep thi work out of the collection. [P. 233, Public Library]

Other librarians simply prefer a short statement about fiction and let it go at that:

The library recognizes the importance of the novel. . . . Novels of serious purpos are purchased, considering a public varying greatly in education, interests, taste and reading skills. [P. 232, College Library]

We never forget the many people to whom reading is a great source of pleasure relaxation and recreation. Our libraries must always provide for the person who just wants a good book to read. [P. 296, Public Library]

The library recognizes that any given title may offend some patrons. However selection will not be made on the basis of any anticipated approval or disapprova but solely on the merits of the work and the interests of the readers. [P. 117, Public Library]

Demand is a valid factor in book selection. To be of any value, best sellers must be chosen in time to meet mass demand. Usually these are selected as soon as they reach best seller lists. [P. 76, Public Library]

The uneasy uncertainty about fiction is reflected in these difficult decision statements. The ultimate solution, for all libraries, is to judiciously weigh demand (selection) with the intrinsic merits (evaluation) of the novel, and buy accordingly. However, in most cases—some would say in all cases—the evaluation should give way to demand.

The Question of Demand

One of the oldest problems in a library is the individual who asks for a book (or anything else) the librarian has decided will not be purchased. The librarian's negative decision is based on an objective evaluation of the book itself and, possibly, the determination that it will be of little value to the public. All goes well until John Q or Mary P wanders into the library and asks for what the librarian has rejected. What to do? Order or otherwise obtain the title requested.

Many libraries follow this procedure routinely. The resulting improvement in public relations alone makes it worthwhile. The comparatively small number of such requests will not open the floodgates.

In addition, precaution should be taken to foresee demand for titles:

1. Purchase any book that is on the best-seller list published in your local

newspaper and in many major review sections such as *The New York Times Book Review.*

2. Purchase enough copies so no one has to wait more than two or three weeks.

3. If the demand is for a form (science fiction, romance, mystery, biography), purchase a specified title when requested. Where there is more demand than titles for a given form, buy more books in that area. Few people will ever be entirely satisfied, but at least the librarian should make a sincere effort to purchase the type of titles wanted.

Another approach to this difficulty is the McNaughton Plan and other leasing plans whereby the librarian may rent or lease larger-than-normal quantities of a given form (see pages 166–167).

Remember, if you have not purchased the book because you think it fails to measure up to a certain standard of quality, spare the person who asked for the title. "The one thing I most emphatically do not ask of a critic is that he tell me what I *ought* to approve of or condemn. . . . The responsibility for what I choose to read is mine."[24] You must know what you think the library audience will enjoy reading. You should not select on the basis of what people *ought* to read, or reject on what they *ought not* to read. You do not change a person's reading habits by saying they are terrible or morally reprehensible.

No one, including children, wants to be protected from books:

Teachers and librarians who "rescue" children from inferior books assume they are God's chosen people, bringing culture to the savages. They often bewilder me and they usually scare the hell out of me, for they are so messianic and so utterly misguided about reading, literature, and kids. Better to leave kids' reading alone and hope for the best. . . .[25]

A Question of Quality

The demand usually is for one of two types of book: (1) a best seller[26] or a book headed for the best-seller list because it has been extensively reviewed or mentioned in the press and on television, or (2) a book in a certain

[24] W. H. Auden, op. cit., p. 5.

[25] Ken Donelson, "The Trouble with Read Only the Very Best," *Media & Methods,* March 1978, p. 33.

[26] A "best seller" is any book that sells in the hundreds of thousands (an average first novel may sell from 2500 to 5000 copies). At the same time it is a euphemism for any book that lacks certain of the basic literary qualities described previously. It is also synonymous with "popular culture," and as such considered acceptable by some circles. For a historical listing and discussion of best sellers see Alice Hackett's frequently revised *80 Years of Best Sellers, 1895–1975* (New York: R. R. Bowker, 1977). There are listings of current best sellers in every issue of *The New York Times Book Review* and *Publishers Weekly.*

general subject area—from gothic novels and science fiction to popular biography. Normally the individual knows the name of the best seller, or at least has a hint as to the author. In the second category there may be a favorite author, but more often it is a sweeping demand (some call it an insatiable hunger) for anything of a given type.

Much of the debate about evaluation is centered around "What is high quality?"

There is, never has been, and is not likely to be consensus as to what constitutes the particulars of quality. One traditionalist will argue with another about, say, the position of Dickens or Trollope in nineteenth-century fiction. At the same time, both would agree in a general way that both Dickens and Trollope at least constitute part of what is known as quality. To complicate matters, today's high-quality artifact may have been yesterday's low-quality artifact. (El Greco told a friend "Michelangelo was a good man, but he didn't know how to paint.") Every reader can point to a critic who at one time or another has badly misjudged an individual, a novel, or a work of art or music or has expressed the type of bias the professional librarian seeks to avoid.

The argument for high quality or culture is essentially antidemocratic in emotional context: it admits to elitism, that all people are not created equal, and both enjoyment and creation of high art is a lifetime project few are willing to undertake. Theoretically, of course, the liberals (from Rousseau to Locke to English communications critic Raymond Williams) would claim that this is a fallacious notion. Quality is not a monopoly of the elite but should be—can be—part of the culture of every person. Between emotion and theory stands the sometimes helpless librarian, who can fall back on this summary:

Elitism of the intellect should be a term of praise rather than disparagement. But the word itself is an unfortunate one that has too many bad associations. There is a tendency, when the word "elite" is mentioned, automatically to equate it with a moneyed elite, or an elite that comes only from birth or high political position. That washes off into the intellectual elite, making any form of elitism "bad" or "undemocratic."[27]

The only really "bad" or "undemocratic" situation is in a library where the user has no choice. Every library should offer a wide variety of materials, both that hailed as the best of its kind and, if necessary, the worst. The latter situation is acceptable when the librarian is purchasing materials for people who do not have the ability to choose, who through lack of reading ability and general education simply cannot cope with what has come to be known as quality materials. It's equally acceptable for people who *can* choose but for some reason prefer a relatively bad novel or biography to a better title.

[27] Harold Schonberg, "Elitism, in the Arts, is Good," *The New York Times*, February 5, 1978, p. D19.

THE RIGHT TO CHOOSE

It is pointless to discuss choice unless the individual really has that choice, and here Herbert J. Gans sums up the much larger argument that is sometimes lost in the narrower battles about demand and value judgments:

American society should pursue policies that would maximize educational and other opportunities for all so as to permit everyone *to choose* from higher taste cultures. Until such opportunities are available . . . it would be wrong to expect a society with a median educational level of twelve years to choose only from taste cultures requiring a college education, or for that matter, to support through public policies the welfare of the higher cultures at the expense of the lower ones. Moreover, it is wrong to criticize people for holding and applying aesthetic standards that are related to their educational background, and for participating in taste cultures reflecting this background.[28]

Americans must be given education so they can have the choices. Until they have that educated choice, there is no choice.

Sometimes it is forgotten that reading is not easy and requires concentration. And concentration, to continue with the larger social issues, depends upon the ability to relax. This presupposes not only an ability to read but also employment and background that allow relaxation and attention to reading.

The kind of attention required by serious literature is both personally and socially only variously possible. . . . More difficult to analyze is the evident distinction between ways of living which stimulate attention and allow rest, and ways which produce neither attention nor rest, but only an unfocused restlessness that somehow has to be appeased. These are radical questions about society as a whole. . . . These problems cannot be solved in the field of publications alone. . . . It is the business of the society to create and maintain the conditions in which this necessarily difficult growth can go on, in particular by the creation and strengthening of institutions based on some more adequate principle than that of quick profit.[29]

This is not to say the librarian should buy nothing but the "best" books or nothing but books of the lowest common denominator. It is to say that the librarian should turn the library into a place in which people can find touches of everything, at various quality and interest levels.

Take, for example, the small public library where the "sin" is not the exclusion of less than good books, but the all-out embrace of local popular culture. Here the librarian is working an equal disservice to the community.

[In the public library] there was a list of about 20 new books a month published in the town newspaper, and a periodical shelf fairly well stocked with "good" magazines. But in many other respects the library was a product, even a cause, of the lapse in information (between the small town and the larger cities). The newspaper list frequently disappointed me; I would scan it eagerly, and perhaps

---

[28] *Popular Culture and High Culture* (New York: Basic Books, 1975), p. 128.
[29] Raymond Williams, *The Long Revolution* (London: Penguin Books, 1965), p. 143.

among the gardening books, and gothics, the auto repair manuals and movie star memoirs, might be an interesting piece of serious fiction or a work of political analysis. Most of it was safe—too safe. . . . For the most part the book collection was to modern literature what AM radio is to modern music.[30]

The plight of the imaginative in the small public library is another side to the often-heard remark that if some librarians buy only what they consider high-quality titles, others are polarized around low quality. Unfortunately, here there is a tremendous misunderstanding because the librarian buying the less-than-brilliant titles often thinks what is being purchased meets the needs of the community. This is either ignorance or an essentially elitist point of view gone mad—the librarian has such a low opinion of public taste that he or she buys accordingly.

THE SOLUTION TO DEMAND

The best way to meet demand is to foresee it by carefully watching reviews, television programs where books and other materials are plugged, radio shows, and the like. Librarians should spend a few minutes a week or each month checking what is available on newsstands and in markets and drugstores as well as in bookstores. This will give the librarian a better notion of what people read than any theoretical articles on the subject. Granted, it is not always uplifting to the spirit or the mind, but there it is—the reading habits of America in the marketplace. (One can argue the habits are dictated by what jobbers make available, but that's another point.)

THE NONPURCHASE DEFENSE

At times the librarian must support the nonpurchase of a book. These times are much fewer than the literature implies, but they do occur. The approach to this challenge is the difference between the professional, skilled librarian and the nonprofessional, less-than-skilled person.

The what-*not*-to-do's in this demand situation are:

1. Do not say that the title was not purchased because the library cannot afford the book. An expensive title aside, the argument won't work because the smart user can quickly point out hundreds of little-used, costly titles in the library. Besides that, the user may (and sometimes does) contribute the title to the library. The librarian is then either forced to accept it or do an abrupt, damaging about-face.

To be sure, budget is a major factor in selection, but it should not be isolated. It should be part of, but *not the only reason* for, the explanation of why the evaluation-selection judgment ruled out the requested title.

2. Do not say that the title was uniformly badly reviewed and therefore

[30] A common complaint is that the small library ignores the aspirations and dreams of the young, and particularly the bright; see Anne Nelson, "How My Hometown Library Failed Me" (*Library Journal*, February 1, 1978, p. 318).

not purchased. The odds are that the person will disagree with the reviews. One may use reviews, but only in conjunction with librarian opinion. After all, the user is paying taxes to support the library, not the reviewers.

(3.) Do not say that the title was rejected because the content was offensive; at this point you are treading the ground of the censor. Admittedly, a children's librarian might make a case here, but it is better to approach the book from other less debatable criteria such as style, difficulty of accessibility, and the like.

The practical solution when a book was not purchased is threefold:

1. Attempt to procure the title on interlibrary loan. And, to speed matters, call other libraries in the area to see not only if the wanted title is there but if it is in the library and available. The patron can then be given the option of the library's getting the book or waiting for it on loan.

2. Suggest a substitute. This works quite well when the demand is not for a specific title but for a type of book (gothic, mystery) or for a novel by a certain author. It is of no value when the person has a specific title in mind.

3. Explain as dispassionately and as objectively as possible why the library cannot buy the specific title. This is easier said than done, although the majority of people will readily understand, for example, that a book cannot be purchased because there is simply no demand for such a work or that it is a title which does not fit into the general pattern established by the library's public.

The Librarian as Selector of Material

Several things characterize the librarian who is a competent selector of materials:

1. Opinion whether to buy or reject must be based on information about the intrinsic worth of the item and about the community being served. This presupposes an interest in books, periodicals, films—all materials being selected—as well, of course, as an involvement with the public.

2. Anyone can afford an honest opinion, but the librarian is hired as a professional to have an informed opinion. The difference between "I know what I like" and "I know what is useful for this library" may be quite different.[31] In the latter case the librarian should be able to justify the decision.

3. An appreciation that a library is a service to a pluralistic society, not a model reflection of the librarian and friends. This point is stressed in other chapters, but is worth repeating here.

4. The more expected qualities can be summarized as follows:

[31] W. H. Auden has an explanation for the much-heard "I know what I like." When someone between twenty and forty says this, "He is really saying "I have no taste of my own but accept the taste of my cultural milieu, because between twenty and forty, the surest sign that a man has a genuine taste of his own is that he is uncertain of it" (loc. cit.).

Media selectors implementing the system must be learner oriented and versatile. They should have a broad educational background and should understand libraries and information systems. Above all, they must be versed in learning theory, curriculum, and instructional development so they can assess curricular needs and search out materials satisfying those needs. In short, they should be qualified to gain the confidence of the academic faculty they serve and consult.

We expect those making media selections to understand the characteristics, advantages, and disadvantages of various media. They must be knowledgeable of current media research and its applications to learning. Selectors with such qualifications produce client satisfaction.[32]

5. An understanding of your own biases and weaknesses. This is of particular importance if you are deeply involved personally in a political, religious, social, or other movement about which you feel the urge to spread the "gospel." Proselytizing must be controlled, both in the sense of what is selected and, equally important, in what is rejected. It is similarly vital to appreciate that a strictly neutral position on any issue is virtually impossible, that objectivity is constantly being shaded by our personal view of the world. What is necessary is constant questioning of your motives for selection.

The best single guiding principle for selection of library materials is the recognition of fallibility. While not all will agree, the modifying principle should be one of humble skepticism. When hard decisions have to be made, it is well to remember that "an analysis of what we take to be good reasons for our beliefs will show that they always depend at some point on a claim to knowledge of an unattainable sort."[33] There are no selection decisions that cannot be questioned.

Not all book selectors are so humble. . . . I once asked a very well-known public librarian how she identified her selection mistakes. She was indignant. "We don't make selection mistakes," she said icily. I said, "Oh, go on, everybody does. Even the best booksellers find themselves returning up to 25 percent of the books they buy. Surely there are books on your shelves that you thought would be in demand but which . . . have never been opened." . . . She said, "There may be books on our shelves that have never been opened, but that's not our mistake, that's our readers' mistake."[34]

RELIANCE ON REVIEWS

Examination of each item ordered is rarely possible in libraries. Most librarians depend heavily upon reviews, at least as the first, major screen in the selection process. The reasons differ, but essentially: (1) The librarian

---

[32] Helen J. Ackerman, "Tips on Nonprint Acquisition . . . ," *American Libraries*, October 1978, p. 558.

[33] Peter Ungar, *Ignorance: A Case for Skepticism* (New York: Oxford University Press, 1975), p. 15.

[34] Dan Melcher, *Melcher on Acquisition* (Chicago: American Library Association, 1971), p. 7.

cannot examine new titles. Few jobbers or publishers will send titles to the library on approval. The result is that the librarian must either go to a large bookstore or jobber to look at the books before buying or make special arrangements with some publishers and some jobbers to receive approval books. The latter is difficult and also depends on the library having a large book budget, although even a substantial budget is no guarantee of cooperation between jobber or publisher and library. (2) There are too many books published each year for even the most avid reader to examine more than a few.[35] Some 20 years ago the average number of books published in the United States was about 10,000. Today the figure is over 40,000.

Other reasons for relying primarily on reviews and other sources are: Lack of subject specialization, particularly in technology and the sciences, by most librarians; lack of availability of many of the books for examination before purchase; and lack of reliance on the once-popular idea that all books had to be read first.

If reviews are the primary method of determining selection, why should the librarian bother to learn rules of evaluation?

1. The prolific output of publishers, coupled with less than adequate reviews (quantitatively or qualitatively) has forced librarians to examine some of the materials, or at least double-check existing reviews.

2. The publishing output is matched by slashes in budgets, which in turn makes necessary much more careful attention to what is added or rejected.

3. Even where books and other materials are recommended, high cost, question of value to the library audience, and similar issues may require the librarian to view the material and make a personal evaluation.

WHO DECIDES?

Both specific and general considerations go into answering the question "Who selects materials for the library?"

Specifically, the head librarian is charged with selection. The librarian is responsible to a board, committee, president, mayor, or principal who must take legal responsibility for problems that arise from selection. Hence, in serious censorship cases, the buck stops with the governing body—which may either stand behind or reject the opinion and action of the librarian.[36]

The system is not usually so bound by chains of command, however. In most libraries day-by-day choices are made by the librarian, the staff, or both. Librarians in turn should solicit suggestions and assistance from those who use the library—faculty, general public, subject specialists, and others.

No matter what system is employed, the librarian should have the final

---

[35] The same argument is true for almost all types of material.

[36] Elizabeth Futas, op. cit. See pp. 9, 22, 44, and 91 for policy statements on responsibility from public libraries and pp. 175, 310, 215, 231, and 242 for similar statements from college and university libraries.

professional word in the selection process. The librarian is responsible to the governing body and to the public served, but it should be perfectly clear to both who is ultimately responsible (and willing to accept the blame and the praise) for the collections. To have it any other way is to invite chaos, with constant in-fighting between groups. Some systems require that the librarian first check with the governing body before a certain amount of money is spent on a single item, or there may be a hierarchy of administrative processes to go through for selection. In any case, these exceptions should be carefully spelled out for all involved.

Committee Selection

Actual selection is generally made by a committee composed of subject specialists, sometimes the library director (or an assistant), heads of branches and divisions, and similar personnel. In university and college libraries that employ the committee system, the panel usually includes faculty representatives, and school libraries try to have representatives of the teaching faculty.

Meetings are held every two weeks, once a month, or (in smaller libraries) even quarterly. The average library tends to have more frequent, rather than less frequent, meetings. Each title is considered and usually someone who is for (or opposed to) the title has a few words about the book. Rejections are normally filed, to prevent consideration of the same book in the weeks or months ahead.

Before the meeting is held the reviews are routed to make certain all concerned have seen them. Each library has its own methods of handling reviews before the meeting, but generally the reviews are circulated to individual subject experts or those involved with divisions or departments. The individual has the responsibility of checking what is to be purchased and what is to be ignored. The marked reviews are then brought to the meeting for discussion.[37]

If the committee cannot reach agreement about a title, the normal procedure is either to order an approval copy for examination and review by a member of the staff or to put the question aside until more outside reviews are available.

In addition to deciding on purchase or rejection, the committee has other decisions to make:

(1) How many copies to order. If a popular book, should there be enough to satisfy demand, enough for all the branches? If a reference book, should another copy be ordered for general circulation? If a science title, will one or more copies be needed for the general reading room? And so on.

(2) Purchase of nonreviewed titles. In most meetings questions will arise

[37] In larger libraries, where committee meetings may be few or nonexistent, the librarian simply checks what is to be ordered and hands the copy to the acquisitions librarian for processing.

about nonreviewed titles, such as specialized books the librarian may have heard of through a publisher's announcement. Depending on individual policy, some libraries wait for reviews or ask for approval copies, but are more likely simply to order without either. The rationale is that the publisher and author are reputable and there is a need for more material on the subject regardless of quality.

Actually, selection goes on every minute of the work day. Any librarian worthy of the name is constantly checking what the library has or does not have and evaluating what new books or replacements to add to the collection.

[The selection meeting] is the culmination of the selection procedure, which had its beginning earlier. In reality, the selection procedure is continuous and unending, somewhat analogous to *The Worm Ouroboros* of E. R. Eddison in which the end is the beginning unendingly and the weekly selection committee meetings simply conclude one phase of this ongoing process, which has its beginning with the arrival of the day's mail.[38]

Once choices are made, the mechanics differ. Many libraries simply check handy review cards for purchase or nonpurchase and these are then passed on to the acquisitions department for verification and ordering.

PATTERNS OF SELECTION

In most libraries the choice of materials is usually a committee decision, but there are variations:

1. Does the library have branches? (or is it a central library in a system of smaller libraries)? Where the answer is "yes," one may observe some standard selection styles:

a. Those in charge of the branches assume an active role in selection. Where the branches are large enough, the heads of the smaller libraries may participate in selection meetings. However, the usual procedure is to send the branches a list of selected titles, which they may order or not.

b. In some situations, particularly where there are many small branches without professional librarians, the actual selection is made by the head of the system—although always with attention to local needs.

One way to cope with lack of experts in all media and lack of budget for many libraries is to establish a formal or informal media selection center for a group of libraries. The centers may function within a large library system or take in a larger geographic area that includes a wide variety of types and sizes of library.[39] The difficulty, for both liberal and pluralistic selectors, is

---

[38] Ronald V. Norman, "A Method of Book Selection for a Small Public Library," *RQ*, Winter 1977, p. 144.

[39] For a good description of such centers see Cora Bomar, et al., *Guide to the Development of Educational Media Selection Centers* (Chicago: American Library Association, 1973). See also an outline of the activities of two centers in Marilyn L. Miller, "Collection Development in School Media Centers . . . ," *Collection Building*, vol. 1, no. 1 (1978), pp. 40–46.

that any system which removes selection to a remote location may mean a corresponding diminution in appreciation of community need. Some librarians therefore do battle against centralized selection.

In the centers trained experts evaluate the media, including books and equipment in some situations, and make recommendations that may be accepted or rejected by individual librarians. Economic and local political-administrative tangles have delayed many of these centers and their development. In a less formal way the idea is employed in local, county, regional, and statewide networks.

In the average school media library (or centralized system), selection is done in committee meetings at the local and district levels. In some, preview films are tested by many teachers over a several-month period and evaluated in terms of effectiveness.[40] Part of the service of the district media center may be to provide regular previewing of films, discussion of books, and the like.

Centralized selection has the advantage of being able to offer a great number of books and nonprint materials for viewing by individual librarians. Equally important, provision is made to find reviews and keep files and bibliographies on needed materials, record evaluations, and the like.

Centralized selection also has disadvantages: (1) The committee may meet at regular intervals, and requests from the local libraries tend to build up until there is a large backlog; (2) the centralization may fail to take into account local needs and preferences, particularly where the committee makeup is not in sympathy with a particular library situation; (3) the committee effort is not worth the effort in that most materials are purchased only after favorable reviews, and selection is little more than automatically ordering from the reviews or accepted bibliography.

Nevertheless, the advantages outweigh the disadvantages, and in most school systems the centralized selection process is favored—as it is in larger county, regional, and state systems serving the general public.

(2.) Does the library have numerous bibliographers, subject experts, and division or department heads? If this is the case, they are the ones who meet, usually biweekly or once a month, to discuss what is to be selected or rejected.

   a. In a really large library, there may be no regular meetings. Here the subject expert simply orders books he feels are necessary for the collection.

   b. Where there are only two or three department, division, or subject heads, they usually meet as a group with other professionals in the library.

(3.) Does the library have a separate acquisitions section or someone in charge of acquisitions?

   a. In smaller libraries the separation may not be evident.

---

[40] The popularity of group selection was evident in the 1978–1979 conferences sponsored by the American Library Association on "Media Evaluation: The Group Process." The programs demonstrated both evaluative skills and the skills necessary to work in a group situation.

b. In a larger library, with an acquisitions section, someone will be in charge of supervising the various problems. Here the acquisitions librarian may do everything from routinely checking reviews, to discussing problems with subject experts, to revising and reorganizing the approval plans, among other duties.

c. In still larger or special library situations, one person may be charged with collection development. This individual will consider all orders for materials and meet with the librarians to discuss purchases.[41]

4. Interlibrary cooperation influences selection. As budgets become tighter, even larger libraries are working more closely together to avoid duplication or purchase of little-used, expensive materials.

In addition to the standard services of interlibrary loan, there is another dimension when one considers expensive audiovisual materials. Here it is not unusual for numerous libraries to band together to share expenses or join systems and associations that make films, slides, and similar items readily available. A large university, public, or state library is usually at the head of the system. The materials are selected (often with the assistance of circuit members), maintained, and circulated.

The Schenectady County Public Library (a medium-sized library) acquisitions policy statement notes of audiovisual materials (phonorecords, films, slides, transparencies, filmstrips, tapes):

The only type currently purchased by the library [is phonorecords]. 16mm films for children and adults are available through the Mohawk Valley Library Association and other sources, such as the New York State Library. A collection of 4,000 color slides on American art is available through the New York State Division of Library Development. . . . Additional slide sets on world art are available through interlibrary loan from the New York State Library.[42]

The Public and Selection

Most libraries encourage requests from the users for materials, a process that tends to be relatively informal. Few libraries have outsiders participating in the actual selection, at a meeting.

Many librarians would like to formalize the procedure of public participation. This author agrees. It is particularly important to have the public

[41] There are numerous titles for such people—Coordinator of Collections, Media Specialist Coordinator, Head of Collection Development, and so on. They differ from subject bibliographers or reference department heads. They are also separate from the traditional Head of Acquisitions, who is more involved with the mechanics of acquisition than with selection. Often, in fact, subject bibliographers and others work through this official. See *Collection Development in ARL Libraries* (Washington, D.C.: Association of Research Libraries, 1974). It was found that 88 percent of the large libraries surveyed had someone in charge of collection development, not simply the Head of Acquisitions, although they might be the same.

[42] Futas, op. cit., p. 16.

involved when the library is seeking new users. This is also a major consideration in school libraries where reading patterns are being formed.

PUBLIC LIBRARIES

Public library users may be encouraged to assist in the selection policy by:

1. Inviting requests for current best sellers or titles likely to be widely reviewed in newspapers and on television. A specific place and form should be provided for such suggestions, and the procedure should be made as simple as possible.

2. Inviting requests for any book or type of material not carried by the library. Signs, posters, brochures, and the like should invite such participation and forms should be readily available.

Invitation should be a library policy and take the form of specific routines and procedures such as forms, access to librarians who order materials, signs, brochures, and the like. Librarians should take an active part in inviting people to select materials. This can be done best at the informal level when the librarian is helping a user find what is needed. If what is wanted is not in the catalog, the librarian should find methods of filling the gaps in the collection.

Other procedures are possible, although little has been done among librarians to involve the public in selection. Much more study is needed in this vital area.

The lack of objective studies may be accounted for by a natural fear that the public may take over the whole selection process, dictating rather than suggesting what the library is to purchase. This in itself, some liberals would argue, would not be bad. However, even the most advanced liberal will agree that the danger is that a few, rather than many, members of the library community could end up commanding the selection process. Only a few will be much involved or interested in constant selection processes.

Such a fear is more a ghost than a fact. The public hires librarians to make the daily selection policy and carry out the routines of acquisition. Most of it is a routine, albeit highly specialized procedure in which the public is not interested. The average user only wishes to think he or she can make a suggestion that will be given serious consideration. Few, if any, have any plans about taking over the selection process.

Where there are formalized procedures to involve the public in selection, it is unlikely that those procedures will be violated by an overeager public. If a special-interest group were to try to encroach on library selection policy, the library board must be asked to become involved in establishing just how far a small part of the public may assault the selection process. More good than bad can come out of active public participation in selection because now the public feels it plays a guiding role in the acquisition decisions. Few will want to be more than guides.

Motivated by a desire to have public participation, librarians are in a better position to seek out nonusers or infrequent users of the library. A librarian, for example, may ask organizations or individuals what types of materials they want in the library to encourage them, or members of their family, to use that library. For the first time, nonusers may feel they have a part in the library, and this could encourage them to use the library.

ACADEMIC AND SCHOOL LIBRARIES

Academic libraries come closer to active participation of faculty in the selection process. This may be done in one of three ways:

1. The most common is to invite suggestions for new books or replacements from the faculty—and the students.

2. Historically, available funds were divided among various academic departments. Here the faculty actually selected the books.[43] This is now more the exception than the rule. Normally the actual selection today is governed by decisions of the subject bibliographer or divisional subject head.

3. A combination of both methods, with one trend quite obvious.[44] The larger the library, the smaller the role the faculty plays directly in selection.

4. Elementary and secondary schools tend to follow a similar pattern, although here again most control remains with the librarian. Suggestions are invited and often formally channeled to the library from the teachers, supervisors, and students.

Many school media librarians go to great lengths to involve as many people as possible in the selection process, although not enough students. One study reveals that while librarians take the final responsibility for selection of materials, there is a substantial involvement of teachers:

who make requests (92 percent), attend previewing exhibits (for audiovisual materials, 42 percent), participate in subject area development of the collection (39 percent), and attend demonstrations of new materials by publishers and distributors (35 percent). Only 17 percent reported teacher involvement in selection committees. . . . When respondents ranked in priority order the most important factors in the selection of materials, they ranked student requests at 3.89 on a scale of five (one being high.)[45]

[43] Barbara Rice, "The Development of Working Collections in University Libraries," *College and Research Libraries*, July 1977, p. 309: "Prior to 1960, responsibility for building comprehensive collections was vested in the faculty, with faculty meaning almost everyone but librarians. During the 1960s there was a shift . . . to librarians . . . a noticeable trend to selection by librarians, primarily by bibliographers . . . or heads of divisional subject libraries."

[44] Rice (ibid.) points out that "at present, current book selection is usually being performed automatically by blanket order with the remainder of titles being selected by [librarians]." This is discussed elsewhere, but by the close of the 1970s there seemed once again to be a return to selection and a backing away from automatic ordering plans.

[45] Marilyn L. Miller, "Collection Development in School Media Centers . . . ," *Collection Building*, vol. 1, no. 1 (1978), p. 40.

5. In a special library the person most responsible for selection is likely to be the clientele, since particular attention is given to their needs.[46]

The involvement of the public in selection can be exhausting and difficult, but it deserves the effort. Why? The best answer is given by a social critic who sees the expert (the librarian) as part of a dangerous movement toward public inertia:

The social order no longer excites a passionate curiosity to understand it. Instead, the attempt to understand it has been deliberately drained of passion and monopolized, moreover, by trained specialists. . . . Social scientists (librarians?) betray no more emotion about society than doctors feel toward the human body . . . and their pronouncements, delivered with an air of detachment in language technical and obscure, hold the same interest for the general public as the pronouncements of physicians—the mild interest that adheres to any statements that seem to promise better health and a sense of well-being.[47]

In too many libraries the public wanders in for this or that but feels no "passionate curiosity to understand" the library because its operation is just another carried on by distant bureaucrats. One of the best ways to shatter the inertia is to involve the public actively with the selection of materials.

In one library it was found "that the innovations and nontraditional services we librarians dream up are not always in tune with what the public wants or needs. . . . By giving citizens a voice in the development of library service, the priorities selected are more apt to be public priorities, and these can get public support."[48] It is important that those in charge of selection keep in contact with the people who do use (and possibly don't use) the library. Size works against this, and in the rush to make libraries larger it is worth considering the value of personalized selection, nicely summarized by a working librarian:

Unfortunately, as collections and clientele increase, the less librarians often know about the individuals they serve. This is especially noticeable in small libraries where growth is beginning. Such facilities change from a small "country store" atmosphere, where staff members have time to talk with and learn the reading needs of individuals, to medium or large "supermarkets," where the volume of demand restricts personalized contact. . . . Patrons especially resent this loss of personalized service in small libraries where it was available a short time earlier. Without adequate personnel to continue individualized service, these libraries become victims of their own success. They have increased the number of people

---

[46] This was the finding of a survey of state-agency libraries where only six of 18 respondent librarians thought they were most responsible for selection (Mary C. Grattan, "Collection Development in Texas State Agency Libraries," *Special Libraries*, February 1977, p. 71).

[47] Christopher Lasch, "The Narcissistic Personality of Our Time," *Partisan Review*, no. 1 (1977), p. 19.

[48] John Berry, "Discovering the Public," *Library Journal*, September 15, 1977. The editor is commenting on an article on a local community survey (Hays, et al., "The Patron and the Public," op. cit., pp. 1813–1818). This is a good introduction for the beginner to a model user study.

they serve, but they are not able to continue the personal contact that means so much to patrons.[49]

It is imperative that as many people as possible who use the library become involved, directly or indirectly, with both the selection and the evaluative process. (Nonusers, too, should be encouraged to speak out about why they don't use the library.) Ideally, every selection committee would have one or more members of the community served on the committee. For example, in a public library this should be nonboard members who are rotated once every year or so. In schools, it should be both teachers and students, and academic libraries must make an effort to involve faculty and students.

[49] Willie Nelms, "Personalized Service in a Growing Library," *Library Journal*, March 15, 1978. This library solved the problem by developing personalized service through reader profiles. When a book comes in that matches the profile, the user is notified.

Part Two

SELECTION OF PRINT MATERIALS

6
Book-Selection Aids

W HEN THE LIBRARIAN speaks of book-selection aids and tools employed for other decisions about print materials, it is usually in terms of *basic bibliographies*, which are employed as much for verification of data as for actual selection, and *basic selection guides*, which review the material and make purchase recommendations.

National and trade bibliographies are covered in reference courses, but it will be useful here to review briefly the basic American bibliographies the librarian is likely to use in selection.[1]

Basic Bibliographies

All are published by the R. R. Bowker Company, New York, unless otherwise noted.

1. When you want to see what titles are going to be published within the next one to five months: *Forthcoming Books* (since 1966; bimonthly) and *Subject Guide to Forthcoming Books* (since 1967; bimonthly).

2. When you want to check what was published last week (approximately): *Weekly Record* (since 1974). This is now a separate publication; between 1872 and 1973 it was a section in *Publishers Weekly*.

3. When you want to check what was published last month: *American Book Publishing Record* (since 1961; monthly). This cumulates the *Weekly Record* and rearranges material by broad subject; there is an annual cumulation. Equally useful, and preferred by some, is *Cumulative Book Index* (CBI) published by The H. W. Wilson Company, Bronx, N.Y. (since 1898, monthly).

4. When you want to check what is in print: *Books in Print* (since 1948; annual with one supplement). The subject approach is *Subject Guide to*

[1] For a detailed approach see any text on bibliography and William Katz, *Introduction to Reference Work* (3rd ed.; New York: McGraw-Hill, 1978), vol. 1, chaps. 2–3.

Books in Print (since 1957; annual). Also useful are such related titles as *Paperbound Books in Print* (since 1955; biannual) and *Children's Books in Print* (since 1969; annual).

5. When you want more information on what a publisher issues: *Publishers' Trade List Annual* (since 1873; annual), literally a collection of publisher catalogs.

All these publications give enough information to ascertain the title and the correct spelling of the author's name. Some include other valuable data: publisher's name, year of publication, price, and sometimes brief descriptive notes and other helpful facts such as the LC or the Dewey number.

Most of these bibliographies are used by the acquisitions departments of larger libraries to verify orders. In smaller libraries, where ordering and selection are done by the same people, bibliographies are more likely to be heavily used by the selector.

Those concerned with selection should also be familiar with the *National Union Catalog* (Washington, D.C.: Library of Congress, since 1955; monthly) and its many formats. The alphabetical-by-author book catalogs represent a running account of what has been published both in the United States and throughout the world. The catalog is used to check and verify, although primarily for retrospective rather than current searches.

For periodicals, the standard bibliographies are:

1. *Union List of Serials in Libraries of the United States and Canada* (3rd ed.; Bronx, N.Y.: The H. W. Wilson Company, 1965; 5 vols.).

2. *New Serial Titles* (Washington, D.C.: Library of Congress, since 1961; eight times a year). Also cumulated for 1950 to 1970 by Bowker in four volumes.

3. *Ulrich's International Periodical Directory* (17th ed.; New York: R. R. Bowker, 1977).

The first two are used to check what has been published, where, for how long, and similar information. For both the *Union List* and *New Serial Titles* you will need the name of the serial or periodical. *Ulrich's* lists periodicals by broad subject and offers a fine subject and name index. In practice, except for medium-large to large libraries, most periodicals are selected from current reviews or, more likely, from what is indexed in basic indexes and abstracting services, with bibliographies used primarily by the acquisitions and ordering departments to check dates, addresses, and so on. A companion to *Ulrich's, Irregular Serials and Annuals* (New York: R. R. Bowker, 1976), lists about 30,000 titles and is updated every two to three years.

These bibliographies, as noted, are of less importance in selection than in acquisition, but with reviews and retrospective selective book lists we are in country dominated by those who select and choose.

Book Reviews

How does the librarian learn about new books?

The principal source is the review, which normally discusses a book's subject, style, and quality and suggests whether it is suitable for a given type of audience or library.

There are other ways of learning about and evaluating new titles, but most librarians rely on reviews that appear in any of one to four or five sources.

The formal review of books goes back to the early seventeenth-century journals. The process has undergone many modifications through the years, and a review today may be defined as a summary description of the book, often (although not always) with a critical evaluation.

Criticism, both of a book and of its place in the literature of the subject area, tends to be limited to longer, scholarly reviews and appears less often in the shorter notes found in library-oriented and popular media. Some purists contend that without detailed criticism a review is not a review at all but only a summary of content, an annotation or abstract. Nevertheless, for our purposes *book review* includes all types of approach that announce publication and give the reader a general idea of content, usually with a comment about the degree of contribution of the book to its purpose—information, entertainment, esthetic enrichment, or something else.[2]

Mechanics of the Review

Most publishers automatically send each new title to one or more of a review periodical's editors. On occasion, the editor may request a specific title or use other channels to get a desired book. Obviously, the publisher is eager to have books reviewed and cooperates with the review media.

But review editors may receive thousands of books each year. How do they determine which books will be reviewed? There are some fairly objective, automatic tests: the audience served by the medium (*The New York Times*, for example, reviews titles that would not be considered by the *New York Review of Books*, which serves a different audience); language (most do not review foreign-language titles); whether or not a title is a reprint, paperback, and so on. Beyond these criteria, whoever selects books for review must rely on a subjective concept of the audience served by the publication: for instance, will our average reader find this review useful? This judgment is not easy, and more than one editor has been embarrassed to discover weeks or months later that a book rejected for review is gaining wide acceptance among readers served by the medium.

[2] Some reviews, particularly those directed to booksellers, estimate whether or not the book will sell well. (See, for example, some *Kirkus* and *Publishers Weekly* reviews.)

Actual methods of acceptance or rejection for review nevertheless remain a point of conjecture among publishers, authors, and librarians. Over the years one becomes fairly certain that a specific periodical is not likely to review the work of author X, while almost everything by Y and published by P will be included. "Unfair" is often a battle cry of critics; there have been—and will continue to be—countless articles on the biases of review editors.[3]

The rule for evaluating reviews is based upon the human fallibility of review editors: trust no single review medium—or, for that matter, even two or three. They may have overlooked the book your library needs.

HOW REVIEWS ARE USED

Use of reviews by libraries may be either formal or informal. The formal approach requires reading of one or more reviews, committee selection meetings in which they are discussed, and a subsequent decision to order the book or not. Informal approaches vary and may be no more than the ordering of a book by a subject expert or librarian on the basis of a single favorable review. This method is often used, even in combination with formal committee selection meetings. For example, in the large Montgomery County (Maryland) school system the procedure is that "all media, print and non-print materials (with the exception of 16mm films and textbooks) are automatically approved for purchase if they receive a favorable review in an approved professional journal or are recommended for purchase in a standard bibliography."[4]

The importance of the review in the selection process is underlined time and time again in studies of how books are selected by librarians. Among 71 public libraries polled in the 1970s, reviewing media were an overwhelming first choice (55), followed by publishers' brochures (18). Much the same was found in a similar survey of 345 academic libraries.[5]

Asked the most effective way of gaining the attention of librarians, publishers rated only one method "most effective"—reviews. "Nearly 90 percent of the responding publishers are . . . aware of the importance of favorable book reviews. . . . In some cases publishers send 500 or more copies of a title into the review stream."[6]

[3] Some magazines, particularly the library-oriented reviews, do make an effort to explain basis for inclusion or exclusion of certain types of titles, but this is always too general to be really useful. See, for example, the *Booklist* editorial policy statement on the contents page of each issue.

[4] John T. Gillespie, *A Model School District Media Program* (Chicago: American Library Association, 1977), p. 81. When the librarian is unable to locate a review, request for the item is sent to the centralized Evaluation and Selection Division to find a review. "If the evaluation is favorable, the school may order it."

[5] Elizabeth Futas, *Library Acquisition Policies and Procedures* (Phoenix, Ariz.: Oryx Press, 1977), pp. xxxi, xxiv.

[6] Sandra K. Paul and Carol A. Nemeyer, "Book Marketing and Selection," *Publishers Weekly*, June 16, 1975, p. 43.

EVALUATION OF REVIEWS

Evaluation of review sources is more game than science. Librarians have one or two—perhaps half a dozen—sources they regularly check for reviews. They grumble about their inadequacy but go on reading because they think, on balance, the reviews are really not that bad—and, besides, nothing else is much better.

Basic reviews, as will be seen, are limited and choice is dictated by the type of audience for whom books are being selected. For example, a children's librarian will not be reading the main selection tool of the research librarian. The urge to bring reviews into line with what librarians want is strong, but nothing much (including canceled subscriptions) ever achieves the ideal.[7]

The good book review is one that promptly gives the librarian an accurate, objective appraisal of the content of the book. In addition, in a review medium for librarians, the reviewer should indicate how the book will fit into the collection and, most important, how it compares with other titles in the same subject area (does it offer new or modified information, is the point of view of the author original, is the material current or dated, and so forth?).

Points to check in evaluating a review medium include:

1. Scope How many reviews are published each week, month, year? Are the materials and subjects reviewed relevant to the library's collection? An important part of scope is not only what is included, but also what is not. Are foreign materials overlooked? Are there reviews of allied print materials (maps, pamphlets) and nonprint materials? Some reviews cover more material than others, but there is no single source in which the majority of titles published each year can be found.

Only 10 to 15 percent of the 40,000 or so titles published each year in the United States are reviewed in the library services, and the percentage becomes considerably smaller if one asks how many of the 100,000-plus English-language titles from other countries are reviewed. A poll of publishers revealed that the majority feel that "currently fewer than 10 percent of all books published in the United States each year are reviewed, and some reviews appear as long as two years after a title is published."[8]

Study after study reveals the truth of this assumption; one survey found that "of 651 reference books published in the United States for one year,

[7] As long ago as 1958, and certainly in other studies 50 years or more before that, a survey of reviewing media found the majority of reviews said nothing, failed to give judgments, normally reviewed only a small part of the book, and in most cases were defective even in description of content. See Leroy C. Merritt, et al., *Reviews in Library Book Selection* (Detroit: Wayne State University Press, 1958).

[8] Sandra K. Paul and Carol A. Nemeyer, op. cit., p. 43.

approximately one-third were not reviewed."[9] Actually, the review of two-thirds of the books in any subject area is rare. Williams found that 50 percent of music books are not reviewed. Also, of the 262 titles investigated only 23 (about 10 percent) were reviewed in the general library press.[10]

The situation may nevertheless not be as drastic as it seems at first. The majority of good to excellent books are reviewed, if not always in the library press, sooner or (usually) later in a specialized source. One can also argue that the decision to eliminate certain titles for review is a major help in reducing the amount of "garbage" to be considered. The author may see it differently, as do publishers, and there is always the chance that a truly exceptional title will be overlooked.

2. Timeliness   Do the reviews appear weeks or months before the book is generally available to the public, or weeks or months after the book has been published? Do reviews appear even years after the book is out?

The gap between the time a book is published and the time it is reviewed varies drastically from one review medium to another. For example, *The Kirkus Reviews* actually publishes reviews that often resemble annotations more than reviews several months before the book is released, while scholarly journals may not issue a review for one, two, or even three years after publication. Popular reviewing sources, such as *Time, The New York Times Book Review, Saturday Review*, and the like, tend to publish reviews about the time the book is available in bookstores. Television and radio (interviews of authors or actual reviews) use about the same schedule.

The importance of timeliness to a librarian varies. In public libraries prompt notices are vital because the reviews serve to alert the librarian to books likely to be popular—and popular titles will be in immediate demand, sometimes long before they are available in the library.

3. Reviewers   Are the reviews signed? If not, is the reputation of the publication strong enough for you to accept unsigned reviews? If reviews are signed, do the reviewers have the qualifications to evaluate the subject matter of the book objectively and with intelligence? Does the reviewer write well, even display a good style?[11]

---

[9] Alma Covey, quoted in Nyal Williams, "Music Reference Materials: An Examination of the Reviews," *RQ*, Fall 1977, p. 34. (*American Reference Books Annual* [Littleton, Colo.: Libraries Unlimited] will eventually review critically at least the majority of American reference titles.)

[10] Ibid., p. 35. At the same time, 14 music periodicals did review 36 titles not covered by the library press.

[11] Much has been written about qualifications for reviewers. See, for example, Elaine Moss, "Pigs-in-the-Middle," *Signal* (May 1977, pp. 59–62), a discussion of children's book reviewers; Jack Forman, "Make Your Point: YA Selection Criteria . . . ," *School Library Journal* (September 1978, p. 51); and Eliot Fremont-Smith on adult reviewers on television in "Up the Placards, Down the Tube," *The Village Voice* (October 2, 1978, pp. 130–131). A cursory check of *Library Literature* will show a continuing barrage of articles on the subject.

There are three basic types of reviewer: (1) librarians and teachers writing for the library press, (2) popular reviewers writing for the popular press, and (3) scholars who pen reviews (which tend to be more essays than short reviews) for the thousands of professional and scholarly periodicals.

4. Recommendations   Are most of the reviews favorable, or is there a balance between "recommended" and "not recommended"? Is the reviewing medium more an alerting service than a review; that is, is almost everything listed recommended? A subject of much debate is the great percentage (65 to 80) of favorable reviews in most of the reviewing media. The urge to applaud everything can be explained objectively, and some journals (*Booklist* is an outstanding example) only list items of which they approve.

Many feel that several factors may be at work: (1) The reviewer is a friend of the author of the book being considered; (2) the reviewer feels a sympathetic link with anyone who has the courage to write; (3) the reviewer thinks he or she may one day be in a position to be evaluated and tends to empathize with the author; (4) the reviewer receives only moderately good or excellent titles from the editor and is inclined to favor the book. Then, too, there seems to be an unspoken understanding between reviewer and the review medium that unless you have something positive to say about the book, don't say it. A bad review is likely to cause restlessness.

Figures on favorable and unfavorable reviews vary from service to service. Favorable usually range from 65 to 80 percent. Unfavorable may be from 10 to 15 percent, while another 15 to 25 percent may be neutral: the review is simply descriptive with no indication of how the reviewer feels about the quality of the title. For example, in a study of three major sociological reviews from 1949 to 1971, of 2378 reviews 68 percent were favorable, 18 percent unfavorable, and 13.5 percent neutral.[12]

Many librarians long for recommendations that stare clearly whether or not the book is likely to offend anyone. This may or may not happen. Some library reviews go out of their way to point out themes or language likely to offend less-than-tolerant readers. Popular reviews, on the other hand, may actually recommend a book because of its forthright style or content. Judicious reviews are likely at least to tell the young-adult librarian whether or not the book has four-letter words scattered through the pages, but today few adult reviewers bother.[13]

5. Comparison   This aspect may be most important for many librarians: Does the reviewer compare the title to similar books in the same field, then

---

[12] Alma Covey, *Reviewing of Reference Books* (Metuchen, N.J.: Scarecrow Press, 1972).

[13] *VOYA* (Voice of Youth Advocates) does indicate so-called offensive language. "We wish there weren't librarians who curled up and died every time they encountered a dirty word, but we specialize in reality and know that there are more who do than don't" (*VOYA*, October 1978, p. 4). Others, such as *Booklist*, avoid the issue by not reviewing the books; still others review but fail to mention the language.

recommend for or against purchase? Does the reviewer consider earlier editions of the same title and compare scope?

6. Format Does the book have an index, a good binding, logical arrangement of materials, and so forth? Are there bibliographies? Is there too much extraneous material—from unnecessary appendices to pieces that have nothing to do with the book itself?

Does the reviewer clearly indicate the importance of illustrations in a particular text or a children's book? Is it stated how good or bad the reproductions are, particularly for art books?[14]

There are three basic types of media in which reviews appear: (1) the library press, (2) popular periodicals (including newspapers), and (3) subject journals.

Library-Oriented Reviews

Booklist. Chicago: American Library Association, since 1905. Biweekly. Circulation 39,000.

Choice. Chicago: American Library Association, since 1964. Monthly. Circulation 6000.

The Kirkus Reviews. New York: The Kirkus Reviews, since 1933. Biweekly. Circulation 5000. (Referred to hereafter as *Kirkus*.) In mid-1977 the service began issuing *Pointers*, a quarterly that contains short descriptions of five to ten books in 16 categories of fiction and nonfiction, guides for general readership.

Library Journal. New York: R. R. Bowker, since 1876. Biweekly. Circulation 32,000.

Publishers Weekly. New York: R. R. Bowker, since 1872. Circulation 32,000. Reviews and notes are found in each issue under "PW Forecasts."

School Library Journal. New York: R. R. Bowker, since 1954. Monthly. Circulation 39,000.

Choice of one or more of the library review media depends as much on personal preference as on objective tests of audience and scope. Traditionally, public libraries prefer *Library Journal*, *Publishers Weekly*, and *Kirkus*, although not necessarily in that order. *School Library Journal* is a favorite for any librarian selecting children's and young people's books, while *Booklist* is often the preference of small to medium-sized public and school libraries. *Choice* usually is a first for academic libraries, followed by *Library*

---

[14] Illustrations are of major importance for judging children's books (and, of course, for art titles or books dealing with graphic material). For a good discussion of the criteria for illustration in children's works see Andrea Emmerson, "The Significance of Book Illustrations for Reading Purposes" (*The School Librarian*, June 1978, pp. 112–117).

Journal.[15] Special libraries depend upon services such as *New Technical Books* (see page 132).

Kirkus and *Publishers Weekly* can be relied on by all types and sizes of libraries when there is any urgency about purchasing a popular book before it is available to the public. Unlike the other library services, both review well before the book is actually in the bookstores, and both indicate when the book will be available, often a month to three months after the review.

The actual number of books reviewed by each of the media varies considerably. In 1976 *Choice* reviewed 6402 adult titles, followed by *Library Journal* with 5819 and *Booklist* with 3014, although 1109 of these were juvenile and 277 young adult books. *Publishers Weekly* noted 3666 adult works and 518 juveniles, followed by *Kirkus* with 2825 adult and 1225 juvenile. *School Library Journal* considered 2117 juvenile books and 313 young-adult works.[16]

In comparison, *The New York Times Book Review* section, one of the most popular in the United States, reviewed 1012 adult titles, and *Time* or *Newsweek* will consider no more than 250 to 300 books a year.

Timeliness of reviews also varies. *Choice* publishes reviews from two to six months after the book has been published; *Library Journal*, one to two months after publication; *Booklist*, four to six weeks after publication; *Kirkus*, two to three months *before* publication; *Publishers Weekly*, one to two months *before* publication; *School Library Journal* reviews usually appear one to two months after publication.

Most of the reviews are written by professional librarians or people closely associated with the book's subject. *Choice* depends heavily upon university and college professors while *Library Journal* uses both teachers and librarians. *Booklist*, *Kirkus*, and *Publishers Weekly* rely upon staff members, most of whom have library, publishing, and subject specializations.

The majority of reviews are favorable; as already noted, *Booklist* includes *only* books it recommends, although the reviews are sometimes mildly critical. Most, at least, will point out weaknesses although they may recommend the title for purchase. Some effort is made to compare the new titles with others in the field, but the only consistently comparative reviews are those found in *Choice*.

All services sometimes or regularly include reviews of materials other than books, although *Booklist* is the most consistent, with regular features on audiovisual materials—films, filmstrips, video, slides, recordings. Books in foreign languages and government publications are often reviewed.

[15] Academic libraries, asked to rank major selection tools in one survey, replied as follows: "In all, 136 libraries picked *Choice*, with the majority (105) picking it first [followed by] *Library Journal* (96), *Publishers Weekly* (40), *Booklist* (39) . . ." (Elizabeth Futas, op. cit., p. xxiv). Among 66 public libraries polled, the most frequently mentioned reviews employed were *Library Journal*, *Publishers Weekly*, *Kirkus*, *Booklist*, *Choice* (ibid., p. xxxii). Other continuing surveys show variety in the order of preference, although the basic reviews inevitably appear on the list.

[16] *The Bowker Annual of Library and Book Trade Information* (22nd ed.; New York: R. R. Bowker, 1977), p. 328.

Added Adult Aids

ASLIB Book List. London: Aslib, since 1935. Monthly.

Bestsellers. Philadelphia: North American Publishing Co., since 1946. Monthly.

New Technical Books. New York: The New York Public Library, since 1915. Monthly.

Science Books and Films. Washington, D.C.: American Association for the Advancement of Science, since 1965. Quarterly.

The index to library periodicals, *Library Literature*, includes close to 180 different journals, many of which contain book reviews as well as reviews of other media. Most of these are library-oriented reviews and range from notices of reference books in *RQ* (Chicago: American Library Association, since 1960; quarterly) to reviews of library science titles only in *Journal of Academic Librarianship* (Boulder, Colo.: Mountainside Publishing, since 1975; bimonthly). Most librarians read several of these specialized journals (more for their own enlightenment than for book reviews), and in the process pick up certain titles missed in more conventional sources. Some examples:

1. *Bestsellers*, found in many public libraries, is primarily a guide for booksellers, but the reviews of existing and probable best-selling paperbacks provide useful information for librarians trying to stay one step ahead of public demand. Valuable, too, for insights into distribution and publishing as well as for notes on magazines.

2. The best single source for reviews of semipopular and likely-to-be-much-used technical books in science is *Science Books and Films*. Approximately 250 to 300 titles, both recommended and not recommended, are considered. Science films have been reviewed as well since 1975. Reviewers recommend only works likely to appeal to the public, not simply experts. Various age groups are considered, child through adult. This is only one of several selection services offered by the American Association for the Advancement of Science, which frequently publishes lists of recommended books. In a standard example—*AAAS Science Book List* (3rd ed., 1970, supplemented by a 457-page list in 1978)—arrangement is by subject with a reading level (from junior high to professional) given for each title.

3. When technical science books are needed, turn to *New Technical Books*, which contains descriptive annotations as well as critical comments. Arrangement is by subject, with emphasis on physical science, mathematics, engineering, and technology in general—except medical titles.[17]

---

[17] Specialized titles are not likely to be reviewed more than once, and only a few of these account for most of the actual reviews. Ching-Chih Chen, *Biomedical, Scientific and Technical Book Reviewing* (Metuchen, N.J.: Scarecrow Press, 1976), reports that in one year (1974) a check of 3347 reviews in various journals of 2067 biomedical books showed 35 percent reviewed more than once, with only 727 of the titles accounting for 2007 of the reviews.

4. The British equivalent of *New Technical Books* is the *ASLIB Book List*. Each monthly issue contains 50 to 75 reviews of scientific books from English or continental publishers, classified by subject and critically reviewed with a good indication of audience level.

5. *British Book News* (London: British Council, since 1940; monthly) is a basic selection aid for English public and academic libraries and can be useful in America; experts select and review 250 to 275 titles per month. Reviews (on the order of those found in *Choice* or *Library Journal*) are arranged by broad subject and tend to concentrate on titles published in England. Each issue opens with a lead article or two, often a bibliography, and there is a special unannotated list of forthcoming books, notes on titles suitable for young adults, paperbacks, and similar items.

Children and Young Adult

Appraisal: Children's Science Books. Cambridge, Mass.: Children's Science Book Review Committee, since 1967. Three times a year.

Bulletin of the Center for Children's Books. Chicago: University of Chicago, since 1947. Monthly.

Horn Book. Boston: Horn Book, since 1924. Bimonthly.

In Review: Canadian Books for Children. Toronto: Provincial Library Service, since 1967. Quarterly.

Interracial Books for Children. New York: Council on Interracial Books for Children, since 1970. Quarterly.

Reviewers' Consensus. San Leandro, Calif.: Willow Tree Press, since 1976. Quarterly.

School Library Journal. See page 130.

VOYA (Voice of Youth Advocates). New Brunswick, N.J.: Dorothy Broderick and Mary K. Chelton (10 Landing Lane), since 1978. Bimonthly.

In the area of professional library reviews of books for children and young adults, choices of what is best or better vary from librarian to librarian. Generally, however, most begin with *School Library Journal* and *Booklist*.[18] Others might prefer *Kirkus*, which has longer reviews and considers books two to three months before they appear in other sources.

In addition to the professional reviews, those in *The New York Times Book Review* are helpful. Some space is given to reviews of books likely to have a wide appeal, and from time to time there are special sections, as there are in *The Times Literary Supplement*. Some also favor *The Christian Science Monitor*, which carries quite splendid reviews—as do several other American newspapers. *Publishers Weekly* is not to be forgotten in this

---

[18] *Marketing, Selection and Acquisition of Materials for School Media Programs* (Chicago: RTSD Office, American Library Association, 1977) found that 98 percent of the librarians questioned used *School Library Journal* and 70 to 81 percent used *Booklist*.

connection. Children's books are an important section of the "PW Forecasts" —and the notices appear a month or so before the book is in the stores.

Arrangement differs in each publication. Standard practice is to have sections on picture books, nonfiction for children, fiction for children, then young-adult listings and sometimes (as in *School Library Journal* and *Booklist*) adult books suitable for young adults.

Librarians also turn for assistance to the following aids, usually in the order listed here:

1. *Horn Book* is considered one of the top three aids. It features 75 to 100 reviews of recommended books suitable for preschool through junior high, with the well-written reviews grouped by age interest. There are several articles in each issue on various aspects of children's books.

2. Another basic selection aid for school libraries (some put it ahead of both *School Library Journal* and *Horn Book*), the *Bulletin of the Center for Children's Books*, annotates 60 to 80 titles per issue. Material is for readers from the primary level through high school, although most emphasis is on the elementary grades. The reviews are some of the best available and are particularly useful because nonrecommended titles as well as recommended books are considered.

3. *In Review* features 70 to 90 critical reviews of Canadian children's books. Reviewers indicate clearly whether or not the book should be purchased. The writing is clearly and incisive, and each quarterly issue includes some articles. Many consider this equal to the top American selection aid.

4. *Interracial Books for Children* fulfills a needed function among children's librarians. The articles, bibliographies, and reviews concentrate on revelation of blatant discrimination in children's books—including texts. Books that measure up to the nonprofit supporting group's standards are given equal space and reviews. While this service has been available for several years, it is much needed. For example, in early 1978 it was found that:

The percentage of children's trade books depicting black characters has doubled in the last decade, but such books still constitute only about one out of every seven published, according to a study conducted at the Graduate School of Education of Harvard University.

Children's literature in this country still tends to portray an "all-white world," said Jeanne S. Chall, the professor of education who directed the survey. "Much still remains to be done with regard to both quality and quantity."

The study examined a representative sample of children's books published from 1973 to 1975 and copied a similar study done in 1965 by Nancy Larrick, a children's literature specialist, of similar books published from 1962 to 1964.[19]

5. Several specialized services review subject areas; one of the most useful is *Appraisal*. Here sometimes difficult-to-find reviews of 75 to 100 science books for children are considered (and rated for audience age and difficulty)

[19] Edward B. Fiske, "Children's Books . . . ," *The New York Times*, January 8, 1978, p. 41.

by experts from Harvard and New England libraries. Equally useful, although only part is devoted to children, is *Science Books and Films* (see page 132).

6. Most of the reviews so far noted concentrate almost exclusively on children. Young adults are duly considered in *School Library Journal* and *Booklist*, but there few periodicals are solely concerned with teenagers. One of these, and among the best for those who have a pluralistic or liberal view of service, is *VOYA* (see page 133). Edited by two outstanding librarians, the magazine stresses articles and reviews of books and nonprint media likely to interest young people, not just librarians. The writers take an intelligent, nonpatronizing attitude about youth, and the result is a first-rate service which should be at the desk of anyone ordering for this age group.

7. *Reviewers' Consensus* is an index to reviews and is used much as *Book Review Digest* is employed by those selecting titles for adults. The quarterly issues list only titles that have been reviewed three or more times. The search for reviews is limited to some 15 basic sources such as *Appraisal*, *Kirkus*, and *School Library Journal*. Short (usually no more than 15- to 20-word) content notes are given "only when it is essential for a knowledge of the contents of the book."

Arrangement is by subject and by age interest, with full bibliographical information given for each title. There are also title and author indexes and other features that make for extremely easy use.

This service offers ratings of new titles based on the reviews: 1 is highly recommended, 3 is satisfactory, and 5 is rejected. Given this feature, a children's librarian may double-check personal reactions to a title, quickly eliminate from further consideration consistently low-rated titles, or simply order directly the high-rated titles as needed. The editor nevertheless correctly urges librarians to read many reviews and to use this service as an auxiliary, not a final method of choice.

See *Children's Literature Review* and *Children's Book Review Index* (pages 145 and 146) for additional help in locating reviews.

Top of the News (Chicago: American Library Association, since 1942; quarterly) concentrates more on articles about children and young-adult service than the others but does include a limited number of reviews and some useful media bibliographies. It is not primarily a reviewing source, nor is the related *School Media Quarterly* (Chicago: American Library Association, since 1951; quarterly), which is concerned with activities of school librarians, although it too includes some book reviews and occasional media bibliographies.

Popular Reviews

New York Review of Books. New York: New York Review, since 1963. Biweekly. Circulation 94,000.
The New York Times Book Review. New York: The New York Times

Company, since 1896. Weekly. Circulation 1 million. *The Times* also prints daily book reviews, which are collected once a month in *Books of the Times*, a separate service available from the publisher.

The New Yorker. New York: New Yorker Magazine, Inc., since 1925. Weekly. Circulation, 493,000.

Newsweek. New York: Newsweek, Inc., since 1933. Weekly. Circulation 3 million.

Saturday Review. New York: Saturday Review, since 1924. Biweekly. Circulation 512,000.

Time. New York: Time Inc., since 1923. Weekly. Circulation 4 million.

The Times Literary Supplement. London: Times Newspapers of Great Britain, since 1920. Weekly.

Popular reviews are separated here from library-oriented reviews and special reviews for clarity, but all are used, most of the time, by librarians. Public librarians and those working with young adults, in particular, have to know what the popular reviewers are considering. After a notice appears in *Time* or *Newsweek*, someone will inevitably be in the library requesting the book. Much the same will happen, although at a later date, when a review appears in a specialized journal. One important task of the selector is to keep ahead of public requests, and this can be done only by careful consideration of all reviews.

The librarian who attempts a comprehensive overview of a subject must rely on several sources, not simply on a single group. For example, in his examination of music-book reviews Nyal Williams discovered that it was not enough simply to examine specialized review sources: "None of the journals cover the field extensively enough to be used as the sole selection tool."[20]

There are many sources of popular reviews, and those listed here are representative of some of the better-known. One should also consider reviews in *Nation, National Review, Atlantic,* and *Harper's Monthly.* Examination of popular reviews shows several common features:

1. Book reviews are only a minor feature, usually tucked in the magazine between more general topics or at the end, in *Newsweek, The New Yorker,* and *Time*—and even in *Saturday Review,* which at one time was devoted almost exclusively to reviews. Only *The New York Times Book Review, The Times Literary Supplement,* and the *New York Review of Books* are entirely devoted to reviews.

2. The reading audience is assumed to be better educated than average, usually profiled as college graduates with relatively high incomes. The degree of sophistication of the supposed reader is reflected in the reviews and notes, as well as the positions of the reviewers. In order of degree of difficulty, supposed involvement in intellectual and cultural matters, and

[20] Op. cit., p. 38.

length of reviews, the publications listed here could be ranked: *The Times Literary Supplement*, the *New York Review of Books*, *The New Yorker*, *The New York Times*, *Saturday Review*, *Newsweek*, and *Time*.

3. None of the popular media attempts to be comprehensive, and concentration is on "newsworthiness" or major titles likely to interest their audiences. For example, *The New York Times* averages reviews and notes on about 1100 books a year, compared to some 350 for the *New York Review*, even fewer for *Time*, *The New Yorker*, and *Newsweek*.

4. The reviews usually appear about publication date or the time the book is available in the bookstore, although the *New York Review* sometimes may not publish a review for six months to a year after the title is out.

5. The majority of reviews are favorable, particularly as only a small number of titles are considered and, except for a maligned best seller or subject specialist's much-discussed book, the editors simply eliminate "bad" books for review.

THE BOOK REVIEWER

Unlike at least some of the library-oriented reviews, most of those in popular periodicals are signed, and the reviewer is often a familiar figure to the general reader or the person who knows a given subject field. (Signed reviews in such mass-circulation publications as *Time* and *Newsweek* are usually written by staff members who specialize in reviewing books; daily reviews in *The New York Times* carry the byline of one of several staff reviewers or of *Times* reporters who regularly report particular subject areas.) The reviewers tend to be professional writers and are given more space for their notices than in the library-oriented reviews. Also, most of them are paid, if not well, at least better than those who write for the library press.[21] A favorite game is to argue which of the popular review media is the best, the worse, the most political, the least political, the most biased, the least biased, and so on. Winners and losers seem to change from season to season. No one reader is ever convinced a popular or even semipopular review medium (such as the *New York Review of Books*) is always good. Reviewers have their weaknesses and strengths, and few will be successful all or even part of the time in the eye of the critical reader.

Some reviewers do little more than revise the book-jacket copy, and certainly do not seem to have opened the book. Reviewers in local newspapers and regional magazines often use this approach, as do some in larger-circulation magazines, and many local newspapers print widely

---

[21] Except for paid staff members, library-directed reviews do not pay reviewers directly, although the reviewer is allowed to keep the book reviewed. Sometimes payment is given for special features, articles, and the like. Subject-oriented, small-circulation specialized journals follow the same procedure.

syndicated reviews. One cynic believes that about 70 percent of the shorter popular reviews are lifted from book-jacket copy.[22]

CRITICISM

One of the most frequent criticisms of popular reviews is that they are little more than "the marketing arm of the publishing industry."[23] Check the advertisements and then the reviews. Inevitably, so the argument goes, the heavy advertisers are better represented in the reviews. The debate highlights a truth: most of the titles considered are popular or semipopular, likely to be commercial successes if not always best sellers. Exceptions are *The Times Literary Supplement* and the *New York Review of Books*, although even here concentration is on better-known publishers and writers.

One result of the persistent criticism is that new popular and semipopular review media appear each year, and a surprising number survive: there are 100 or more others in the field. Many of these serve regions, such as *Books West Magazine*; others are directed to specialized better-educated audiences, while some may be involved with lesser reviewed books, as is *Book News*.

Aids for Subject Specialists

Library-oriented and popular reviews are adequate for the needs of most libraries. Large research libraries, special libraries, and an occasional unusual situation nevetheless require subject selection aids. For example, a survey of subject specialists and their selection needs found:

Title by title selection in a large research library involved the checking of about thirty selection aids by specialists in subject fields where most of the orders consisted of language monographs. . . . Book reviews in professional or book review journals did not appear to be the most productive selection sources of the subject specialists.[24]

The larger and the more specialized the library, the more likely the need for reviews that reflect the specific interests of subject divisions. The number of specialized reviews may run anywhere from half a dozen to literally

---

[22] Elliot F. Smith, "The Mystery of Flaps or How Critics Wing It," *The Village Voice,* February 28, 1977, p. 45. Smith tells how, as a former jacket-blurb writer, he helped compile "about 300 descriptive words" which often are found in reviews. Smith's column is worth reading, if only to compare these much-used words against a few of the descriptions you may recently have read in your favorite review medium.

[23] *The Cultural Watchdog Newsletter*, December 1977, p. 4.

[24] Geza A. Kosa, "Book Selection Tools for Subject Specialists in a Large Research Library: An Analysis," *Library Resources and Technical Services*, Winter 1975, p. 18. The two most "useful types of sources for selection were bibliographies, including LC proof slips and publishers' advertisements."

thousands, when titles in academic, scientific, technical, business, and other journals are considered.

Anyone oppressed by the number and variety of possible sources of specialized reviews can take comfort in the fact that, for better or worse, only a few sources are actually used. Out of the scores or thousands of periodicals in a subject area, only a handful (usually from six to twelve) are employed regularly. A study of scientific reviews found that "Nine general science reviewing journals provided reviews of more than 50 percent of the total output of new science books."[25]

Sources of information differ, but subject experts generally rely upon:

1. Word of mouth, particularly from experts they are serving.

2. Advance news of books as found in *The Weekly Record* and its cumulation, *American Book Publishing Record*; publisher catalogs and announcements; and other national and trade bibliographies such as the *British National Bibliography*.

Both 1 and 2 are preferable to specialists because they solve the most pressing problem: timeliness. "The usual criticism of book reviews was that there was a longer time lag between the appearance of a book and its review than the specialist could tolerate."[26]

3. Where speed is not a major consideration, the third major source is the review that appears in professional journals of the field.

By definition a subject specialist will know the major journals, certainly which ones carry reviews. A librarian will learn, for example, that library history reviews are in the *Journal of Library History*, and that the *Medical Library Association Bulletin* is an obvious place for medical-library book reviews, just as *RQ* is a selection aid for reference books. In addition to knowledge and memory, there are a few simple ways to learn about periodicals that cover certain subject areas:

1. *Magazines for Libraries* (3rd ed.; New York: R. R. Bowker, 1978) lists some 6000 titles under broad subject headings, annotates the titles, and as part of the bibliographical information indicates which periodicals carry reviews, how many, and of what length. A cursory check of this feature, as well as the list of recommended basic titles at the head of each section, gives an excellent overview of the major reviewing journals in a subject field.

2. Similar information can be found, often in more detail, in a number of such specialized lists as *Periodicals in Education, Education/Psychology Journals*, and *Author's Guide to Journals in Psychology, Psychiatry and Social Work*. These lists are found in Sheehey's *Guide to Reference Books* (Chicago: American Library Association, 1976) and in the *American Reference Books Annual* (Littleton, Colo.: Libraries Unlimited). Most are

[25] Ching-Chih Chen, op. cit., p. 123. This is an astonishing figure when one considers that estimates are that there are from 50,000 to 100,000 scientific journals. See also Nyal Williams, op. cit., pp. 33ff. Williams found about 50 percent of the books examined were reviewed in a few sources.

[26] Kosa, op. cit., p. 18.

also reviewed in the library-oriented review sources as they appear. Also major bibliographies of a subject field such as Carl White's *Sources of Information in the Social Sciences* (2nd ed.; Chicago: American Library Association, 1973) give the major subject review sources.

3. A check of the most-cited journals listed in *Science Citation Index* and *Social Sciences Citation Index* annual often indicates the journals with the major reviews.

4. Robert Broadus, *Selecting Materials for Libraries* (Bronx, N.Y.: H. W Wilson Company, 1973), devotes about half to "selection by subject field" and offers the basic guides and selection aids for all major areas.

SCHOLARLY BOOK REVIEWERS

Unlike writers for the library-oriented review media or the popular magazines, those who write for specialized journals have several advantages They are not pushed for time; most subject reviews appear six months to two years after a book is published. Most, although not all, are given almost limitless space for reviews. And the scholarly or specialized book reviewer is writing for peers who are presumed to know the subject well and will not be offended by technical, sometimes less-than-lucid language.

"Logrolling" or "you rub my back and I'll rub yours" is often the major criticism of scholarly reviews, summarized in a scathing look at such reviewers by another scholar:

The safest strategy calls, of course, for the generous dispensation of undeserved praise in your reviews of colleagues' books. Generally, your colleagues will reciprocate. It is difficult not to think highly of somebody who thinks highly of you. . . . Nasty reviews are, of course, much more amusing to write and to read than complimentary ones, and they have the added merit of greater validity. However, the fear of retaliation restrains all but the most brilliant and senior academics. . . . But generally, alas, book reviews are nearly as dull as other genres of academic writing. The victim of unfair reviews (and most truly witty reviews are unfair) should find solace in the fact that book sales seem unaffected by the quality of reviews. Bad reviews are better than no reviews at all. In the words of Chairman Mao, "the absence of attacks from the enemy is a bad thing." In the long run, everybody wins except the impecunious student who has to buy the blasted book.[27]

This points up an important consideration of specialized reviews: just because they are specialized, long, and in impressive journals is no indication they are any better than those found in other types of publication. The journal itself must be constantly examined. Has the editorial policy changed? Who selects the reviewers, and what qualifications are required? How current are the reviews; if not current, is there an excuse for the tardy appearance? How many reviews are published—more or less than in preceding years?

[27] Arthur P. Young, "Scholarly Book Reviewing in America," *Libri*, no. 3 (1975), p. 179.

Finally, the busy librarian has to consider the amount of duplication of reviews between one journal and the next, which reviews appear first, and which of the early notices are better written, and so on.

REFERENCE BOOKS

In the author's *Introduction to Reference Works* (3rd ed.; New York: McGraw-Hill, 1978, vol. 1, pp. 36–45) there is a wider discussion of the current and retrospective selection aids for reference books. For purposes here it is sufficient to note that the majority of standard review services, from *Choice* and *Library Journal* to *Booklist*, include reviews of reference works, normally under that subject. The standard retrospective source is Eugene P. Sheehy's *Guide to Reference Books* (9th ed.; Chicago: American Library Association, 1976), and an annual annotated listing of American reference books is found in the splendid *American Reference Books Annual* (Littleton, Colo.: Libraries Unlimited, since 1970).

Some of the best current reviews are to be found in the *Wilson Library Bulletin*, which grades reference titles suitable for most libraries. The *Reference Services Review* is a quarterly that, after a lag in both quality and style, can be recommended as source of subject reviews of reference books as well as an index to reviews of reference books elsewhere.

GOVERNMENT DOCUMENTS

Space here does not allow a discussion of government documents, but they are vitally important for the smallest as well as the largest of libraries. The author's *Introduction to Reference Works* includes a discussion of selection aids (Chapter 10). As with reference books, many review journals include special sections on government documents, among them *RQ*, *Reference Services Review*, *Serials Librarian*, *Booklist*, *Library Journal*, and *Choice*. The *Government Publications Review* (New York: Pergamon, since 1973; quarterly) is devoted exclusively to the subject and includes a "What's New in Documents" section.

Libraries Unlimited frequently revises several standard works, the most important being Joe Morehead's basic *Introduction to United States Public Documents*. Other titles include *Subject Guide to Government Reference Books* and *Government Reference Books*.

For most small to medium-sized libraries the single most useful selection guide is the free *Selected U.S. Government Publications* (available from the U.S. Superintendent of Documents, Washington, D.C.). This monthly has undergone many changes through the years, but it lists and annotates government documents likely to be of the broadest interest to users.

Government documents have no competition, so one must either accept or reject the subject matter and hope that the presentation will be suitable for the audience.

Paperbacks

Paperbacks are so much a part of the American book scene that mos libraries now purchase them routinely. Of the 42,780 titles published i America in 1977, 12,569 were paperbacks. The genre is usually divide into: (1) mass-market paperbacks, which consist of the typical mysterie westerns, science fiction, and general fiction found in drugstores, super markets, and airports, and (2) trade or scholarly or "quality," which includ reprints of everything from university press books to literature and religio and are sold most often in bookstores.

A common misconception is that most paperbacks are reprints of popula titles. Actually, of the 12,569 titles issued in 1977, only 3288 were reprint The fallacy arises because the general public is primarily concerned wit mass paperback titles which often (although not always) are reissues o once-popular hardback books. Libraries may have no choice as to format some titles are available only in paperback.

The average library is likely to treat the paperback as a hardback, an often makes arrangements through the publisher or jobber to have th paperback rebound. Many trade paperbacks are offered in both hardbac and paperback, or in reinforced covers. Several large jobbers and binder have special arrangements to supply reinforced paperbacks for librarie Conversely, in other school and public libraries (as well in popular readin rooms of academic libraries), the paperback may be treated as an expendabl item that is not cataloged. A rack is put out for paperbacks, from whicl they are circulated until they fall apart and then are discarded. This i particularly true when the library is dealing with donated paperbacks an with mass-market titles that augment the fiction collection.

At this late date it seems pointless to list the advantages of paperbacks i libraries, particularly as much of the early hostility to the form has passed Still, those who are seeking persuasive arguments for their use, particularl with children and young people, can turn to John T. Gillespie's *Paperbacl Books for Young People* (2nd ed.; Chicago: American Library Association 1977), which lists and describes distributors, publishers, and guides. Gillespie' *The Young Phenomenon: Paperbacks in Our Schools* (Chicago: Americar Library Association, 1972) is a detailed discussion of the paperback and it use in libraries. See also Nancy Larrick's "The Paperback Opportunity" (*School Library Journal*, April 1975) and Suzanne M. Coil's "Paperback and Progress against Illiteracy" in the same journal (April 1978). A cursor check of *Library Literature* will indicate the impressive number of article written about paperbacks for all types of libraries and age groups.

EVALUATION

Paperbacks are evaluated as other books are, at least in terms of content. Beyond that are other considerations:

1. The binding may be a "perfect" binding, an ironic name. This binding technique is far from perfect and too often the covers separate from the body of the book or the individual signatures simply fall out when the glue cracks and parts. This same "perfect-bound" process is used for many hardbound books as well, often with the same results. (See "Perfect Books Prove Less than Perfect" in *American Libraries*, March 1979, p. 109.)

2. The size of the type and the margins. The type may often be characterized as advertisement size without extra space between lines and impossible to read as there is little or no margin, which often disappears into the center. The result is a disaster for almost anyone over twenty-one with less than perfect vision.

3. The paper may be little more than newsprint—which is not bad in itself, when the library plans to keep the book for only a few months. If the book is going into the collection as a permanent addition, check the paper first.

4. The cover may be too lurid for some readers: *Little Women* in one edition several years back featured two or three less-than-little, less-than-fully clothed women on the cover. It is not by accident that some publishers prepare two paperback covers—one for libraries and cautious readers, another for newsstands.

When a paperback costs more than the standard $1.95 to $2.95 for the mass-market variety, examine the book first if possible. This can be done for many titles at a bookstore, particularly when the library does not have access to books from a jobber. The more reputable trade or quality publishers of paperbacks, quite aware of the aforementioned problems, now design books of a quality much better than that associated with the typical mass-market type.

Asked how to evaluate a collection of paperbacks as to quality, Mary K. Chelton of Rutgers gave this commonsense reply:

I would suggest separating the paperback originals from reprints because all the reprints can then be checked against standard tools.

Secondly, I would suggest calling in a local science fiction expert. I've seen too many libraries ignorant of the genre blithely destroy or sell off classics.

The originals may have to be handled either as ephemera or as titles to be reviewed by staff since they are so poorly covered in our review media. If Palliser has been smart enough to subscribe to the *Kliatt Paperback Book Guide* these last 12 years, some evaluation may be possible through that source.

If the collections are mainly media tie-in potboilers, Harlequin romances, and Barbara Cartland, I suggest creating a display area called "Popular Culture on Demand" and letting the public evaluate them by reading some more than others.[28]

[28] "Action Exchange," *American Libraries*, February 1979, p. 68.

Paperback Selection Aids

B-J Paperback Book Guide. Cedar Falls, Iowa: Barbara Blow and Maragaret Juhl, since 1975. Quarterly.
Growing up with Paperbacks, 6th ed. New York: R. R. Bowker, 1977.
Kliatt Paperback Book Guide. Newton, Mass.: Doris Hiatt and Claire Rosser, since 1967. Quarterly.
Wynar, Bohdan. *Reference Books in Paperback*, 2d ed. Littleton, Colo.: Libraries Unlimited, 1976.

No one service covers the majority of paperbacks published each year, but almost all of the regular popular and library-oriented book review sources include sections on them. For example, in each issue of *The New York Times Book Review* there is a listing of best-selling paperbacks, and chitchat about the publishing of such titles, and *Publishers Weekly* "Forecasts" includes the genre. Special issues are devoted almost exclusively to new paperbacks. This is much the pattern in other reviews as well, from *Booklist* (with its regular feature on paperbacks) to *Library Journal* and *Choice*. *School Library Journal* usually devotes one issue a year to paperbacks. The basic bibliography in the field is *Paperbound Books in Print* (New York: R. R. Bowker, since 1955; biannual). More than 150,000 titles are listed by author, title, and subject.

Both the *Kliatt* and the *B-J* services are directed to younger people. *Kliatt's* 45- to 55-page periodical contains 100- to 200-word summaries of titles recommended for young adults, ages twelve to nineteen. Only recommended works are listed, although the descriptive summaries indicate certain reservations about some books. The editors key potentially controversial paperbacks with an M, which warns the text contains explicit sex, excessive violence, or the like. The *B-J* service covers much the same territory for much the same age group, differing in that it tends to concentrate on other titles and often includes books for younger readers. Most school and public libraries subscribe to both services.

Many retrospective lists of selected books do include paperbacks, but Wynar's compilation is one of the few lists devoted solely to paperbacks in a subject area. Now in its second edition (with a third promised), there are about 1500 titles mentioned or annotated under 37 broad subject headings. Author, title, and subject index give it an added value. Many paperbacks are somewhat more than reference books and may be used in the general reading collection. Another work in a subject field is Georgette Dorn's *Latin America, Spain and Portugal: An Annotated Bibliography of Paperback Books* (2nd ed.; Washington, D.C.: Library of Congress, 1976). Listed are some 2300 titles suitable for high school, academic, and public libraries.

Growing up with Paperbacks is representative of numerous lists. It is only 32 pages long, consists of about 200 titles for children and young people, and covers a wide variety of books, from current best sellers to classics. There is a brief annotation for each item. Numerous other lists of this type are listed and annotated in *Paperback Books for Young People* (see page 142).

There are many other considerations in paperback selection, though it can be said that almost all libraries will benefit from the purchase of paperbacks. Precisely how they are employed, how many are purchased, and so on depends upon the imagination of the librarian and the needs of the public being served.

Indexes to Reviews

1. General

Book Review Digest. Bronx, N.Y.: The H. W. Wilson, Company, since 1905. Monthly.

Book Review Index. Detroit: Gale Research Company, since 1965. Bimonthly.

Current Book Review Citations. Bronx, N.Y.: The H. W. Wilson Company, since 1976. Monthly.

2. Subject and specialized

Children's Literature Review. Detroit: Gale Research Company, since 1975. Biannual.

Index to Book Reviews in the Humanities. Williamstown, Mass.: Phillip Thomson, since 1960. Annual.

Reviewers' Consensus. See page 135.

Technical Book Review Index. Pittsburgh: JAAD Publishing Co., since 1935.

The librarian is looking for a review of a book published and reviewed last month or five or even more years ago must consult several indexes to find it. This information may be needed to double-check the proposed purchase of a less-well-known or controversial title or to remind the librarian what was said about an older book being considered for reordering. (It is quicker to check a basic recommended list, but if this fails the book review indexes are a tremendous help.) Use of such indexes by the reference section, checking to find material for a user, is constant.

Today the librarian has a choice of three general review indexes and several subject indexes. The most popular and widely used is *Book Review Digest*, favored because it is the only one of the three to offer a subject approach to reviewed titles. The subject index serves both the generalist and the subject expert, who may routinely check each issue under subjects for titles possibly missed in the regular purchasing routine. It is also the only one of the three that offers descriptive and critical excerpts from reviews.

Many librarians go through each monthly issue to look for books that may be of value to the collection. In this sense the *Book Review Digest* is a major buying selection device in many libraries.

The shortcoming in the *Digest* is that it indexes reviews in only 75 periodicals and requires at least two reviews of nonfiction and four of fiction before a book is listed. The result is that a new author will not be included until the review media recognize him or her in quantity. Conversely, the conservative approach to listings does insure that most of the titles are of general interest.

Lacking both excerpts from reviews and a subject approach, *Book Review Index* and *Current Review Citations* are useful because: (1) They list any book that has received even one review, no matter how short or critical; (2) they cover hundreds more magazines than *Book Review Digest—Book Review Index* analyzes about 300 periodicals and *Current Book Review Citations* checks more than 1200 for reviews; (3) they, particularly *Book Review Index*, tend to be more current.

Small to medium-sized libraries will find *Book Review Digest* enough, but as the library becomes larger or as the demand for book reviews increases, it is necessary to take both of the other services. (There is duplication, but not so much that both are not useful.)

With these three general services, only a few libraries need turn to more subject-specialized indexes. The exception may be *Technical Book Review Index*, which is taken by even medium-sized libraries. This is a type of *Book Review Digest* for technical and scientific works. Review excerpts are included and many libraries use it as a buying guide in a difficult field. Also, it nicely complements the standard review medium in this area, *New Technical Books*.

Children's librarians prefer *Children's Literature Review* for the same reason, since it also includes excerpts from reviews, although the reviews may be not only of current titles but also of books published several years ago. For current citations to reviews, without the review excerpts, the same publisher offers the annual *Children's Book Review Index* (Detroit: Gale Research Company, since 1975). The best of the lot, though, is *Reviewers' Consensus*, discussed on page 135.

Index to Book Reviews in the Humanities selectively indexes titles by author. It is useful in special situations as it sometimes manages to find reviews of books on architecture, drama, literature, music, and the like overlooked by the other services.

There are several similar titles. See, for example, *Index to Book Reviews in Historical Periodicals* (Metuchen, N.J.: Scarecrow Press, since 1975; annual). *Reference Services Review* (Ann Arbor, Mich.: Pierian Press, since 1973; quarterly) regularly indexes reviews of reference books, and since 1973 the citations have been cumulated in a three-year index by the same publisher as *Reference Book Review Index*.

A number of periodical and newspaper indexes include special sections on book reviews. One of the most useful, because it is usually more current than the others, is *Readers' Guide to Periodical Literature*. A separate section in each biweekly issue lists reviews that have appeared in the magazines indexed by the *Guide*. (Most of the other basic Wilson indexes, from *Business Periodicals Index* to *Social Sciences Index*, include the same indexing feature.)

Beyond Reviews: Information on New Titles

Neither librarians nor the public relies entirely upon published reviews for news about new books and other printed materials. Many learn about a new title from a publisher's advertisement, a television show, or from a friend. Among the standard nonprint sources for information on new titles are those discussed below.

PUBLISHER BROCHURES AND ADVERTISEMENTS

While reviews are the most popular way of selecting books, second choice for most librarians is the publishers' catalogs, brochures and advertisements.[29] This noncritical selection method is tempered by the fact that experienced librarians do know authors and publishers and rarely err by selection based upon either or both—with, of course, the subject matter given first consideration.

Still, this remains an issue of debate, one that can elicit such opposite remarks as these, both from public librarians:

Catalogs and publishers' notices are also used routinely. It must be stressed that catalogs are used for publishing information only. Any critical claims in the catalogs are treated as sales promotion, not as evaluative opinion.[30]

Perhaps we are wrong . . . [but] we make extensive use of [catalogs and publishers' notices]. We realize, of course, that these are promotional materials, but in many instances they summarize contents very succinctly, and through this summary we get a pretty good idea of whether or not we wish to pursue our interest in the book. Generally, catalogs and publishers' notices are our first glimpse at books to come. Later, a variety of reviews from a number of sources either confirm our feelings or prompt us to reevaluate them.[31]

"Our first glimpse at books to come" is probably the most-often-heard reason for relying on catalogs and advertisements. When speed of selection

[29] Futas (op. cit., p. xxxi) found that of 71 public libraries questioned about selection aids, publishers' brochures ranked second, followed by advertisements (9 gave the ads a third place). Academic libraries follow the same pattern. Interestingly enough, while brochures and advertisements are of primary importance in selection, "no library readily admits this in their written policy statement" (p. xxiv).

[30] Dem Polacheck, "A Method of Adult Book Selection for a Public Library System," *RQ*, Spring 1977, p. 232.

[31] Ronald Norman, "A Method of Book Selection for a Small Public Library," *RQ*, Winter 1977, p. 144.

is essential, this method is a vast improvement over reviews that may not appear until long after the book is published.

No matter what the point of view of the librarian about the use of publisher brochures and catalogs, almost all librarians rely upon them, if only for information about new titles. It is no surprise that, as already noted, "85 percent of the publishers . . . believe that direct mail [brochures, advertisements, catalogs, etc.] is an effective promotional device for reaching libraries."[32]

An extension of the advertisement is the sales representative. Almost all large American publishers, and not a few smaller ones, field a sales force that calls on libraries.[33]

Sales people and advertisements are useful guides to what is likely to be popular and in demand, and a tipoff of just how much a publisher is likely to invest in promoting a book helps the library to decide the probable demand factor. This can be learned from the sales representative, by watching the size and number of advertisements, and from *Publishers Weekly*, which regularly reports on advertising activities, book-club selection policies, and the like. (This is particularly true of the special announcement issues where such information is given after short descriptive annotations of "the major books of the season selected from publishers' lists.") Other good sources of news about books likely to be promoted are *Kirkus*, which regulary picks, with alarming accuracy, the best sellers; and the "PW Forecasts," which has equal success in choosing more popular titles.

Somewhat in the same category as publishers' brochures are publications of major American book jobbers. For example, Baker & Taylor publish *Directions*, which lists uncritically and briefly annotates titles of value to academic libraries and, naturally, available from Baker & Taylor.

Used wisely, publishers' catalogs and advertisements can be useful in the selection process. Where possible the blurbs should be supported by reviews and examination of the titles by the librarian. However, in a real world of lack of time and pressures for early purchase (particularly of popular titles or works in a subject area with limited materials) it is difficult to question the wisdom of reliance on the publisher. Always, however, with the warning that the librarian examine the book when it comes into the library. If then the decision has proved wrong, the title should be returned.

BOOK EXHIBITS

Book exhibits, extremely useful sources of information about new titles, are of two basic types: the national exhibit found at conventions and meet-

---

[32] Sandra Paul and Carol Nemeyer, op. cit.

[33] Oddly enough, "Only 28 percent of the publishers queried believe that direct sales visits are effective, and librarians regard this method to be among the least successful employed by publishers" (ibid).

ings of librarians and teachers,[34] and the local exhibit, such as collections of certain types of children's books sent by the school district media center to librarians and schools throughout the district.

THE BROADCAST MEDIA

At one time it was thought that television would kill an interest in reading. Actually, nothing promotes a book more than being mentioned (or "plugged" blatantly) on television, radio, or by word of mouth. Librarians can count on demand for a title when a film is made from the book. The same obtains when a book is adapted for a television or even a radio show.

The obvious way of staying ahead of such requests is to be alert to the media, but another, even more satisfactory solution is offered by *Get Ready* (Utica, N.Y. [1600 Lincoln Ave.]: Mid-York Library System, since 1977; weekly). This 4- to 6-page library-published newsletter gives a two- to three-week lead on what books are going to be on television, tied in to a film, or even when they are going to be reviewed in a popular magazine. There are also useful bibliographies on current topics of interest.

Other suggestions of possible electronic activities connected with books: (1) The "Media" section of *Publishers Weekly* and also, of course, in general news items in that same publication. (2) *Media & Methods* (page 241) often has special sections on television or radio tie-ins to books and other print materials. (3) *American Bookseller* (New York: Booksellers Publishing, since 1977; monthly), which is similar to *Publishers Weekly*, reports on tie-ins under "The Screen and the Tube."

LIBRARY OF CONGRESS PROOFSHEETS

This is a list of books represented by catalog cards in the Library of Congress. Many of the books, although not all, are new and frequently the information is ahead of what the library will find in reviews. For this reason the slips are sometimes used as advance warning of new titles.[35] More often they are a back-up device for double-checking subject-area titles that may have been missed.

The service is available in 18 subject classes and may be purchased in a flat form or in a cut form the same size as the LC catalog card. The copy is "an exact replica of the cataloging data contained on the card—indeed, it is a photo-offset reproduction of the printed catalog card."[36] Larger libraries

[34] Edward Malinowski, "The Combined Book Exhibit: An Institution, and How to Use It," *American Libraries*, June 1978, pp. 354–355. An explanation of the exhibit featured at most American Library Association conventions.

[35] Futas (op. cit, pp. xxxi, xxiv) notes that of 71 public libraries only three listed LC proof slips as part of the selection process; among 164 academic libraries only 11 mentioned them.

[36] Mary Ganning, "Library of Congress Cataloging Distribution Services, 1901–1976," *Library Resources & Technical Services*, Fall 1977, p. 321. A clear explanation.

may subscribe to one or several of the subject series which, as they are received, are checked against orders and holdings by the subject bibliographer.

Select Retrospective Lists of Books

Books for College Libraries, 2nd ed. Chicago: American Library Association, 1975.

The H. W. Wilson series:

Public Library Catalog, 6th ed. 1973.

Children's Catalog, 13th ed. 1976.

Junior High School Library Catalog, 3rd ed. 1975.

Senior High School Library Catalog, 11th ed. 1977.

Fiction Catalog, 9th ed. 1976.

The Reader's Adviser, 12th ed. New York: R. R. Bowker, 1974–1977; 3 vols.

The purpose of most general or subject retrospective book lists is to provide the librarian a suggestion of what constitutes part of a basic book collection. There are possibly hundreds of lists of "best books," which the librarian uses in various ways, but primarily: (1) to check against holdings to determine what is missing and should be added to the collection and (2) to evaluate the collection. If the library has a certain percentage of the books on a given respected list, it must be in fairly good condition. If the library lacks most of the titles, the collection needs to be re-examined. A third purpose has fairly well faded with the booming 1960s—the "core" list, such as *Books for College Libraries*, from which the librarian purchased almost blindly to start a library from nothing. A fourth purpose is as an aid in weeding. If the librarian thinks the book is of little value, a quick check of a standard list will indicate if the opinion is valid or not.

No matter what they are called or who puts them together, the lists are only guides that never should be considered final authorities. There are too many variables: usually too-early cutoff dates for entry, particular needs of various libraries, sometimes questionable standards for selection, too few (or too many) titles. The list of exceptions to the ultimate authority of any list can be spun out almost indefinitely by the librarian who wishes to do so.

EVALUATION

When considering the worth of a retrospective selection aid or bibliography for your needs, you may ask many of the same questions you ask about review media.

1. Scope How much material is listed and for what subjects? Is the subject matter relevant to the library? Is material limited to books, or are other media considered?

2. Audience   Is this aid directed to adults, children, teenagers, specialists? Does it fit its audience, or does it contain too much or too little material?

3. Annotations   Are there annotations, or simply lists of titles? Are the annotations truly descriptive of content or simply publisher quotes? Are there any critical remarks?

4. Timeliness   Is the material currently available? How much of it is out of print or can no longer be purchased? Do entries cover a broad period of time or concentrate on a given period? Are current titles well represented?

5. Selection   Who chose the titles? Was it a committee, an individual? Is the selector authoritative? Is the publisher trustworthy?

6. Recommendations   Is everything in the list recommended? If not, is it clear what is not recommended?

7. Format   Is full bibliographical information given? Are out-of-print titles indicated? Is the arrangement easy to follow and to use? Are there adequate indexes—author, title, subject?

Good lists can be judiciously employed in the selection process. A few are regularly used in most libraries not only as a check on its holdings and their quality but also as guides for people seeking books in certain subject areas. The best known of these lists are published by The H. W. Wilson Company in their standard catalog series.

PUBLIC LIBRARIES

1. *Public Library Catalog*. Each year a supplement is issued to update the work, and the total is revised every fifth or sixth year. The basic volume is arranged alphabetically by author. After full bibliographic information there follows a descriptive, and sometimes evaluative, annotation. There is a useful author, title, and subject index as well as a directory of publishers.

The nearly 9000 nonfiction titles chosen for entry and the 3000 books in the supplements represent the work of a committee of librarians who meet regularly to evaluate what to include in the supplement and what to include in or exclude from the basic volume.

Users often go through the annual volume when it appears to see if anything has been overlooked or to fill in a subject area where there is great demand.

The arrangement and method of selection are followed by the other standard catalogs.

2. *Fiction Catalog*. Four annual supplements before a new edition. Arrangement is by author, with an extremely useful subject index that allows a librarian to find novels on a wide variety of subjects from science fiction

and mysteries to fiction centered in a certain historical period or about a given type of occupation. Here some 5000 titles are selected and annotated with another 2000 added via the supplements. Titles are for adults, although many are suitable for high schools, and the list is equally valuable for academic libraries.

ACADEMIC LISTS

The Wilson lists stop at colleges, and for that area one must turn to what is essentially a listing without annotations. The basic list for four-year liberal arts colleges is *Books for College Libraries*. This is a simple listing of 38,651 titles, most published before 1973. Not only is the list dated, but the number of books is also less than half the approximate 100,000 recommended as basic for college libraries. Arrangement is by LC classification number, with an author, title, and subject index in the sixth volume. There are no annotations and the subject indexing is poor.[37] The first edition of this work appeared in 1967 and listed 53,400 titles issued prior to 1963. It remains a useful, although obviously dated, guide.

Choice is the companion review to the sets and in itself is an excellent retrospective list, particularly the nine-volume cumulation, which lists and annotates more than 58,000 titles reviewed in the magazine between 1964 and 1974. Arrangement is by subject and there are good, appropriate title and author indexes. The set was published between 1976 and 1977 by Rowman & Littlefield.

The so-called opening day collection is another feature of *Choice*. Originally published in 1968, it has been revised many times and is a list of about 1800 titles deemed essential for every academic library. The list normally appears over several issues of *Choice*, as do specialized subject lists from time to time.

SELECT LISTS FOR SCHOOLS

1. *Children's Catalog* is a classified arrangement of about 5500 titles. There is a superior author, title, and subject index. Many of the annotations, as in other Wilson catalogs, are taken from reviews and the source of the reviews noted.[38] The work is updated by an annual supplement.

2. *Junior High School Library Catalog* has four supplements prior to a new edition and considers books for students in the seventh through ninth grades. Arrangement and approach are similar to the *Children's Catalog*.

3. *Senior High School Library Catalog*, which has five supplements before

---

[37] For a detailed review of what has almost become a classic among college libraries, see the Reference and Subscription Books Review in *Booklist*, May 1, 1976, pp. 1284–1286.

[38] This and other retrospective lists are briefly described in Moira Evans, "Selection Tools for Building a Children's Literature Collection," *Texas Libraries*, Summer 1975, pp. 73–79.

a new edition, includes 5281 titles and follows much the same arrangement and approach as the other two Wilson catalogs in this field.

A fault with the Wilson catalogs, as with most retrospective lists, is pointed out by a critic:

An analysis of the 1975 *Junior High School Library Catalog* was made to determine the number of out-of-print titles in a stratified sample of 413 titles, representing slightly more than ten percent of the collection. When titles were checked against the 1976 *Books in Print*, a range of from 3 percent of the short story collection to 35 percent of the "200's" was found to be out-of-print. . . . Added to this is the year-by-year attrition expected before the 1980 edition of the Catalog.[39]

This is true of most retrospective lists, even the current editions of *Books in Print*, where an alarming number of titles actually are out of print but not so reported by the publisher.

There are numerous other lists of books for elementary and secondary school libraries. Among some of the favored:

1. *Books for Secondary School Libraries* (5th ed.; New York: R. R. Bowker, 1976). (National Association of Independent Schools.) Frequently revised, this is a simple listing of about 6000 nonfiction titles in subject categories. A related title is *Core Media Collection for Secondary Schools.*

2. *The Elementary School Library Collection* (New Brunswick, N.J.: Brodart, since 1965; annual). Edited by Mary Gaver, an expert in the field, this is a reliable listing. There are about 10,000 titles, but no annotations, for grades K–6. In addition to books, select nonprint material is included.

3. *Guide to Reference Books for School Media Centers* (Littleton, Colo.: Libraries Unlimited, since 1973; biennial supplements). This differs from the other lists given here in that there are critical annotations for almost everything included and the materials are for kindergarten through high school. Limited to reference works, this guide includes a major section on "media sources," and "media selection" aids are to be found throughout the carefully organized book.

4. *Building a Children's Literature Collection* (rev. ed.; Middletown, Conn.: Choice, 1978). This is a children's literature collection to be used in academic libraries. The list is not annotated but opens with a lengthy, informative essay on the subject by Harriet B. Quimby. It is followed by a list of children's books for the literature section, with an essay by Rosemary Weber.

GENERAL

The *Reader's Adviser* lists in three volumes more than 30,000 titles considered the "best" for the general public. First published in 1921, succeeding

---

[39] Marilyn L. Miller, "Collection Development in School Media Centers . . . ," *Collection Building*, vol. 1, no. 1 (1978), p. 39.

editions have appeared every four to six years. In the present set, the most valuable is the first volume, devoted to American and British fiction, poetry, essays, literary biography, and reference works. Most entries are first by author with a list of the author's works—usually briefly annotated—and a selected bibliography of books about the writer.[40]

In the same category are such basic lists as *Good Reading* (New York: R. R. Bowker, 1978), now in its 21st edition. Selection here, as in the other Bowker entry, is by subject experts who build on entries in previous editions. *Good Reading* lists and annotates 2500 titles under 35 broad subjects, and the entries are usually as suitable for high school as for adults.

Readers Advisory Service (New York: Science Associates, since 1973; quarterly) "publishes topical subject bibliographies, reading lists . . . and booklists." Subjects move from China and linguistics in one number to zero-based budgeting and a selected bibliography of Coleridge. Most are short, prepared by working librarians, and are relatively timely.

AWARD LISTS

Most useful for checking previous selections, and sometimes to increase the number of titles chosen earlier, are the numerous award-winner lists. The obvious ones are the annual National Book Award and Pulitzer and Nobel prize winners. Librarians watch the prizes each year and check to see if the winners are well represented in the library. Additional better-known award lists include:

1. Notable Books of 19—. A list 40 to 50 titles chosen each year by a committee of the American Library Association. Titles are "selected for their significant contribution." Criteria include wide general appeal and literary merit. The list is widely published in the library press.

2. "Best Books of the Year," which appears in the December issue of *School Library Journal*, is a carefully chosen list of what the magazine's editors consider suitable for children and young adults.

3. "Best Books for Young Adults" is a list chosen annually by the American Library Association's Young Adult Services Division.[41] A useful compilation of most of the prizes for children's books is *Children's Books: Awards and Prizes* (New York: Children's Book Council, since 1969; annual).

4. *Library Journal* frequently devotes special issues to "best" titles in subject areas. The March 1 number normally includes roundup articles on "Recommended scientific, technical & medical books of 19—" and "Outstanding business books of the year." The April 1 issue contains "Reference books of 19—," a select list compiled by the American Library Association. This list also appears in other ALA publications, including *Booklist*.

---

[40] The arrangement is actually more complex; for a good overview of the set see the Reference and Subscription Books Reviews, *Booklist*, March 1, 1978, pp. 1129–1131.

[41] For a critical summary of how the list is chosen, see Lillian L. Shapiro, "Overdue," *Wilson Library Bulletin*, June 1977, pp. 803ff.

7
Ordering Books

THE DISCUSSION so far has been limited to selection and evaluation of materials. The equally important parallel operation in any library is
acquisitions: acquiring materials after they have been selected.[1]

Acquisitions work includes obtaining materials by purchase, gift, or exchange; paying for or acknowledging receipt; and maintaining appropriate records. . . . The
work may also include . . . work related to binding and rebinding, the recording
of serials, precataloging and allied operations. . . . The terms "acquisitions work"
and "order work" are sometimes used interchangeably. Usually, however, order
work applies to purchasing, while acquisitions work includes obtaining material by
[other means as well].[2]

The average individual acquires a book from a bookstore, a book club,
or the publisher. Librarians also follow these procedures, but they depend
primarily on a third source, the book wholesaler, also called jobber or
vendor.

The Book Wholesaler (Jobber)

A jobber procures books from the publisher at a discount, stores them in a
large warehouse, and then sells them to bookstores and to libraries. The go-
between in the publishing-library transaction, the jobber is a familiar enough
part of the capitalist system and has counterparts in many aspects of trade.
Ideally, the wholesaler provides efficient, fast service. The librarian should
be able to order any book in print and secure it from the jobber at a
minimum delay. A large jobber has books from several thousand publishers.

---

[1] This book is concerned with selection rather than acquisitions, but every librarian
needs some understanding of how books are procured for the library. What follows is an
outline of practices likely to affect the person in charge of selection.
[2] Stephen Ford, *The Acquisition of Library Materials* (rev. ed.; Chicago: American
Library Association, 1978), pp. ix–x.

Some specialize in certain types of books, but most offer: (1) Trade books or general books, found in an average bookstore or library; (2) textbooks, and (3) specialized professional and technical titles less likely to be in the average bookstore.[3] Most book wholesalers *do not* offer periodicals or other types of materials. There are special jobbers for periodicals and other print and nonprint materials, discussed in Chapter 10.

Librarians prefer to deal with jobbers for books and serials because, among other reasons, (1) a single source for an order saves writing individual orders to individual publishers and (2) the jobber not only places the orders, but follows up on problems that may arise. One source means less paperwork and fewer headaches, hence less cost.

Ease of ordering and less hassle with paperwork were reasons librarians cited for preferring jobbers. "Faster service; and postage is cheaper because we can batch orders"; "speedy delivery and economy of getting many titles from single source"; and "quicker and more accurate in reporting on out-of-stock and out-of-print titles" were typical responses from librarians all over the country.[4]

Jobbers are listed in many standard reference sources (among them *Literary Market Place* and *American Book Trade Directory*). However, most librarians have no problem finding a jobber. Distributors send representatives to libraries, and the question about who is best at one service or another is a topic of much discussion among librarians.

PRIMARY JOBBERS

Among the best-known book jobbers in the United States are:

(1.) The Baker & Taylor Companies, the nation's oldest and largest book wholesaler. Much favored by public and school libraries, they have five distribution centers—in Illinois, Nevada, New Jersey, Georgia, and Texas. The eastern division office is at 50 Kirby Ave., Somerville, N.J. 08876. Telephone 800-526-3811.[5]

(2.) Brodart, Inc., equally well known and almost as large, has headquarters at 1609 Memorial Avenue, Williamsport, Pa. 17701. Telephone 800-233-8467.

(3.) Stechert Macmillian, Inc., 866 Third Ave., New York, N.Y. 10022 (telephone 212-935-4262), offers service to larger academic and special

[3] Of the $4.6 billion worth of books sold in America each year, trade (general) books account for $537 million, but textbooks are the leader, with $1.2 billion. In third place are the technical and professional titles: $559 million. Other categories include paperbacks (divided between mass market and professional), university press publications, religious books, subscription and reference books, and children's and juvenile titles ("Association of American Publishers Report," *Publishers Weekly*, August 22, 1977, pp. 32–36. The report is updated each year).

[4] "A PW Survey," *Publishers Weekly*, February 6, 1978, p. 73.

[5] For a sketch of Baker & Taylor see "Side Tripping," *American Libraries*, May 1978, pp. 260–261.

libraries, specializes in foreign purchases, and is one of the major periodical jobbers.

(4.) Blackwell North America, Inc., took over a large jobber (Richard Abel) in the 1970s and is a branch of Blackwell's of Oxford.[6] Main office is at 10300 SW Allen Blvd., Beaverton, Ore. 97005 (telephone 503-643-8423) and the eastern regional office is at 1001 Fries Mill Rd., Blackwood, N.J. 08012 (telephone 609-629-0700).

(5.) Bookazine Co., Inc., 303 W. 10 St., New York, N.Y. 10014 (telephone 212-675-8877), distributes trade titles, with about 40 percent of its sale going to libraries, the rest to bookstores.[7]

(6.) Ingram Book Company, 347 Reedwood Dr., Nashville, Tenn. 37217 (telephone 800-251-1200), is especially useful for academic titles, particularly those of independent presses.

(7.) Book Mail Service, Inc., 82-87 164 Street, Jamaica, N.Y. 11432 (telephone 212-380-4000), is a major independent paperback distributor that specializes in both trade and mass-market titles. They issue special lists and aids for librarians; Baker & Taylor, Brodart, Bookazine, and Ingram also publish material of various levels of usefulness to librarians.

These seven are only a representative sampling of the scores of jobbers throughout the United States and Canada, and in no way begin to exhaust the possibilities open to librarians—as a glance at the listings in *Literary Market Place* alone will show.

Dependence on a jobber increases with the size of the library.[8] The larger the library the more likely it is to employ a jobber for domestic titles, one or more others for foreign titles, and several for subject specialities. The small library may rely solely on ordering from one jobber, a few publishers, and the local bookstore. Often a small local jobber will go to extraordinary lengths to provide comprehensive, accurate, and satisfactory service. While the discounts may not be as great as those offered by larger jobbers, the efficiency may nevertheless make the small jobber's efforts more cost-effective.

Librarians evaluate jobbers on many points, but essentially they separate one from another on the basis of extra services, discounts, delivery time, and general fulfillment of orders.

---

[6] Richard Abel & Company offered one of the finest approval plans in operation, so fine that it was unusually costly and the company was forced into liquidation. Librarians still speak fondly of the Abel service. Blackwell's is one of the most famous bookstores in the world. For a detailed view of its operations see A. P. U. Millett's "A Librarian's View of Blackwell's," *New Zealand Libraries*, Spring 1977, pp. 8–15.

[7] For a sketch of Bookazine see "Approaching 50 . . . ," *Publishers Weekly*, October 3, 1977, pp. 73ff.

[8] Estimates vary with individual studies and the year, but the consensus is that among all libraries about 75 to 80 percent of the books purchased come from one or more jobbers. Jobbers also serve bookstores, and some are better organized to sell to bookstores than to libraries; most, however, serve both. Bookstores use jobbers primarily for the 20 percent of their titles that account for 80 percent of sales (popular trade books).

EXTRA SERVICES

Beyond the standard services, larger jobbers offer numerous acquisition aids:

1. About two-thirds have an approval plan for libraries.

2. Cataloging and processing of books. Several offer books processed with catalog card kits. There may be problems, such as using Library of Congress subject headings and Dewey classifications, but this can usually be worked out with the jobber.

3. Book catalogs. Almost all offer catalogs that keep the library advised of recent publications. Some have magazines, which can be useful in selection, and still others supply selected lists of both current and retrospective titles.

4. Some sell a variety of library supplies, from bindings to furniture.

5. Audiovisual supplies and equipment are offered by a few jobbers, but most concentrate on books.

DISCOUNTS

1. Almost all jobbers and publishers offer a discount off the list price of the book. Discounts vary with:

   a. Volume of purchases made by the library.

   b. Type of materials ordered. More specialized materials may have a lower discount or none.

   c. Services offered by the jobber. Where many services are offered, such an approval plan, the discount will be less.

2. Discounts may range from a high of 40 percent for trade titles to none for highly technical volumes, foreign books, and many reference books.

   a. Trade books. On the average the library may expect a discount of 35 to 40 percent from a jobber for trade books. If the book is ordered from the publisher the average discount is less—20 to 30 percent, with an average of about 24 percent.

   b. Scholarly titles and technical works. This varies with the jobber and publisher, but on an average the discount is from 5 to 20 percent, with the average closer to 10 percent.

   c. Foreign titles and some esoteric works. There usually is no discount, and the library may have to pay a service fee to the jobber for securing the works.

   d. Out-of-print, relatively difficult-to-find titles. Here the library usually pays the net figure quoted by the dealer, often greater than the initial publishing price. Discounts are rare.

Discounts are a constant source of friction.[9] Some states and communities, for example, force the library to throw open its annual book and serials budget for bid. The jobber with the lowest bid gets the contract. The jobber who does no more than supply the books is likely to receive the contract, which then actually costs the library more because it must pay for services otherwise available without extra charge from better jobbers.

DELIVERY TIME

Fulfillment time of orders is the basis of the greatest number of complaints among librarians about jobbers—and publishers. Some jobbers can deliver a book within three to ten days after the order is received, but the average for most orders is four to six weeks (for books available from the jobber's warehouse). When the jobber must order books from the publisher, the delay time is greater—90 to 120 days.

Publishers are much slower than jobbers, as a rule. Publishers generally take from three to six weeks to fill an order.[10]

FULFILLMENT

No jobber has all of the books needed by a library. As a result the average fulfillment of an average library order will be about 50 to 70 percent of the titles ordered—an alarming percentage of unfilled orders. The reasons jobbers give include: (1) The book is no longer in stock, or no longer available from the publisher. (2) The book is available from the publisher, but the jobber does not handle it. (3) The book has not yet been published (although the librarian may have every reason to know it has). The result is that larger libraries tend to deal with several jobbers, avoiding those who do not handle the type of books needed. (Some librarians try to solve the problem by ordering directly from publishers. Unfortunately, they may have no better luck and are almost certain to have to wait even longer for a reply.)

There is no real solution to the problem of fulfillment, at least at the close of the 1970's, when too many jobbers and publishers consider the time element of no real importance—at least when it comes to serving libraries.

Except for more popular foreign titles, most domestic jobbers do not offer foreign books. The library usually deals directly with foreign pub-

[9] Publishers discriminate against libraries: an average bookstore will get a discount of 40 percent, while the library may expect no more than 24 percent. This rightfully irritates many librarians. For a good survey article on the situation see Audrey B. Eaglen, "Out of Patience—Indefinitely," *School Library Journal*, February 1978, pp. 23–26. For an equally excellent overview of jobbers, see the same author's "Book Wholesalers: Pro and Con," *School Library Journal*, October 1978, pp. 116–119.

[10] In a survey of booksellers and publishers ("A PW Survey," *Publishers Weekly*, February 6, 1978, p. 76), Doubleday and Random House were the publishers most frequently cited as giving the fastest order fills, with McGraw-Hill and Harper & Row taking the second spot. Simon & Schuster, David McKay, Grosset & Dunlap, Crown, and Scribners were listed most often as the slowest where fulfillment was concerned.

lishers when the orders are limited or specialized or deals with a foreign jobber.

As already noted, there normally is no discount on foreign titles, and, if anything, the library must pay a service fee to the jobber and be burdened with the added cost of postage, currency conversion, and the like when working through the publisher.

Publishers

There are various types of publishers, but a general definition is a firm that takes an author's manuscript, edits it, and produces it in book form.[11] Once the book is issued, the publisher tries to make it available as widely as possible through bookstores, libraries, jobbers, and other channels. Estimates differ, but there are close to 6000 publishers in the United States, although fewer than about 50 sell the majority of titles.

If any one trend was obvious among publishers in the past 20 years it has been mergers. There have been more than 300 such mergers in that period so that today "Seven paperback publishers now control the bulk of the mass paperback industry . . . and 40 of the hard-cover trade houses in the country" sell the vast majority of books.[12] The significance of these mergers is both cultural and bureaucratic. The cultural aspects are evident in more publishers turning from the adventure of publishing to the sure thing of a smash hit in a best seller. From the point of view of ordering, the larger publishers are becoming increasingly bureaucratic, and ordering has become a major headache. Publishers spend millions on advertising, but when one tries to obtain a book it may seem as if nothing is spent on delivery.

There are numerous reasons that librarians must order, if only on occasion, directly from the publishers.[13] Some publishers do not deal with jobbers, and the only way to get their books is to go directly to the publisher. Also, some jobbers will not be bothered with some publishers, particularly those in the small-press world who must rely upon direct sales or special jobbers to distribute their works. Then, too, there are standing-order and blanket-order plans (to be discussed below) whereby the library works directly with the publisher. On the whole, though, the librarian prefers to bypass the publisher because of numerous problems.[14]

[11] Many library schools offer courses in publishing; here we suggest briefly how publishing is related to acquisitions.

[12] Ann Crittenden, "Merger Fever in Publishing," *The New York Times*, October 23, 1977, section 3, p. 1. For a detailed discussion of mergers see "The Question of Size in the Book Industry Today," a special report in *Publishers Weekly*, July 31, 1978, pp. 25—55.

[13] A useful title in this area is Jung Kim's *Policies of Publishers: A Handbook for Order Librarians* (Metuchen, N.J.: Scarecrow Press, 1978), which tabulates data on discounts, returns, buying plans, prepayments, and so forth.

[14] "The Prepayment Dilemma: A Consumer's Guide," *American Libraries*, November 1977, pp. 571—572. The insistence of some publishers on prepayment is only one of the headaches of working directly with publishers.

SMALL PRESSES

There are now more than 3000 small-press publishers in America, and the numbers increase as the commercial publishers merge and become more profit-conscious. A small press may be anything from a mimeograph machine in a basement to a sophisticated print center. The small presses publish everything from little magazines, to poetry, to political and social pieces, to fiction. In fact, they do anything done by commercial presses, but usually gravitate more to the less popular, the esoteric, and the truly creative.

Len Fulton's *International Directory of Little Magazines and Small Presses* is the basic guide in the field. The fourteenth edition, covering 1978–1979, gives complete information on the presses, including to names of editors and owners and types of materials published. Fulton offers other services for small-press bibliography, and interested librarians can write for details to Dustbooks, Paradise, Calif. 95969.

In the political and alternative scene there are several useful guides. The best is *From Radical Left to Extreme Right* (2nd ed.; Metuchen, N.J.: Scarecrow Press, 1976), a multivolume summary of various publishers. Includes an objective summary of the purpose, scope, and audience for the publishers' works. Emphasis is almost entirely on periodicals. *Alternatives in Print* (San Francisco: Glide, 1975), frequently updated, represents the work of an American Library Association group and is a list of organizations devoted to social change. Listing of liberal periodicals can be found in the *Alternative Press Index* (Baltimore: Alternative Press Center) and the *Guide to Alternative Periodicals* issued by Don Carnahan (Sunspark Press, Box 91, Greenleaf, Ore. 97445). One of the best ways of keeping up with such works is to check the annual summary of American reference books in the *American Reference Books Annual*. See, too, the author's section "Alternatives" in *Magazines for Libraries*, third edition.

The small press depends heavily on three sources of income: readers who buy their books; federal and state grants; and libraries. Libraries certainly should purchase the output of local small presses, and the librarian should make an effort to pinpoint these publishers (which can be done in the geographic index of the *International Directory*).[15]

The small-press movement is likely to grow in the United States. As one critic observed:

There is some industry speculation that if current trends continue, with book publishing companies growing larger and increasingly profit-conscious, more and more experimental, high-risk works will be published by the small regional pub-

[15] Many librarians are actively involved with small-press titles. *Booklist* has an irregular column on small-press titles, and *Library Journal* has an annual column on the some subject. Within libraries there are various ways of making small-press titles evident. See Paul Fericano, "Small Press Racks in Libraries," *The Serials Librarian*, Winter 1976–1977, pp. 135–138, and articles on the alternative press and little magazines in many of the library journals.

lishing houses that seem to be cropping up all over the country, particularly in the West. These publishers, which may produce as few as five books a year, may well become farm teams, in effect, developing new talent for the majors.

Similarly, as the larger publishers place increasing emphasis on the mass market, such works as poetry and translations of important foreign books will gravitate more and more to the university presses—much as cultural television programming has been relegated largely to public television.[16]

A recurrent difficulty with the larger general jobbers is that they do not handle small-press books, or, for that matter, highly specialized titles where they are likely to get only a few orders.

Since the mid-1970s a number of specialized jobbers have developed out of this reluctance of the majors to stock small-press books, and there are now about a dozen. A typical example, one of the largest and earliest, is Bookpeople.

This Berkeley, California, jobber carries most small-press titles as well as a number of alternative books from establishment publishers. By 1979 they had more than 3000 bookstore accounts and were doing much to carry the message of the small press to the nation.[17]

Paperback Distributors

The average relatively popular or scholarly trade paperback is likely to be available from your regular book jobber. However, because of the rapid increase in the number of paperback publishers and titles over the past few years, specialized jobbers who handle only paperbacks have emerged, and many librarians now turn to these dealers for service. Another source is the more traditional news dealer, who may limit service to mass-market titles and is probably more interested in working with retail outlets than with libraries.[18]

A state-by-state listing of paperback distributors, as well as information on what types of books they handle, will be found on pages 126–209 of *Paperback Books for Young People*. This list is equally suitable for other types of libraries, and thanks to the diligence of the compiler is the best of its type.

Discounts vary. A regular book jobber who stocks select mass-market and trade paperbacks is likely to have a special discount rate for paperbacks but

16 Crittenden, op. cit.

17 Roy Akers and Morrie Gelman, "Bookpeople: The First Alternative Jobber," *Books West*, June 1977, pp. 11–14. A good background article on both the firm and all such jobbers. For a list of distributors see pp. 453–454 of Len Fulton's *International Directory of Little Magazines and Small Presses*, 14th ed.

18 For a discussion of a typical news dealer see Roger M. Smith, "Milligan News Expands Paperback Sales . . . ," *Publishers Weekly*, March 5, 1979, pp. 82–83. For an overview of the industry see Smith's *Paperback Parnassus* (Boulder, Colo.: Westview Press, 1976).

may simply lump paperbacks into the overall order for all types of books. News dealers asked to supply single copies will give no discount and sometimes add the cost of mailing and invoicing. Independent paperback distributors may or may not give discounts, depending on the volume and the type of book ordered. Publishers rarely give discounts except on volume orders of the same title.

Information about jobbers may be had from the Educational Paperback Association, c/o Ludington News Co., 1600 E. Grand Blvd., Detroit, Mich. 48211. Organized to assist schools and librarians, the association is involved with all aspects of improving service to libraries.

Books, of course, may be ordered directly from the publisher; for a list see *Paperbacks for Young People* (pp. 1–122) and *Paperbound Books in Print*.

As discounts rarely are given, lucky the librarian who has quick access to a large paperback bookstore. Here arrangements may be made to buy the books directly from the bookdealer, who, because he or she buys in volume, actually may be able to give faster, more efficient service than the usual jobber. This is particularly true where the library may want only one copy of a single title of a mass paperback or a relatively popular trade title.

Finally, there are several book clubs that specialize in paperbacks. Possibly the best known are the Scholastic Book Services, the Xerox Educational Publications (both for schools), and the layperson's Quality Paperback Book Club. The latter issues a monthly bulletin and offers 20 percent discounts. Most titles are reprints of hardbacks the library is likely to have already, but this is a good source of duplicates at a reasonable price.

Order Plans

Today libraries have a number of order plans that help streamline the acquisitions and selection process. Whether developed as approval, blanket-order, or standing-order plans, all have several common elements:

1. A great number of books are delivered to the library from the jobber or publisher almost automatically.

2. The procedure allows publisher and jobber to save money, and hence the discount to libraries is higher.[19]

3. The librarian is given an opportunity actually to examine the books before they are shelved or rejected.

4. The jobber or publisher may send titles that are not likely to be reviewed, at least within a reasonable time. This allows the librarian to consider books that otherwise might be overlooked.

There are distinct drawbacks to the plans, but first consider how they operate. Let us say, for example, the library has been ordering individual

---

[19] It also saves much paperwork. Processing a typical single order today costs from $30 to $40, possibly even more. Much of this is eliminated with the order plans.

titles from Harvard University Press. Each time a new title is published and reviewed the library enters an order. Under a purchasing plan the library has an agreement with the press whereby one copy of each new Harvard Press publication is automatically sent to the library.

example

Each month, shipments are made in one lot from books that have arrived in the warehouse [of the press] the preceding month. Special discount of 10 percent applies [to such orders]. Libraries may exclude a limited number of subject classifications such as Law and Medicine. Occasional returns are permitted but publisher does not establish a standard order with the understanding that each and every book is subject to return. A blanket standing order may be set up on a trial basis and canceled at any time.[20]

The various kinds of plans became important in the 1960s, when book budgets increased in size and trained librarians decreased in number. Most of the early plans were received enthusiastically, but now are considered merely another way of helping to build collections.[21] Thanks to more rigorous budgets and an equal need for rigorous selection, some larger libraries have reduced the scope of their plans or canceled them altogether.

There are three major type of plans employed by librarians:

A. APPROVAL PLAN

Under the approval plan, the library sends the jobber or publisher a *profile* of the library.

A profile is a detailed listing of criteria governing the inclusion and exclusion of titles. The profile delineates the scope of the plan in such areas as subject matter, language, geographic area, level, publisher, price and format. The profile is subject to review and adjustments as needed.[22]

1. On receipt of the profile the jobber or publisher sends the library all books (and other materials) that match the profile.[23]

2. An important aspect of the approval plan is that the librarian reserves the right to return any titles not considered in keeping with the library's needs (and thus with the submitted profile).

Where the approval plan is operating efficiently, less than 12 percent of the books should be returned. If returns are more than 12 percent the profile should be modified or the plan dropped.[24]

---

[20] Jung Chon Kim, *Policies of Publishers* (Metuchen, N.J.: Scarecrow Press, 1976), p. 54.

[21] For a review of articles and books on the subject see Rose Magrill and Mona East, "Collection Development in Large University Libraries," in *Advances in Librarianship* (New York: Academic Press, 1978), vol. 8, pp. 6–7.

[22] Gloria Moline, *An Evaluation of Approval Plan Performance* . . . (San Jose, Calif.: San Jose State University Department of Librarianship, 1975), p. 6.

[23] The vast majority of approval plans are with jobbers, although a few publishers offer the same approach.

[24] There is disagreement on the percentages of returns. Some vendors and librarians say the percentage of returns should be no more than 4 percent.

The approval plan is primarily suited to larger or specialized libraries where the size of the book budget and the multiple or specialized needs of the users justify the expense of establishing and maintaining a plan.

A survey of 101 academic libraries found that approximately 80 percent "have or have had approval plans." Most of the respondents still with plans have total acquisition budgets of half a million dollars or more.[25] Both librarians and jobbers believe that only a library with a book budget of from $300,000 to $500,000 plus should consider an approval plan.[26] Needs of smaller libraries are met easier by routine selection and other types of purchase plans.

There is ongoing debate about the effectiveness of approval plans (see pp. 167–168) and many meetings and conferences to discuss the subject, such as the fourth annual international conference on Approval and Gathering Plans for Academic and Research Libraries in October 1979. Questions range from the ability of the plans to reduce acquisitions costs to technical service problems.

B. BLANKET ORDER

The blanket order is similar to the approval plan, although here the order is somewhat less sophisticated:

1. There is no profile. The librarian simply tells the publisher or jobber to send everything published under a given price, or everything within a given subject area, or all trade books, or special requirements, details worked out with each publisher.

2. The library normally cannot return titles to publishers, although there may be some agreement with jobbers to do so.

A famous version of the blanket order is the Greenaway Plan—named for Emerson Greenaway, former director of the Free Library of Philadelphia, who originated the plan in 1958. A publisher automatically sends the library one copy of almost every trade title published. (Some limit may be set on price; for instance nothing over $15 is to be sent.) The discount ranges from 35 to 40 percent to as high as 70 percent. The title usually may not be returned.

The advantage of this plan is the large discount and the rapid acquisition of titles. The librarian may examine the title before cataloging, sometimes file it in a wastebin when not suitable. If a decision is to purchase, multiple copies may be ordered. A basic problem is convincing the selection staff that titles should be subjected to the same rigorous selection tests as those items ordered individually.

Today it is usual for a large library to have 20 or more such contracts with publishers. Since emphasis is on trade books, most of this type of purchasing is done by public and school libraries.

[25] Kathleen McCullough, et al., *Approval Plans and Academic Libraries* (Phoenix, Ariz.: Oryx Press, 1977), p. 1.
[26] Gloria Moline, op. cit.

Most publishers have plans by subject areas; Doubleday, for instance, has a wide variety of programs suited for various types and sizes of libraries. The publisher routinely sends out a monthly annotated book list which tells the librarian titles to expect in the next shipment.

A similar approach, although often with differences in discounts and ordering procedures, is the:

C. STANDING ORDER

The librarian who uses a standing order simply gets everything published by the publisher, although there may be a few exceptions; for example, anything over x dollars may be excluded. The standing order is most usual with smaller technical and professional firms that issue much the same type of material year in and year out in relatively small quantities. (Blanket orders usually are used with larger trade publishers, where the quantity is so diverse and large that definite exceptions have to be established.)

Standing orders are fairly common among university presses and specialized publishers. For example, many libraries have a standing order with the American Library Association publishing department for all or nearly all its books. The librarians reason that books published by the ALA are likely (about 95 percent of the time) to be a desired purchase for the library. Larger academic libraries have similar arrangements with university presses, particularly those specializing in history, English, art, and similar fields.

Time-Life Books has a standing-order plan that saves the library 30 percent off retail prices. The library simply puts in a standing order for the publisher's various series (e.g., The Great Cities, The Westerners, Wild World of Animals). The books are sent either twice a year or quarterly. Under this plan the library may return books when not satisfied.

To add to the semantic confusion, however, there are other plans.

RENTAL PLANS

One way to handle best sellers is for the library to subscribe to a rental plan such as the well-known McNaughton Plan.[27] Under this system: (1) The library rents, does not actually buy, high-demand books; (2) the books are delivered fully cataloged and processed for the shelf; (3) the collection is constantly revolved.

The rationale is that this saves the library the expense of buying and processing ephemeral books not likely to be added to the permanent collection. It also solves the problem of duplicates, at least among best-selling titles. There are several ordering approaches, including a way whereby the librarian can order a certain percentage of mysteries, westerns, science fiction, and light romances. The librarian can select specific titles each month from an annotated listing or simply leave selection to the jobber.

[27] Sold through Brodart.

Costs vary. For example, a basic collection of 100 titles with 10 new titles added each month would cost $61.50 per month; a basic collection of 5000 titles with 500 new titles added each month would cost $3075 per month.

There are many variations on the McNaughton Plan. For example, Josten's (a Minnesota jobber) has a lease plan whereby multiple copies of a single best-selling title may be leased rather than purchased as well as a general-order plan similar to the McNaughton.

The cost efficiency of these approaches is debated, but they are common, particularly in public libraries and in recreational reading rooms in smaller academic libraries.[28]

Some public libraries finance the plans by renting the books to the public, and it is not uncommon to find a rental section in many libraries. There is debate about whether or not this should be done, but it is so prevalent that the argument is now more academic than real. If the rentals are low enough, there seems absolutely no reason not to have such a system in operation.

DISADVANTAGES

The primary argument against many plans is that the library that adopts them has given up selection for efficiency.[29] Approval and some standing-order plans do allow the librarian to return what is not suitable. However (and this is the crux of the debate, which has little to do with the plans per se but much to do with the operation of the library), many librarians simply do not return the unwanted books because:

1. In some libraries the acquisitions department makes little or no effort to have a subject evaluate the books as they come into the library—evaluation is done by the acquisitions librarians. This may work, but is not particularly good unless the acquisition librarians are all-around experts.

2. Even where the staff and laypersons examine the books as received, some titles are not returned when rejected because it is easier to catalog and shelve the books than return them to the jobber or publisher, and may actually be less costly.

All this can be disastrous to some degree, not only for large libraries but also for central systems where a plan is in operation and where the librarians in branches or smaller libraries have little to say about what is purchased. Some see it as a dehumanization of book selection.

Beyond failure to evaluate and select books sent through the various plans, there are other drawbacks. There tends to be a tremendous number of snags and duplication of effort. For example:

[28] Application to academic libraries will be found in Ruth Cushman's article on such plans and a letter to the editor, in *Journal of Academic Librarianship*, March 1976, pp. 15–19, and September 1976, p. 190.

[29] The survey of academic libraries found that "more than a third of the libraries . . . do not formally display approval-plan books for review. . . . In most libraries the time given for review is one week. . . . Persons who review books are not always the persons with authority to reject" (McCullough, op. cit., p. 5).

PROBLEMS

1. No one is ever sure just what books are coming or not coming on the approval plan.

To order or not to order is the librarians' daily dilemma associated with approval plans. . . . Some vendors have offered to check regular orders against their approval title file to eliminate unwanted duplication while others offer no solution other than "wait and see." With computer and microform technology currently available, it is difficult to believe that this problem is yet unsolved. Meanwhile, librarians spend time and energy maintaining extra files and double-checking questionable titles that are requested.[30]

2. To get one of the plans working properly requires six months to a year. Meanwhile, the overall collection may suffer.

3. Unless the profile is constantly watched, the library collection is likely to get out of balance and no longer reflect the real needs of the community served.[31]

The various plans themselves do not cancel selection and evaluation. Used wisely, they do much to improve selection because the librarian may now actually examine the book before deciding to add or not to add it to the collection.

The objections to the plans—and particularly the approval plan, which sweeps in vast numbers and various types of books—really are admissions of failure on the part of the library.

All plans should be carefully monitored. When the people who are ultimately responsible for selection use the plans wisely, they can be recommended.

Other Sources of Books

In addition to publishers and jobbers, librarians are likely to spend some money with local book dealers and with book clubs. This is a minimal amount compared to the part of the budget that goes for relatively mass purchases. Business with bookdealers may be significant when: (1) A small library, with a limited amount of money and staff, selects many of its current titles from the local bookstore, or (2) a large library employs a book dealer to secure hard-to-find materials, particularly out-of-print items (see page 173).

[30] Jane Maddox, "Approval Plans—Viable?," *The Journal of Academic Librarianship*, January 1976. Problems with coverage of subject areas and the profile was the most often-named headache librarians encountered with approval plans in the McCullough survey (p. 2).

[31] There are scores of other points pro and con for such plans; see, for example, McCullough, op. cit., pp. 123–146, where librarians and jobbers discuss the various points of disagreement.

BOOK CLUBS

An estimated 7 to 7.5 million Americans are members of book clubs, and many librarians find it advantageous for price, selection, and convenience also to join one of the clubs. The best-known two are the Book-of-the-Month Club and the Literary Guild. The former has an estimated 20 percent average discount and offers a wide variety of both fiction and nonfiction. The Literary Guild's discount is higher, about 30 percent, but concentration is on more popular fiction. Both have bonus plans whereby after a certain number of copies are purchased the customer gets a free book.

Titles, and a way to reject books, are offered each month.

Most of the clubs issue newsletters or bulletins in which the next choices and alternative choices are annotated. Also, most clearly state if there is going to be anything offensive in the books chosen. For example, the Literary Guild noted that Erica Jong's *How to Save Your Own Life* had "explicit sexual details [that] may offend some readers." The practical reason for the warnings: to keep members from complaining and dropping out of the club.

In addition to the well-known giants there are about 150 other adult book clubs, most of which cater to special interests—from cookbooks to mysteries and horses.[32]

Many things might be said about the effects book clubs have on reading tastes, but generally:

[They are] both tastemaker and taste-follower. There are the obvious main choices for the multitudes—the big reads by the big names—and the alternate choices, some of which are daring and surprising. . . . In books outside the main selections and featured alternates [the editorial directors] indulge their personal preferences regardless of potential popularity.[33]

There are distinct problems with many of the clubs, but most offer enough advantages to warrant consideration by smaller to medium-sized libraries. Larger libraries generally find the services not worth the bother.

BOOKSTORES

Book clubs are a major source of books for laypeople, but they are secondary to bookstores. The number of book dealers is increasing each

---

[32] Several of these are evaluated in the September 1977 issue of *Consumer Reports* (pp. 505–513). Among some of the specialists: American Garden Guild, Cook Book Guild, Doubleday Book Club, Military Book Club, Mystery Guild, and Science Book Club—all subsidiaries of Doubleday.

[33] Herbert Mitgang, "More Readers Using Clubs as Bookstores in Mailboxes," *The New York Times*, October 23, 1977, p. 61.

year, and several reports indicate the increase has been close to 50 percent in the past six or seven years.[34]

Other than bookstores and book clubs, the major commercial channels for book distributions are paperback bookstalls in supermarkets, drugstores, and other mass-market outlets. These channels serve more Americans than bookstores. Mass-market paperbacks are available at between 60,000 and 80,000 outlets in the United States.[35]

Given the importance of bookstores to American ways of reading, what part does the library play with the bookstore? This depends. Smaller libraries, particularly in equally small communities, may rely upon the local dealer almost exclusively for the purchase of books. Discounts usually are worked out and the relationship can be helpful to all concerned.[36] Larger libraries look more to antiquarian dealers for out-of-print materials, although they may rely upon a local dealer for regional history, small-press items, and related titles. The library, in fact, may have a standing order with the dealer for all such materials.

Advantages of a library working with a book dealer are many, but Carole Roberts lists some major ones:

(1) The bookseller is often aware, because of publishers' newsletters, etc. which books are to be heavily promoted, which authors will be holding autograph sessions and which books will therefore be in demand. He can order extra copies so that the library can also have the book available at the time of demand. . . .

(2) The books arrive promptly, since the publisher will probably be quicker in filling an order for ten copies from a bookstore (knowing that delaying will likely mean cancellation of the order) than he is in filling a single-copy order from a library. Libraries seldom cancel orders even if there is a delay of several weeks. Thus the readers can have the books without a long wait.

[34] Gordon B. Neavill, "Book Distribution and Marketing in the United States: A Review Article," *Library Quarterly*, January 1977, pp. 62–70, a review of the $450 volume by Benjamin M. Compaine, *Book Distribution and Marketing, 1976–1980* (White Plains, N.Y.: Knowledge Industry Publications, 1976). Actual numbers: 2468 to 3498 bookstores that concentrate on books. Other retail outlets (which may have more greeting cards, for example, than books) total about 12,000. The 3498 general bookstores compare with 2600 college bookstores and 1421 dealing with religious books. Figures from *The Bowker Annual of Library and Book Trade Information*, 22nd ed. (New York: R. R. Bowker, 1977), p. 327. See also Paul Doebler, "Bookstore Growth since 1954," *Publishers Weekly*, September 11, 1978, pp. 40–48.

[35] There are other sources, including discount jobbers who offer high discounts to the laypublic. Several of these (Bookpost, New World Books, Bookquick) are listed in *The New York Times Book Review* "Book Exchange" classified advertisement section each week. Discounts for best sellers are about 30 to 35 percent and drop to 10 percent for technical titles. These are useful for popular titles, but the dealers tend to be more of a headache than a solution for individuals or smaller libraries seeking the out-of-the-way title. Still, most are reliable and, for a person or library buying more than a dozen books a year, well worth the trouble.

[36] Actually, larger bookstores such as Barnes & Noble now regularly offer 10 to 20 percent discount on best sellers for both librarians and the public, and the discounting of these few titles is more the rule than the exception in large chain stores with book outlets where, however, the discount is limited to best sellers.

(3) Probably this should have been first on the list, as it is possibly the most advantageous aspect of bookseller/library co-operation. The librarian can see and handle the book before making the purchase (in most cases) and can make a more accurate assessment of how the book will fit in with the stock requirements of the library than he can do by just reading reviews.[37]

Finally, keep your eye on the sales table in the bookstore. Often a title you could not afford at an earlier date shows up at a much more reasonable price on sale. And this, in turn, leads to another source of savings—remainders.

REMAINDERS

Almost every reader is familiar with the offerings of Marboro and Publishers Central Bureau, two of the largest, certainly the most heavily advertised, remainder firms in America, but there are many more who offer cut-rate books.

Remainders are excess inventories of books that were printed in quantities much larger than their sales potential warranted. They are books that sold poorly due to limited interest or overpricing, or they may be books that have simply run their course at full price and have been or are about to be issued in paperback editions. Remainders also include titles that have become dated or have been replaced by newer publications. Two specific examples of a true remainder are *Grand Ole Opry*, which was originally published at $35.00 and was remaindered for $14.98; and Gore Vidal's *1876*, first published at $10.00, remaindered for $2.98.[38]

The discount rate of many remainders is higher than even the largest jobber or publisher can duplicate. This alone warrants careful consideration of remainder lists.

The difficulty is that most of the legitimate titles have already been purchased by the library. Remainder lists should nevertheless be followed because (1) they are the source of inexpensive duplicates of standard popular titles that may have been worn out through constant use and (2) more likely, the library will find inexpensive titles that, for one reason or another, were not purchased when first published but are now so inexpensive as to warrant consideration.

A useful guide to remainders is offered by Pierian Press in *Best Buys in Print* (since 1978; quarterly). This is a title, author, and series listing of remainder titles. Unfortunately, it has no subject approach. The listing is

---

[37] "Libraries and Bookstores, Mutual Friends," *Expression*, Autumn 1977, pp. 44–45.

[38] Robert McGee, "Remainders, Reprints and Imports," *American Bookseller*, April 1978. The entire issue is devoted to remainders and is an excellent overview of the subject. See also Genevieve Stuttaford, "Bargain Remainders . . . ," *The Village Voice*, December 15, 1975, p. 68.

updated quarterly and is little more than the grouping of offerings by about a dozen large remainder houses.[39]

REMAINDERS AND REPRINTS

Many of the so-called remainder books are actually reprints of standard titles, often under a different publisher's name.[40] The remainder houses in fact publish the reprints, although the unwary buyer may think they are no more than remainders.

Here is how it works:

Let us say that McGraw-Hill published an art book to retail for $24.95. They printed 5000 and only sold 2000, remaindering the rest. The remainderer might buy the book for $4 a copy, with return privileges, and retail it for $9.95. Because of his dynamic sales approach and merchandising savvy, it sold quickly and successfully. In fact, it became obvious that he could sell 50,000 at $9.95. He examined the cost factor of producing the book and discovered that if he made an arrangement with McGraw-Hill, he might buy the rights for $4 a copy. Authors, of course, were excluded from this new arrangement for reprint—no additional royalties.[41]

There are numerous reprints selling as remainders. An example is *Norman Rockwell: Illustrator*. It has been a reprint (on remainder lists) since 1971, and has sold close to a million copies as a so-called remainder. The same procedure may be used for old classics reprinted in a new format and sold as remainders.

A confusing reprint practice is the taking of a book that is in print and subdividing it into different parts, issuing each as a new book. Unless the librarian knows the initial book, it is difficult to relate a part to the original.

If you know remainders, you will probably be familiar with these examples of original promotional publications: *Gray's Anatomy*, Special $7.98; *Tracing Your Roots*, Special $2.98; *50 Norman Rockwell Favorites*, Special $7.98; and *Treasury of Beatrix Potter*, Special $3.98.[42]

The library, of course, probably has all of these as parts of larger, original works.

---

[39] C. Edward Wall, "Budget Stretching: Remainder Books for Libraries," *American Libraries*, June 1978, pp. 367–370. The editor of Pierian Press explains the remainder business and his service.

[40] For a discussion of standard reprints see the sections on out-of-print materials (p. 173) and microform (pp. 201–204).

[41] Dusty Sklar, "Books for a Buck," *Bookviews*, July 1978, p. 29.

[42] McGee, op. cit., p. 5.

Ordering Other Materials

Unlike books one orders through a jobber, most nonprint materials are ordered directly from the distributor, publisher, or producer. There simply is no one jobber for these items, although there are some (such as Brodart) that handle multiple types of nonprint media for school libraries.

Stephen Ford points out that "the librarian can expect that it will cost more to acquire audiovisual than print materials: there will be fewer items per purchase order because there are not many wholesalers supplying them."[43] Another problem: equipment and nonprint materials are usually on separate budgets, separate lines, even under separate departments. And to make it more difficult, kits (which can contain both equipment and media) may sometimes cause terrific administrative problems.

Throughout this text attention is given to the ordering of materials only briefly, with enough discussion to make the individual responsible for selection aware of acquisition problems.

Out of Print

What does the librarian do when a book is needed, but it no longer is available from the publisher because it is out of print?[44] This problem is common to all types and sizes of libraries. The school media center may need an out-of-print reference work, the public library a local history, the special library a report, and the academic library may need the book for a wide variety of reasons. All may need an o.p. title as a duplicate, to replace a missing or stolen item, to put on reserve, to meet the needs of a reader.

There are several answers to the o.p. problem. The traditional approach is to look for the book, periodical, pamphlet, or whatever through an antiquarian (used-book) dealer. As a routine aspect of selection, many librarians regularly visit their local dealer or have correspondence with numerous bookpeople all over the United States and the world. In fact, this is one of the joys of being in selection, of being a librarian. What normally happens when a particular print item is needed is:

1. The librarian knows the type of used-book dealer likely to have or be able to find the required title. The dealer is contacted, given the title or titles, and the librarian waits for a reply—usually from 30 days to years, depending on what agreement is reached. (It is bad form to post the same list with other dealers unless, of course, you have notified them that you

---

[43] Op. cit., p. 132.

[44] A good deal of work with out-of-print materials is a matter of acquisition rather than selection. Once the selection is made, it is customary for the acquisitions section to take over. However, working with book dealers is likely to be shared between selection and acquisition.

are doing so. The reason is that all might suddenly turn up the book, after great effort, and the library could buy only from one. The result would be to alienate the others.)

The success rate of searches differs, but given the average list of o.p. books and the average dealer is likely to come up with 40 to 90 percent of the titles. (The o.p. catch is what is meant by "average list." If this is no more than popular titles only recently out of print, the rate of success will be higher than for, say, nineteenth-century American art books which are both rare and difficult to locate. Actual accomplishment of the dealer depends so much on the type of titles sought that, as one critic points out, it really is not possible to chart a percentage of success.)

There normally is no cost for the service itself, although some dealers charge for a single or a difficult search. Time to find a book is usually three to six weeks.

2. Most antiquarian and used-book dealers issue catalogs. If there is no great rush for the wanted item, many librarians simply scan the catalogs as they come in and order when they find a needed item. The catch here is that if many other people want the book, it may be gone before the order is placed. (Some librarians, of course, use the phone for rush orders, but even then a particularly desirable item may be snapped up before the librarian is able to reach the dealer.) Actually, this system is not often used. The scanning of catalogs is more relaxed mnemonic device because a subject librarian is likely to see a book or other item useful to the collection,[45] and order it—although only after the file is searched to see that the library does not have the book or does not have it on order from another dealer.

Names of dealers are easy enough to find in the *American Book Trade Directory,* and o.p. book and periodicals and serials dealers are regular advertisers in the classified section of such library magazines as *Library Journal* and *American Libraries.* The single best system is to read *AB Bookman's Weekly* (P.O. Box AB, Clifton, N.J. 07015; since 1948). The basic periodical for the antiquarian booktrade, it consists of three parts: (1) Editorial, which reports on everything from auctions and the history of books to matters of concern to dealers. (2) "Books wanted," a listing of books wanted by other dealers and by libraries. (3) A much shorter "Books for sale." The librarian who regularly reads *AB* will never be at a loss to find a dealer for a particular type of wanted item. Any librarian selecting materials should read it as a matter of course; it is a vital link for librarians to the world of books and bookpeople. (An annual listing of o.p. and antiquarian dealers will be found in the *AB Yearbook.*)[46]

A directory of some 750 o.p. dealers can be found in Ruth Robinson *Buy Books Where . . .* (Morgantown, W. Va.: Ruth Robinson Books, 1978)

---

[45] It is also great fun and an education. Fun in that it is always enjoyable to find an item the library can use, particularly at a reasonable price. Education in that any librarian who spends several years scanning antiquarian catalogs is likely to know much more about books in general, and a subject area in particular than at the start.

[46] Another way to advertise for wanted materials is through *The Library Bookseller*

The list is particularly useful because some 2300 collecting specialities are listed, as well as authors on whom the dealers concentrate. To date this is by far the best directory of its type.

3. A more rarefied way to obtain rare items is through the antiquarian book auctions at such well-known houses as Sotheby Parke Bernet, Swann Galleries, and Christie's (all regularly advertise their auctions in *AB*). However, this is primarily for the librarian with a good income, and here it is usual to work through a dealer.

4. The most rewarding approach for librarians is browsing. Some libraries actually finance buying trips for librarians or faculty. In most situations, however, the librarian simply takes time out each week or month to visit the local bookstores and, of course, when on a trip, the bookstores in the area visited.

All of these routes presuppose a librarian with an interest in books and an equal involvement with bookpeople.[47] Unfortunately, this is not always the case, and a serious fault of some librarians is an apparent lack of empathy with their fellows in the antiquarian book trade. (Much the same shortcoming is evident among some librarians in nonprint situations, where they show lack of curiosity about filmmakers, recording artists, and the like.)

5. A favored approach is to order the book on microform. This is done when it is apparent that the o.p. titles will be too costly to replace with a print work, or the o.p. titles simply can't be located by dealer, or there is so little demand for the title that it is considered more economical to order on microform.

Here the librarian would search the various bibliographies and lists (see page 208), as well as the individual catalogs issued by microform publishers, such as *Books on Demand* (see page 208). If what is needed can't be located in this fashion, the next step may be the *National Register of Microform Masters* or *Directory of Library Reprographic Services*.

For a title cannot be found in these sources, a search will be made by University Microfilms (publishers of *Books on Demand*). Fees differ, but if they do locate what is needed they make a master microfilm copy and then either send the library a microform or a printout as requested.

There are both advantages and disadvantages of buying o.p. books on microform. The advantage of the microform—at least the microform printed out as a book—is that the printout is on paper likely to outlast regular book paper. Second, of course, is that the book may be had almost immediately and no search of o.p. dealer stocks is necessary. The disadvantages:

1. *Price*. While it is difficult to prove or even be consistent, much depending upon individual titles, experienced librarians tend to find that an o.p. title, once located, may be considerably less costly than the microform

[47] This is stressed in two excellent articles on o.p. materials: Felix Reichmann, "Purchase of Out-of-Print Materials in American University Libraries," *Library Trends*, January 1970, pp. 342ff, and Ernest R. Perez, "Acquisition of Out-of-Print Materials," *Library Resources and Technical Services*, Winter 1973, pp. 40–59. A good overview of antiquarian and rare books is offered by Jean Peters (ed.), *Book Collecting* (New York: R. R. Bowker, 1977).

printout. For example, the 1978 cost per page of a title from *Books on Demand* was twelve cents and binding charges another $5 per volume.

2. *Quality of reproduction.* While the type reproductions are passable, the reproductions of photographs and other illustrations are not always acceptable. (A new process is supposed to solve this problem).

In general, then, if an o.p. title can be found without undue difficulty and is not a rare or near-rare book, it is a much better "buy" than microform for most libraries. And, in any case, unless there is a tremendous rush for the materials, the o.p. market, not reprint and microform publishers, should be the beginning place for searches.

6. Reprints offer another solution, although a poor one in that many reprints are listed in *Books in Print*, a first place to search for o.p. titles. If the librarian does not find the title listed there, it is likely not to be available as a reprint anywhere else. However, a second place to check is *Guide to Reprints* (since 1967; annual), which lists books, journals and other materials issued in reprint form. This, however, is primarily of value for journals.

The International Bibliography of Reprints (New York: R. R. Bowker) is updated every two or three years. The edition for 1976–1978 includes both books and serials, with most emphasis on serials. Originally published in Germany, the guide is of limited use to most U.S. libraries since the focus is on foreign-language titles and the cutoff date is 1974.

One fascinating aspect of reprints is that they are rarely if ever reviewed. An occasional note or review is found in the library-oriented journals, but only when the reprint includes some new introductory material or is of such importance as to warrant special mention. *Choice* does tend to review a few outstanding reprints, but is not consistent.

When a decision is made to purchase a reprint, the price should be compared with a used (or rare) original. Sometimes the reprint is, literally, many times more expensive than the same original title from an antiquarian bookperson. In this case, it may pay to wait until the original is available.

The actual pricing of antiquarian books is a matter of experience—knowing whether or not the price asked is at least near the fair market price. Equally it is a matter of knowing dealers. For example, any experienced bookperson will tell the novice that the price of a title from Quaritch in London is likely to be higher than the same titles purchased from the Phoenix Book Shop in New York. (*Likely* needs to be stressed; this is not always the case, and much depends on the particular title.) The librarian should also check the price against the such standard works as *American Book Prices Current* and *Bookman's Price Index*.

7. Through gifts and exchanges (see p. 176) it may be possible to turn up the missing title(s). In fact, many libraries regularly put out want lists on the gift-and-exchange circuit.[48]

[48] The Universal Serials and Books Exchange (formerly the United States Book Exchange) is a nonprofit clearing house for duplicate serials and books. They usually have some 100,000 books and 3 to 4 million issues of some 35,000 periodicals and serials. Member libraries pay a fee and so much per item purchased, usually about $6.

WHY O.P.?

There are two further aspects of out-of-print titles worth consideration:

1. Is the title really o.p.? Jobbers and even *Books in Print* (by omission) may report to a library that a title is no longer available. On other occasions the publisher will respond "o.p." but a jobber may still have many copies in stock. Again, sale tables or general stock in your local bookstore may yield an elusive volume.

When the publisher is queried as many as half a dozen may still be available, while others are simply in another edition or binding. The librarian should double-check so-called o.p. titles.[49]

2. If it is o.p., why did the publisher let it go out of print? Lack of sales is the best reason, but the o.p. signal goes up quite fast—too fast for many libraries. One study found "both in Britain and the United States, that after ten years less than half the original publication is recorded as remaining in print." The author then poses a question:

One has no way of knowing whether those which remain in print as original editions are the duds which the publishers cannot sell or whether they are best sellers which the publisher reprints frequently, but one is inclined to suspect that it is the former and that enterprising publishers will ensure that there is always a new edition of a best seller to hand.[50]

[49] For a report on one study of o.p. see *The Unabashed Librarian*, no. 18 (1976), p. 14.
[50] R. Moss, "Book Obsolescence," *New Library World*, July 1978, pp. 130–131.

8
Periodicals

No PRINT FORM except the book is as important in most libraries as the periodical. In large research or special libraries, 80 to 90 percent of the holdings may be devoted to periodicals.

The form is important because: (1) Periodicals are the source of current material that often cannot be found in any other place. (2) Periodicals are the source publication for new theories, discoveries, trends, and viewpoints that do not appear in books for many months or years later, if at all. (3) The magazine is good for ephemeral information, from how-to-do-it articles to personality sketches.[1]

Three out of four Americans buy a magazine in the course of a year. The reasons for purchase parallel those for library use—28 percent read for entertainment, 27 percent for information and about 45 percent combine a search for entertainment and information.[2]

Types of Periodical

Of the some 60,000 current selected titles listed in *Ulrich's International Periodical Directory*, probably close to 55,000 constitute what may be called specialized titles, periodicals edited for (and often by) a narrow-interest audience—from scientists to businesspeople to zookeepers. The readership will be limited to those actually involved in the specialized field. The majority of such periodicals are supported by subscriptions or a sponsoring organization. A good example of the latter is *American Libraries*, issued by the American Library Association and of interest only to librarians and those closely connected with the operation of libraries. Others range

majority of periodicals are

---

[1] In policy statements librarians often note that periodicals are also purchased "to provide aids for the professional staff in selection of materials and for professional reading."

[2] "Why and How People Buy Magazines," *Folio*, February 1977, pp. 80ff.

from the *American Journal of Physics* and the *American Bar Association Journal* to the *Transactions of the Czechoslovakian Mathematical Society*.

Often considered part of the specialized periodical circle is the scholarly or scientific periodical. The latter group is by far the most numerous, with some estimates running as high as 50,000 titles. Further subdivisions may be made of government periodicals (both federal and state), which run into the thousands.

At the other extreme is the general magazine, the one likely to be encountered on the newsstand and indexed by *Readers' Guide to Periodical Literature*, *Access*, and *Popular Periodicals Index*. Here, of course, special interests are considered, but the emphasis is more on recreation and bits of useful information than on scholarship, yet they are often the major sources on current social and political issues, since the scholarly journals rarely emphasize contemporary analysis. Perhaps a better term is "consumer magazine," because the primary source of support is advertising, and the editorial material backs up the advertisers. The Standard Rate and Data Service has 51 subject classifications for this type of magazine, with a spread from airline in-flight titles through crafts and hobbies, television and radio to youth.³ᐟ Some 2000 of these are published throughout the world, although if one stretches the category to include some more popular business, trade, and scientific titles the actual number is nearer 5000 to 6000.

The number of titles with over 500,000 circulation is much less—probably no more than 100 or 120—and it is with these that Americans are familiar. Whether it is *American Home* or *Bride's Magazine* or *Rolling Stone* or *Time*, the average consumer title differs from the average specialized journal, which concentrates on a narrow field of interest by and for experts in one field.

Between the special and the general is the business, trade, technology, and house organ. Actually, some librarians consider these specialized, but sometimes they are grouped separately and probably include from 10,000 to 20,000 titles. The Standard Rate and Data Service also has a special monthly publication for business titles with nearly 160 subject entries. These include such topics as tobacco, ports, nut culture, manufacturing, pets—in fact, just about any area where there is likely to be a business involved.

Another category is the little magazine, which concentrates on literature, politics, or both and is outside the mainstream. This type has a small circulation, normally is subsidized by the publisher and government grants, and includes about 2000 titles in America alone.

There are, of course, other ways to categorize periodicals: by readership, advertising or lack of advertising, circulation, type of subscription schedule, sponsoring organization, and so on.

Public and school libraries tend to concentrate on the general, consumer title. Academic libraries draw more heavily from the scientific and scholarly

³ *Consumer Magazine and Farm Publication Rates and Data* (Skokie, Ill.: Standard Rate and Data; monthly). The service is used primarily by advertisers.

group, and special libraries focus on titles of direct specialized interest to users.

In terms of selection, it is necessary to be able to categorize (if only generally) various types of periodicals in order to work out the formula that title type X will interest reader type Y. For example, a general commercial title (X) will appeal to males under thirty (Y), whereas a specialized title may appeal only to plumbers over fifty. The categorization is really not difficult most of the time; even a cursory glance at the contributors, editorial policy, and publisher will tell the librarian what type the periodical is.

SERIALS

Experienced librarians frequently refer to "periodicals" and "serials" in the same breath. There is a game of sorts in which the effort is made to define both terms, but they defy totally objective definition. For most purposes:

Serial is an umbrella term for any publication issued in parts, with a numerical or chronological designation, and usually published over an indefinite period of time. There are three or four primary types of serials. One type is the periodical and the newspaper. A second is the continuation, or series . . . a third type is what is really a separate division—the government document that may or may not be a serial but is likely to be one. Finally, sets in progress may be considered serials when they are to be published over a long period of time.[4]

In this chapter the focus is on the periodical, with a glance at newspapers. Government documents and other types of serial are important in selection, but present so many distinct problems that they are studies in themselves, particularly government documents.[5]

Another type of serial, proceedings and transactions, may be annual or a continuation, or may be issued as irregular serials. As publications, they represent the material delivered at a meeting and are usually made up of papers and discussion topics. Such titles as "Transactions of the Institute of Mining Engineers" or "Proceedings of the Section for Linguistics and Literature of the Hungarian Academy of Sciences" are representative. These are important in selection because they may constitute as much as 25 percent or more of the content of a specialized scientific library. Others in this area would include reports, minutes of international congresses, bulletins, newsletters, business services, memoirs, and the like. Each has its distinctive selection problem.[6]

[4] William Katz and Peter Gellatly, *Guide to Magazine and Serial Agents* (New York: R. R. Bowker, 1975), p. 4. For a longer definition, read on in this chapter. See also a more detailed study: Doris M. Carson, "What Is a Serial Publication?," *The Journal of Academic Librarianship*, September 1977, pp. 206–209.

[5] The standard text for government documents is Joe Morehead, *Introduction to United States Public Documents* (2nd ed.; Littleton, Colo.: Libraries Unlimited, 1978).

[6] Various forms of serial are discussed in Katz and Gellatly and in Andrew Osborn's *Serial Publications* (2nd ed.; Chicago: American Library Association, 1973).

HOW MANY?

The expansion in the number of periodicals over the past two decades has equaled that of the book and other materials, and no one can be quite certain how many journals are currently being published in the United States or worldwide.[7] As already noted, the latest edition of *Ulrich's International Periodicals Directory* lists some 60,000; a beginning collection of 36,000 serial titles is envisioned for the proposed National Periodicals Center (see page 192). Researchers believe that about 6000 journals cover original research; 1500 to 2000 is the figure given for general-interest magazines in the world, and some estimate the grand total of all types to run as high as 100,000 to 200,000.

The gross number is of little real concern to either the user or the librarian. Collections vary with the size of the library and may range from as few as a dozen titles to 50,000 or more in large research libraries. As a result of escalating periodical prices and less money for acquisitions, the emphasis is not on casting a net to take in all the journals but on formulas that will allow the library to function with a minimal number of essential titles.

The highly selective approach is satisfactory to users so long as they can consistently find the majority of titles they use (or are in much-employed indexes and abstracting services) in the library. Most people are willing to wait a few days to secure articles from lesser-used titles through interlibrary loans, from private organizations, or eventually from a National Periodicals Center.

By Type of Library

Some of the standards and guidelines hint at what constitutes the average-size collection of periodicals for a library.

PUBLIC LIBRARIES

While dated, the guidelines for public library systems give a relative notion of the quantitative standards for periodicals: "At least one currently published periodical title should be available for each 250 people in the service area."[8] A mid-1970s survey shows large public libraries have holdings from 1000 to 1999 titles, medium to large 300 to 399, and small under 19.[9]

In terms of selection advice, the standards call for the headquarters library to receive all current titles indexed in *Readers' Guide to Periodical Liter-*

---

[7] Authors give various estimates as to the number of serials, but a good approach is suggested by Henry Drennan's "The Numbers of Serials," *The Serials Librarian*, Spring 1977, pp. 215–219.

[8] *Minimum Standards for Public Library Systems* (Chicago; American Library Association, 1967), p. 43. The new guidelines do not offer quantitative assistance.

[9] William A. Katz, *Guide to Magazine and Serial Agents* (New York: R. R. Bowker, 1975), p. 182.

ature "and the most frequently requested items indexed in other indexing services," but, selection is not to be limited only to indexed titles.

A more detailed explanation of typical public library collections and how they are selected will be found in Chapter 9, "Selection as Practiced," in the author's *Magazine Selection* (New York: R. R. Bowker, 1971).

ACADEMIC LIBRARIES

The "Standards for College Libraries" offer no quantitative assistance for periodical selection. The "Guidelines for Two-Year College Learning Resource Programs" are no more specific. Both, of course, do call for periodical and newspaper collections, the college library guidelines noting that "The journal has become the common medium for scientific communication and usually represents more recent information."[10]

The author's mid-1970 survey found that university libraries average from 2000 to 4000 titles, college libraries average 700 to 799 titles, and two-year colleges have from 400 to 499 titles.[11] However, among the large research libraries the collections usually begin at 6000 to 7000 titles and go 60,000 (Yale), 65,000 (Columbia), or more than 100,000 (Harvard). Given these gigantic collections, it is understandable why from 30 to 45 percent or even more of the academic acquisitions budget may be for serials.

SCHOOL LIBRARIES

The guidelines call for a minimum of 50 to 175 periodicals and newspapers in a library with 500 or fewer users. Where there are more students the requirement is enough titles to meet the "access to research capabilities" of the audience serviced.

An important provision of the standards is that purchased titles need not necessarily be indexed. Also, duplicate titles are purchased for heavy demand.[12]

WHO SELECTS?

The procedure employed for selection of periodicals is much the same as for books and other materials. The primary responsibility is that of the librarian, but opinions from users and experts is welcomed.

About half the larger academic and research libraries have serials departments, sections, or divisions, and actual selection may or may not be made by the head of the section. In most small to medium-sized libraries, serials work usually is the direct responsibility of the person in charge of acqui-

[10] "Standards for College Libraries," *College and Research Libraries News*, October 1975, p. 278.

[11] Katz, op. cit., p. 182.

[12] *Media Programs: District and School* (Chicago: American Library Association, 1975), p. 71. In the mid-1970s the average number of titles for a school system was between 200 and 300.

sitions and technical services. In libraries in which the number of titles is between 300 and 400, a part-time clerk usually takes care of the routine record keeping. Where there are over 400 titles, a professional librarian will be in charge, usually assisted by a clerk. Anything over 1000 titles warrants a separate serials unit.

There are various approaches to actual periodicals selection, but in general: (1) The book selection committee, where it exists, takes part in the selection of periodicals, normally at intervals of several months. (2) The serials librarian, if there is one, may advise, but actually selects only about half the time. (3) In academic and school libraries, the faculty may assist formally (as member of a selection committee) or, more likely, informally (by giving advice to the librarians). (4) In many situations the librarian or the subject-division heads make suggestions that are passed on for ordering without a meeting.[13]

Various plans have been suggested to make the selection of serials and periodicals more systematic. Generally emphasis is put on informal advice from the public rather than having the public on formal committees. It is rare to have a serials selection committee.[14]

In large and academic libraries selection may be left to divisions and departments, at least initially. This situation exists only where the library has budget allocations.[15]

When it comes to regular evaluation of the periodicals collection, and, more especially, the need to weed out titles, the responsibility should be assumed by the librarian (although, ideally, always with help from users).

Librarians rarely view the weeding process as the ongoing task it must be. And a collective effort of professional librarians oriented to the necessity of careful justification for serial commitments will themselves become the obvious source of personnel to undertake a title by title evaluation as required.[16]

Evaluation

A concise rationale for evaluation of periodicals is found in the selection policy of Texas A&M University Library System:

[13] Geraldine Wright, "Current Trends in Periodical Collection," *College and Research Libraries*, May 1977, p. 235. In 147 moderate-sized academic libraries "Faculty participate in the selection process in 95 percent of the libraries; students . . . play an active role in only 9 percent of the libraries; serials librarians select new titles in 58 percent of the libraries."

[14] Jane E. Fowler, "Managing Periodicals by Committee," *Journal of Academic Librarianship*, November 1976, pp. 230–234. It was found that the library director makes the final decision on subscriptions at college libraries but that most suggestions for new titles come from faculty and libarians. See also Nancy Buckeye, "In the Library Serials Committee," *Serials Review*, July-September 1975, pp. 5–7.

[15] Ibid., p. 233. A survey of 27 college libraries found that about half had subscription allocations by department.

[16] Buckeye, op. cit., p. 6.

The multiplicity of new serial titles, the potential obligation to maintain a serial title in perpetuity, escalating costs of serials, cost of binding, and maintenance and storage costs make a high degree of selectivity mandatory.[17]

What rules, then, should the librarian follow in evaluating a periodical? One beginning to evaluation is to quantify. Here the librarian (and committee of experts) should ask: (1) Is the title absolutely necessary to have in the library? (2) Is it highly desirable to have in the library? (3) Is it simply not necessary?[18]

To reach one of these four decisions requires an understanding of the intrinsic worth of the title and how it fits—or does not fit—into the library collection.

INTRINSIC EVALUATION

The periodical itself must be evaluated first. The evaluation principles are much the same as for other materials:

 1. Purpose, scope, and audience for the periodical are of first concern. These should be obvious from a glance at the table of contents, the type of writers, and the contributions.

2. One must judge content as one would a book: (a) Accuracy and relative objectivity of the content within the stated purpose and scope. (b) Reputation of the publisher and the writers. (c) Quality of the writing and its suitability for the intended audience. (d) Subject matter and its relevance for the intended audience.

3. Reference or research value is often given as a criterion for selection, although it is difficult to be more precise because almost any magazine has some research or reference value. Still, there is a core (from *Harper's Monthly* to *Scientific American*) that does have general reference value in that they are widely indexed.

4. Often a title of less than impressive quality is purchased when it is of local interest. This may be a periodical published about the community, or even a general title published locally. Particularly recommended for consideration are local history, genealogy, and little magazines.

5. Standard format items should be checked: quality of paper and printing, illustrations, special features, and the like. Advertising, too, may be a headache—there may be more ads than copy.

6. A magazine should not be rejected for a particular article, editorial stand, or illustration. All points of view (as with books and other materials) should be represented. Nor should a magazine be turned down on the basis of a single issue.

[17] Elizabeth Futas, *Library Acquisition Policies and Procedures* (Phoenix, Ariz.: Oryx Press, 1977), p. 244.

[18] Fowler, op. cit., p. 232. Each department of a college library was supplied with a form that asked the four questions (which also are applicable in other situations).

SELECTION

Beyond the intrinsic value of the periodical, the librarian must consider selection principles. The selection decision is based on what is indexed, what is requested, and what is found in approved lists. Most librarians also touch other selection bases. A periodical may pass all tests for intrinsic quality, yet not be selected if it fails to meet any of these tests.

(1.) Many librarians buy only what is indexed or abstracted in a few services, particularly those published by The H. W. Wilson Company, beginning with *Readers' Guide to Periodical Literature*. This is hardly sophisticated, but if the periodical collection does not exceed 200 or 300 titles (an average for most small to medium-sized libraries of any type) the index approach is adequate, if a bit primitive.[19]

The decision to purchase only indexed periodicals is based on the notion that most, if not all, periodicals selected by a library are for research and hence need to be indexed. This is hardly true. The indexing test bars new periodicals—and thus new ideas—that are not considered by the indexing publisher. What happens, in effect, is that actual selection is made by an indexing firm, not by the library. Many periodicals have their own annual indexes—of widely varying detail and quality.

Library leaders concede the basic error of the indexing test. Where periodicals are mentioned in the standards, there normally is a warning: "Magazines and newspapers that contribute to the satisfaction of user needs are considered for acquisition although they may not be indexed."[20] The presence of a periodical in an index or abstracting service is useful. However, it should only be one test—not the beginning and end-all of selection.

(2.) Generally, the periodical collection should support the book collection; it will include approximately the same type and balance of subject matter as accepted by books and other media. As one librarian put it: "Since the library operates on . . . limited periodical funds, it must in its selection of periodicals as in its selection of books emphasize standard materials and services of first importance in the broad pattern of operation."[21]

(3.) Cost must be weighed, particularly in terms of the potential use of the periodical. If likely to be little used and the price is above average, it should not be purchased.[22]

[19] Futas, op. cit., p. 18. Inevitably where a library has a periodical-selection policy statement, it is related to what is indexed. A typical public library policy stated: "All periodicals indexed in *Readers' Guide* . . . are acquired. Indexing in any of the other periodical indexes received by the library is the most important criterion for the addition of other periodicals."

[20] *Media Programs: District and School* (Chicago: American Library Association, 1975), p. 71.

[21] Futas, op. cit., p. 78. This is a public library.

[22] Cost is a major consideration, and can be charted in numerous articles, particularly the annual price indexes in *Library Journal*, plus the three-year comparative studies that appear each year in the fall. See also Frank Clasquin's "Financial Management of Serials

Between 1970 and 1975 alone the price of serials almost doubled, and the same trend is expected for the last five years of the decade. In 1977 the average price of an American periodical was $22.52, with titles in chemistry and physics at almost $100. Price is by far the most important consideration governing periodical selection today, and is discussed later in this section.

(4.) Appearance of the title in special bibliographies and lists is of help. Some of the lists are considered later in this section.

(5) Scarcity of material on the subject will dictate consideration, particularly if it is a subject in heavy demand by users.

(6) Demand, as for books and other materials, must be given serious consideration. If a user takes the time and effort to ask for a particular periodical, the librarian should give special consideration to its purchase. Where the title is not purchased, a substitute should be suggested, especially if it is in the area of general reading and recreation.

(7) The availability of the periodical (in the form of articles from the periodical) on interlibrary loan must be considered. If the title is readily available from other libraries and is little used, it need not be purchased.

8. There are selective rules for special situations: (a) Foreign-language areas in the community or the curriculum of the school or academic center requires supporting titles. (b) Large-print titles should be selected for readers with partial vision.

9. Except for special situations, most libraries do not purchase duplicates unless the title is heavily used and one or more extra copies are kept for later binding or for circulation.[23]

10. Back files. For the most part, libraries purchase missing back files of periodicals only on microform. Cost and storage problems of hardbound copies (when available) make microform preferable.

An examination of selection policy statements, articles, and discussions with librarians demonstrate that these tests are often modified. Jane Fowler found that the most important factors in *selection* were: relation to curriculum, 12 libraries; need, 10 libraries; faculty priorities, 8; available nearby, 7; indexed, 6; faculty research interest, 4; good reviews, 3; new faculty or new courses, 3; cost, 3; and nine more reasons of lesser importance.

BEST-SELLING MAGAZINES

Just as there are best sellers among books, so there are among magazines— and so the librarian has the same decisions to make. For example, if *Reader's Digest* and *TV Guide* top the list of favorites, should the librarian purchase?

---

and Journals through Subject Core Lists," *The Serials Librarian*, Spring 1978, pp. 287–297; Richard De Gennaro, "Escalating Journal Prices: Time to Fight Back," *American Libraries*, February 1977, pp. 69–74; and William H. Huff, "The Periodical Collection in Times of Tight Budgets," *Illinois Libraries*, February 1978, pp. 98–100.

[23] The cost squeeze is working more and more against duplicates. See Peter Gellatly, "Cancelling Duplicate Serials . . . ," *The Serials Librarian*, Summer 1977, pp. 399–402.

Today most librarians (including this author) would say yes because they are popular, because they are best sellers. The real difficulty comes when one has to consider almost equally heavily read titles such as comic magazines (which constitute a major readership category, topped only by a few individual titles), *Playboy*, *Penthouse*, *National Enquirer*, *Modern Romance*, and so on.

Actually, it need not be a problem. Most communities are conservative to middle-of-the-road enough not to want the girlie and gossip magazines in their school or public libraries. The librarian should ascertain whether this is the case. If it is not and if there really is popular demand for, say, *Playboy*, it should be purchased.

Most of these titles pass selection requirements of large academic and research libraries because they are representative of popular culture, a topic for many universities, and must be purchased for research—as well, of course, for some just-passable editorial material.

Any heavily read title should be given consideration, no matter what its editorial content. It should be accepted or rejected on community need. For example, comic magazines are now used for poor readers—and even for good readers in school and public libraries.[24] There is no nonsense about trying to justify their editorial content, only the recognition that they do help the beginning or poor reader by attracting attention. There is no reason the *National Enquirer* or *Playboy* or whatever cannot be used in the same manner.

Collection Development

Between budget cuts and serial price increases of 80 to 200 percent over a decade, the primary attention of larger and special libraries in the late 1970s has been how to maintain a viable serials collection. This is a pressing concern in science and technology collections, where serials are the major resource.[25]

Libraries have handled the crisis in numerous ways, the most common being the shifting of funds from books and other materials to serials. Ac-

[24] Laurel F. Goodgion, "Comics in the Children's Room," *School Library Journal*, January 1977, pp. 37–39. This includes a justification and explanation for the use of comics as well as complete information on ordering.

[25] There are numerous articles in this field. Representative is Christine Bolgiano and Mary King, "Profiling a Periodicals Collection," *College and Research Libraries*, March 1978, pp. 99–104. Evaluative methods are outlined to check the scope, quality, accessibility and usefulness of a collection in a university library. Evelyn McDaniel's "The Use of Periodicals in Blount County Library" (*Tennessee Librarian*, Fall 1977, pp. 17–27) gives results of a study of a small public library. A good general article is Nancy Buckeye's "Evaluating Periodical Collections," *The Idaho Librarian*, October 1977, pp. 163–165. For a specialized situation see Marilyn Williamson, "Serial Evaluation at the Georgia Institute of Technology Library," *The Serials Librarian*, Winter 1977, pp. 181–191.

cording to some reports, research libraries spent twice as much for books as for serials in the late 1960s, but by the late 1970s there had been a reversal.

WHO READS WHAT?

Since there is a limit to the periodicals budget, the librarian is faced with a simple decision: (1) Periodical titles that are not used, or used only occasionally, must go. (2) New titles that may be used extensively must be added. The solution: (1) Establish a core list of titles to which the library must subscribe. (2) Work out methods of adding new titles as necessary.

How the librarian ascertains what to purchase and what to cut depends upon both general and specific considerations. Generally, librarians consider these factors:

1. The cost of starting (and canceling) a subscription is substantial, so much so that it sometimes is more economical to continue with the subscription.

2. Back issues of serials are difficult or impossible to locate. It is therefore better to temporarily cut the budget for books because these may be more easily obtained when money is once more available (and they tend to stay in print much longer than a single issue of a journal). In most cases, of course, it is possible to secure single-issue microform copies.

3. Serials are of more importance than other materials in certain disciplines, particularly technology and the sciences. Where the audience dictates, the serials must be maintained even at the expense of books.

SPECIFIC EVALUATIVE STEPS

A variety of methods may be employed to determine the specific titles in a journal collection. Among those favored:

1. A journal-use study Here the library, through a variety of means, checks which journals are used in the library, which are checked out, what is frequently photocopied, and which are requested on interlibrary loan. The difficulty is that a use study measures only the journals available in the library, not the entire journal literature of value to a patron.[26]

2. Circulation statistics Here there is a measure of how often the journal circulated in the past three or four years, as well as how often it is used in the library itself. This, of course, is little more than a variation or a part of the use study.

Since most journals do not circulate (or if they do no record is kept), some librarians have developed ingenious methods of circulation count. For ex-

[26] There are hundreds of use studies. Typical is Dianne Langlois and Jeanne Von Schultz, "Journal Usage Survey," *Special Libraries*, May-June 1973, pp. 239–244.

ample, one technique distinguishes used from unused titles among bound volumes:

The study is restricted to bound journal volumes that users are encouraged not to reshelve. The use data are generated by applying a small pressure-sensitive label to the spine of a bound volume the first time it is reshelved by library personnel after the study is initiated. This tag indicates that one volume of the periodical title was used at least once during the study period. These data are collected periodically during progressively expanding time periods. For each title, the total number of bound volumes, the number of used volumes, and current date are recorded. Thus, for each title, the fraction of volumes used during any time period can be calculated. This calculation may be made for individual titles, groups of related titles, and/or the entire collection. In the latter case, data collection is quite simple, since only the total number of volumes and volumes used must be counted. The fraction of bound volumes used in a selected time period serves as a simple measure of the relative utility of the collection.[27]

3. Citation studies This is much favored, and is essentially no more than counting how often an article (or journal or author) is cited in other journals. The assumption is that a core list of journals may be established from citation counts because:

1. The value of a periodical to a professional worker is in direct proportion to the number of times it is cited in the professional literature.
2. The journal or journals used as the base for the tabulation are representative of the entire field.[28]

Citation studies are useful in a general way because they normally provide a list of periodicals ranked in order of use. With modifications, the list can be used as a jumping-off place for selection, at least in a subject area.[29]

The problem with citation studies is that the journal most often cited may be so cited because: (1) it is published more frequently than other titles; (2) it is well known to the writers and readers; (3) it is cited because it is more available; (4) it is indexed in one or more major indexing or abstracting services. Other journals may be used as much, if not more, but do not appear in the citation studies because they are scanned for current awareness but not frequently cited.

There are other reasons that seriously qualify citation studies and make

[27] Karen Brewer, et al., "A Method of Cooperative Serials Selection . . . ," *The Journal of Academic Librarianship*, September 1978, p. 206.

[28] K. Subramanyam, "Criteria for Journal Selection," *Special Libraries*, August 1975, p. 366. Representation of the "entire field" does come close in the annual citation counts made by the publisher of *Science Citation Index, Journal Citation Reports* (Philadelphia: Institute for Scientific Information, since 1973).

[29] For example, see the lists of journals for economics and political science in Robert Goehlet's "Periodical Use in an Academic Library: A Study of Economists and Political Scientists," *Special Libraries*, February 1978, pp. 51–60. For a citation study of information science journals, see Andrew Pope, "Bradford's Law and the Periodical Literature of Information Science," *Journal of the American Society for Information Science*, July-August 1975, pp. 207–213.

one suspect that many factors other than quality account for frequent citations.[30] In fact, few librarians use a citation study alone, although most rely upon them as directives in collection development.[31] They may be corrected by the other evaluative methods.

4. Comparative techniques The collection is compared with similar collections in similar librarians or with citation studies.

5. Interlibrary loan data This is checked to see from which periodicals articles are most often requested. The same data show the availability of low-use journals.

6. Questionnaires Questionnaires are employed to ask users what they cannot find but think they need (both by specific title and by subject) and their reaction to journals being considered for cancellation or for purchase.

7. Recommendations This may be one of the more satisfactory and easy techniques: the librarian simply asks other librarians, subject experts, and anyone who uses a certain subject area which titles they recommend. One comparative study found that "librarians did as well as citation count" in predicting the most-used titles. At least this was the case when the librarians "were familiar with the test journals."[32]

8. Circulation Circulation in itself is no guarantee of quality (as noted, the two most popular magazines in America are *Reader's Digest* and *TV Guide*). However, in subject and professional fields it at least suggests the title most likely to be read, and there is almost always a correlation between circulation and the findings of evaluative studies.

Another indicator of high usage was the number of subscriptions to the journal. One might expect that journals having a large number of subscriptions would not be in great demand in a library since users would be more likely to have their own copies. The findings, however, indicated the opposite, i.e., journals which were highly subscribed to were more likely to be the ones frequently used in libraries.[33]

[30] Pauline Scales, "Citation Analysis as Indicators of the Use of Serials . . . ," *Journal of Documentation*, March 1976, pp. 17–25. A well-documented refutation of citation studies.

[31] Maurice Line and Alexander Sandison, "Practical Interpretation of Citation and Library Use Studies," *College and Research Libraries*, September 1975, pp. 393–396. A clear explanation of the use of citation studies and their limitations. See also Sandison' "Reference/Citations in the Study of Knowledge," *Journal of Documentation*, September 1975, pp. 195–198.

[32] Elizabeth Pan, "Journal Citation as a Predictor of Journal Usage in Libraries," *Collection Management*, Spring 1978, p. 33.

[33] Ibid., p. 32.

9. Number of articles Oddly enough, there seems to be a correlation between value and the number of articles in a journal. Elizabeth Pan discovered that

the total number of articles published in a journal during a specified period of time is just as accurate an indicator of potential usage as its citation count. A simple but possible explanation for the finding is that journals which contain more articles have a greater probability of being used. Note that the number of articles is not the same as the number of pages. Everything else being equal, and given the same total number of pages, a journal with brief articles is more likely to be used than one with long articles. This finding, intriguing though it may be, needs to be further tested before it should be accepted.[34]

All these tests and methods are used to check on one another, particularly as the task of building a core periodical list becomes more complex. In small to medium-sized libraries, one suspects the same results might be achieved, as Pan suggests, by an experienced librarian's recommendations.

Given the core collection, no matter how tentative, the next step is to add or to delete titles. In these days of tight budgets, the primary decision is going to be to weed.

THE WEEDING RESPONSE

Once it is determined what is little used, the library first cancels as many duplicate subscriptions as possible and then little-used titles and those easily locally available on interlibrary loan. The latter move, of course, requires close cooperation between libraries.[35] Less frequent methods: (1) For every new title ordered an old one must be canceled, usually in the same subject area. (2) The no-growth situation is magnified by holding the number of serials down to a certain budgetary amount, canceling when rising costs go over that figure. (3) Where tear sheets or reprints are readily available for specific articles (as from the Institute for Scientific Information) the signal may go out to cancel.

Networks and Selection

The bottleneck to most research with periodicals is that while citations are easy enough to locate (either manually or through computerized bibliographical data bases), it is another thing to find the actual article. The periodical may be in the library, but in name only—it has been stolen or mutilated. Or it just may not be shelved properly, or is being used else-

---

[34] Ibid.

[35] Some libraries now have special committees to review cancellations and new orders to see all members within the group of libraries are aware of what is being ordered or killed. Meetings of such committees can be painful and vociferous, particularly when there is disagreement over which of the libraries is to cancel or order a serial.

where, or. . . . Rather than begin a major search, most librarians solve the problem by asking for the article on interlibrary loan. The National Periodicals Center would speed this up considerably, particularly when an article was requested from a hard-to-find periodical.

At this writing there is a plan to develop a National Periodicals Center, a key link in a proposed national network of periodical service. The primary objectives of the Center are:

1. To provide a reliable method of access to a comprehensive collection of periodical literature (originally about 36,000 titles, to increase to 60,000).

2. To reduce the overall costs of acquiring periodical materials by interlibrary loan. (It is envisioned that requests for material will be sent to the Center from individual libraries and systems.)

3. To reduce the time required to obtain requested material.[36]

What this means is that by means of an extended interlibrary-loan service the user in any part of the country will be able to locate an article in almost any periodical and have it within 24 hours or less. Inexpensive telefacsimile, use of the cathode ray tube (television screen), and similar media may make for almost instant response. There are problems, not to mention cost, but eventually this type of center will have a strong influence on periodical selection and weeding.

Meanwhile, the standard interlibrary arrangements do much to shade selection policy, as do, of course such ongoing plans as CONSER (Cooperative Conversion of Serials project), which will be a vital link in a national and international serials data base.[37]

All of these networks and interlibrary-loan plans are a method of distributing the burden of selection and acquisition of periodicals, but there are other methods. A favored one is the cooperative or consortium. Here a number of libraries, usually in a single region, share collections as well as experience and contribute to or establish union lists of holdings. These range from the Research Libraries Group (Harvard, Yale, Columbia, and the New York Public Library) to a number of public, college, school, or even special libraries in a region or urban center.[38]

---

[36] Council on Library Resources, *A National Periodicals Center* . . . (Washington D.C.: The Council, 1978), p. x. There are seven other objectives, less related to selection. For a summary of the project see Nancy Gwinn, "A National Periodicals Center," *Library Journal*, November 1, 1978, pp. 2166–2169.

[37] There are numerous articles on CONSER, but a good overview is suggested by Glen R. Witting, "CONSER . . . ," *UNESCO Bulletin for Libraries*, September–October 197 pp. 305–310.

[38] See Karen Brewer, et al., "A Method of Cooperation . . ." (*Journal of Academi Librarianship*, September 1978, pp. 204–207) for an outline of the experience of seve academic libraries in northeast Ohio who joined to establish a cooperative consortiur

Ordering

Serials are normally purchased through a subscription agent, and in America this usually means one of three or four large agents, Ebsco, Faxon, Moore-Cottrell, and Stechert-Macmillan.[39] The librarian enters an order (often on a form supplied by the agent), and the agent then passes the order on to the publisher. A good jobber with solve numerous problems that are likely to arise (from failure of the publisher to deliver an issue to a forwarding company's failure to note the beginning of a subscription). The best of the agents help the librarian with the single greatest serial problem—the claiming of missing issues of a particular magazine—and they do many other things. All help possible is needed because:

Serials, as we all know, are cranky, unpredictable, changeable, erratic, and individual to the extreme. They require particularly close attention to detail, and that sixth sense which alerts one to the awareness of that something "not quite right"— which if not caught will soon compound geometrically. Late publication, title changes or variations, mail delays [or complete nonarrival due to strikes, wars, etc.], changes in numbering, date, frequency, or format, splitting of titles, mergers, recalcitrant publishers or agents, payment problems, renewals, cancellations, replacements, claiming, cataloging, binding—all take an incredible amount of time, detective work, phone calls, letter writing, and records changing. And even after all that, one can never be certain that the desired result will occur; that the problem will be solved; that the ordered replacement will arrive; that the records are up-to-date.[40]

The ordering and maintaining of serials is a study in itself, one usually left to acquisitions sections and serials divisions. In smaller libraries, however, it is not so easy to consign the problem to others, and here the librarian should do as much as possible to: (1) Become familiar with serial jobbers and the difficulties they and the librarian must face together in order to keep serials moving smoothly from publisher to library. (2) Become familiar with the literature on the subject, which is impressive. In fact, just a cursory glance though any issue of *The Serials Librarian* or the less specialized *Library Resources and Technical Services* will reveal at least one

[39] Katz and Gellatly, op. cit., is a detailed study of how serials are ordered, the problems encountered, and serial agents to consider; it includes an evaluative listing of the major periodical subscription agents. An updated unevaluative list can be found in *American Book Trade Directory*. The standard listing for foreign subscription agents is Nancy Buckeye (ed.), *International Subscription Agents* (4th ed.; Chicago: American Library Association, 1978). See also the chapter on serials in Stephen Ford's *The Acquisition of Library Materials* (2nd ed.; Chicago: American Library Association, 1978).

[40] Kathleen Kuhns, "Serials Librarians and Their Discontents," *The Serials Librarian*, Winter 1976–1977, p. 174. A good overview of the whole problem of ordering and maintaining serials.

article on the subject of ordering and maintaining serials. See, for example, Harry Kuntz, "Serial Agents: Selection and Evaluation" (*The Serials Librarian*, Winter 1977, pp. 139–150).

General Aids

Brown, Clara D. *Serials: Acquisition and Maintenance.* Birmingham, Ala.: Ebsco, 1971.

Davison, Donald. *The Periodicals Collection*, rev. ed. Boulder, Colo.: Westview Press, 1978.

Katz, William. *Magazine Selection.* New York: R. R. Bowker, 1971.

"Development in serials: 19—," *Library Sources and Technical Services*, summer issues.

Folio. New Canaan, Conn.: Folio Magazine Publishing Corporation. Monthly.

The Serials Librarian. New York: Haworth Press, since 1976. Quarterly.

The Serials Review. Ann Arbor, Mich.: Pierian Press, since 1975. Quarterly.

Title Varies. P.O. Box 704, Chapel Hill, N.C. 27514. Since 1973. Bimonthly.

Although now dated, *Magazine Selection* offers a general philosophy of selection for public libraries, and to a lesser extent for all libraries. Emphasis is on selection philosophy and techniques with particular sections on censorship, the little magazine, indexes, and so on. Also included is the result of a survey of selection practices among public librarians.

Brown's work is a basic approach to the acquisition of serials and to maintaining records. It is only incidentally concerned with selection, being much more involved with what constitutes a good serials section in a library. The practical advice is of special help to the novice who must set up a record system for serials. The veteran serials librarian's work is much more to the point in the better-known Osborn, *Serial Publications.* (2nd ed.; Chicago: American Library Association, 1973).

Davison's revised edition of *The Periodicals Collections* offers a brief working account of building and maintaining a collection. The drawback is that here an English librarian is writing about practices in English libraries, and while the general information is useful, many of the particulars are of limited value to readers outside Great Britain. The excellent writing style and practical approach to the selection of titles nevertheless make this a classic in the field, one of the best of its type available.

PERIODICALS

The best single place for a critical annual survey of periodicals and serials is in the summer issue of *Library Resources and Technical Services.* The 16-to-20-page summary covers most aspects of the serial world for the preceding year and ends with a good bibliography.

There are two periodicals devoted solely to serials. The oldest is *The Serials Review*, which has several distinctive features: (1) Notes and sometimes good essays on individual magazines. (2) Articles that highlight the new titles in certain areas and subjects; one number included informative and critical material on science-fiction magazines, reference works, and government publications. (3) Review articles on indexes and tools of the serial trade. (4) "The Serial Review Index," which indexes reviews of serials. The writers are primarily librarians and have a solid background in the subjects covered. It is an important aid for selection and, while always a trifle late, a good source for checking given subject areas for periodicals which may have been overlooked in routine selection.

The Serials Librarian is a journal that features five to seven articles on all aspects of serial work, not merely selection. It differs the *The Serials Review* in its emphasis on the control and selection of serials, not simply reviews. Under the editorship of a veteran serials librarian, Peter Gellatly, the magazine is essential for keeping up in this area. It has several standard features, including Gary Pitkin's excellent annotated listing of articles and books about work with periodicals.

Folio magazine is a solid source of information on what it takes to succeed in magazine publishing. There are notes on publishers, articles on methods and readership, and so forth. As a type of *Publishers Weekly* of the periodical world it is a good nonlibrary introduction to magazine publishing. It is useful for the careful tracing of trends and events. In addition, the publishers issue *Folio: New Magazine Report*, a four-page annotated listing of new magazines. However, about half of each issue is given over to notes about people, and the title is of limited value to all but the largest of libraries.

Title Varies is a running account of the horrors of the title changes that drive many serial librarians mad. They even have the "Worst serial title change of the year" award, and regularly chronicle even mild changes so the librarian may keep up with the field. Failure to keep up may well have the librarian reselecting magazine Y (now under title X) as X, only to find when X arrives that it is only Y, and there are now duplicates. In addition it is truly amusing, a rarity to be treasured.

REVIEWS

Katz, William. "Magazines," regular column in *Library Journal*.
Farber, Evan. "Periodicals for College Libraries," regular column in *Choice*.

The number of places where the librarian will find consistent periodical reviews is limited. For current titles the author's magazine column in *Library Journal* is useful; an effort is made to annotate periodicals of a wide general use or of particular value to a given subject field. *Choice* concentrates on journals of interest to college and university libraries and to collections serving large research organizations. Actually, of course, neither is rigid and in one review column the reader is as likely to find a title as in another.

Neither is timely. *Choice* has the advantage of more lengthly reviews, *Library Journal* the advantage of more titles mentioned. Both rely on outside experts.

Other library periodicals (*American Libraries, Booklist*) occasionally review magazines, but on a more limited scale. *The Serials Review* consistently has long, detailed reviews of periodicals by subject areas; these tend to be more retrospective than current and are of little real assistance in evaluating new titles. The same journal offers the only consistent index to periodical reviews, and through it one may often find specific notes, if not always critical evaluation, of particular titles.

Periodical Bibliographies and Lists[41]

International Directory of Little Magazines and Small Presses, 1978–1979 (14th ed). Paradise, Calif.: Dustbooks, 1978.

Irregular Serials and Annuals, 1978–1979 (5th ed.). New York: R. R. Bowker, 1978.

Sources of Serials. New York: R. R. Bowker, 1977.

Ulrich's International Periodical Directory, 1978–1979 (17th ed.). New York: R. R. Bowker, 1978.

UNION LISTS

Union List of Serials . . . (3rd ed.; New York: The H. W. Wilson Company, 1965). 5 vols.

New Serial Titles. (Washington, D.C.: Library of Congress, since 1961). Eight issues a year.

Revised and updated every two years (with quarterly supplements) *Ulrich's International Periodical Directory* is the basic bibliographic aid for libraries. The latest edition lists, by subject, over 60,000 periodicals. In addition to complete bibliographic data, the guide usually indicates whether or not the periodical is indexed in basic, better-known indexes. There is a subject and title index.

Ulrich's is often supplemented by *The Standard Periodical Directory* (6th ed.; New York: Oxbridge, 1978), a subject listing of the same type limited to publications of the United States and Canada. It includes ephemeral titles (such as newsletters and house organs) not found in *Ulrich's*.

Some 32,000 serials are listed under approximately 250 subject headings in the latest edition of *Irregular Serials and Annuals*. This includes titles not found in *Ulrich's* because they are annual or irregular. This is the ideal place to look up serials such as continuations, conference proceedings transactions, and the like. The work is updated every two years.

[41] For more detailed information on these basic titles see Katz, *Introduction to Reference Work* (3rd ed,; New York: McGraw-Hill, 1978).

Trying to find the publisher of a periodical can be extremely difficult, as can trying to match up several titles by the same publisher. The problem is solved by *Sources of Serials*, which lists some 50,000 publishers of both periodicals and irregular serials. Under each name is a complete listing of all serial titles published and a full address for the publisher. It is useful for dealing with associations and organizations that publish a vast number of individual titles.

Who has what periodical is found in the basic *Union List of Serials*, supplemented by *New Serial Titles*. Here titles are listed alphabetically (there is no subject approach) with a key to what library has a run, or a number of volumes of, a given periodical. A helpful compilation is the ten-year cumulation for 1950–1970 of *New Serial Titles* in four volumes.

Most libraries have access to other regional and local union lists, which should be checked when a decision to select or reject is based upon the holdings of other libraries.

SUBSCRIPTION AGENT PUBLICATIONS

Serials Updating Service. Westwood, Mass.: F. W. Faxon, since 1974. Quarterly.

Ebsco Bulletin of Serials Changes. Birmingham, Ala.: Ebsco, since 1975. Bimonthly.

Stechert-Macmillan News. New York: Stechert-Macmillan, since 1975. Bimonthly.

Periodical Update. North Cohocton, N.Y.: Moore-Cottrell, since 1978. Monthly.

In terms of selection, the Stechert-Macmillan publication is primarily useful for "Periodicals," an annotated listing of new titles. The 50-to-75-word descriptive annotations do not include the publisher's address. There also are short articles and information on books.

The Faxon *Serials Updating Service* is one of the more thorough of the group. It alphabetically lists titles with information about such things as claims information, delayed publication, and suspended titles. It does not include new titles, but after the title listing there is a subject index. The drawback is that this is a computer printout, and quite difficult to read. The Ebsco service follows much the same procedure, but it has a large section on new titles. This is particularly useful because, alone of all the services, it does include the address of the publisher. The librarian is free, then, to write for sample copies from the publisher without going through an agent.[42]

Periodical Update follows much the same pattern as newsletters of other jobbers, but differs in one major respect: the annotations. Each title listed is carefully analyzed and described. Indication of audience is given and type

[42] Publishers' addresses can also be obtained by checking *Sources of Serials*.

198

of library often indicated. Editor Ruth Kanner is responsible for the outstanding annotations, and for this reason alone it is a service well worth considering. It also contains the standard information on delayed publications, title changes, and so on.

There are numerous nonevaluative sources for new titles. A standard, which simply lists the title, although usually with the publisher's address and bibliographical data, is *Bulletin of Bibliography and Magazine Notes* (Westwood, Mass.: F. W. Faxon Company, quarterly). In the regular column "Births, Deaths and Magazine Notes" one finds the titles for the preceding quarter.

LITTLE MAGAZINES

The basic nonevaluative guide to little magazines in the United States (with some attention to other parts of the world) is Len Fulton's *International Directory of Little Magazines*. Revised every year, the latest edition includes about 2000 entires. Titles are listed alphabetically with complete bibliographical information about each title. There usually is also a short paragraph explaining types of materials accepted or rejected. The geographical directory by state is useful for libraries that concentrate on local littles, and there is a subject index.

How does a librarian recognize a little magazine?

The editor tends to concentrate on poetry, possibly a bit of fiction, and even some startling graphics. The writers are generally unknown to the librarian—or, for that matter, to many of the readers. A few of the more enterprising editors manage to persuade a major poet or writer to contribute, usually to the first issue, but this rarely continues. The reason for the professional's lack of enthusiasm is that he or she is rarely paid for the work, and few of the little magazines have circulations of more than 500 or 1000. Most professional authors want more recognition than that type of circulation provides.

Little magazines are more than poetry or literature, however. As expressions of individualism, normally divorced from the commercial world, they dare to be themselves in almost every area of human activity and interest. They are political (left to right), literary, feminist, black, Chicano, dance, ecology and environment, film, music, occult, and voices from prisons and hospitals. Today almost all professions have their own little magazines, which run counter to the mainstream opinions expressed in the professional journals. The scientist has *Science for the People*, the psychologist *State and Mind*, and the librarian *Emergency Librarian* and *The Unabashed Librarian*, to name only two.[43]

Few little magazines are profit-making, and most lose money. They sur-

[43] Sanford Berman, "Alternative Library Lit," *Library Journal*, January 1, 1978, pp 23–25. An annotated listing of more than a score of small-press-movement publications in librarianship. Note the bibliography at the end of the article.

vive economically primarily through the ingenuity of the editors, who work long hours for no wage, persuade writers to do the same, and usually have access to some funds, often from their own pockets or the resources of friends. Today some receive outside local, regional, state, or even federal support, although rarely enough to insure much more than that the next two or three issues will be published. Survival finally depends upon the subscribers, and—depending on the drive of the publisher—the little magazine may survive with only 500 subscribers. A more comfortable figure is 1000 to 1500, and magazines with real ambition require 5000 to 6000 paid readers.[44]

From a purely economic point of view, the little magazine may at least break even if given limited library support. Fewer than 100 library subscriptions are normal, and most come from academic centers and a few larger public libraries. Still, even with 100 libraries on a subscription list the editor is assured of at least much-needed exposure to readers who often subscribe themselves or (equally as often) quickly submit manuscripts.

SELECT LISTS

Farber, Evan. *Classified List of Periodicals for College Libraries*, 4th ed. Westwood, Mass.: F. W. Faxon Company, 1972.
Katz, Bill, and Berry Richards. *Magazines for Libraries*, 3rd ed. New York: R. R. Bowker, 1978.
Richardson, Selma. *Periodicals for School Media Programs*. Chicago: American Library Association, 1978.

For the librarian looking for a annotated listing of selected periodicals, there are three basic sources. The first and the one with the most titles (more than 6000) is *Magazines for Libraries*; the third edition represents the "best" titles chosen by subject experts in basic subject areas. Both descriptive and evaluative annotations are to be found for each title, and there is a clear indication for which type of library audience the periodical is recommended. The listing is updated every five or six years and is directed to all types and sizes of library.

The other two bibliographies are narrower in scope, compiled for specific types of library. Farber's title has 1000 periodicals, evaluated for college libraries; there is a full annotation with clear recommendation. Even more narrow in approach, although certainly equal to the other two lists in quality of selection and annotation, is the Richardson school media list. This includes about 500 titles for elementary through high school, arranged alphabetically by title with a subject index.

Representing various points of view, certainly various opinions, the three lists may be used together when there is a question about a single title

[44] For a detailed study of the little magazine see Katz, *Magazine Selection*, and the much more comprehensive and up-to-date *The Little Magazine in America* (New York: Pushcart Press, 1978).

found in two or more of the bibliographies. None is entirely satisfactory as a selection aid by itself, any more than are the lists of "best" books. However, they are all a vast improvement over the method of simply blindly selecting for the library what happens to be indexed in, say, *Readers' Guide to Periodical Literature.*

There are numerous other lists, many for subject areas, most of them nonselective and certainly noncritical. These are useful for checking what basic titles are available and for the annotations or other bits of information exceeding what is to be found in *Ulrich's.* Some examples, by title only: *Periodicals in Education, Education/Psychology Journals, Author's Guide to Journals, Management and Economic Journals.*

Critical reviews or indications of publication of select lists will be found in *Serials Review,* more particularly the regular "Tools of the Serials Trade," and in the annotated listings and book reviews in *The Serials Librarian.* These also tend to be reviewed in *Library Journal, Booklist,* and *Choice* and regularly appear in the annual *American Reference Books Annual.*

Newspapers

The selection of newspapers in most libraries follows a basic pattern: (1) The local newspapers and those in the region and state are purchased. Only the major state titles are considered. (2) Thanks to its status as almost a national newspaper, *The New York Times* is purchased—and it has an index. (3) The next category is significant regional newspapers from major sections of the United States. Most are indexed in the separate *Newspaper Index.* (4) As it grows larger in size or more specialized in service to a community, the library may purchase foreign-language papers. This is particularly important when the library is serving a non-English-speaking community. It is advisable to get advice from users before purchasing.

Some care must be exercised about the selection of local newspapers (and some national or international ones) that represent the official voice of an organization, religion, or political group. If there is demand for such titles, they should be purchased—although they are likely to be given to the library by the involved group. On the other hand, selection basics must be exercised so the library is not flooded with special-interest papers.

The basic directory of American and Canadian newspapers is *Ayer Directory of Newspapers, Magazines & Trade Publications* (Philadelphia: Ayer Press [since 1880; annual]), which lists newspapers by state and by city. The Library of Congress publishes the *Newspapers and Gazette Report* (since 1973; three times a year), which reports on developments in the location, microfilming, and preservation of newspapers. There is also the Library of Congress *Newspapers in Microform* (since 1973; annual), the best single source of who has what. The list is arranged alphabetically by state and includes the master as well as the service microforms of close to 35,000 U.S. and 9000 foreign titles held by some 1200 libraries.

9
Other Print Materials

THE LIBRARIAN must deal with a variety of print forms in addition to periodicals and books. The division by form is arbitrary but useful for selection purposes. Each form may have its own selection aids, bibliographies, and even reviews. Print forms tend to encompass various subject areas and are more easily treated as forms than divided by subject. Too, many libraries have separate collections by form—a place for pamphlets, another for microform, a third for reports. (This may not be the best way to handle the materials, but it is generally done in this fashion.)

In this chapter these forms of printed material are considered:

1. Microform, which is little more than another version of a printed form, although it is sometimes listed as a nonprint or nonbook material.

2. Pamphlets.

3. Manuscripts and archives, which are not published works but are an important part of many larger libraries, particularly in terms of local history and dissertations.

4. Reports which are a major consideration for special libraries and large research collections.

Out-of-print, discussed in Chapter 7 (pages 173–176), not a form at all but a technique for acquiring hard-to-find titles, should be kept in mind in the context of this chapter because o.p. may be translated into microform and reprints.

Not treated here are government documents (too involved a subject for a few pages) and reference works (although many reference titles are listed throughout the book).

Microform

Microform[1] is a method of reducing printed materials to a small space on film. Almost everyone is familiar with the microfilm and the microfilm

[1] *Microform* is a generic term that includes all forms of material photographed and reduced in size.

reader. Microform is a common format in most libraries.[2] Periodicals and newspapers are often on microform, as are major sets of government documents, reports, court decisions, genealogical records, and the like. Many dissertations and theses are now available only on microform or printed out from a microform master.

Purchase of microform rather than print is usually a decision based upon need to conserve space, save money, duplicate materials, or purchase out-of-print, rare, and otherwise unavailable items. Sometimes, of course, there is no choice; the material is available only on microform. Microform is widely used to replace deteriorating books, newspapers, and periodicals. A valuable title may be reduced to microform for interlibrary loan.

The use of microform in libraries is relatively common, although there are some disadvantages: (1) The library must have some type of reader, which, while increasingly less expensive, remains a major cost. And various forms of microform call for various types of reader. (2) The use of microform for any length of time tires the eyes.

It is often suggested that one method of saving money on periodicals, books, and other materials would simply be to "publish" the material on a single microform master copy—and then print out the book or periodical (or parts thereof) when needed. This is already being done by several non-commercial firms, which will produce a hard copy or a microform of a report not otherwise available in printed form. *Wildlife Disease* is an irregular serial published since 1959 only on original microform.

The possibilities of microform in a library are virtually unlimited. One librarian put it this way:

It's fun to talk about the future of microforms in libraries. (My vision, which is shared by many, is that academic libraries will be microform *dispensing* libraries—that is, they'll consist mainly of browsing collections, and if students want to check out books, we'll just hand them microfiches to read and keep. There'll be a master file of microfiches that are never circulated, but which can be quickly and cheaply duplicated. It will be—it is now—cheaper to duplicate a microfiche and give it away than it is to circulate a book. Also, of course, this can obviate the problem of books being ripped off, or even of books being signed out when needed.)[3]

He is talking about a college library, but this situation does exist in many special libraries today. "The Consumer Association library, which has been purchasing and producing microfiche for a little over three years, has nearly

---

[2] But not until 1978 did a style manual for microform citations appear: Eugene B. Fleischer, *A Style Manual for Citing Microform and Nonprint Media* (Chicago: American Library Association, 1978), which includes style for other nonprint material as well.

[3] Evan Farber, "The Administration and Use of Microform Serials in College Libraries," *Microform Review*, March-April 1978, p. 81. The assumption here is that the average person will settle for microform rather than print, one that has proved wrong more often than not. Of course, the time may come when microform and readers have improved to a point where they are as easy to read and use as a book, but it has not yet arrived.

40,000 items on microfiche and a mere 8000 books and pamphlets in hard copy."[4]

Microform has two basic forms: the roll and the flat transparency or card. Probably the best known, certainly the most often used, is the familiar 35mm reel or roll.[5] In fact, it has been in libraries for so many years that many librarians and users think only of this format when microform is mentioned.

There are several types of microform: (1) Microfiche or fiche, available in several sizes, but the standard 4-by-6-inch size with an average of 98 pages per sheet is favored. (Different reductions increase or decrease the number of pages.) (2) Ultrafiche, an ultrafine reduction, usually on a 4-by-6-inch transparency. One card may contain 3000 to 5000 pages. (3) Microprint, a 6-by-9-inch card that contains up to 100 pages of text in ten rows and ten columns.

Other, more esoteric approaches are familiar to most spy-story readers.[6] Aperture cards, with one to scores of microimages mounted in the aperture of the card, are often found in special libraries and where unit records are maintained, but are less used in the average general collection.

The forms (and the equipment necessary to read them) change from year to year in a highly innovative and competitive industry. There are many sources of current information on these modifications and changes; see the note on *Microform Review*, p. 205. For the generalist, a good journal to follow is the *Journal of Library Automation*, which regularly considers developments in microform—as in the December 1978 issue, where Carl Spaulding gave "An Update on Micrographics."

Microform can be reversed and used to print out books or periodicals as needed. This "xerographic printing" allows the library to obtain hard copies of otherwise difficult-to-find books. Another even more common practice is to use computer output microfilm (COM) for compiling indexes, bibliographies, and other reference works. (COM is now used for some card catalogs and similar purposes about the library. These fall into a category now usually left to acquisitions.)[7]

---

[4] Peter Thomas, "Micropublishing and Libraries in the Future," *Aslib Proceedings*, May 1978, p. 165.

[5] Most microfilm is on 35mm frames, but some is now available on 16mm. When ordering be sure to know the difference; reading equipment may not be compatible for both forms.

[6] Microfiche is used for many purposes. One of the more bizarre was in the June 26, 1978, issue of *Publishers Weekly*, where on page 25 Ballantine Books included a microfiche of "Linda Weintraub's new novel *Runaway* in its entirety" as a publicity stunt.

[7] Much continues to be written about the miracle of COM. This topic is outside the scope of this book, but any reader interested in a basic, clear explanation could do no better than read William Horner, ". . . Microfiche Catalogs," *North Carolina Libraries*, Winter 1975, pp. 31–33. A longer, equally lucid explanation is in William Saffady's *Computer-Output Microfilm: Its Library Application* (Chicago: American Library Association, 1978), which includes an excellent glossary of terms that beginners will find helpful.

Where there is a choice between the familiar 35mm microfilm reel and the microfiche card, which is best?[8] Users prefer microfiche. Librarians historically have tended to lean toward microfilm because it is easier to control. Actually, choice is likely to be dictated by the publisher. In addition to regular hard copies, the publisher may make microform available in only one format: (1) Most periodicals and newspapers are available only on microfilm; (2) most reports, surveys, government documents, and the like may be available only on microfiche. In the few cases in which the library does have a choice the decisions must be based upon the user's preference and equipment requirements and relative cost.[9]

EVALUATION

The first point of evaluation is whether or not what is available on microform is wanted.[10] Here one would apply the yardstick used for other print materials. Beyond that, given a choice between the printed (hard) copy of a work and a microform version, most users and librarians prefer the print copy. A standing evaluation rule in most libraries is therefore always buy the print copy when it is available (exceptions: back files of newspapers, low-use items, materials that deteriorate rapidly, or when the hard copy is considerably more expensive or not suitable).

Not everything should be put on microform, even when that is possible. Valuable, much-used older newspapers and periodicals, for example, should be kept in original form (with microform for heavy use). A unique copy of a periodical, book, or newspaper should not be consigned to microform. Art periodicals and books, or any other work in which illustrations are a major factor, should not be put on microform. (Microform has yet to be a satisfactory medium for illustrations. Some types have been developed for art reproductions, but not for art books and periodicals.)

Generally, a negative candidate is any material in high demand. Most users prefer hardbound copies and do not want to be given microform when the print version is available.

Evaluation of microforms is not usually concerned with such standard items as ongoing microfilm of *The New York Times* or of *Time* magazine, and rarely with reports and government documents found through ERIC, which surface as microfiche. Library evaluation is concerned with significant

---

[8] The microcard, sometimes called micro-opaque card, has fairly well passed out of library use and should be purchased only when the material is available in no other form.

[9] The debate as to which is preferable for daily use—microfilm or microfiche—continues, and there is no really satisfactory blanket solution. A useful discussion, with pros and cons, will be found in Homer I. Bernhardt's "Formats" in *Microforms in Libraries* (Weston, Conn.: Microform Review, 1975), pp. 32–34.

[10] Evaluation of the quality of both microform and equipment is of interest to the microform industry. A directory of the numerous standards will be found in Don Avedon's "Micrographic Standards," *IMC Journal*, Third Quarter, 1978, pp. 11–16.

microform collections that may range in price from $1000 to $50,000 or more. Many of these, listed in *Guide to Microforms in Print*, may range from a well-over-$20,000 collection of Britannica's *Library of American Civilization* to KTO Microform's *Meet the Press* series. There are much more expensive series, such as Xerox's ambitious program to put more than 1000 eighteenth-century periodicals on microform and titles from *Short Title Catalogues*.

What is needed to evaluate microform has been suggested by Mark R. Yerbugh:

> The ideal armory of prerequisite skills possessed by the competent evaluator includes, but is not limited to, a thorough understanding of librarianship, a clear awareness of collection needs in his/her unique institutional setting, familiarity with microform trends, standards, and technologies, a generous measure of common sense, and finally, subject competence reflective of the particular collection under consideration.[11]

Few can lay claim to such expertise, so most librarians must rely on reviews. Unfortunately, however, the basic review sources usually do not consider microform, nor do the media reviews. The best single answer is the *Microform Review* (Weston, Conn.: Microform Review, since 1972; quarterly), which is a systematic approach to detailed evaluation of new microform offerings. Collections, series, and sets are considered, as are individual works. Both technical quality of the reproduction and actual content are examined. There are also articles on microform publishing and the industry as well as book reviews and news notes.

The same publisher issues the monthly *Microlist* (a listing by author, title, and subject; covers microforms announced for publication the preceding month). This is a list, not an evaluation.

THE COLLECTION

Collections of microform tend to be centralized, although for practical purposes it would be better to have them integrated into the total holdings. It would be much better, for example, to have the microform holdings of a periodical on the same shelf as the current issues of the periodical, or easily available nearby. Much the same holds true for books on microform.[12]

Theft, microform deterioration, physical handling and other reasons are sometimes given for isolating microform. Most have proved groundless, at least in most libraries, and as one librarian concluded after working out a method of open shelving for microforms:

[11] "Academic Libraries and the Evaluation of Microform Collections," *Microform Review*, January-February 1978, p. 15, which goes into great detail but also serves as a good introduction to the purpose, scope, and audience of *Microform Review*.

[12] A convincing argument for the integrated collection is given by Susan Nutter in "Microforms and the User . . . ," *Drexel Library Quarterly*, October 1975, pp. 17–31.

Open shelving can be an efficient, effective, and economical means of housing journal microfilm. It may well provide small academic and research libraries with a viable alternative to microfilm storage in cabinets or in nonuser areas, provided the library is in a temperate climate or is environmentally controlled. It should work as well for libraries that classify their journals as for those that arrange them alphabetically. It is not suggested for libraries that have extensive microfilm collections, long runs of newspaper microfilm, or large package collections.[13]

EQUIPMENT

Several sources evaluate equipment used with microform. The American Library Association's *Library Technology Reports* and *EPIE* (see page 250) report on new developments; other studies are found in the library press.[14] The best single source of objective reviews of microform equipment is *Micrographics Equipment Review* (Weston, Conn.: Microform Review, since 1976; quarterly), a companion to *Microform Review*. Here detailed data, including illustrations, are presented for all types of micrographic equipment. Each piece is thoroughly tested and a full report given. The review should be consulted if any major investment in micrographic equipment is contemplated.

MICROREPRODUCTION

The *Guide to Micrographic Equipment*, published by the National Microfilm Association and updated about every three years, is a definitive report on specifications and capabilities of various pieces of equipment. Data are given without evaluation, and for approval or disapproval one must turn back to *Micrographics Equipment Review*.

Librarians should consult other librarians who already have equipment and should also consider: (1) *Clarity of image*. Can you read the magnified film or fiche without strain? Do the lights have to be put out, or can it be used in a lighted room? Is the lamp too bright, not bright enough? (2) *Ease of use*. Does it take a mechanic to operate the equipment, or can one learn how to use it in a matter of seconds? Can it be repaired quickly (in

---

[13] Jacqueline A. Maxin, "The Open Shelving of Journals on Microfilm," *Special Libraries*, December 1975, p. 594.

[14] Once a year, for example, *Library Journal* devotes an issue to microform.

There are two standard collections of articles on microforms: Albert Diaz (ed.), *Microforms in Libraries* (Weston, Conn.: Microform Review, 1975), covers many aspects of the genre, including three articles on acquisitions; Patricia Walsh (ed.), *Serials Management and Microforms* (London: Mansell, 1978), concentrates on how microform is used in the management of serials.

For a history of the home reader (a still-to-be-realized dream) see Carl Spaulding, "The Fifty Dollar Reading Machine," *Library Journal*, October 15, 1976, pp. 2132–2138. At one time it was thought that every home would have a microform reader or that readers could be borrowed from libraries. Neither has happened.

other words, is there a service organization near)? Some equipment has an automatic device to turn microfilm reels rapidly—but is this needed and, if it is useful, is the device likely to need constant repair?

BY TYPE OF LIBRARY

Guidelines for microform must be general: "types and quantity vary with program needs."[15] The kind and amount of equipment vary, too, although usually there are at least one or two readers and a reader-printer available.

ORDERING

There are several hundred commercial micropublishers in the United States. Better-known names include: Xerox, Bell & Howell, and Readex. Other names will be found in the bibliographic guides discussed in the next few pages.

Publishers issue various types and formats of microform. Some concentrate on books, others on periodicals, still others on government publications. The price and the quality of the work differs from publisher to publisher, and one soon learns whom to trust and whom to avoid, achieved through: (1) discussing publishers and their products with other librarians who have medium to large microform collections; (2) considering carefully the evaluative reviews of microform in *Microform Review*; (3) and, of course, experience—a marvelous teacher.

The actual ordering of microform is no different than ordering books, although it is generally the practice to go directly to the publisher, not through a jobber or agent. Discounts, arrangements for payment, speed of delivery, and the like differ from publisher to publisher.

Noncommercial institutional publishers usually produce works at somewhat lower prices than the commercial publisher. Among these are the Library of Congress, numerous historical societies, museums, and libraries.

Publishers are identified in both *Guide to Microforms in Print* and *Subject Guide to Microforms in Print*. For an extensive coverage see *The Micropublisher's Trade List Annual* (Weston, Conn.: Microform Review [since 1976; annual]), which offers on microfiche the catalog of major micropublishers throughout the world.

General Microform Aids

A Basic Guide to Microfilms. Washington, D.C.: Government Printing Office, 1973.

LaHood, Charles, and Robert C. Sullivan. *Reprographic Services in Libraries:*

---

[15] *Media Programs: District and School* (Chicago: American Library Association, 1975), p. 75.

Organization and Administration. Chicago: American Library Association, 1975.

Rice, E. Stevens. *Fiche and Reel.* Ann Arbor, Mich.: University Microfilms, 1976.

Saffady, William. *Micrographics.* Littleton, Colo.: Libraries Unlimited, 1978.

Of the several basic guides for the microfilm neophyte, the best is the Army technical manual *Guides to Microfilms.* This concentrates on record keeping, but in the process offers valuable insights into the use of microfilm in libraries. There is solid advice, for example, on how to set up miniaturization systems, and the appendices explain the terminology used. Another basic guide is *Fiche and Reel*, available free from the publisher. Numerous illustrations and good style suit it well for the person who wants a quick overview of various forms of microreproduction and micropublishing.

Even the novice will be able to follow LaHood's *Reprographic Service*, which is directed to librarians and administrators and moves from a history of the subject to equipment and staff needs. There is a useful glossary and bibliography as well as reproduction of the American Library Association Standard Photoduplication Order Form.

Micrographics, the most comprehensive title listed here, offers a textbook approach to the basics of microform and is particularly strong in showing how librarians may adopt microform for library use. *Reprographics*, a companion volume by the same author and publisher, considers full-size document "reproduction transmission and storage systems."

Microform Bibliographies and Lists

Guide to Microforms in Print. Weston, Conn.: Microform Review, since 1961. Annual.

Books on Demand. Ann Arbor, Mich.: University Microfilms, since 1975. Annual.

National Register of Microform Masters. Washington, D.C.: Library of Congress, since 1965. Annual.

Dodson, Suzanne. *Microform Research Collections: A Guide.* Weston, Conn.: Microform Review, 1978.

Directory of Library Reprographic Services. Weston, Conn.: Microform Review, various dates.

The basic subject guide for microform is *Guide to Microforms in Print*, which lists more than 60,000 titles from approximately 200 American and foreign publishers.[16] Titles include not only books but also serials and

---

[16] With the 1977 edition, scope was broadened to include foreign publishers, and the guide now includes *International Microforms in Print.*

other forms, such as government documents, published in the medium. *Microform* is used broadly to include the range of forms from microfiche to microfilm. The same publisher (rearranges) the titles by subject and brings out *Subject Guide to Microforms in Print* annually.

Books on Demand, limited to books, is the catalog (actually three separate volumes) of a single firm, in this case the largest—University Microfilms. It is an author, title, and subject catalog that lists 100,000 titles. They may be purchased either on microfilm or as hard-copy xerographic prints of the microform.

The title indicates the unique quality of the trade bibliography. Instead of printing copies and waiting for orders (the normal procedure), the publisher has master copies on microform and prints out one copy at a time as ordered; either hard copies or microfilm may be purchased. This procedure eliminates costly warehousing and a large investment in inventory and is a common practice among larger microform publishers.

There are scores of publisher catalogs. Readex and Bell & Howell, for example, publish catalogs of their offerings at regular intervals and KTO Microform (Kraus-Thomas) issues an annual *General Catalogue.* Most libraries have these on file along with the other bibliographies in the field.

University Microfilms publishes several other useful lists and catalogs, of which one of the best is the frequently updated *Serials in Microform* (the title changes from time to time). This is a listing by title of periodicals, newspapers, and other serials available on microform. There is a short subject index. Each entry contains information about the length of the back file, place of publication, current volumes, and indexes available.

One of Bell & Howell's best catalogs is the annual *Newspapers on Microfilms and Special Collections,* which lists some 5500 titles, primarily newspapers, listed by state, city, and name, but also some periodicals, listed by title.

The *Directory of Library Reprographic Services* gives the name and address of libraries that have photoduplication services and list charges, regulations, and the like. Since much material required by one library is already in another, this is a handy way of ascertaining the relative costs and difficulty in securing a microform copy of what is needed. Frequently revised, the sixth edition (1976) has 438 entires and includes a handy section of some 60 charts on various reprographic services. This can be searched after the librarian has looked at the next listing.

The National List of Microform Masters is a union catalog that tells who has what microforms. It lists holdings of approximately 300 American and foreign libraries as well as commercial publishers. Arrangement is alphabetical by author, and by late 1975 320,000 titles were listed, including 70,000 serials. Each year some 50,000 titles are added to the basic set. (A six-volume cumulation covers 1965–1975).

A more refined effort is *Microform Research Collections.* Here the compiler lists major collections (not individual periodicals or newspapers) held by research libraries with an author, editor, compiler, title, and subject index that permits the user to search out hard-to-find materials. The volume also serves as a buying guide; it lists collections that may be purchased. The compiler includes citations to reviews, at least of more expensive sets.[17]

Numerous individual lists of materials on microform are listed in *Guide to Reference Books* and in subject reference guides, but there is no single place where these are listed, although most are reviewed in *Microform Review*.

Pamphlets

There is no entirely satisfactory definition of the term *pamphlet*, but generally it is understood to be anything in a paper binding and less than 49 pages long.[18] Librarians tend to treat the average pamphlet as ephemeral and to put it in the vertical file under an appropriate subject heading. If it is important or has lasting interest, it may be rebound and catalogued, much as a book would be.[19]

The content of pamphlets is as varied as that of books and periodicals and covers every conceivable subject from as many viewpoints. Pamphlets have several distinct advantages over the traditional book: (1) Because they can be produced quickly, they tend to be timely. (2) Since they are short and without hard covers, they tend to be relatively inexpensive or free. (3) Brevity results in concentration on a single subject or a significant part of that subject, thus saving the reader a search through extraneous material.

While pamphlets are treated separately here, they normally are part of the vertical file arrangement. The librarian responsible for keeping the files current and weeded will also select other types of materials, from clippings and certain government documents and pictures to maps and author and vocational materials.

Selection is usually done by (1) the librarian in charge of the vertical

---

[17] Suzanne Dodson, "Toward Bibliographic Control: The Development of a Guide to Microform Research Collections," *Microform Review*, July-August 1978, pp. 203–212. An excellent article about how the guide was compiled and the need for additional national and international controls of microform bibliography.

[18] The American Library Association notes that some libraries define a pamphlet as anything under 80 pages, others prefer about 100 pages, while binderies say 64 pages or less. So far as format is concerned, therefore, it is what the librarian describes as a pamphlet (*ALA Glossary of Terms*, Chicago: American Library Association, 1973, p. 96). Another definition is by cost: anything priced under $2 (or free) may be considered a pamphlet.

[19] Readings cover the whole field—that is, vertical file collections and maintenance— not just selection of pamphlets. The basic aids: Shirley Miller, *Vertical File and Its Satellites* (Littleton, Colo.: Libraries Unlimited, 1977), and G. N. Gould, et al., *How to Organize and Maintain the Library Picture/Pamphlet File* (Dobbs Ferry, N.Y.: Oceana Publications, 1968). Articles: Kathryn Schultz, "The Development of a Vertical File," *California School Libraries*, Summer 1977, pp. 16–25, and Adeline Whetsel, "Using Vertical Files," *Hoosier School Libraries*, December 1977, pp. 17–22.

file, (2) the subject bibliographers and division heads, (3) a special committee, (4) the regular selection committee, or a combination of these. Normally, members of the staff simply make suggestions and one or more people are responsible for checking over the standard lists and the *Vertical File Index*.

In larger libraries there may be a special committee to handle pamphlets. The Free Library of Philadelphia has such a group, which meets every two weeks to review titles and welcomes suggestions from staff members.[20]

EVALUATION

A pamphlet is evaluated much as other printed materials are, and most of the rules for books are equally applicable here (see pages 91–96). There are also a few points that are peculiar to evaluation of the pamphlet as a form:

1. *Selection.* The librarian should be highly selective, particularly of free or inexpensive material that could soon fill the files and serve no real purpose. Selection means asking (first and foremost): Is this necessary, does it contribute something to the collection not just as easily accessible in a book or periodical articles?

2. *Objectivity.* The majority of pamphlets are published by business organizations, institutions, or individuals and thus usually have a distinct point of view—which is sometimes blatant propaganda. For example, a large industry may issue a pamphlet in support of using waterways that conservationist groups think should be protected. The conservationists may publish another pamphlet from their viewpoint. It is unlikely that most pamphlets will be even close to objective. The real question, then, is: Regardless of the special viewpoint, is the material still useful for the library?

Lack of objectivity can be overstressed, however. Many pamphlets with the proverbial axe to grind are still acceptable because the amount of information is considerably greater than the bias—which may hardly be noticeable, as in titles from UNESCO, the Red Cross, the Association of American University Professors, and the like.

There are several approaches: (1) If the material is outright propaganda, do not use, or be sure to balance with a pamphlet that argues the other side of the debate. (2) If the pamphlet is free or inexpensive, don't hesitate to remove what can be used (photographs, charts, bibliographies) and put the rest in the wastebasket. (3) Avoid anonymous pamphlets. In fact, some librarians underline the sponsor of the work so it is perfectly clear to the intelligent reader that it does have a viewpoint; a red pencil mark under U.S. Steel and under a Ralph Nader group will be of assistance to readers. And don't let your own biases show. If the material is useful, don't ban it

[20] Elizabeth Futas, *Library Acquisition Policies and Procedures* (Phoenix, Ariz.: Oryx Press, 1977), p. 330. When pamphlets are mentioned in selection policies most of the concern is with content, particularly propaganda.

simply because you happen to disagree with the point of view. Let your readers choose for themselves.

3. *Format.* This is relatively unimportant for free material, but if cost is involved be sure the pamphlet is well printed if possible, illustrated, and stapled or otherwise held together so it will last for more than one circulation.

WEEDING

Since most pamphlets are put into file drawers and there is a natural limit to what a drawer will hold, be sure to have some plan for annual weeding. What to dispose of is simply a matter of checking such criteria as: (1) *Timeliness.* A fast way of checking this is to date-stamp the material as it comes in—in a place where the date can be read easily. (2) *Duplication.* Where there are several pamphlets on the same subject, dispose of the lesser ones. (3) *Use.* If the pamphlet has been in the file for more than a year and shows no use, it is safe to weed.

ORDERING

Most jobbers can't take the time or effort to handle pamphlets, and libraries must order them from the publishers. Since many cost less than a dollar, the ordering procedures sometimes cost much more than the actual material. Then, too, while publishers of pamphlet lists try to give accurate ordering information, it is not unusual to find the wrong address, wrong price, and so on.

Given the lack of jobbers, many libraries employ a simple form (title of pamphlet, publisher, and query as to cost if not clear). The postcard or letter is then sent to the publisher and, unless the material is quite expensive, usually bypasses the acquisitions department.

PAMPHLET LISTS

Educators Guide series (see below).
Free and Inexpensive Learning Materials. Nashville, Tenn.: George Peabody College for Teachers, since 1941. Biennial.
Vertical File Index. Bronx, N.Y.: The H. W. Wilson Company, since 1935. Monthly.

The most frequently consulted list for pamphlets and related material is the *Vertical File Index.* The items are arranged by subject, cover a vast area of interests, and are suitable for all types of situation and all levels of instruction, from pregrades through the university. Approximately 2000 items are listed each year; some of these are free, but many are quite expensive.

In the *Educators Guide* series there are several listings that include pamphlets: *Educators Guide to Free Guidance Materials;* . . . *to Free Health;*

. . . Physical Education and Recreation; . . . to Free Science Materials; . . . to Free Social Studies Materials. Arrangement is by type of medium, so the pamphlets may be isolated. Most of the titles are for elementary and secondary schools, although a number are suitable for adults. All are free and consequently all are propaganda to some extent.

Next to *Vertical File Index*, the *Free and Inexpensive Learning Materials* list is one of the most frequently used in elementary and secondary schools. It gives information on some 3000 pamphlets and related publications which can be used in the class. This differs from the other lists in that all items are recommended and have been screened by the publisher.

A useful ongoing critical report of current materials in this area is the regular column by Kathleen Weibel, "Free and Inexpensive Materials" in *Collection Building.* Each source is explained carefully, and full ordering details are given. Other listings will be found in *Booklist, Library Journal, The Wilson Library Bulletin,* and almost any of the other standard library periodicals.

Government is a good source of pamphlets, and current offerings can be found in *The Monthly Checklist of State Publications* (Washington, D.C.: Government Printing Office) and the monthly *Selected U.S. Government Publications* (Washington, D.C.: Government Printing Office).[21] Contact with local or county government offices will put the library on the mailing list for their materials. The quality of these, and more particularly the state publications, will vary greatly. However, as many of the state titles are inexpensive or free, the librarian can take the chance. Unfortunately, most are never reviewed, although some are noted in columns mentioned above. Then, too, there is always the checklist of materials indexed in *Public Affairs Information Service Bulletin,* which is a trifle too specialized for all but the largest libraries.

There are numerous other pamphlet sources. A useful listing will be found in Mildred L. Nickel's *Steps to Service* (Chicago: American Library Association, 1975), pp. 31–32.

Manuscripts and Archives

One speaks of manuscripts and archives in the library in terms of a special situation. Large research libraries have sections or even major parts of the library devoted to the collection of manuscript material, and historical societies may have little but manuscript material.

A manuscript is usually a unique document in that it is not published, printed, or widely distributed. Aside from the ubiquitous private letter, a manuscript may take many forms—from a business record or an unpublished diary to the original draft of a novel.

---

[21] There are numerous guides to government pamphlets, from the definitive *U.S. Monthly Catalog* to the *Subject Bibliographies*—the latter replacing the *Price List* series and offering a subject approach to documents in scores of fields of interest.

"Archives" often is used to describe manuscripts. Technically, however, archives are associated with records and reports, which may or may not be published material. Also, archives are often the by-product of an office, institution, or organization, while a manuscript is more likely to be synonymous with an individual's efforts.[22]

"Archives" has nevertheless become the umbrella for both types of material, and the official journal of those in charge of manuscripts and archives is *The American Archivist*, a publication of The Society of American Archivists and a necessary addition for any library with an interest in the subject.

By implication, if not strict definition, archival collections are primarily of historical and some legal value. This contrasts with collections of current records and reports (which, of course, in time are likely to be designated as archives).

There are numerous collections of archives and records in the United States and throughout the world; among the best known, if only for size, is the National Archives and Records Service, which has been characterized as a "housekeeper for the federal government's own records."[23]

ACQUISITIONS

Smaller libraries, particularly those associated with local historical societies before World War II, began collecting archives and manuscripts with little thought about how they should be handled or preserved. In public and some college and university libraries manuscripts may have been donated over a period of time, again with little thought to their actual use in the library. Then, too, there is the all-too-common situation in which, lacking anyplace else, the university or the town government will use the library to store archives.

Fortunately, provision has been made in the past 20 or 30 years to reassign these records and manuscripts to larger historical societies, research and academic libraries, or other places where they may receive the proper care. This is not always the case—one finds small libraries jealously holding on to a handful of materials—but at least there is agreement among professional librarians that manuscripts should be collected only by those able to handle them properly.

School librarians should not be involved with manuscript collections. Whenever this does arise—when someone wants to donate letters, diaries,

[22] And there are other distinctions. For a discussion see Frank B. Evans, "A Basic Glossary for Archivists, Manuscript Curators and Records Managers," *American Archivist*, July 1974.

[23] Edward Weldon, "Lest We Forget: Setting Priorities for the Preservation and Use of Historical Records," *The American Archivist*, July 1977, p. 299, a good overall view of manuscript collections in America. One of the best guides for librarians is Edward G. Kemp's *Manuscript Solicitation for Libraries, Special Collections, Museums and Archives* (Littleton, Colo.: Libraries Unlimited, 1978).

or other personal papers to the library—the librarian should put the donor in touch with the nearest academic library or the local historical society or state library. There more experienced librarians can evaluate the worth of the material and indicate how best to handle the disposition of the manuscripts.

Many colleges and universities solicit the papers of prominent public officials, authors, and alumni, but this should only be done when there is an adequately developed archives department or section in the library. The solicitation may go on anyway, for—as one expert has pointed out—this is an ego trip for those who are asked to donate papers, and in the process the school may hope that this will "also help them fund improvement such as, perhaps, a new wing on the library."[24]

Archives and manuscripts, then, are a highly specialized type of collection, in-depth discussion of which is outside the scope of this book.[25] Still, even the least involved librarian should realize the importance of such collections and know where to find materials the library itself may not collect.

LOCAL HISTORY COLLECTIONS

Public and smaller college libraries should be encouraged to maintain local history collections, with size and value as the important consideration. Once the collection becomes larger and more valuable than a basic collection of local books, clippings, and county histories (once it takes on manuscripts and archives), the librarian should give serious consideration to a special section for local history and manuscripts or give the manuscripts to larger libraries in the area.

Striking the proper balance is not easy, particularly when the collection begins to take on a monetary value. Valuable historical documents deserve a serious commitment on the part of the library to maintain them safely. Nevertheless, the dedicated smaller public or college library can—and should —do much to help establish a working local history collection.[26]

DISSERTATIONS

Dissertations written by students of a given university are housed in that university library—as a separate collection, part of the collection of the school that gave the degree, or interfiled by subject. No matter how they are handled, dissertations are an important consideration in larger research libraries.

[24] "Archival Research Centers," *The American Archivist*, July 1977, p. 341.

[25] It is a field with many interesting aspects, such as the necessity to be able to separate out true documents from forgeries. A fascinating discussion of this little-considered point is offered by Cheryl Price, "Document Examination in American Archives," *Special Libraries*, September 1977, pp. 299–304.

[26] See Jane Ratner, "Local History Collections . . . ," *Library Journal*, November 1, 1976, pp. 2231–2235.

Most students and teachers will want more than is available in the library itself, and often the library will be asked to acquire a dissertation in a given subject field. This may be relegated to the interlibrary loan office and only under certain situations will it be considered a type of material to be purchased.

University libraries differ on policy about circulating dissertations, particularly on interlibrary loan.[27] Many do not loan, reasoning that the library where the dissertation is needed may purchase it at a reasonable price, either on microfilm or in hard copy, from University Microfilms, publisher of *Dissertation Abstracts.*

Where a dissertation cannot be obtained on interlibrary loan, the acquisitions librarian must determine, along with the user (individual, academic department, or graduate school), whether it should be purchased. If the dissertation is likely to be used more than once or twice, it should be purchased on the less expensive microfilm; if more than casual use is likely, it should be acquired in hard copy.

Methods of purchase are clearly explained in *Dissertation Abstracts,* or the librarian may write or call University Microfilms, which has a virtual monopoly on dissertations as well as many master's degree theses.

While dissertations are listed under subject and often by author in many of the major indexes, the single best source for information is *Dissertation Abstracts International* (Ann Arbor, Mich., University Microfilms, since 1938; monthly). This both locates and gives short abstracts of works accepted for a higher degree in American and Canadian universities. (A few European institutions are listed, too.) While published monthly, it is often cumulated.

Actually, rather than begin in the abstracts, it is faster and more satisfactory to start the search with the *Comprehensive Dissertation Index, 1861–1972* (Ann Arbor, Mich., University Microfilms), which is just what the title indicates. The index, in multiple volumes by discipline, is a key-word subject approach to the basic set. (The last four volumes in the set offer an author entry). One must be careful in searching these volumes by subject: only subjects that appear in titles are included and often it is possible to miss what is wanted. The best way is to try to find a specific dissertation by author or, if a subject approach is the only thing available, search the subject under numerous synonyms.

ARCHIVE BIBLIOGRAPHIES AND LISTS

National Union Catalog of Manuscript Collections. Publisher varies. Since 1959. Annual.

[27] This is considered, along with many other questions, in one of the few articles on dissertations and libraries: Kelly Patterson, et al., "Thesis Handling in University Libraries," *Library Resources and Technical Services,* Summer 1977, pp. 274–284.

U.S. National Historical Publications Commission. *A Guide to Archives and Manuscripts in the United States.* New Haven: Yale University Press, 1961.

In the field of manuscripts and archives there are countless guides, bibliographies, and catalogs. Most of these are highly specialized, and are listed generally in guides to a subject field such as the *Harvard Guide to American History* (Cambridge, Mass.: Harvard University Press, 1974, 2 vols.). The more general aids are to be found, of course, in Eugene Sheehy's *Guide to Reference Books* (9th ed.; Chicago: American Library Association, 1976.)

While there is no one national guide to repositories, the most comprehensive in the United States is the *National Union Catalog of Manuscript Collections.* The multivolume set contains reproductions of catalog cards for well over 40,000 manuscript collections. Supplements give information on some 2000 collections each year. Entry is made possible by cumulative and annual indexes which allow the user to search out a collection through a name, place, subject, or historical period. The difficulty with this general approach is that the catalog card normally gives the broadest indication of holdings, and only after examination can the researcher actually tell how much of the manuscripts, letters, memoranda, diaries, log books, and so on is pertinent to the subject. After 1970 the catalog includes records of oral history interview transcripts and some sound recordings.

Even more general, the *Guide to Archives and Manuscripts in the United States* is nevertheless a good place to begin, since material is listed by state and then by city. There is a discussion of the holdings of 1300 libraries and a detailed list of materials from 8000 individuals. The detailed index is useful, as is an indication whether or not the manuscript collections have issued guides. This is now almost 20 years old, however, and can be used only as a beginning.

Once a collection of material is spotted, of most help is the individual library's archives catalog or guide. For example, *Manuscripts Guide to Collections at the University of Illinois at Urbana–Champaign* (Urbana: University of Illinois Press, 1976) describes in detail records and manuscripts from those in the rare book room to the business archives. Annotations are to be found for most items and there is a detailed index. As more than one critic has observed, this is a model for libraries planning their own guides to collections.

Reports

The report is a valued and increasingly important aspect of government, technology, and science.[28] Specialized libraries may turn over a large per-

---

[28] A. H. Holloway, et al., *Information Work with Unpublished Reports* (London: André Deutsch, 1976). While this has a definite British slant, it gives basic general information on selection and acquisition of reports. The selected bibliographies and "Other Relevant Literature" lists are useful.

centage of their budgets to the acquisition of reports, and even smaller libraries will from time to time rely upon reports.

There are two basic types of reports. The first is usually internal, private, and a report on the progress of research. Sometimes so-called R&D (research and development) activities produce such reports. Usually typewritten or mimeographed, they have limited circulation and may never find their way into a library. The second type is the published report—published in the sense it is available to a wider public. This may be no more than the culmination of the R&D report in another form, or the first report issued after work had been completed on a project. Again, it may be no more than a mimeographed copy, but today it is likely to be in a microform format or in a hard copy produced from microform.

Reports range in form from a few duplicated pages to a fat printed book and in subject matter from advanced science to workshop practices, from scientific research and technical materials to economics, commercial or administrative. They are issued by all kinds of bodies from small laboratories to Government departments. They may be published, semi-published or issued only [on] a limited scale and [as] confidential. They may be issued free or sold.[29]

No one knows how many reports are issued each year—particularly as probably one-half or more are secret, or, at best have limited circulation among a select few. Still, it is estimated the number in the United Kingdom runs to well over 100,000 titles annually, and that total may be multiplied by at least 10 or more for the United States. (This compares with an average of 40,000 books published in the U.S. each year.)

Reports tend to center around the sciences, business, and technology and, to a lesser extent, the social sciences. The humanities depend more upon published books and periodical articles. In the sciences there are a number of journals devoted almost exclusively to reporting on reports. For example, *Accounts of Chemical Research* reviews fundamental studies in progress.

ACQUISITION

In a company, government agency, or research institution many of the R&D and final reports are produced internally by staff. Arrangement must be made between the librarian and management and individuals as to how to handle the reports in the library and whether, in fact, all of them are to be acquired, or only acquired when in a finished state.

Beyond the internal situation, which differs from library to library, is the more controlled external acquisition of published reports. How does the librarian learn about published reports likely to be of interest?[30]

[29] C. W. Hanson, *Introduction to Science Information Work* (London: Aslib, 1971), p. 74.

[30] The library is almost completely concerned with published reports; the R&D type are not likely to be available and may be carefully kept secrets or, at least, circulated only to a limited number of people.

1. At least some of the information will come from the people served by the library—people whose business it is to keep up with and ahead of published materials by means of reports.

2. Most of the basic abstracting and subject indexes—from *Public Affairs Information Service* to *Nuclear Science Abstracts*—index published reports and give information as to where they may be ordered.[31]

3. The single largest publisher of reports is the United States government, and many of these may be located through the Monthly Checklist (see page 141) as well as through more refined services such as the *Congressional Information Service*, which offers an index to congressional publications.

4. Individuals, and to a lesser extent libraries, often may obtain reports through the "invisible college":

. . . a kind of friendship, gossip, grapevine network which, especially through mobile people in key positions, allows news to travel quite rapidly. Contacts are made by telephone, luncheons, letters, meetings, parties, conferences and committees. This network may well extend overseas. When one hears on this jungle telegraph about a new study or report, one rings or writes the chief investigator concerned to obtain copies of his instruments and "a confidential copy of the first draft" of the report.

A researcher who does not have access to this informal network is handicapped in that he does not know the latest developments in his field and may be embarrassed by such ignorance. He is also handicapped in that he may never see some reports because many of them are not distributed or published in any formal way after they have been submitted to the sponsoring body.[32]

There are, however, at least two major ways of gaining access to reports through formal channels.

REPORT BIBLIOGRAPHIES AND LISTS

Government Reports Announcements. Springfield, Va.: National Technical Information Service (NTIS), since 1946. Semimonthly.[33]
Resources in Education. Washington, D.C.: U.S. Educational Resources Information Center (ERIC), since 1966. Monthly.

With emphasis on science and technology and a slight nod to the social sciences, *Government Reports Announcements* lists and abstracts about

[31] The amount of report literature indexed is limited. For example, Inspec (which includes three abstracting services in physics, computers, and electronics) is made up primarily of journal articles. "Nearly 80 percent of the abstracts . . . are of journal articles, 15 percent are of conference papers, and 5 percent are books, monographs, reports, dissertations and parents" (*Database*, September 1978, p. 70).

[32] Roy Lundin, "Access to Research: What Happens to All Those Reports," *Australian Library Journal*, January 1978, p. 10.

[33] For a representative list of NTIS reports as well as a brief introductory statement on how to use the reports, see Rao Aluri, "Reference Sources among NTIS Technical Reports," *Reference Services Review*, April-June 1978, pp. 53–56.

70,000 reports each year. All are the results of moneys given to individuals or to organizations by more than 300 federal agencies for research on a wide variety of topics. As part of the grant or funding the individual or company usually is required to write a report—which eventually finds its way here.

Librarians who want to scan the service for possible materials can do so by looking under one or more of 22 subject headings, all of which have major subdivisions. Actually, the way to search for specific materials is to use the *Government Reports Index*, which comes out with the abstracts as a separate publication, lists material by subject, personal and corporate author, contract number, and accession report.

For smaller to medium-sized libraries, there is a cut-down version of the service, *Weekly Government Abstracts*, which gives information both on published and to-be-published works. There are also subject divisions: *Library and Information Sciences* is issued weekly and abstracts reports in this subject area. It gives brief information, too, on related aspects of the subject.

Selection as such may not be exercised by large research libraries because the announcements and the index are backed up by a standing-order microfiche service the library may buy in part (by subject) or complete. On the other hand, the ease with which reports may be purchased is such that smaller libraries should use an on-demand type of service and withhold orders until a request is made for a specific item.[34]

Much the same backup of documents on microfiche is offered by ERIC through *Resources in Education*. Most of the reports are available on standing order, but may be selected individually as needed by the library. Larger libraries will have a file of the microfiche reports within easy distance of the index.

Resources in Education abstracts about 15,000 reports each year. (It also includes selected books as well as dissertations and other related papers.) The reports cover all aspects of education, including related fields such as library science and sociology. (A twin aid to ERIC is *Current Index to Journals in Education* which indexes educational periodicals, as does *Education Index* in a somewhat overlapping way.)

Both ERIC and NTIS services are available for online computer search and are among the top ten or so favorite resource tools for larger reference libraries throughout the United States.

CONFERENCE PAPERS

A related area is conference papers. These are products of thousands of meetings held each year, and while some may be later published as books or monographs, many remain as issued—photocopied, mimeographed, or

[34] Joseph Mihokovich, "On Demand Publishing at NTIS," *Journal of Micrographics*, July-August 1978. This is a summary of NTIS publishing activities, which run to about 12,000 copies of reports each day.

otherwise limited-reproduction papers delivered as talks or discussed at a conference. Many are indexed in the standard indexing and abstracting services. From the addresses given (if not always the price) the librarian with a need for a given paper in a given subject area can often locate it through an index.

A more systematic approach is offered by *Conference Papers Index* (since 1973; monthly), which has listed over half a million reports and annually indexed about 100,000 more. Some 5000 conferences (many of which are held at regular intervals) are covered. The index, which is cumulated both quarterly and annually, is to papers in the life sciences, chemistry, engineering, and related fields. There are author, subject, and title indexes. Another helpful feature for acquisitions librarians is the fact that data for almost all the papers is given: where they may be purchased, price, and format. The index is available for search through a computer-data base.

Part Three

SELECTION OF NONPRINT MATERIALS

IO

Media Selection and Evaluation

Librarians are talking about well-known methods of communication—film, television, recordings—when they discuss nonprint or media (or nonbook and audiovisual materials). And the average librarian (who, like almost everyone else, watches television, goes to movies, and listens to recordings) knows something about the media from everyday activity. But in terms of library selection and evaluation, there is much more to media—or nonprint, as we shall be calling it in this book.[1]

A broadening communications spectrum requires a new array of practical knowledge, insight and handling skills, particularly in the areas of sound and images. Its role in support of educational programs in secondary schools has brought about the development of "media," "instructional" or "learning resources center." The significance of the audio-visual culture is increasing as nonprint forms join the book in providing information and learning. An awareness of the possible implications through these new vehicles of information, together with the competence necessary for their organization and servicing, has become indispensible information for a large sector of modern librarianship.[2]

---

[1] Librarians have not yet found an umbrella term for materials that are neither books nor periodicals. Films, recordings, video cassettes, slides, and the like are clearly understood as to their format, but how to describe them as a family? Schools favor "media"; public librarians are torn between "media" and "audiovisual"; college and university libraries use both, but sometimes favor "nonprint." Sanction for the terminology is found many places, particularly in the standards for school libraries, which has been renamed *Media Programs: District and School* (Chicago: American Library Association, 1975). The related *Guidelines for Audiovisual Materials and Services for Large Public Libraries* (Chicago: American Library Association, 1975) considers much the same material but calls it audiovisual. Not to be forgotten for public libraries is *Media and the Young Adult* (Chicago: American Library Association, 1977). Then there is *Recommendations for Audiovisual Materials and Services for Small and Medium-Sized Public Libraries* (Chicago: American Library Association, 1975). Somewhat similar guides for college and university libraries use even other terms; see *Nonprint Media in Academic Libraries* (Chicago: American Library Association, 1974).

[2] Mathilde V. Rovelstad, "The Changing of Dimensions of Library Science," *Libri*, vol. 27, no. 1 (1977), p. 16.

Books remain its major medium, but today's library also has much to offer in a variety of nonprint items. The major ones we consider are films, recordings, television, filmstrips, slides, pictures, and related media.[3]

The relative importance of each of the forms can be measured in terms of sales to schools and colleges. According to the 1978 edition of *Educational Media Yearbook* (New York: R. R. Bowker, pp. 108ff), nonbook sales totaled about $260 million in 1976 compared with book sales of $4.6 billion for 1977. Sixteen-millimeter films account for $63 million, led only by sound filmstrips at $65 million. Next are multimedia kits (two or more kinds of media such as filmstrips and recordings), with sales of $55 million. In relative order, other media include games, manipulative and realia ($17 million); cassettes ($16 million); silent filmstrips ($9 million); and transparencies ($9 million). Other media, all under $8 million: precorded videotapes, recordings, 8mm silent and sound films, slides, prerecorded tapes, and study prints.

Figures for public libraries are less current, although here too films lead the list of most popular media, followed closely by filmstrips and recordings.

The Media Debate

James Alcott, publisher of *Harper's* magazine, sums up a feeling some librarians have today about the new media: "The written word is no longer pre-eminent as a shaper of thought. It has been usurped by electronics. . . . By the year 2001, the United States will be well on its way to becoming a post-literate society."[4]

Reaction to this statement takes several forms:

1. The antimedia people point out that the library is one of the last, best hopes to retain and guard literacy. The media may dominate the environment, but that is no reason to give in and automatically to call readings and books obsolete is to join the yahoos and anti-intellectuals.

2. Some media people take an opposite tack, asking for understanding of the media, not fear of them. They point out that this is one more way to information, knowledge, and esthetic enjoyment. They ask that the librarian keep the proper relationship between what is happening outside the library (reliance on television, film, and recordings) and what is going on inside the library (reliance on traditional print resources).

These two basic arguments have numerous modifications. It hardly needs to be said, but is often forgotten by both camps, that the media are neither

---

[3] Not considered here: the computer and the bibliographic data base, and programmed instruction and teaching machines. Both are of importance, particularly the first, but selection is usually left to specialists when room for selection exists at all.

[4] "Magazines Sacrifice Content . . . ," *Folio*, August 1978, p. 23.

good or harmful in themselves. What is important is how they are used.[5] Even advocates of nonprint materials are willing to admit many media have been abused:

Perhaps, in the past decade, too many influential persons became hooked on the notion that the media would become the salvation of learning. All too many embraced the media as a cop-out—a means of handling difficult students or unfamiliar content. . . . This led . . . to large quantities and collections of nonprint media which were supposed to insure that through exposure to them every child would learn something.[6]

A backlash was to be expected, particularly when the new media did not automatically solve the problems of education. The reaction against nonprint came in the late 1970s. Closely related to the so-called return to basics, inflation, and the desire for tax cuts was an outcry (in some communities, a polite murmur) in opposition to spending money for media other than books and periodicals. Librarians quite properly are fighting this move, defending justified expenditures on materials that have added to, not detracted from the learning process. It is nevertheless important to realize that "The school media program and its personnel become targets for budget cutting when administrators make bottom line funding decisions."[7]

AUDIENCE FOR THE MEDIA

No matter the role the different media play, each should be represented in the library. The library serves the communication needs of the whole community; as part of that communication pattern nonprint material must be included in the library. If the library is to serve "all current and potential individuals and groups in society,"[8] it is necessary to find ways to reach people who can't read, do not choose to read, or (more likely) read only when necessary. Serving this group with both books and nonprint material, the library acts "as an agency to guide the user at all levels to the most significant representative materials [necessary] to meet each individual's need for information, knowledge and ideas."[9] Some of the nonprint material in a library may "allow easy access for people previously excluded by lack of education, lack of language facility, lack of cultural backgrounds, age, physical or mental handicaps, and apathy."[10]

[5] Even this is open to debate. Marshall McLuhan's insistence on the "medium is the message" is sometimes difficult to refute when the average American watches several hours of television each day.

[6] D. Philip Baker, *School and Public Library Media Programs* (Syracuse, N.Y.: Gaylord, 1977), p. 48.

[7] Stanley R. Wrinkle, "The New ABCs of Our Schools . . . ," *American Libraries,* November 1978, p. 588. This and several other articles in the same issue point up the less than encouraging developments in media centers.

[8] "A Mission Statement for Public Libraries," *American Libraries,* December 1977, p. 618.

[9] Ibid., p. 617.

[10] Ibid., p. 620.

While the preceding argument for media is primarily addressed to public libraries, the same points can be made for the school and academic libraries. Both are involved with the educational and cultural aspects of the individual, and both should be anxious to extend services.

THE REAL ARGUMENT FOR NONPRINT

Having recalled the traditional reasons for opening the library to materials other than books and periodicals, consider several other realities of selection, justifications for including nonprint materials in the library. As one critic observed, each of the media has its own unique esthetic merit; each has its own method of communicating information and providing entertainment. This is an important part of existence, and to reject, say, films is to reject a major experience for millions of Americans.

One may stress the use of the nonprint media for disadvantaged people, for those unable to cope with reading, but it is harmful and somewhat condescending to imply that a nonreader should forsake literacy for television, recordings, or films. The nonreader should be able to enjoy all media and should be given every opportunity in the library to learn how to use and enjoy books as well as films. Also, to imply that it does not require a certain type of judgment and literacy to enjoy certain types of film and music, just as it does for print materials, is to totally misunderstand the media and goes a long way to explain the disenchantment with media mentioned earlier. If nonprint materials are seen solely as a way of solving educational problems, they are bound to fail. They are, after all, only another way, not the way to solve educational difficulties. The error is probably due as much to overenthusiastic media salespeople as to anything else, but it is a mistake librarians (even those opposed to the nonprint materials) should appreciate.

No one medium will meet all the needs of all the people all of the time. Individuals prefer different media for different purposes. The library has an obligation to provide many types of materials to meet the needs of users.

There are unfortunate misunderstandings about media in some libraries. The librarian, for example, does not order a film to lure a person to read a book. The film is sufficient unto itself, as is any medium. Certainly, one may go from a book to a film to a record, but the sequence does not necessarily follow, nor is it really necessary other than to enhance pleasure and understanding. The book can be complemented by nonprint materials. The word is *complement, not replace.*

The point is that "media properly understood, includes book and nonbook, print and nonprint."[11] The librarian who enjoys recordings, films, and other nonprint materials enjoys the world and must show others the dimension.

[11] Lillian Wehmeyer, Media and Learning: Present and Future," *Catholic Library World*, November 1978, p. 152. A good, solid argument for media, particularly as the author introduces less frequently employed justifications. The second part of the article is in the December issue.

of that world. This requires understanding by the librarian and competence in evaluating nonprint materials—skills as difficult to master as evaluating books. Even a cursory glance at the variety and number of film critics will show the skeptic that it takes something more than being able to identify a film to evaluate one.

By Type of Library

Various types of library treat the media in equally various ways, so much so that it is difficult to make generalizations, but approach to the media is best outlined in the various library standards and guidelines.

SCHOOL LIBRARY MEDIA CENTERS

The nonprint media are closely connected with elementary and secondary schools—so closely that some librarians think of "schools" and the "new media" as synonyms.[12] At the same time, too many librarians believe that because nonprint is so much a part of the school library it has little or nothing to do with other types of library. This neat rationale for minimal involvement of the typical academic or public library with nonprint materials is a fallacious argument.

Aside from the public served, there are differences between selection for the typical school library and other types:

1. The media must be closely connected to current curricula and probable changes in those curricula. This means selected media for educational purposes, although with some attention to recreation. Kits are a favored medium in many school libraries, in addition to filmstrips and instructional tapes.[13]

2. There is likely to be stress on linguistics and language recordings and tapes, which requires special knowledge (particularly for selection and often for use in a laboratory situation) on the part of the librarian.

3. There is more than a passing need to integrate the various media carefully, particularly for certain courses. This means evaluation of how a book, film, or recording may be used independently or in coordination with a learning program.

4. Ideally, the librarian will make materials and equipment available as necessary to both the students and the support staff. However, as with other library services, it is sometimes necessary—indeed, considered part of the educational process—to teach students how to find the materials needed,

[12] For a good history of the development of the school media center see Marilyn L. Miller, "Collection Development in School Media Centers: National Recommendation and Reality," *Collection Building*, vol. 1, no. 1 (1978), pp. 25–48.
[13] *Marketing, Selection and Acquisition of Materials for School Media Programs* (Chicago: American Library Association, 1977).

how to use equipment, and how to relate specific material to specific needs. This requires constant attention and training, usually by the librarian, for both students and staff.

5. Librarians, at one time or another, compile bibliographies. If full use is to be made of the media, the school librarian will be required to compile more than a normal number of media lists for use by both students and staff.

6. In addition to simply learning how to operate equipment, many librarians take part in or lead courses in television or film production, which requires added skills. At a minimum, librarians will be expected to help create certain materials for certain situations, if only a tape or a video-recording.

7. There are numerous outside activities—from applying for grants and funding from local, regional, state, or federal agencies to initiating and developing local or regional networks for purchase and distribution of some media.

The guidelines give quite specific quantitative standards for nonprint materials, including equipment and personnel. These should be studied carefully. They go into considerable detail but may be summarized:

Visual images include 500 to 2000 filmstrips, ten projectors and 20 viewers; 2000 to 6000 slides and transparencies, six slide projectors, ten slide viewers and ten overhead projectors; 800 to 1200 graphics (posters, art and study prints, maps and globes); access to a minimum of 3000 films (16mm or super 8mm and videotapes) plus equipment; 1500 to 2000 recordings (including records, tapes, cassettes, and disks) and equipment. Beyond this, precise figures are given for games and toys, models and sculptures, specimens, closed-circuit television, and other media likely to be found in a well-equipped library.

Budget recommendations for school libraries are equally specific. The school should spend a minimum of 10 percent of the national per-pupil operation cost on the media center. No percentage within this is given, as in the public library guidelines, for particular nonprint materials.[14]

While the budget figure is recommended, the actual amount spent on materials for school media centers is somewhat less than ideal:

In 1974 school library media centers held 520 million volumes of books and 100 million items of nonprint audiovisual materials including such materials as games, kits, and specimens. . . . The acquisitions [of print materials] are still only about 40 percent of indicated need . . . and while 100 million items of nonprint items were owned by school library media centers, guidelines would indicate the need for one billion such items.[15]

14 *Media Programs: District and School* (Chicago: American Library Association, 1975).

15 *National Inventory of Library Needs, 1975* (Washington, D.C.: National Commission on Libraries and Information Science, 1977), pp. 110–111.

PUBLIC LIBRARIES

Public library involvement with nonprint materials has had a varied history, culminating (some would say just beginning) with standards, adopted in 1975, that officially recognize the place of the new media in public libraries.[16] The guidelines for large public library systems call for audiovisual resources to take "between 10 percent and 15 percent (or $1.50 per capita) of the unit's total materials budget." The same recommendation was made in the guidelines for small and medium-sized libraries.[17]

Quantitative standards are given in the guidelines, usually by size of the library. For example, in a population of 150,000 to 299,999 there should be a minimum of 300 16mm films and about 30 purchased per year. When the population served goes to 5 million and over, the minimum jumps to 3000 films and 200 new ones per year.[18] Similar estimates are given for other media and for personnel, space, and the like. While somewhat dated, the quantitative figures remain useful as at least a rough guide for beginners and for librarians attempting to justify a budget for nonprint materials.

ACADEMIC LIBRARIES

College and universities were among the last to adopt nonprint for educational purposes.

As a result of this reluctance, separate university audiovisual libraries grew up on the campuses. They were often underfunded and relegated to odd corners . . . [only] a few university library administrators included audiovisual materials in the library collection.[19]

During the late 1950s and 1960s these centers became increasingly well funded and began to take on other duties, from television to production of slides and photographs for instruction. Today these centers may be under the jurisdiction of the library but are more likely to be independent, a part of the basic instructional program of the college or university. The division of labor (from selection and acquisitions to servicing of equipment) is often welcomed by librarians or (particularly true today) a battle rages to win back the nonprint materials for the library.

The larger the library the less likely it is to have a nonprint collection and

---

[16] The best overview is James W. Brown, *New Media in Public Libraries* (Syracuse, N.Y.: Jeffrey Norton/Gaylord, 1976), a detailed analysis of a survey of 50 states and 235 public libraries made during 1975.

[17] *Guidelines for Audiovisual Materials and Services for Large Public Libraries. Recommendations for Audiovisual Materials and Services for Small and Medium Sized Public Libraries.* Both published 1975 by the American Library Association, Chicago.

[18] *Guidelines for Audiovisual Materials*, p. 16.

[19] Jerome K. Miller, Introduction to "Films in Public Libraries," *Library Trends*, Summer 1978, p. 4.

the more likely the collection is to be under the jurisdiction of the audiovisual center. At the same time, librarians without any direct dealings with nonprint are normally going to be the ones most vehement in their denunciation of the nonbook media. How much of this is justified reaction to the threat to the book or a recognition of diminution of power lost to the audiovisual center depends on the situation.[20]

Today it is unusual for an average-size academic library not to have at least some form of nonprint materials or access to them through audiovisual centers. Still, there remain some problems of selection peculiar to an academic situation:

1. As the majority of the nonprint media are focused on the needs of elementary and secondary-school-age people, is the item about to be purchased appropriate for the academic audience? Obviously a health cartoon made for children is not likely to succeed in college; on the other hand, a film on the structure of the body may be equally applicable for high school and college students.

2. Many of the selection aids, retrospective lists, directories, and other media reference aids are also directed to elementary and secondary schools, with a nod to public libraries. This is changing somewhat, but for some of the media it is difficult to find adequate aids.

Guidelines or standards for academic libraries are of little help with nonprint materials. As early as 1959 the "Standards for College Libraries" recognized the importance of audiovisual materials but did little more. The 1975 standards give no precise rules or quantitative or qualitative guidelines. The rationale is that this is not possible because there is no consensus "among educators as to the range, extent and configuration of nonprint services."[21]

Evaluation

In the broadest sense, the selection principles that govern nonprint materials are similar to those that govern selection of print materials, but there are differences—or, more properly, variations.

With these variations, the ten objective points for evaluation of books may be employed for nonprint media. They include:

[20] Another not-often-expressed reason for antagonism to nonprint materials by academic librarians is that these are closely connected with elementary and secondary, as well as public, libraries.

[21] "Standards for College Libraries," *College Research Libraries News*, October 1975, p. 279. The standards for junior colleges are no more explicit, although they recognize the importance of nonprint materials; see "Guidelines for Two Year College Learning Resources Programs," *College Research Libraries News*, December 1972, pp. 305–315. For further discussion of this subject see Evelyn G. Clement, "Standards," in Pearce S. Grove (ed.), *Nonprint Media in Academic Libraries* (Chicago: American Library Association, 1975), pp. 66–78.

1. Purpose, scope, and audience

The purpose is usually clear from both the form (recording or film) and the instrinsic material (jazz or classical; educational or feature). The scope may be measured in terms of length, depth of coverage, and similar criteria.

The audience may be judged much as one would for print materials. However, audience determination is more complex here in that even a child may enjoy a film based on an adult book or an adult enjoy a film based on a child's classic. Young adults may be more than able to cope with material they could not appreciate in print, both in terms of the complexity of the vocabulary and the emotional aspect. For example, *War and Peace* as a novel may be too complex for the average fifteen-year-old but within grasp as a film or even as an abbreviated voice recording.

While a book is for the individual, much nonprint is for a group. The librarian must ask: Will what is useful for one person be equally useful for many? The basic reason for the query is economic. It is one thing to spend $10 for a book for an individual or a few readers, quite another to spend several hundred dollars for a film that will be enjoyed by only a few people.

This question leads to another, concerning programs. When the librarian purchases most nonprint material, is must be evaluated in terms of group use, or programming. These questions must be considered:

a. Does the media program address itself to basic learning skills (such as reading) in such a way as to encourage students to master a discipline? If a public librarian is asking the question, he or she should consider the dimension of entertainment and recreation as well as education. Put another way: Does the program fulfill a need, or is the librarian simply buying this and that more for form than for content? What is the relationship between this medium and that medium in terms of program objectives?

b. Does the media program allow a change in direction, a modification, even abandonment when it proves of little or no value? Unfortunately, once committed to, say, a film program that may or may not work, too many librarians become more involved with the program than with the results. The librarian should be intelligent (and brave) enough to say "I [we] made a mistake."

c. Does the media program really involve the audience, or is the video-tape, for example, the librarian's notion of what the audience should find enjoyable and instructive? This poses the nice question of how much critical authority the librarian (and teachers and others involved with the program) must exercise over choice and change in direction. Ideally, it is a meeting of the needs and desires of the audience and the skills, ability, and experience of the selectors.

2. Difficulty

As with print materials, clear signals are given by distributors and producers of nonprint items that certain ones are prepared for certain age groups. The typical child's recording is not suitable for the chamber music fan.

Some librarians draw a line between popular and classical in music and will purchase only the latter. This is an error, particularly in the average community serving people who love all types of music or serving the average teenager, who may find more in a rock-concert album than in a classical composer's work.

One must argue that "difficulty" really is not the word to use in this connection; it is more a matter of taste. Anyone can listen to a rock recording or see a film about automobiles without having difficulty comprehending the overt sounds and sights. (Difficulty in reading may be just that, and block the poor reader from getting past the first paragraph.) The best way to evaluate the relative difficulty of a nonprint item for the audience the librarian has in mind is to know both the audience and the medium well. Fortunately, most reviews, distributors, and producers indicate sophistication level.

Related to this criterion is the difficulty involved in using audiovisual equipment. Some librarians, and certainly teachers and laypeople, may shy away from the use of films for lack of experience with the equipment. Where nonprint media are provided there should be equal provision for instruction in the use of basic equipment. This may be done through individual assistance, written instructions, and workshops. (The librarian may also offer instruction in the production of audiovisual materials, particularly 16mm and 8mm films. See also item 7, page 236.)

3. Authority, honesty, and credibility of producer, director, and performer

There are certain basic questions to ask about the media: Are the facts, esthetic qualities, or whatever presented in a reliable fashion? Is there any overtone of propaganda, particularly if the material is free or inexpensive? If propaganda is present, is it objectionable?

Over a period of time the librarian learns which distributors and producers are to be trusted, which are to be considered with care. One may say the same thing about recording companies, film directors, and popular performers, but it is impossible to make a list. This only comes with experience and conversations and exchanges with other librarians—by far the best way to ascertain the reliability of this or that media producer.

4. Subject matter

The rules for print materials apply here. The librarian purchases or rents the nonprint items that have a subject interest for the audience served and buys heavily in areas of particular interest.

Subject matter alone in the media is hardly enough. Unfortunately, too many library reviews concentrate solely on content to the exclusion of presentation. For example, film X may be ideal for a library in that the content is focused on development of dams, but the presentation may be so poor as to lull to sleep even the most avid dam builder.

Beyond that is a related question: What are the advantages of one particular medium as contrasted with another? Are they different enough to warrant purchase of another medium?

Sometimes the answer is evident: A picture is worth a thousand words— or is it? A recording is a better investment than an explanation of what constitutes a composer's work—or is it? Much depends on the audience, purpose of the library, and the elusive value judgment. For example, in one notorious case a university spent thousands of dollars on oral history tapes, dutifully transcribed them, and then destroyed the tapes. Why? Because it was felt (wrongly) the best format for oral history was the typed transcript, not the voice of the person. Actually, both formats serve different purposes and different audiences.

The value judgment of which medium is best for which situation or audience is hotly debated and unlikely ever to be resolved.[22] One must know one's own biases, either in favor or in opposition (or neutral) regarding one medium as opposed to another. Even the most objective judge is likely to have difficulty deciding, for example, whether to purchase a film on Egyptian history or a dozen books about it. True, the film may present materials more graphically, but will it be as lasting, as often used as the book? Doesn't the book offer more information? Or are there possibly too many repetitive books on a subject that could be nicely balanced by a film? The answers to these questions depend on many variables, and the librarian must realize he or she can make mistakes, even with the best of intentions.

Any decision regarding any kind of medium must be predicated on knowledge and not preference. The most beneficial method of making a determination would be to identify all the media formats applicable to a particular piece of information, list them in order of how well they present the information, and find if indeed the information is available in the forms identified.[23]

5. Comparison

How does this work compare with others in the same medium? This is an important aspect since there may be many versions of the same thing— scores of renditions of a piece of music or approaches to an educational

---

[22] True believers in one or other of the media do not feel this doubt. They are convinced, for example, that book or film is the true approach. If it comes to deciding which is more important, it is the book or the film—depending on what banner is overhead. Fortunately, most librarians are not so sure, only asking to be convinced that in this or that case medium X is better than medium Y.

[23] James Cabeceiras, *The Multimedia Library* (New York: Academic Press, 1978), p. 20. The author supports this conviction with considerable skill, but one must ask just when does a librarian have either the time or the patience to go through the multiple steps suggested to judge the relative value of one medium over another. Cabeceiras' book is useful in that it does analyze steps that for many librarians and experts in media are now taken at a subconscious level.

problem in a film. The vast amount of nonbook material requires valid comparisons.

A correlation to comparison is the tendency of duplication among the media:

A particular filmstrip may be repackaged with other materials, reissued with changes in title or captions but not in frames (without identification of its origins), or made available for distribution through a film [source] whose catalogs omit producer and copyright information. We need a standard means for identification of the item.[24]

The situation is familiar enough to book sélectors, who sometimes choose a book published in England or reissued in this country as a new work only to find it is an older book reissued in a disguise, innocent or otherwise.

6. Timeliness

This is a consideration, particularly of such things as educational films and slides used for social studies. Generally, the same rules apply here as for print materials.

7. Format

The format of nonprint material raises a twofold question. First, how good is the quality of the film or the record? For example, many librarians avoid certain record companies because the disks tend to warp easily, are badly marred in terms of sound quality, and so forth.[25] Much the same may be said about the quality of some films, kits, and slides.

Equally important is the fact that most nonprint media require additional equipment.[26] It is not enough to rent or buy a film; one must also know what equipment is necessary to show the film.

A few factors are similar in every equipment evaluation:[27]

a. Is the equipment portable, easy to carry, reasonably easy to connect?

b. How durable is the equipment? A cassette, for example, tends to last longer than a record, although when used badly it can be destroyed.

c. Is the equipment easy or difficult to use and maintain? Also important: How many people are likely to use it?

[24] Mary Johnson, "Media Selection: Six Concerns," *Catholic Library World*, May-June 1976, p. 416.

[25] See almost any issue of a music magazine for the poor state of American records. This has even become a popular issue: Sylvia Porter's column "Snap, Crackle, Pop . . ." (Albany [N.Y.] *Times-Union*, October 15, 1978, p. E11) points out that the boom in the production of records has resulted in "a steady decline in the quality of American-made records."

[26] *Media Programs: District and School* (Chicago: American Library Association, 1975). Chapter 6, "Collections," gives specific minimum requirements for equipment as well as the media themselves. This is a good overview of the types of equipment connected with media collections.

[27] Need for equipment helps to explain still another term for library: resource learning center. This nicely weds the equipment factor and the media, and for this reason is favored by some over media library center.

d. In a rapidly changing technology (such as the current struggle over video playback equipment) it is best to purchase as little as possible until a decision is reached as to best and better.

e. What is the life expectancy of the equipment? Based on use, how well will it hold up? Can it be easily serviced and repaired?

Regular courses, workshops, and programs should be provided to train both librarians and the public in the use of nonprint equipment. Money should be provided for this in the budget, as should funds for maintenance, checking, and replacement. Most nonprint materials should be checked for damage when they are returned, and time and money must be set aside for necessary maintenance.

8. Price

The librarian must have a fairly good idea of the relative cost of each of the media. This is particularly true in times of tight budget; as Robert Broadus points out: "If a color motion picture film is purchased, it means some thirty books or twenty filmstrips must be rejected. . . . Assumptions as to value have to be made in spite of the fact that no one has enough information to make decisions with a great degree of assurance."[28]

The cost plot thickens when the media advocate counters "Yes, but if two periodical subscriptions, five art books, and three science titles . . . are purchased, a good color film cannot be purchased." The librarian must make some choice based as much on the media, needs of users, and budget as on individual bias for or against a certain type of media.

Equipment such as that used to record video or show motion pictures can be extremely costly. Equipment used to play recordings may be modestly priced or run into the thousands of dollars. In almost all areas there is a wide choice of prices, which does not necessarily mean a wide choice of quality. Any consumer realizes that high price is not automatically equal to high quality, and the same rule is applicable here—even more so, as dealers who sell to institutions sometimes have the mistaken impression that any price goes.

The librarian should ask several basic questions: (1) Does the distributor guarantee the equipment for a reasonable length of time? (2) Is maintenance available? (3) How expensive will special storage facilities be? Books fit nicely onto shelves, but what is to be done with films, games, recordings? (4) How much space must be allocated for media repair, for listening and viewing, and for countless other things connected with nonbook materials?

Cost plays a major role in the degree of acceptance of nonprint materials in a library. Media advocates argue that too often the budget is balanced in favor of print. According to one critic:

If you look in the latest *American Library Directory*, you'll see that a library with a $200,000 materials budget allots $5000 for media, and out of that comes

---

[28] "Selection and Acquisition," in Pearce S. Grove (ed.), *Nonprint Media in Academic Libraries* (Chicago: American Library Association, 1975), p. 56.

both nonprint and microfiche. That's showing up as a very strong trend and you can imagine what percentage is being spent on microfiche. . . . Where you have a sizable materials budget, all too often only one to ten percent goes for nonprint.[29]

Surveys support this view; a study of Wisconsin public libraries found that 60 percent of the librarians "look at non-book materials in the same way as books—all are sources of information and entertainment." At the same time, regular funding for nonbook materials is scarce. "With low funding for all library services, audiovisual services are most often considered an extra, or the icing on the already undernourished cake."[30]

9. Curriculum support

As the media are most extensively employed in elementary and secondary schools, a major question concerns how they support the curriculum. Some would say that too much of the media is dedicated to this one cause: when one looks about for films, sound records, kits, and the like, the vast majority are curriculum-oriented, so much so that quality is often sacrificed for content. In any case, the librarian should always try to obtain the best medium for the audience.

10. Demand

There is some demand for recordings, which the librarian should evaluate much as he or she does printed materials, but there seems to be little demand for other media. This is likely to change when and if video cassettes are widely available, and one can well imagine the day when the cassette will be as popular as the best-selling novel.

WHO SELECTS?

Nonprint media are selected much as books are. Librarians rely primarily on reviews. Individual media specialists make suggestions to the library selection committee or to a system center. The suggestions in turn are supported by reviews and are discussed by the librarians charged with selection.

Schools and some larger academic centers have distinct sections, divisions, or departments charged with the selection and maintenance of nonbook materials. They work closely with the involved librarians, who may be checking out the material to users. Most librarians prefer the integrated

[29] "Media Censorship and Printist Librarians," *American Libraries*, November 1977, pp. 543, 545. The quote is from Don Roberts. Lest one think Roberts is exaggerating, consider another statement—by Jan E. Cureton in "Films in Public Libraries," *Library Trends*, Summer 1978, p. 93: "It came as something of a shock recently, upon visiting a library, when the librarian proudly pointed to the 'audiovisual room.' It consisted entirely of microfiche readers and files."

[30] Kandy B. Brandt, "Audiovisuals in Public Libraries," *Wisconsin Library Bulletin*, July-August 1978, p. 178.

system; the feeling is that the people who choose print materials must have control over nonprint as well because the two are so closely linked.[31]

Media specialists make individual decisions based on reviews for the library and meet in a committee when needed to preview, discuss, and decide. Where reviews cannot be located, the material must be evaluated by the individual or the committee. Most distributors will send films and other expensive nonprint materials on approval. If not, the librarian should try to examine it somewhere else, in another library or in a district media center.

Substantially more nonprint material than books will be requested for examination. The reason includes high cost, lack of reviews, and necessity to be sure the material suits the audience, particularly in schools where special attention is given to vocabulary and concepts appropriate for given levels and grades. Another reason for examination is that some librarians who feel perfectly comfortable judging print material may want to see or hear nonprint items before purchase.

General Nonprint Selection Aids

The importance of nonprint materials in libraries is not reflected in bibliographic aids. The development of these tools has been slow and not always satisfactory. Today they are vastly improved over a decade ago (and unquestionably will improve) but many gaps remain.

Not the least of the reasons for this situation is the relative recency of nonprint media in libraries. A second reason—as we have seen—is the historic placement of the field as uniquely instructional, related almost solely to elementary and secondary schools. The historic "major concern on the instructional frame negatively influenced the control of the media."[32] It is no accident that most of the bibliographic aids today are still strongly influenced, if not governed, by the needs of schools.

General Aids

Rufsvold, Margaret. *Guides to Educational Media*, 4th ed. Chicago: American Library Association, 1977.

NICEM (National Information Center for Educational Media). *Various services*. Los Angeles: University of Southern California, National Information Center, since 1967.

Sive, Mary. *Selecting Instructional Media*, 2nd ed. Littleton, Colo.: Libraries Unlimited, 1978.

[31] There are numerous discussions of the integrated against the decentralized collection, such as Doris A. Hicks, "Management of Non-Print School Library Materials . . . ," *Catholic Library World*, April 1978, pp. 386–388.

[32] Jane Anne Hannigan, "A Conundrum of Our Times: Access to Media," *School Media Quarterly*, Summer 1977, p. 257.

There is no overall bibliography to the media comparable to *Books in Print*, or even a comprehensive guide such as *Guide to Reference Books*. Lacking these, media experts depend on a few time-tested general identification lists and bibliographies and the specialized lists considered under various media.

The best guide to bibliographies and media publishers' catalogs is Rufsvold's *Guides to Educational Media*, which has clear annotations, with complete information on basic books, lists, bibliographies, and catalogs of films, instructional materials, recordings, slides, and videotapes. Arrangement is alphabetical by title with a good author, subject, and title index.

The Rufsvold title should be a first in any collection of nonprint materials; its careful selection of aids will serve any type of library as a basic bibliography. In fact, the list is so carefully constructed that the inexperienced librarian may order almost everything without fear of duplication.

Another version of the *Guides to Educational Media* is Mary Sive's *Selecting Instructional Media* (first published in 1975 as *Educators' Guide to Media Lists*), which lists the various aids with outline bibliographic information and content descriptions. Much of this is a repeat of the Rufsvold listing, and is necessary only for larger collections.

Somewhat more limited in scope but of great importance to media centers is Christine Wynar's *Guide to Reference Books for School Media Centers* (Littleton, Colo.: Libraries Unlimited, 1973; supplement, 1976). Updated by new editions or supplements, this is primarily a guide to reference books suitable for kindergarten through grade 12. The first section, Media Sources, lists and annotates basic titles of value to any media person.

The nearest thing to a bibliography of everything available in the media is the NICEM indexes, which list uncritically what is available in nonprint materials.

The indexes are a series of individual works, not a single title, that list about half a million items. The breakdown is four volumes on 16mm films; two volumes on 35mm filmstrips; two volumes on overhead transparencies; and single volumes for audio tapes, videotapes, records, and 8mm motion picture cartridges and slides. In addition to listing by title, the indexes analyze the entries by subject. An additional volume, *Index to Producers and Distributors* (4th ed., 1977), gives addresses for producers and distributors.

There are some problems with the NICEM indexes: the lists are two to three years behind what is actually available;[33] the subject headings tend to be too general; the annotations are noncritical, thus of little or no help in selection; the data are not always accurate. These indexes are the product of an underfinanced organization that lacks funds to remedy the lack of timeliness and other faults.

NICEM is nevertheless one of the few media bibliographies now available

---

[33] New editions are revised every two years but are often one to two years late. Some effort at updating is done through *Update of Nonbook Media* (free with the purchase of any of the NICEM indexes), which supplements all the indexes. Arrangement is alphabetical by title under the major media categories.

as a data base, through Lockheed's Dialog system. The approximately 500,000 records may be searched by computer, but as of mid-1979 online service has not solved the problem of updating, and while 40,000 to 50,000 records are added each year, the center is still far behind currency.

NICEM should not be confused with NICSEM, the National Information Center for Special Educational Materials. Confusion is doubled by the fact that NICEM personnel work with this federally funded service to provide information on education for the handicapped, and many of the records are furnished by NICEM. (For a summary see *Educational Media Yearbook*, 1978, pp. 12–13.)

ANNUAL AND CURRENT OVERVIEWS

The best general annual overview of the nonprint field is provided in the standard *Educational Media Year Book* (New York: R. R. Bowker, since 1973). This is useful for up-to-date information on funding, research and development, and government programs. Directed to primary and secondary levels, it can also be used by those in public and academic libraries. Another, less detailed annual is the *ALA Yearbook* (Chicago: American Library Association, since 1976). This includes a section on multimedia materials and several subsections on films, media centers, and related subjects.

Several columnists help the less involved reader keep up with major developments in the field. Deidre Boyle, one of the best, is a co-editor of the *Wilson Library Bulletin* and is a frequent contributor to library journals. She sometimes reviews specific new works. *American Libraries* has a regular column, "Mediatmosphere," which features various writers on as many forms of the current media.

TEXTBOOKS AND GUIDES

There are numerous textbooks and guides in the media field, and more are published each year. Representative titles include Deidre Boyle's *Expanding Media* (New York: Neal Schuman/Oryx Press, 1977), a collection of 45 articles that includes material on selection; Emanuel Prostano's *The School Library Media Center* (2nd ed.; Littleton, Colo.: Libraries Unlimited, 1977), a basic text with some useful tips on selection; and *How to Start an Audiovisual Collection* (Metuchen, N.J.: Scarecrow Press, 1978), a collection of articles relating to the media as employed in libraries.

General Media Reviews[34]

Previews. New York: R. R. Bowker, since 1972. Nine times a year.
Media & Methods. Philadelphia: North American Publishing Company, since 1965.

---

[34] Almost all educational journals now carry some reviews, and certainly articles on the media. Basic titles are listed and annotated in *Magazines for Libraries* (3rd ed.; New

Audiovisual Instruction. Washington, D.C.: National Education Association, Department of Audiovisual Instruction, since 1956. Ten times a year.

Educational Screen and AV Guide. Chicago: Educational Screen Inc., since 1922. Monthly.

Media Mix. Chicago: Claretian Publications, since 1974. Eight times a year.

The approach used for books applies to evaluating nonprint reviews: consider first the broad aspects of the service, then the specific qualities of individual reviews.

1. Scope

How many reviews are published, and are they relevant to the library's collection? What is left out? In the case of nonprint materials, does the source include all media, only some of the media, or only one medium?

A media expert has summarized scope: "Overall, reviewing services are haphazard. At the same time, many worthwhile media are never reviewed. . . . The contents of the major media indexes also duplicate each other, yet none seems to be totally comprehensive."[35]

There is a natural screening process insofar as only the so-called relevant and better materials tend to be reviewed. This saves the librarian going through thousands, instead of hundreds of film reviews, for instance. On the minus side: some of the more innovative, imaginative titles are simply overlooked.

2. Timeliness

Do reviews appear about the time the film or the record or other medium is released?

Most of the reviews found in such basic services as *Previews* have about the same timeliness record as book reviews: the material is reviewed about one to three months after release.

3. Reviewers

Are the reviews signed? How competent are the reviewers? This is reminiscent of the situation with books, but here many of the review sources indicate the judgment is by a committee (EFLA) or rarely indicate which of the magazine's staff actually reviewed the work. Library-oriented periodicals tend to have signed reviews, with an indication of the reviewer's background.

York. R. R. Bowker, 1978). A nonselective key to reviews is found in the list of periodicals regularly indexed by *Media Review Digest.*

[35] Margaret Chisholm, "Selection and Evaluation Tools for Audio and Visual Materials" in *Reader in Media, Technology and Libraries* (Englewood, Colo.: Microcard Editions Books, 1975), p. 383.

4. Recommendations

Are the reviews generally favorable? Are critical remarks noted? There is little difference between print and nonprint reviews, and the majority of nonprint reviews are favorable. Some sources simply do not review poor materials, with the result that the reader can't be sure a nonprint item was not reviewed because it was overlooked. Rarely is there any indication of the criteria for the value judgments.

The reader is usually unsure as to the ultimate effectiveness of the material. Just how good is a film on the history of Egypt for instructing high school students? This critical point may be missed by the reviewer, who otherwise gives an exhaustive opinion of content, authority, and age suitability. Often "the reviews that do appear in [*Booklist* and *Previews*] concentrate on the content to the almost virtual exclusion of the way in which content is translated and transmitted."[36]

5. Comparison

The reviews generally fail to tell the reader how the item compares with similar items in the field. This is particularly troublesome because there is much duplication and the material is sometimes extremely expensive.

6. Format

In nonprint materials a format evaluation may be particularly needed. The librarian wants to know the quality of a film, a recording, or a kit. For example, a cassette may pass all the other tests but fail because of poor recording quality.

The reviewer should look closely for possible bias in content.[37]

1. Does the content support a positive, nonstereotyped portrayal of human roles? Among typical questions to ask: Are parents and children of each sex involved in household tasks? Are fathers shown in roles other than going to work or doing "male" chores? Do girls have a variety of choices and aspire to a variety of goals?

2. Does the content support minority groups? Is the material true to people depicted, or caricatures or stereotypes? Are the characters real people portrayed in various aspects of life and work? Is the language appropriate? (Heavy use of words or expressions that carry connotations of disrespect and contempt is hardly suitable.)

THE REVIEWS

Previews offers the best single approach to the media as a whole. Each issue features about 150 descriptive, often critical reviews, categorized by medium, of 16mm and 8mm films, filmstrips, transparencies, slides, recordings, prints, maps, academic games and multimedia kits. The reviews are written by

[36] Jane Hannigan, op. cit., p. 256.
[37] Paraprased from Marilyn L. Miller, op. cit., pp. 52–53.

librarians and other subject experts and there is critical appraisal of equipment. Most of the material is for the elementary level through high school, which makes this an absolute necessity for school and public libraries. It is of more limited value to academic and special libraries, although librarians will profit from the numerous filmographies and discographies as well as the occasional article and the equipment reviews.

Previews is the overwhelming favorite of school librarians (and doubtless an equal number of public and academic librarians). A poll of school librarians found that 95 percent preferred *Previews* for selection of nonprint materials, followed by *Booklist* (81 percent), *Audiovisual Instruction* (65 percent) and the retrospective list *Elementary School Library Collection* (56 percent).[38]

The most popular general media magazine for elementary and high schools is *Media & Methods*. (Thanks to its innovative, well-written articles, it is also extensively read and used by academic audiovisual centers and public libraries.) Articles usually feature outstanding films, recordings, filmstrips, and the like. There are also regular reviews of educational films, television programs, recordings, and books. Reviews are secondary, although the reader will often find reviews of items not found in the standard general review sources.

Although they are not primarily reviewing sources, several periodicals include some reviews and are required reading for anyone trying to keep up with the field. First is the official publication of the National Education Association, *Audiovisual Instruction*, directed to elementary and secondary schools. Primarily made up of articles, it does have notes about equipment, book reviews, and a valuable index to audiovisual reviews in other publications. Equally valuable are the theme issues devoted to such things as media and the behavioral sciences, competency-based education, and technology and the exceptional child.

An independent effort, *Educational Screen and AV Guide* is directed to the same audience but includes regular evaluations of film, filmstrips, and television. (Numerous reviews give it a lead over the NEA entry, at least for purposes of evaluation and selection.)

Of a number of "one man/one woman" reviewing services, *Media Mix* is one of the best. This is an eight-page review of films, filmstrips, records, tapes, teacher aids, television programs, and the like. It differs from many in that the audience is seen primarily as the high school, and to a lesser degree the college. This newsletter also includes useful tips on teaching.[39] Another individual effort is *Media Monitor* (Pearl River, N.Y.: Informedia, since 1977; four times a year). The 16-page newsletter lists and often

---

[38] *Marketing, Selection and Acquisition and Materials for School Media Programs* (Chicago: RTSD Office, American Library Association, 1977).

[39] "Jeff Schrank, the editor of this monthly eight-page journal, is nothing less than a media magician. . . . Several times in the last year I have asked audiences . . . to rate the publications they use. In each case, *Media Mix* has been voted the overall favorite of those who know it" (C. B. Doak, *Catholic Library World*, December 1976, p. 231).

annotates materials for use in primary and secondary-school classrooms. Included are filmstrips, slides, maps, and cassettes, and there are special quarterly bibliographies on items in the news. The editor is Mary Sive, an experienced and trustworthy authority in the field.

Educational Technology (Englewood Cliffs, N.J., since 1961; monthly) is given over almost entirely to the media. There are good to excellent articles that discuss both the theoretical and the practical. Hard-hitting evaluations of programs are accomplished by devoting each issue to a special topic. There are no reviews, but anyone concerned with media would want to read this monthly regularly.

Social Education. (Arlington, Va.: National Council for Social Studies, since 1937; monthly) is typical of the specialized periodicals that examine the media in their particular areas—in this case, social studies teachers from elementary through high school. Less typical is the fact that the reviews and articles are innovative and often go into detail not found in general review sources. In fact, *Social Education* is one of the best of the specialized sources.

MEDIA REVIEWS IN PRINT-ORIENTED JOURNALS

Primarily devoted to books, the six basic library-oriented publications (*Booklist, Choice, Kirkus, Library Journal, Publishers Weekly*, and *School Library Journal*) give varying attention to other media. The best for non-book material is *Booklist*. The editors consider basic materials in the media regularly, and almost every issue has several sections compiled by experts. As everything listed in *Booklist* is recommended, and as the media lists are conservative in terms of length, significant numbers of school librarians use it almost exclusively—at least in libraries where nonbook materials are not the center of the collection but are an important consideration.

Public and academic libraries may find use for the *Booklist* listings, but they are of limited value for the college or university situation.

Among the frequently appearing lists in *Booklist* are those of 16mm films and selected films for young adults, filmstrips, multimedia kits, recordings (the section with the widest interest), slides, and video.

School Library Journal makes no effort to review the media because this is done in its sister publication *Previews*. Nevertheless, in such departments as "SLJ Professional Reading," "Check Lists" and "Product Showcase" the reader will find much of value. More important, many of the articles are geared to developments in the media.

Library Journal follows the same pattern as *School Library Journal* and does not have media reviews although it considers books in the area and has a useful "Buyer's Guide." *Choice* does not review the media, nor do *Kirkus* or *Publishers Weekly*, although each may mention nonbook materials in passing.

Most of the periodicals devoted to children and young people usually have columns, features, or irregular notices about audiovisual materials. *Horn Book*, for example, is primarily made up of articles about children's literature but has numerous notes on books as well as audiovisual reviews. *School Media Quarterly* has a column of media reviews and devotes many pages in each issue to the subject.

VOYA offers the best single approach to nonprint materials for young adults. Each issue features quite impressive reviews of films, recordings, and audiovisual aids. It is particularly valuable for the sensible reviews of popular films and records and can be a valuable source of information for any library serving young adults—including many college libraries.

Indexes to Media Reviews

Media Review Digest. Ann Arbor, Mich.: Pierian Press, since 1970. Biannual with annual cumulation.

International Index to Multi-Media Information. Pasadena, Calif.: Audio-Visual Associates, since 1970. Quarterly.

Media Index. Pleasantville, N.Y.; since 1977. Biweekly with annual cumulation.

Approximately 50,000 reviews of various media are indexed annually in *Media Review Digest.* They represent what has appeared in more than 200 periodicals and cover most of the media, from films and recordings to transparencies and kits. Some short excerpts from reviews are given and there is a key to whether the review was favorable or not. Information for each item is complete insofar as it represents what was in the review. However, in too many items there is not complete bibliographic data. Arrangement is by media and there are numerous indexes. The index concentrates on 16mm films, filmstrips, and videotapes, which make up one section. A second section is devoted to recordings, tapes, and miscellaneous items. The emphasis is primarily on educational materials. The service is useful for librarians who wish to check out materials for purchase or rental, but it tends to be late and incomplete.

The more timely *International Index* has several problems. While it uses much the same approach as *Media Review Digest*, it too sometimes fails to give full bibliographic data and checks reviews in only 110 periodicals. It nevertheless includes more review extracts. Large libraries would want both services; smaller ones would probably be best off with *Media Review Digest.*

Media Index is limited to indexing reviews of materials employed in elementary-school libraries. The six-page newsletter has some evaluations, news about the media, and cumulations that give excerpts of reviews for various media. A handy subject, title, and publisher index pulls the whole together.

General Bibliographies and Lists

Core Media Collection for Elementary Schools, 2nd ed. New York: R. R. Bowker, 1978.

Core Media Collection for Secondary Schools. New York: R. R. Bowker, 1975.

Educators Guides. Randolph, Wis.: Educators Progress Service, since 1934. Annual.

A Multimedia Approach to Children's Literature. Chicago: American Library Association, 1978.

Except for the NICEM indexes, there are no total general lists of media.[40] Most librarians work with specific medium lists and a few select lists of the media as a whole.

Selected or core lists for the media are the same as similar lists for books and periodicals. They are useful but must be used with caution. As one reviewer put it:

In no way . . . [is a core list] intended to be utilized exclusively for selection of media. The laborious task of previewing all material prior to purchase can be eliminated for those materials, which have already been reviewed by authoritative sources; but librarians, with help from classroom teachers, must still preview other materials to meet the demanding needs of the ever-changing curricula.[41]

The two basic core lists, published by Bowker, are just that, although for most of the items there are a few words regarding content when the title is not self-explanatory. The collection for elementary schools includes 5000 titles for grades kindergarden through eighth. The secondary-schools listing is limited to 2000 titles for grades 7 through 12.[42] Both are arranged by subject with title indexes. The choice was made by the editors (Lucy Brown for the secondary schools and Brown and Betty McDavid for the elementary schools) based on favorable reviews in professional journals and bibliographies.

When the librarian wishes to connect a book with other media, a useful guide for preschool through the sixth grade is the *Multimedia Approach to Children's Literature*. The compilers, Ellin Greene and Madalynne Schoenfeld, have annotated more than 500 books. There are also separate annotations

[40] See also *Audiovisual Instruction*, which does a limited amount of indexing.

[41] Linda C. Roberts, in a review of *Core Media Collection for Secondary School*, 1975 (*School Media Quarterly*, Fall 1975, p. 63). This is a favorite review, but to check the hazards of lists, or for that matter differences in opinion about such lists, see the "not recommended" review of the same title in "Reference and Subscription Books Review," *Booklist*, May 1, 1976, pp. 1287–1288.

[42] The Reference and Subscription Books Review (p. 1288) failed to recommend this list because it "contains a preponderance of elementary level materials, a dearth of media on many subjects . . . and a limited number of titles in formats other than the filmstrip."

of 16mm films, filmstrips, and disks and tapes which are in some way related to or based on the books. Carefully indexed by author, subject, and media.

Several of the basic book lists also include media, although particular attention is given to the area in *The Elementary School Library Collection* (see page 265). Among items listed are films, maps, filmstrips, multimedia kits, games, and cassettes. Another book-selection title with a section devoted to the media is *Guide to Reference Books for School Media Centers* (see page 240).

Totally nonselective lists of media are to be found in a much-used series. Individual volumes of the *Educators Guides* cover free films, filmstrips, and tapes.[43] Within each of the annual volumes *free* materials are listed under broad subject headings. Each of the alphabetically arranged entries within the subject heading contain brief descriptions of content. There are separate indexes for title, subject, and source. While the series is useful, it has the drawback of representing primarily materials of mild propaganda nature (whether put out by private firms or the government). As long as this is realized, however, the listings can be used. The series is well known to librarians as one of the favored approaches to free and inexpensive curriculum-support materials. While focused primarily on the schools, some of the guides may be used by public libraries and even in academic libraries. Unfortunately, the grade level of most of the material is not indicated.

The National Audiovisual Center, a federal agency, offers an extremely useful listing with its *A Reference List of Audiovisual Materials Produced by the United States Government* (Washington, D.C.: National Audiovisual Center, 1978). This lists and briefly annotates some 6000 films, videotapes, slide sets, and multimedia kits. Complete bibliographic information is given for each item, including sales and rental data. Almost all areas are covered, as are various grade and age levels.

Directories and Supplier Catalogs

Audiovisual Market Place. New York: R. R. Bowker, since 1964. Annual.

Educators' Purchasing Guide. Philadelphia: North American Publishing Company, since 1970. Annual.

Index to Instructional Media Catalogs. New York: R. R. Bowker, since 1974. Irregular.

North American Film and Video Directory. New York: R. R. Bowker, since 1977. Irregular.

Children's Media Market Place. Syracuse, N.Y.: Gaylord, since 1978. Annual.

---

[43] The series includes eight parts: *Educators Guide to . . . Free Films*; *Free Filmstrips*; *Free Guidance Materials*; *Free Health, Physical Education and Recreation Materials*; *Free Science Materials*; *Free Social Studies Materials . . .* ; *Free Tapes, Scripts and Transcriptions . . .* ; and from time to time others are likely to be added or modified in the series.

Audio-Visual Equipment Directory. Fairfax, Va.: National Audio-Visual Association, since 1953.

CONSUMER AIDS

EPIE (Educational Product Report). New York: Educational Products Information Exchange Institute, since 1967. Monthly.
Library Technology Reports. Chicago: American Library Association, since 1965. Bimonthly.

In considering acquisitions of nonbook materials, due consideration must be given to the hardware often required—record player, film projector, and so on—usually sold by another dealer.[44] In looking for a reliable equipment dealer, follow the same rules applied when seeking any merchandise. Will the dealer service the equipment, and when called, not two years later? Is there a warranty on the equipment, and how limited is it?

Dealers may be found in the directories as well as the classified pages of the phone book, although the best method is to solicit opinions from other librarians in the area. This is particularly true for expensive investments. The search is made easier because most equipment dealers also sell to the public, so there is more than a narrow range of recommendations from which to choose. You can also go to the local and national library conventions, where major dealers display equipment, and be on the lookout for exhibitions and trade shows.

So-called software is important to librarians, and just as they rely upon publishers' catalogs and advertisements for advance news of books and sometimes simply as direct buying guides, they should do the same in the media field. Often these sources "contain valuable information in background and technical data from which the professional profits by reading." For example, the catalogs of Pyramid Films, Janus Films, Films, Inc., and Contemporary/McGraw-Hill, to name only a few, are modes of published data one might need to know in order to answer specific user inquiries.[45]

How do you locate these various catalogs and dealers? A select list is found in Rufsvold's *Guides to Educational Media* and in Mary Sive's *Selecting Instructional Media,* but the basic, comprehensive listing for both hardware and software is in *Audiovisual Market Place.* The publisher lists some 5000 firms and individuals involved with the media under 25 or so broad subject headings. The librarian looking for a catalog or information on anything from a film distributor to an overhead projector manufacturer would turn here first. Complete information is given, including addresses and phone numbers. This annual includes overview articles and information on events and people.

[44] A useful article on this topic is Edward J. Hingers' "The Audiovisual Supplier . . . ," *Library Trends,* April 1976, pp. 737–748.
[45] Hannigan, op. cit., p. 256.

Another standard aid is the *Educators' Purchasing Guide*, a comprehensive list of education suppliers that includes nonbook-material sources. Arrangement is by subject and the guide is quite easy to use.

Several related titles are published by Bowker:

1. *The Index to Instructional Media Catalogs* covers about 150 subject areas with information on producers and publishers of 40 types of media (from films to workbooks).

2. *The North American Directory* is a geographically arranged listing of more than 1500 college, public, special, museum, or archival libraries with media centers. This is a type of *American Library Directory* limited to media.

The *Children's Media Market Place* is a listing of audiovisual producers and distributors with directory information on publishers, bookstores, book clubs, and organizations. There are sections on grants, a calendar of events, and selection aids. Libraries taking *Audiovisual Market Place* are not likely to need this, although it is useful when budget allows.

The *Audio-Visual Equipment Directory* is a nonselective guide to a wide variety of hardware items associated with media. The listings include more equipment than found in the other directories and should be readily available in any media library.

Useful as the directories and lists are, it is not for lack of information that most librarians have difficulty. They are bombarded with advertising, catalogs, and ubiquitous salespeople.[46] In case you are overlooked, it is simple to get on mailing lists of various companies and concerns about whose products you have an interest.

The real difficulty comes in trying to select equipment. Here several consumer guides can be useful.

A good general source is *Consumer Reports* and allied services that objectively test equipment, much of which can be employed in the library. There are other services too, but EPIE (The Educational Products Information Exchange Institute) is the most reliable single source of information about media equipment. Comparative data are given for products in much the way as in the more familiar *Consumer Reports*. The equipment is carefully tested and impartial reports offered. Various issues cover everything from film projectors and tape players to study carrels and even textbooks. While directed specifically at elementary and secondary schools, much of the tested equipment (if not the instructional materials) is part of the academic-library media scene.

Equally useful, although restricted to equipment, are the *Library Technology Reports*. These tend to be more complete than those found in the other sources mentioned, but suffer from lack of timeliness and only a

---

[46] Catalogs are an important help, and many of them are carefully constructed to assist the librarian in selecting media. Examples may be had from such firms as Demco Educational Corporation, Baker & Taylor, Brodart, and most of the jobbers who deal with books.

limited number appear each year. The in-depth reporting is nevertheless extremely useful—particularly for expensive equipment—and the reports should be carefully checked.

It is worth repeating that whenever the library is involved in a large purchase, some guidance will come from other libraries with similar equipment. A few phone calls usually will do the trick, and a check of the *North American Film and Video Directory* or the *American Library Directory* should help you locate libraries in similar situations.

II
Recordings

RECORDINGS have been part of libraries for decades. The service increased and improved with the introduction of long-playing recordings in the 1950s, reasonably priced high fidelity equipment for the home in the 1960s, and the availability of cassettes and tapes in the 1970s.

The large number of cassette players already owned by patrons [especially young people], coupled with their portability and ruggedness . . . and with the tendency of professional people to listen to cassettes while driving to and from home or business appointments, combine to generate high demand for materials in this format.[1]

The ubiquitous recording may now be more a part of American life than the book; bookshelves are partly being replaced in most American homes and apartments by record and cassette storage areas.[2] Avid readers are likely share the enthusiasm for recordings.

Use by Type of Library

How many recordings should there be in the library? There are no figures for college and university libraries, but school-library guidelines call for 1500 to 2000 items (tapes, cassettes, disks, and audio cards), or three to four

---

[1] William J. Speed, Los Angeles Public Library, quoted in James W. Brown, *New Media in Public Libraries* (Syracuse, N.Y.: Jeffrey Norton/Gaylord, 1976), pp. 172–173. Experience of other librarians is recorded pp. 173–177. For a short history of the development of record collections in academic libraries, see Gerald Gibson, "Sound Recordings," in Pearce S. Grove (ed.), *Nonprint Media in Academic Libraries* (Chicago: American Library Association, 1975), pp. 79–85.

[2] George Steiner, speech at Bennington College, Vermont, October 3, 1978. Between 1973 and 1977 gross sale of record albums went from $1.2 billion to $2.2 billion. Annual book sales are about $4.5 billion.

per user, with access to 5000 items from the individual school's collection and loans from other sources.[3]

For public library systems it was recommended in 1966 that:

> The basic collection of recordings for the system should consist of one disc or reel of tape for each 50 people in the service area, but no collection should contain less than 5,000 discs and reels. Selected recordings should be duplicated to meet needs and to supply rotating collections for the system, if such are desired.[4]

More than ten years later, standards for large libraries call for the same ratio of recordings to people but add: "Twenty percent of a public library or system's audio collection should consist of nonmusical tapes or records. Examples are: language instruction, secretarial instruction, sound effects, and the spoken word."[5]
Normally the balance among types of recordings and cassettes will be about 50 percent classical, 20 percent nonmusical, and 30 percent popular, although in a public library primarily serving young people it might be 50 percent or more for popular and 30 percent or less for classical.

Evaluation

Choice of recordings is a three-part decision based on three questions: (1) What form (record, cassette, tape)? (2) What type (classical, popular, folk)? (3) What audience, with how much attention to a balanced collection?[6]

FORM

Three types of recording format are found today in libraries and homes:
1. The *33⅓ rpm (long-playing) record*, which has displaced the earlier 78rpm recordings. Some popular music still is available on 45rpm records, as is children's work, but 45s are rarely a viable choice for most libraries.
2. *Cassettes*, which are built-in reel-to-reel audio tapes that the user can place in a player (or recorder) without threading. They come in lengths from 30 to 120 minutes and are blank or prerecorded. Libraries concentrate

---

[3] *Media Programs: District and School* (Chicago: American Library Association, 1975), p. 79. Equally explicit and detailed is *Guidelines for Audiovisual Materials . . . for Large Public Libraries* (Chicago: American Library Association, 1975).

[4] *Minimum Standards for Public Library Systems, 1966* (Chicago: American Library Association, 1967), p. 45.

[5] *Guidelines for Audiovisual Materials and Services for Large Public Libraries* (Chicago: American Library Association, 1975), p. 18.

[6] James B. Coover, "Selection Policies for a University Music Library," in Carol Bradley (ed.), *Reader in Music Librarianship* (Washington, D.C.: Microcard Editions, 1973), pp. 236–243. Concludes with a detailed selection policy statement that is a good beginning point for someone who wants specific details on evaluation of recordings. There is still very little on selection of materials for music libraries.

on two-track prerecorded tapes (which are so manufactured that they cannot be accidentally erased). Also available is an eight-track cartridge, often used for popular music, which is larger than the two-track and cannot be played in the average cassette player. Cassettes were once useful only for voice reproduction, but now come close to records in quality for fine music.

3. *Open tape reels*, which are familiar to anyone who has seen a tape-recording machine. These come in various sizes, must be threaded, and have the advantage of great length for hours of recording. Most libraries do not lend tape reels, although they may have them in connection with video or radio material.

Arguments continue whether tape or disk recording is more faithful to the original sound, but for the average library it is wise to buy both formats. Lacking great experience with cassettes, most librarians today are striking a balance in purchase between the record and the cassette, both of which offer problems of maintenance and circulation. Many users find less damage (scratching in particular) likely to happen to the cassette than the circulated record, but many pieces are still available only on records.

TYPE

For our purposes recordings may be divided into classical and popular music and the spoken word. Subject categories encompass a vast amount of material; the *Schwann-1 Record and Tape Guide* lists more than 45,000 recordings, divided between classical and popular.

Types of recordings selected are evident in library policy statements. Here is a typical public library view:

Many types of phono-records for both children and adults are acquired. . . . Collections of classical and folk music, jazz, musical comedies, film sound tracks and educational recordings (such as demonstrations of musical instruments) are maintained. . . . Nonmusical recordings include drama, poetry and prose readings, speeches, documentaries of historical events, nature sounds, sound effects and teaching and practice records, e.g., language and business techniques.[7]

University and college libraries tend to be more selective:

The library will purchase audio cassettes . . . selected by the music department staff for use by students enrolled in music courses . . . containing oral texts needed in instruction and research programs. . . . The library will purchase music records as requested by the music department staff.[8]

School libraries are liberal in their approach, although the range is likely to be less wide than in many public libraries; the guidelines simply state that records should offer "content ranging from music to documentaries to drill

---

[7] Elizabeth Futas, *Library Acquisition Policies and Procedures* (Phoenix, Ariz.: Oryx Press, 1977), p. 16.

[8] Ibid., p. 182.

materials, [which] promote individualized development of listening skills and aural literacy."[9]

AUDIENCE

When the librarian considered selection of recordings only in the light of the classical music there was little problem about what titles to select. (Evaluating the best recording of a classic work is another matter.) By the late 1960s and the 1970s most librarians, wishing to serve an audience beyond those who appreciate classical music, broadened the scope of the collection to take in the best of all types—from Broadway musicals and jazz to rock and country music. Today record-selection policy parallels that for popular books: more effort is made to buy what the community uses and requests than what the community should want.

But even while selecting what the majority wants, most librarians feel (as they should) that some balance is needed, that at a minimum the recording collection should be representative of the best types of music (classical or jazz) and represent the spectrum of types available, from music to spoken records.

Quality

The most important evaluative test, as with books, is the intrinsic quality of the recording. The recording should be evaluated in terms of the performance; the importance of the orchestra, soloist, conductor, and so forth; the quality of the recording itself—qualities difficult to agree on. Further, a librarian with little or no music training simply is not qualified to judge a recording of a work by Charles Ives, and a classicist sometimes does not appreciate rock music. And someone who can evaluate the spoken word well may be tone-deaf.

For many classics and some other titles there are two to as many as a dozen records available. Which is best? Preference enters the picture, but final decision should depend upon the librarian's evaluation of the quality of the recording, date of production, the artists, conductor, and similar factors.

In evaluating quality: (1) Almost always turn to current reviews. (2) If a backlist of recordings is required, consult some basic critical list. (3) Only librarians with an understanding of music and the spoken word (and breakdowns within these categories) should actively select records. (4) And in all cases, if possible, the public should be involved—particularly that part of the public that knows, loves, and probably collects recordings. Advice should be sought from those who use the collection on how it may be improved and kept current. This may be done informally by conversations

[9] *Media Programs: District and School* (Chicago: American Library Association, 1975), p. 79.

with users, or formally by establishing an apparatus whereby printed forms are passed out to listeners to encourage them to list recordings not in the library which they consider "basic" and list new titles as they are released.

The physical condition of the tape, disk, or cassette is important, particularly because many American companies have shown a steady decline in recording quality. Each title should be listened to after being received; if inferior, send it back to the distributor.

Another quality point of particular interest to educational librarians: If the recording is for instructional purposes are there suitable supplementary materials—texts, guides, music scores, and so forth?

Adding to the difficulty of record selection, at least for the next few years, is the development of the so-called digital recording. The sound on these disks closely resembles concert conditions, but the technique may mean eventual scuttling of old record forms and considerably higher cost for recordings. The industry is always trying to improve recorded sound, which in turn often means the library has to consider new equipment and new recording formats.

Equipment

There is an amazing array of equipment on which to play and record audiotapes and recordings.[10] Most librarians are familiar with the basic elements either as separate units or as high fidelity components: amplifier, receiver, speaker (or headphones) and player (record and cassette or eight-track).

Actually, a public library can get by without playing equipment (except for a staff set to check recordings) while the school or academic library may have multiple players because the recordings are an integral part of instruction.

A few practical approaches have been found successful in equipment selection:

1. Another librarian who has the equipment in his or her library can tell you what to avoid, what to purchase, and give you a good notion of price ranges. If one of your own librarians is an expert on high fidelity, consult with him or her—and with experts in the community.

2. *Consumer Reports* regularly runs articles on tested equipment in a variety of price ranges and for a variety of uses. One may not always agree with the findings, but the advice is based upon objective testing. Other useful sources are the American Library Association's *Library Technology Reports*, which sometimes consider equipment, and the EPIE reports (see page 250).

3. Commercial magazines such as *High Fidelity* monthly carry comments

---

[10] A useful basic discussion of equipment will be found in Richard Halsey's *Classical Music Recordings* (Chicago: American Library Association, 1976), chap. 6.

(usually less than critical) about new equipment. These are useful for keeping up with developments, but for more critical reviews one should turn to *Gramophone* and *Audio*. *The New York Times'* Thursday edition features "Sound" by Hans Fantel, who gives good tips on equipment and suggestions of the best for less.

4. Several specialized journals that deal with expensive equipment and evaluations for the experts are useful for comparison. One of the best is *The Absolute Sound* (P.O. Box 115, Sea Cliff, N.Y. 11579; quarterly), which includes detailed analysis.

Listening Programs

When the library gives record concerts, good to outstanding equipment is necessary for both volume and tonal excellence. The librarian should take considerable care in selection, particularly if the room where the concerts are to be given is oversized, has too little or too much furniture, or has high ceilings. Local dealers are usually willing to help and will set up various arrangements until the maximum situation is reached within the available budget.

Listening programs follow several patterns.
Conventional orchestral programs are:

made up of three to five works, balanced in weight, flavor and texture. A brilliant curtain raiser . . . is succeeded by an established masterpiece. . . . After this, a challenging piece is brought in . . . and the concert concludes with an amiable, affirmative statement.[11]

The librarian who regularly attends concerts will have no problem in working out programs. In fact, unless you do regularly listen to music, leave the program to others—possibly enthusiasts in the community or among the teaching faculty. Much the same holds for setting up *opera programs* and *popular-music programs*. The latter can be developed into a type of disco, but only if the library has the space to accommodate dancing as well as listening.

Finally: (1) Assure comfortable seating for the listeners. (2) Listen to the recordings before you have the music program. (3) Sit in different parts of the room to identify any "dead" areas for sound.

Ordering

Librarians purchase recordings, cassettes, and tapes directly from major record distributors, rarely from the manufacturers.[12] Discounts vary, al-

---

[11] Ibid., p. 23. Halsey gives sample programs, and his chapter on listening programs is a good beginning for a librarian.

[12] Actually, some libraries may profit from joining the manufacturers' record clubs, although the problem here is lack of real selection.

though they may be no more than the standard ones so associated with recordings that no one is really certain any more of the "real" price of a record. Advertisements often carry discounts of 25 to 40 percent, the same offered libraries.

Smaller libraries with budgets between $300 and $1000 a year for recordings will do well to buy locally, if the local dealer is able to supply most of what is needed. Libraries with larger budgets should turn to national dealers and wholesalers who can offer more complete service and usually larger discounts.

Major national distributors of recordings advertise extensively in music magazines and in the Sunday edition of *The New York Times*. Among the better known, certainly the largest:

1. Sam Goody has several New York City stores, but recordings are ordered from 46–35 54 Rd., Maspeth, N.Y. 11378. Goody is one of the best known of the dealers, particularly for cut rates on both equipment and recordings.

2. King Karol Records, Box 629, Times Square Station, New York, N.Y. 10036. Particularly good for hard-to-find classical recordings.

3. Chesterfield Music Shops, 12 Warren St., New York, N.Y. 10007.

4. National Record Plan, P.O. Box 568, New York, N.Y. 10008.

Names and addresses of other national dealers are listed in such guides as the *Audiovisual Market Place* and can be obtained, at least locally, by simply scanning the newspapers. The largest dealers are listed, too, in most of the basic guides. Halsey's *Classical Home Recordings* has useful special sections, "Where to Buy" and "How to Buy" (pages 238–249).

A few larger and specialized libraries have adopted various approval and blanket order plans, which are discussed briefly by James B. Coover.[13]

Scores

Music scores, particularly those of the great composers' works, are usually purchased as part of a basic collection.[14] The library is also likely to have single scores representative of all genres of music catalogued by period (contemporary, Renaissance), nationality (American, Russian), type (popular, folk), and instrument (keyboard, chamber music).

Scores and books about music are normally purchased from special dealers who often sell recordings as well. The librarian who follows the standard music magazines will find ample information on scores as well as new books

[13] Op. cit.
[14] H. P. Dawson and B. R. Marks, "The Ordering and Supply of Sheet Music," in Carol Bradley (ed.), *Reader in Music Librarianship* (Washington, D.C.: Microcard Editions, 1973), pp. 232–233—a useful summary. See too the short article by Duckles on buying music books. See also Olga Buth, "Scores and Recordings," in *Library Trends*, January 1975, pp. 427–450. *A Basic Music Library* (Chicago: American Library Association, 1978) is the best single source of selective lists of scores and books about music of value to the small and medium-sized library.

in the field. Lacking a *Books in Print* for scores, the librarian's best general source for this type of information is the Library of Congress' *Music, Books on Music and Sound Recordings.*

Oral History

Many libraries, of different types and sizes, have taken an interest in oral history. Thanks to inexpensive recording devices it is now possible to capture the memories and words of both the locally and the internationally famous, and video cassettes now offer the added dimension of a picture as well as sound.

A number of local, regional, and national projects devoted to oral history exist, but guidance for both the beginner and the expert has come in good part from the Columbia Oral History Project, established in 1948 by Allan Nevins to tape the recollections of famous Americans. This takes the form of an interview (which when transcribed may run to well over 1000 typewritten pages).

Oral History in the United States (New York: Oral History Association, 1971) is an index by topic and by name of more than 20,000 notables. Both the Columbia project and the work of 230 other projects are indexed.

Often updated, *Bibliography on Oral History* (Denton, Tex.: Oral History Association) by 1975, with the third edition, had a list of 306 entries. Updatings are carried in *The Oral History Review.*[15]

A. M. Meckler's *Oral History Collections* (New York: R. R. Bowker, 1975) is a useful annotated listing of interviews on tape. The first section is arranged by name and subject, the second lists American and foreign oral history centers. This is actually a reference work for historians, but the type of material indicates what can be done and the section on oral history centers is a useful guide for the librarian looking for additional information on the process.

General Record Aids

Duckles, Vincent. *Music Reference and Research Materials*, rev. ed. New York: Free Press, 1974.
Bradley, Carol (ed.). *Reader in Music Librarianship.* Washington, D.C.: Microcard Editions, 1973.

The basic source of reference materials in the music field is Duckles. Often revised, the guide lists and annotates some 2000 titles conveniently listed under form (dictionaries, bibliographies, etc.) with appropriate subdivisions. Good indexes.

[15] There are now numerous articles on oral history, but for a good overview see the October 1975 issue of *Catholic Library World*, devoted exclusively to the subject.

Reader in Music Librarianship is an excellent source of opinion about various aspects of the profession. Each chapter, written by a subject specialist, covers everything from recordings to sound equipment. There are useful bibliographies after each chapter and in the opening section.

Beyond *Music Index*, which provides current articles on all aspects of music librarianship, the basic sources are updated by special issues of *Library Trends* devoted to music and related subjects, among them "Trends in Archival and Reference Collections of Recorded Sound," edited by Gordon Stevenson (July 1972), and "Music and Fine Arts in the General Library," edited by Guy Marco and Wolfgang M. Freitag (January 1975). *Choice* often has specialized bibliographies on music, and the *Reference Services Review* for September 1978 has a fine survey of basic aids—from indexes to texts—by David D. Ginsburg, "Reference Sources in Pop, Rock and Jazz."

Record Reviews

Notes. Ann Arbor, Mich.: Music Library Association, since 1943. Quarterly.
Gramophone. London: General Gramophone Publications, since 1923. Monthly.
High Fidelity. New York: ABC Leisure Magazines, since 1951. Monthly.

Recordings are regularly reviewed in the general media services such as *Previews* and in some of the book review sources. *Booklist* considers recordings. All the others—from *School Library Journal* to *Choice*—review books about music that often are useful in selection.

In medium-sized or larger libraries or in libraries where multiple recording reviews are sought, there are some basic sources that review only recordings and tapes.

Gramophone, the outstanding English record and tape magazine, features about 2500 detailed reviews a year, discographies,[16] and articles. Most of the magazine is devoted to reviews and can be used by librarians with large collections to determine what has been issued abroad. The labels represent international companies, but with a little use one may easily discover American equivalents. *Gramophone* has the advantage of often reviewing titles weeks or even months before they are noticed in America. It is also a good place for checking attitudes of counterparts.

High Fidelity is one of two magazines about equally divided between articles on music and equipment and reviews. (The other is *Stereo Review* [New York: Ziff-Davis, since 1958; monthly].) Both are written for the general reader and neither is particularly critical in reviews of tapes and recordings. Each runs about 1000 reviews a year.

---

[16] The term *discography* is widely used to loosely identify various types of lists, catalogs, and bibliographies of sound recordings. Gordon Stevenson, "Standards of Bibliographies of Discographies," *RQ*, Summer 1976, p. 309, is a splendid discussion of the subject.

Libraries serving children and high school students will want to watch the fair to good reviews the young people themselves will be following in such popular musical magazines as *Crawdaddy* and *Rolling Stone.* The adventuresome (and it is hoped most librarians fit into this category) can try "Riffs," a series of reviews of popular music and musicians in *The Village Voice.* See, too, the reviews and articles on everything from disco to rock in *The Soho Weekly News.*

High Fidelity cumulates its reviews, published once a year as a separate book, *Records in Review.* This is a handy guide, particularly for retrospective titles.

One of the best, both an index and a review, is *Notes.* Similar to *Book Review Digest,* it gives excerpts from reviews of both recordings and tapes found in more than 30 music periodicals. About 200 different recordings, both popular and classical, are to be found in each issue. Books are also included. The "Index to Record Reviews" is cumulated annually as *Record Ratings,* a separate publication.

Indexes to Reviews

RILM Abstracts. New York: City University of New York, since 1968. Quarterly.

Music Index. Detroit: Information Coordinators, since 1949. Monthly.

Record and Tape Reviews Index. Metuchen, N.J.: Scarecrow Press, since 1972. Annual.

The standard indexes to reviews of recordings are *Media Review Digest* (page 246) and *Notes* (see above). Several more general indexes to music which include not only reviews of recordings but, also index material other than records. The most ambitious is the RILM Abstracts, which covers more than 180 national and international periodicals. Arrangement is by about a dozen subject areas, with numerous subdivisions. Abstracts are quite complete and this service is a necessity in any library with more than a modest music collection. Equally important is *Music Index,* which covers more than 300 periodicals and has references to reviews as well as almost any other conceivable subject in the area.

Limited to classical reviews, *Record and Tape Reviews Index* analyzes from 20 to 25 periodicals and lists the reviews by composers, music in collections, spoken recordings, and performer. For the popular field, see the *Annual Index to Popular Music Record Reviews* (Metuchen, N.J.: Scarecrow Press, since 1972) for material found in more than 60 periodicals. Arrangement is by various subject categories (rock and country to band and humor) and there are indexes to artists and to anthologies and concerts.

Record Bibliographies and Lists

Schwann-1 Record and Tape Guide. Boston: ABC Schwann, Inc., since 1949. Monthly.

NICEM (National Information Center for Educational Media). *Index to Educational Records.* Los Angeles: University of Southern California. Revised biennially.

Harrison Tape Guide. New York: Harrison, since 1955. Bimonthly.

National Center for Audio Tape Catalog. Boulder: National Center for Audio Tapes, University of Colorado, since 1954. Irregular.

Chicorel Index to the Spoken Art on Discs, Tapes and Cassettes. New York: Chicorel Publishing Co., 1973. Various updates.

U.S. Library of Congress. *Music, Books on Music, and Sound Recordings.* Washington, D.C.: Government Printing Office, since 1953. Semiannual.

Educators Guide to Free Tapes, Scripts and Transcriptions. Randolph, Wis.: Educators Progress Service, since 1955. Annual.

The single most confusing problem in record selection is locating the needed recording:

The difficulties of determining what has been recorded, what is currently available, and where and at what price it can be obtained consume much of most collection directors' time. To the uninitiate it is a simple task. All one needs to do is obtain a current Schwann Catalog, make a decision, and give the order to a local dealer.[17]

There is considerably more to selecting records than this example, which is equivalent to telling a novice that book selection consists of no more than locating the title in *Books in Print.* Some of the complications include: (1) Failure to locate the label in *Schwann* because the catalog does not list many regional, esoteric, educational, or foreign releases. (2) Decision on which available version of a recording will best suit the needs of the audience served. (3) Having the recording delivered. It may be in *Schwann* or another source, but by the time the order is given it may no longer be available. Or it may take weeks or months for a dealer to secure the recording. And there are other problems—from lack of proper subject and form approaches in most of the lists to faulty bibliographical data.

The *Books in Print* of the record and tape medium is the famous *Schwann-1 Record and Tape Guide.* Published since 1949, the monthly lists about 45,000 available stereo long-playing records and both eight-track cartridge tapes and cassettes on domestic labels. Arrangement is by area of interest, with the largest single sections devoted to classical and popular music.

[17] Gerald Gibson, "Sound Recordings," in Pearce S. Grove (ed.), *Nonprint Media in Academic Libraries* (Chicago: American Library Association, 1975), pp. 90–91.

Subsections cover jazz, folk music, musical shows, ballet, and opera. New releases appear in a separate section each month, and there are feature columns on new books.

The discerning record collector checks it to find the best version of a classical music selection before purchasing a disk.

Some record store owners shelve their product by manufacturer's number alone, confident that customers will use it to guide them to desired items.

Music critics, scolding the producers of yet another Beethoven's Fifth, consult it to see just how many predecessors actually exist.

Musicians use it as a miniature *Grove's Dictionary* in which to find composers' dates, spellings, and opus numbers.

Bargain hunters check it to compare list prices with so-called retailers' discounts.[18]

A close relative of the music guide is *Schwann-2 Record and Tape Guide* (since 1969; semiannual); the 2 distinguishes it from the first title. Both have the same approach and are used in much the same way. The *Schwann-2* listing, however, is used to locate spoken-word tapes and records and it includes religious titles, classics on lesser-known labels, and monophonic and reprocessed stereo recordings. There is also an international popular music section. Librarians will use this primarily for the spoken-word listings.

There are two NICEM indexes for recordings and tapes. The basic *Index to Educational Records* lists about 25,000 titles in the same fashion as the other NICEM indexes. The main listings are alphabetical by title, with a separate subject index and producer and distributor section. Most of the records are nonmusical, with heavy stress on the spoken word. Much the same focus is also found in the *Index to Educational Audio Tapes*, where language and literature (as in the recording list) account for at least one-fifth or more of the works. Emphasis is on material for elementary and secondary schools, although much of it (particularly the foreign-language-instruction recordings and tapes) may be used with adults. Both services suffer from lack of critical reviews, lack of full coverage (not all distributors and producers send NICEM information), lack of timeliness, and failure to give complete bibliographical data.

In the *Educators Guide* series there is *Educators Guide to Free Tapes, Scripts and Transcriptions*, which includes some 1800 titles under 16 subject headings. Although scripts are listed, most of the material is on recordings and tapes. As in others in the series, the free listings are primarily of interest to teachers in elementary and secondary schools.

Harrison may be used to supplement *Schwann*, and while there is much duplication, the *Harrison Guide* is a bimonthly (rather than semiannual) listing of some 30,000 spoken-word, language-lesson, poetry, and similar recordings. Emphasis is on popular music and only about one-sixth of the

[18] Ellen Pfeifer, "Schwann at 25," *High Fidelity Magazine*, October 1974, p. 45. A short history of the catalog and its founder.

listings can be classified as classical. It lists reel-to-reel recordings, not found in its competitor.

Another often-used guide to tapes is the *List-O-Tapes* (Los Angeles: Trade Service Publications; weekly), a loose-leaf catalog, found in most dealer stores, that lists about 60,000 cartridges, cassettes, and tape reels. It is organized by subject, with a special section on new releases. While primarily for dealers, it can be of use in large libraries.

The same company issues *Phonolog Reporter*, a similar loose-leaf service for recordings. Published since 1948, the more than 6000-page book is as familiar in record stores as *Books in Print* in bookstores, and serves much the same purpose. The publisher issues numerous other services. Interested librarians should write for a description of these works (One-Sport Publishing Division, 701 E. Prospect Ave., Mt. Prospect, Ill. 60056).

All of these listings have peculiarities that require more than a cursory glance. For example, the *Phonolog Reporter* lists the full contents of a record under the title of the record, not the performer, with a cross reference from the artist and composer entries. Numerous subject divisions are updated weekly by a card service and triweekly by inserts.

The frequently updated *National Center for Audio Tapes Catalog* lists about 15,000 noncommercial tapes by subject and title. Emphasis is on educational tapes that can be duplicated—after purchase. The subject areas are closely allied with foreign-language teaching, children's literature, speeches and lectures in series, and even music. The advantage to libraries is not only the subject matter but also the cost, which is usually much lower than commercial pricing. Tapes are for all grade levels from elementary through university. Several other universities offer this kind of service, and some are listed in the general guides to media.

The *Chicorel Index* lists about 3000 titles limited to literature and the performing arts, but with a nod toward social studies. Most commercial and noncommercial recordings are included under broad subjects such as readings from novels, political speeches, and similar areas. Listing is alphabetical with numerous indexes: author, poems by title and first line, speeches, and novels by title. Full ordering information is given for each entry.

The Library of Congress catalog includes material catalogued by the Library and several cooperating libraries. Content, as indicated by the printed cards, includes music in most of its aspects, from recordings to scores to books. One of the most complete listings available, it is of major help in cataloging and in trying to trace elusive materials.

From time to time the Library of Congress issues helpful bibliographies and lists in this area, among them *Spoken Recordings* . . . (1974), a listing of twentieth-century poets reading from their works, and *Folk Recordings* . . . (1974), a list of folk music.

Select Lists

Halsey, Richard. *Classical Music Recordings for Home and Library*. Chicago: American Library Association, 1976.

Discovering Music . . . New York: Scholastic Magazines, 1974.

Recordings for Children, 3rd ed. New York: New York Library Association, 1972.

Roach, Helen. *Spoken Records*, 3rd ed. Metuchen, N.J.: Scarecrow Press, 1970.

The best single approach to a select list of records is the Halsey title, which also includes good chapters on the problem of selection, ordering, and organizing recordings in the library. A 4000-item listing rates records in a variety of ways and indicates clearly the age or listening levels of each recording. Numerous other features make this a valuable guide, particularly as a base for building or evaluating a collection in the school or public library.

Directed to young people, *Discovering Music* is an effort to personalize the "best" of recordings. After interviews, prominent musicians recommend basic titles for a record collection. Next comes another listing of fifty basic composers and their works, followed by a listing of modern composers and musicians with lists of their best recordings. This particularly useful listing • for beginners strikes a good balance between popular and classical.

Many state or regional library organizations publish local lists of recordings. *Recordings for Children*, a good example, lists about 450 carefully selected titles for listeners (from preschool to thirteen years of age) that can be counted on as basic for most collections. The similar *Records and Cassettes for Young Adults*, issued by the same group, is revised every five or six years. "Recordings for Children" is issued and revised about every two years by *Illinois Libraries*. Some basic book collections, such as Mary Gaver's *The Elementary School Library Collection*, include recordings. Particularly useful, too, is the annual "Notable Children's Recordings" list of 20 to 30 titles chosen by a committee of the American Library Association. *Top of the News* publishes the list in the spring.

Librarians looking for guidance on nonmusical recordings should turn to Roach. While somewhat dated, the basic information remains useful, as do the numerous basic lists for different purposes and age groups. (Some of the records are no longer available, but other versions of those recommended may be purchased.)

Each year numerous special lists or discographies are published, and most of these appear in the standard book review media or are picked up in one of the review magazines previously discussed. Among typical titles one will find *All Together Now: The First Complete Beatles Discography* (New York: Ballantine Books, 1976) and *A Selected Discography of Solo Songs* (Detroit: Information Coordinators, 1976), a supplement to a basic list, covers 1971 through 1974 and lists solo song recordings by composer.

12
Film and Television

FILM, like its counterpart, television, is so much a part of American life that it is difficult to imagine that less than 50 years ago "one early educational film catalog advised teachers, in case the projector caught on fire, to throw it out the window. The thought of throwing a blazing 50-pound projector through a school window was not designed to encourage film use."[1] Encouragement was given by the federal government in the 1950s and 1960s. Generous funding to schools for films as instructional aids was followed by grants to public and academic institutions to build film collections. Federal support has now fallen off, but film remains a priority item in libraries.

Several factors nevertheless weigh against film use: (1) The necessity not only to purchase (or rent or lease) costly films but also to maintain expensive equipment; (2) the necessity to train personnel for selection, acquisition, and constant checking of the film; and (3) the necessity of deciding how much of an ever-tighter budget should be taken away from traditional selection and given over to film.

Film and television are grouped together in this chapter, and while they do have much in common, there are definite differences. (This territory is covered well by Marshall McLuhan in almost any of his titles.) Anyone who has seen a fine movie in color on a large screen in a theater with good sound recognizes the difference of impact between that presentation and viewing the same film on television: "Yes, it's fine on TV, but it isn't like watching the movie on a big screen." Much the same may be said of watching opera, ballet, baseball, or any other "event" on television, in person, and in a film.

Ultimately it may fall to the librarian to point up these real, quite important variations by making available in the library as many forms of the media as possible so users may discover the differences for themselves by comparing the same material on video cassette and on a 16mm film.

[1] Jerome K. Miller, Introduction to "Films in Public Libraries," *Library Trends*, Summer 1978, p. 3.

There is already some antagonism between video and film, between librarians who champion one over the other. It seems a pointless argument: they are equally as bad or as good, depending on what is shown, how it is shown, and who is viewing.

The effects of films and television are also points of ongoing debate, although really separate issues. Few people argue any more about effect of movies per se on adults, but there is considerable discussion of the effects of television on children. It is well, of course, to keep up with such discussions, since they may eventually have a strong influence on what is or is not selected by the library in the area of television video cassettes and library programming.

Use by Type of Library

Film is used in different ways in different types of library. In schools it is essentially an educational medium, as much entertainment as information in public libraries. Use dictates the type of film purchased, but film is little mentioned in most selection policy statements.

Theoretically, most professionals agree that a written film policy should exist, and the rationale for it is easy to establish. In practice, however, many of these same professionals prefer "No Policy" as policy.[2]

In her examination of selection policies in public and academic libraries, Elizabeth Futas found specific mention of film less than a dozen times in policy statements, and where statements were included they tended to be general and brief.[3]

The explanation may be in the organization of film services, often not directly connected with the library. Also, even when the library does administer its own films, the size of the collection, narrow definition of use, and the like mitigate against a policy.

PUBLIC LIBRARIES

Guidelines for large systems and public libraries give specific minimums for a number of films, staff, space, and the like that can be useful as suggestions for smaller libraries and systems serving groups of libraries. The number of 16mm films recommended is from 300 for populations under 300,000 to 2000 films for populations from 1 to 2.5 million.[4]

There now are well over 1000 public-library film collections in the United States. Today it is unusual for a public library not to have some type of film

---

[2] George Rehrauer, *The Film User's Handbook* (New York: R. R. Bowker, 1975), p. 43; there follows an outline for a selection policy and several examples.

[3] *Library Acquisition Policies and Procedures* (Phoenix, Ariz.: Oryx Press, 1977).

[4] *Guidelines for Audiovisual Materials and Services for Large Public Libraries* (Chicago: American Library Association, 1975), p. 16.

program or at least access to a collection. In New York, for example, some 1000 films a month are shown in various public library branches, and films are shown in libraries throughout the United States each day.

The role of the public library in film is worth stressing because film is all too often discussed solely in the context of schools. Actually, it has been the public librarian who has accepted the challenge of showing feature films, welcomed classic documentaries, and encouraged independent filmmakers.[5] Among the conclusions of a 1976 survey on the film and public libraries was:

an increase in the library use of films, greater interest by the public in serious film study, film as an art form, the social documentary and interest from all ages in the improvement of cinema literacy, and the ability to interpret the film, the language of the present.[6]

More than any other of the nonprint media (recordings aside), public libraries have adopted films. This became "official" in 1967 with the formation of the Film Library Information Council to serve public library interests.

ACADEMIC LIBRARIES

Writing about film in academic libraries, Burlingame and Farmer note that "Major film collections were not established in academic libraries until the 1950s. Even the Library of Congress was not actively involved. . . ."[7] Today the role of films in many academic libraries is far from evident, at least at the instructional level. But if one considers films employed in formal classes on the history and development of motion pictures or, even more often, in showings for students during off hours, film is a major part of campus life.

Even where films are an important consideration in instruction they often are under the jurisdiction of a media center or audiovisual center rather than the library. As previously noted, academic librarians were not anxious to consider nonprint materials, and to fill this gap the media center was created.[8] Another reason for the center is community relations. Some colleges and universities make films available to the general public, and this type of public relations is seen by librarians as outside of their jurisdiction.

Today, cost of both equipment and film and the problem of cut or static budgets prevent many academic librarians from getting more than mildly

[5] For a history of film and the public library see Ronald F. Sigler, "A Rationale for the Film as a Public Library Resource and Service," *Library Trends*, Summer 1978, pp. 9–26.

[6] James W. Brown, *New Media in Public Libraries: A Survey of Current Practices* (Syracuse, N.Y.: Jeffrey Norton/Gaylord, 1976), pp. 131–132. Also useful is Clara DiFelice, "Film and Public Libraries: A Survey of the Literature," *Film Library Quarterly*, no. 4 (1978), pp. 26–28.

[7] Dwight F. Burlingame and Herbert E. Farmer, "Film," in Pearce S. Grove (ed.), *Nonprint Media in Academic Libraries* (Chicago: American Library Association, 1975), p. 122.

[8] The functions of the centers "are almost identical to those used to characterize the necessary activities of the library" (Ibid., p. 127).

excited about taking over films. Even if the opportunity presented itself, librarians at the college and university level seem to prefer that film remain with the audiovisual centers.

Apart from major film collections (which include those at the Library of Congress and the University of Southern California), few academic libraries have extensive holdings. Burlingame and Farmer found in 1971 that of 64 libraries polled, only 13 had film collections "within the library—one had videotapes. In this group . . . only six had collections that numbered over 200 prints."[9] The important phrase here is "within the library." Actually, most universities and colleges have instructional films and most have some videotapes, collections of broadcasts on tape, and the like, usually in audiovisual centers.

SCHOOL LIBRARIES

Films are heavily used in schools, where they have received almost unanimous endorsement by librarians, teachers, and administrators. When teachers are given a choice of nonprint media film ranks first, especially among secondary-school teachers. School media librarians are equally enthusiastic.[10] Probably more has been written about the film in schools than in any other context.

The guidelines are quite specific as to quantitative evaluation. Grouping together 16mm, super 8mm, and videotapes, the media standards for school libraries call for access to at least 3000 titles in a school with 500 or fewer users. Super-8mm silent film (which can be the filmloops in cartridges) is separated out; here the standards call for 500 to 1000 items, or one to two per user.[11]

Aside from the educational 16mm and 8mm films (as well as filmstrips and other teaching devices) available from the typical school media center, there is now increased effort to purchase or rent films of a broader nature. It is not unusual to have in schools film programs that include shorts, documentaries, animated cartoons, and even more sophisticated "adult" films that actually have no age limitations, such as those of Norman McLaren and works that trace the adventures of Jacques Cousteau.

Film selection in schools may be done by the media librarians alone, but more likely choices will be made by staff, with the help of teachers and librarians, at a central school district media center or by committees made up of teachers representing various grade levels and subject specialties plus media librarians.

[9] Ibid., p. 128.

[10] A study of a large school district was found that "30 percent of the teachers use [film] service extensively, another 35 percent indicate considerable use" (John J. Gillespie, *A Model School District Media Program* [Chicago: American Library Association, 1977], p. 108).

[11] *Media Programs: District and School* (Chicago: American Library Association, 1975), pp. 76–77.

Film Programs

Films are used in many ways in libraries, or simply checked out to an interested teacher or general user. If this is the only film function of the library, there is little need to worry about programs. However, in most situations the viable film collection is maintained by library-sponsored programs.

Programs may be built around directors, subjects, actors, series, and the like. There is no limit to the type of presentation, but attention should be given to continuity, length, and type of film to be shown. There are several articles on this subject, and George Rehrauer devotes a chapter to programs.[12] Anyone involved with film should investigate the various approaches and discuss programs with other librarians.

Evaluation

Mediocrity, if not downright lack of intellectual or artistic merit, dominates too many films. Their second- or third-rate quality should be apparent to even the most uninvolved librarian, although the continual sale of such films makes one wonder just who is evaluating them.

The librarian may argue that he or she does not have enough training or experience to review or evaluate a film adequately. In that case it is imperative to check the standard reviews and bibliographies listed in this chapter and discuss the would-be purchase, lease, or rent of a questionable film with other librarians, teachers, faculty—and with students who may be forced to watch the film. Today it is difficult to imagine any but the least aware not being able to distinguish between "best" and "better" in films. There will be honest differences of opinion about what constitutes the top-rank films in "better," but there should be a consensus (and there usually is) about the really bad or really extraordinary film.

The basic evaluative questions are: (1) What type of film to rent or purchase (educational or feature). (2) How to evaluate the intrinsic worth of the film. (3) What audience to consider.

TYPES OF FILM

The most common type of film found in the elementary or secondary school is the educational or instructional film, usually an effort to make a single point about a given situation. This can be well done, but is it normally more concerned with educational purpose than with entertainment or artistic

---

[12] Op. cit., chap. 7, "Designing Film Programs." See also "Evaluation of Library Film Programs" in the appendixes.

aspects. An almost sure way to tell an educational film from others is that it inevitably has a voice-over narration that sounds vaguely like a teacher.[13]

Libraries include the feature work for both education and entertainment, but are prone to treat it as they would books and periodicals—something the general public is likely to view and even borrow. A feature film is longer than the educational form (90 to 120 minutes against 10 to 30 minutes) and is the best-known form, since it usually opens in commercial film houses or on television.

The independent film (sometimes called "art" film) is the antithesis of the commercial or educational film. It is usually the work of people not connected with major companies. A good definition is suggested by *Sightlines*:

Independent films are as personal films produced by filmmakers who want to explore a particular cinematic form or subject. These are noncommissioned films: not produced for television or a major studio, not sponsored by government or industry, not made to fill a curriculum slot (although many can be used very appropriately in the classroom). Independent films cover a range of genres and techniques: experimental, social documentary, cultural documentary, animation, and narrative, and come in both short and feature lengths.[14]

In some respects the independent film might be compared with the small press or little magazine. It represents imaginative, often quite advanced thought by filmmakers who see film as an art form, not totally an entertainment or instructional form.

The three categories hardly exhaust the possibilities of description, but they are shelter terms for other related forms such as animated cartoons, the entertainment film for children, documentaries, and other types of motion picture.

Format

Film is also described by format. The most common is 16mm—the width of the film. The 35mm film is familiar to commercial movie fans but is too costly for libraries; most 35mm feature films are eventually transferred to 16mm for library use. Today they are also reduced to videotape or video cassettes (which some see replacing 16mm).

---

[13] Some distinguish between the educational film for children and young adults and those for adults. The latter is sometimes called the "information" or "idea" film, although its objectives are much the same as the typical educational film. The content, however, is more advanced and may even be quite controversial in an effort to spark a discussion after the film is shown. A classic example is the American Library Association's *The Speaker*.

[14] Deidre Boyle, "The Independent Film and the Library: A Workshop Report," *Sightlines*, Summer 1978, p. 12. An excellent summary article that points up a basic fact: independent films are not fairly represented in libraries. Librarians are reluctant to show or borrow experimental films. See Amos Vogel, "Independents—Smiles and Tears," *Film Comment*, January-February 1976, pp. 56ff. A basic book in this field is Hollis Melton (ed.), *A Guide to Independent Film and Video* (New York: Anthology Archives, 1976).

Another type is the 8mm or super 8mm film, or film loop in a cartridge. Projection equipment is inexpensive, light, and easy to operate, and super-8mm normally has a sound track that increases its versatility.

One way to distinguish among these formats is by viewing. At equal projector distance 35mm film will fill the largest space, 16mm the next largest, 8mm the smallest. For example, the difference in size of the clear projected picture for the average 8mm is 50 percent less than for super 8mm.

One cannot evaluate the best format by itself. Equipment is a major consideration; each format requires a different type of projector, so the librarian must consider the cost of the equipment as well as the cost of the film.[15]

Intrinsic Evaluation

Format and type of film aside, the librarian must come to terms with the intrinsic quality of the film. It is difficult to set rules applicable for all three types; what is acceptable in an educational film may not be in a feature or an art film. There are nevertheless some general rules:

1. Technical quality   In some ways this is the easiest to judge: a librarian can quickly evaluate the quality of the sound, the photography, lighting, editing, color, black-and-white, and the like.

2. Voice   How convincing are the actors or the voice-over narrator? Sometimes this is the weakest point in the film, especially in poor education and feature motion pictures where the voices are less than appropriate.

3. Timeliness   Art films and many features are literally timeless. But in educational films it is imperative that a film making a political point or scientific hypothesis do so with an eye to the present (from the clothing styles to manner of presentation).

4. Objectivity   Is the film purposefully trying to make a point—as do many free films available to libraries from commercial and business concerns? If so, is it clear to the audience that the point being made is the purpose of the film? There is nothing wrong with selling an idea, or even a product or country, so long as this intent is clear to all who are viewing. (The library may not want to show such a film, but that is another matter.) If the film purports to be objective, does it give both sides of an argument, show objections to a thesis?

5. Content or subject matter   The content may defeat the best of films in that it is almost worthless or, at best, of no interest to the viewers. And even the best of films may not be relevant to a particular library's audience.

[15] Jan W. Cureton, "Establishing a Film Collection," *Library Trends*, Summer 1978, p. 95.

6. Audience No matter how good the film, it will be a failure unless the audience is receptive. Much the same can be said about books, and recognizing this fact may help librarians to appreciate that not all films will draw a large audience. Yet really good feature and educational films should be shown, if only to a small group of enthusiasts.

The real test of a film being considered for purchase or long-term lease is simply "Will it be used again?"

This is not to be interpreted as it might come in useful some day. This negative approach shelves the responsibility of the librarian. . . . It should always be possible to say why a particular piece of film has been selected for the library.[16]

In the early years there seemed to be some need to justify films in the library, and this was met by using films as "bait" to attract the reader to allied books. This theme is rarely heard today; film has come to be understood as having its own intrinsic worth. Still, public librarians rightfully continue to tie books to many of the motion pictures, sometimes in terms of an exhibit or reading list. Film serves the dual purpose of being good in itself and of helping the viewer relate to other materials in the library.[17]

A useful practical approach to criteria for selection will be found in many of the select film lists. The New York Library Association's *Films for Children* includes a practical set of rules for evaluation and adds a list of good sources for reviews.

The following checklist is for children's films but applicable to films for any age group. If the librarian used only this to judge the intrinsic quality of a film, choices would be considerably better.

1. The film should offer the child an esthetic experience.
2. It should have respect for the child's intelligence and taste.
3. It should be authentic and original.
4. It should have beauty of language.
5. It should have integrity and appeal to the age and interest of the intended audience.
6. Films for children should allow the child to explore the world and his relationship to it.
7. Stories that are adapted from book to film should retain the original spirit.[18]

[16] Helen P. Harrison, *Film Library Techniques* (New York: Hastings House, 1973), p. 37.

[17] Charles Suhor, "The Film/Literature Comparison," *Media & Methods*, December 1975, pp. 56–59, a comparison between the short story, novel, drama, and film. Suhor stresses that the media complement each other rather than compete and suggests how they can be used in libraries.

[18] Julie Cumings, "Children's Films . . . ," *Library Trends*, Summer 1978, p. 46. Actually, the author points out, few children's films measure up to these criteria because not that many are made with any sense of conviction and creativity. Not only are film producers to blame, but so are badly trained librarians.

EVALUATION PROCEDURES

Thousands of films are produced year by year, and the possibility of viewing them all is no more realistic than reading all books or listening to all recordings. Therefore, the same selection technique is used with films as with other media: (1) The librarian filters out what is likely to be purchased or rented by examining reviews and bibliographies and talking to salespeople and other librarians. (2) Once a short list of films is established, they are generally previewed by the librarian, often with the assistance of teachers and other interested persons.

"The high cost of 16mm films . . . makes it mandatory that they be previewed before purchasing. Most reputable film distributors provide free film preview service for a period of one to two weeks."[19] Other arrangements include purchase of the film; if not accepted it may be returned and the company credits the library account. Producers and distributors hesitate to grant too many free previews because some librarians request previews without intent to purchase, keep the film beyond a reasonable limit, or damage the film.

The actual previewing and decision whether or not to buy may be made by an individual film librarian, but is more likely to be done by a screening committee made up of various interests in the library, from subject specialists to curriculum experts. Screening may be done once a month, every few months, or even as little as once a year, when the librarians in the area or region get together to make decisions on what to purchase.

A record should be kept of films that have been previewed. This must include the name of the film, distributor, when the film was viewed, and evaluations. If a complex or long film, some indication might be given of content, audience, and the like.

The library should have a standard evaluation form that can be used during the previewing by those evaluating the film. A widely used form is available from the Educational Film Library Association (EFLA).[20]

Film Acquisition

Librarians complain about the rising costs of books and periodicals, but the price of an average 16mm film comparatively is astronomical. The average 16mm film costs from $7 to $9 a minute for black-and-white with sound; for color the figure jumps to $15 to $17 per minute—and the cost rises each year. As a result librarians must make some basic decisions about general budgeting for films:

[19] Jan W. Cureton, "Establishing a Film Collection," *Library Trends*, Summer 1978, p. 97.

[20] George Rehrauer, op. cit. (pp. 84–88) includes several evaluation forms, including the one suggested by EFLA.

1. If the film is likely to be used more than five or six times a year for any length of time, it is cheaper to purchase than to rent.

2. If the film is likely to be used only a few times a year, it is best to rent the film.

3. If the cost of a single film, no matter how often it is used, is over $1000, it is best (except in a large library) to lease or rent the film in cooperation with other libraries.

4. A good part of the budget must be set aside for replacement footage of worn or damaged reels as well as for duplicating popular prints.[21]

Each time a film is checked back into the library it must be inspected. Necessary repairs should then be made, and the film should be cleaned on a regular basis. All of this requires adequate equipment and personnel.

Too often, these basic facts [about film care] are ignored until the need for care and maintenance has reached a critical point. In planning a budget for a film collection, one must include funds for replacement footage, duplicate prints, inspection equipment, supplies and required personnel in order to assure successful utilization.[22]

The need for inspection is sometimes overcome by the trust factor, whereby the librarian trusts the user to report any damage he or she has caused or found when the film was shown. This may be done through a standard form, and librarians report that the trust system normally works well enough, particularly when the film is checked out by teachers or administrators.

But trust may not be enough. A writer for the *Chronicle of Higher Education* (January 22, 1979; page 55) reports "a new piracy" among borrowers who cut out sections, then neatly splice the film together again. The pirates want highlights of such films as *Gold Diggers of 1935*, sections that are costly "and not easily replaced."

There are alternatives to purchasing a film:

1. Lease An arrangement whereby the library leases the film for a given period, usually four to five years. There are enough clauses in a contract of this type to warrant careful scrutiny by the librarian, and generally leasing is not recommended.

2. Rental Rental of films is favored in most situations, at least where the film is not likely to be used often. Rental conditions and terms vary considerably from distributor to distributor, particularly as to how long the film may be retained, the cost of shipment, and insurance. While rental is primarily done through large distributors, smaller libraries should look to

---

[21] In one large system, "about 60 percent of the new films purchased each year . . . are either replacements for worn or damaged film (13%) or duplicate prints of films already in the collection (47%)" (John T. Gillespie, *A Model School District Media Program* [Chicago: American Library Association, 1977], p. 112).

[22] Cureton, op. cit., p. 98.

film rental procedures often offered by large universities and other public outlets.

3. Free Except for postage, many corporations and some government agencies offer libraries free films. These are listed in specialized bibliographies and in the *Educators Guide to Free Films*. Sometimes the message is hardly worth the effort because the film is too loaded with propaganda to be shown, but some are worthwhile and well worth the postage—so long as they are previewed before being shown to the public.

Cooperative Efforts

The high cost of films has caused most librarians to adopt cooperative purchasing plans. Systems cooperate with one another for either cooperative purchase or long-term leasing of desirable 16mm and feature films.[23] Ideal as cooperative purchasing-leasing may sound, it does have its problems and the whole concept, while accepted by librarians, is subject to constant modification.[24]

The *North American Film Directory* includes a section on film circuits and cooperatives, and anyone looking for additional information on this aspect of film will find it useful.

Equipment

The possibilities for film equipment are almost limitless, particularly if one includes video, but the basic requirements include projectors, projection screens, and usually some type of editing and repair outfits for checking and maintaining the film.

As with recordings, the basic sources of information on film equipment for libraries are the EPIE reports, the American Library Association's *Library Technology Reports*, and to a more limited degree *Consumer Reports*. Also, consult other librarians about specific equipment to be purchased.

[23] Help is often extended to cooperative efforts by the distributors: "If, for example, a film normally rents for $100 per showing, many libraries would find it impossible to fit into their limited budget. However, if four libraries decide to band together . . . the distributor might offer the film for that period for $150. For $37.50, therefore, each library would be able to show the title that would normally cost $100. This is the type of deal that can be worked out through individual negotiation" (Edward J. Hingers, "The Audiovisual Supplier . . . ," *Library Trends*, April 1976, pp. 741–742).

[24] There are numerous articles on the subject, although a good overview of one plan is Herbert P. Braselman, "Cooperative Purchasing," *Sightlines*, Winter 1975-1976. For a less than encouraging response, see a distributor's letter to the editor in the Spring 1976 issue.

There is no lack of dealers in this field, and manufacturers' catalogs are a part of any good film library collection. Film review magazines often review equipment, or at least carry advertisements for manufacturers.

The librarian must decide whether to make projectors available to those who want to use the film. This is almost always the case in school and academic libraries but rare in public libraries. If equipment is going to be used, the librarian may have to suggest trained individuals to operate the equipment. In fact, in some libraries the librarian is the projectionist or is responsible for training students and teachers.

Another aspect related to the type of program offered by the library is instructional equipment used in the actual making of films by students and members of the public. Many libraries offer instruction or at least help teachers with equipment. Thanks to super-8mm film and movie cameras, motion pictures can be produced with precision and a minimum of cost. For the amateur or paraprofessional, there is a wide variety of equipment available (from cameras and films to projectors and sound-recording and editing equipment), some of it now suited for videotape copies. Numerous stores and distributors carry this type of equipment, and almost any issue of a standard film magazine has articles about 8mm motion pictures.[25]

Ordering

Films are purchased, rented, or leased from distributors who have purchased the films from the producer (who is sometimes also the distributor).

Lacking basic bibliographies or many select lists, the film librarian must pay particular attention to film distributors, compiling a list of distributors and obtaining as many useful catalogs and lists as possible for consultation. One tip about organization is suggested by Jan W. Cureton:

One method of handling [film source files] is with a double filing system. The first file should contain catalogs arranged alphabetically by source. The second is a subject file into which brochures or circulars on new releases can be placed for reference at the time of selection. The subject file is also a convenient place to store filmographies on specific subject areas.[26]

In addition to writing for catalogs, Edward J. Hingers suggests:

1. Be sure that you get on a lot of mailing lists and that your files are kept up to date.

2. Whenever a salesman calls (in person or on the telephone) ask for the latest catalog or list of his recent releases.

3. Since no one can possibly preview all the films released in any given year, ask the salesman which films have been good sellers to other libraries. This is a

[25] Don Sutherland, "Super 8 for Para-Professional Filmmakers," *The New York Times*, November 12, 1978, p. D46. A good roundup article on the state of the art.
[26] Op. cit., p. 97.

valuable checkpoint and *not* a substitute for regular previewing; the bandwagon approach is not always valid.[27]

Film distributors are listed in many places, among them *Audiovisual Market Place*, the NICEM *Index to Producers and Distributors*, *Feature Films on 8mm and 16mm*, and *Film Programmer's Guide to 16mm Rentals* (Albany, Calif.: Reel Research), to name only a few.

General Film Aids

Rehrauer, George. *Cinema Booklist*. Metuchen, N.J.: Scarecrow Press, 1972, 1974.

Rehrauer, George. *The Film User's Handbook*. New York: R. R. Bowker, 1975.

Harrison, Helen. *Film Library Techniques*. New York: Hastings House, 1973.

The management and budget aspects of film is the topic of the best all-around book on the subject for librarians—the *Film User's Handbook*, which covers almost all aspects of film likely to be of interest to librarians in any type of situation or library. Topics from how to prepare a program to the physical organization of the collection are covered, always in a way understandable to the beginner. In addition there is a good bibliography of some 200 basic books in the field as well as a listing of approximately 175 film or film-related periodicals.

Published first in England, the Harrison title has a definite British slant, but much of the information on the practical aspects of cataloging, administration, and selection is applicable to American libraries. In fact, most emphasis is on administration of film libraries of all types, from those in schools to television stations.

Also compiled by Rehrauer, *Cinema Booklist* (and its supplement) provides an excellent select listing of basic books in the field of film. Entries are by title and a brief content note is given for each. There is a subject and author index. Educational films are considered, but most of the focus is on the feature or commercial film and books suitable for courses in the study of film. (The list is further updated in Rehrauer's *Film User's Handbook*.)

Film Reviews

Landers Film Reviews. Los Angeles: Landers Associates, since 1956. Nine times a year.

EFLA Evaluation. New York: Educational Film Library Association, since 1946. Monthly.

[27] Op. cit., p. 74.

Film Library Quarterly. New York: Film Library Information Council, since 1967. Quarterly.

Film News. New York: Film News Company, since 1939. Bimonthly.

Sightlines. New York: Educational Film Library Association, since 1967. Quarterly.

Governed by limited budget, the librarian must be particularly careful in the selection of films. In evaluating the various reviews and selection aids, the librarian should expect, at a minimum, full bibliographical description—the cost (rental, lease, or purchase), length, date, director, and so forth. The evaluative criteria used to check print and nonprint reviews are applicable here as well.

Below is a discussion of the basic film selection aids edited specifically for librarians. The general media reviews such as *Previews, Booklist,* and *Media & Methods* include film reviews. Several have regular columns on films and related media. One example is Jana Varlejs' "Cine-Opsis" in the *Wilson Library Bulletin.* The dedicated film librarian will no more be confined to film-oriented library journals than would the book selector to *Booklist.* The film librarian must be familiar with a wide variety of general film periodicals and reviews, from such standards as *Sight and Sound* to *Film Comment* and *Film Culture.* The film librarian must also be a regular reader of other basic periodicals in the area, titles that are not part of the selection process itself but are absolutely necessary for development of evaluative skills.[28]

For evaluation of films for elementary and secondary schools, the best-known source is the *Landers Film Reviews*, a sort of *Kirkus* of educational films, with critical reviews of about 150 to 200 films per issue. The reviews are timely as well as some of the best available because they weigh content in terms of for whom the film is intended. There are notes and reviews of related media—recordings, slides, filmstrips—as well as information on film festivals and other activities of interest to libraries.

The source most generally used by primary and secondary school librarians for educational film reviews is *Film News*. Edited by Rohama Lee, the magazine includes articles on film and a main section of about 40 reviews of instructional films, mostly documentaries and short educational titles but some features are covered. Films are often grouped under a current topic of interest, and appropriate audience is noted for each one. The style is lively, critical, and always informative, and related media (from filmstrips to video) are considered. Along with *Landers Film Review*, this is basic in school libraries and can be of some value for public and academic collections.

Film News Omnibus, a book compilation of reviews from *Film News*, is issued about every three years; the one covering 1973–1975 reprints reviews of some 80 feature films and close to 500 shorts. There are good critical notes with suggestions about audience use.

---

[28] A basic list of film magazines will be found in William Katz, *Magazines for Libraries* (3rd ed.; New York: R. R. Bowker, 1978), and in Rehrauer's *Film User's Handbook*.

Sightlines opens with articles on film, then moves to authoritative reviews of 16mm and 8mm films for use by schools and public libraries. It often has special bibliographies covering topical subject areas, and each issue features profiles of leaders in the field. Published by the Educational Film Library Association, *Sightlines* is one of two major services offered by that organization.

The other EFLA service consists of loose-leaf evaluation sheets on which are individual film reviews. The 40 to 60 reviews are for all age levels and some of the best available, critical as they are descriptive, the work of committees who screen and discuss the film before it is evaluated. The comments are useful in public libraries and in some academic situations. There is a monthly and annual subject index. *Sightlines* and the related service cover not only the standard educational film, but also take note of independent filmmakers' work, include some features, and go beyond the basic school-oriented titles.

Film Library Quarterly is primarily concerned with films in a context wider than that of most reviewing periodicals. Here attention is given to the standard 16mm educational film, with equal focus on the feature film, major directors, camera experts, and so on. Films are reviewed, although nowhere so many as in the school review media. More attention is given on how to use films in the public, academic, and school situation than reviews.

INDEXES TO REVIEWS AND FILM LITERATURE

Film Literature Index. Albany, N.Y.: Filmdex, since 1973. Quarterly.
Film Review Index. Monterey Park, Calif.: Audio-Visual Associates, since 1970. Quarterly.
Film Review Digest Annual. Millwood, N.J.: KTO Press, since 1977. Annual.

The basic index to film reviews, *Film Review Index* covers 700 to 1000 reviews in each quarterly issue. Arrangement is by title and there is a subject index. Approximately 90 periodicals are analyzed for reviews, and while most emphasis is on 8mm and 16mm education films, some feature-film reviews are included. The best place to check for commercial film reviews is *Film Literature Index* and *Film Review Digest Annual.*

The *Digest* analyzes about 25 periodicals for reviews. Arrangement of the 300 or so feature films considered is alphabetical by title. Reviews are listed under each title. There is a useful index of reviewers, a general index, and an award section.

Media Review Digest, mentioned previously, has devoted about half of each number to reviews of films. It is most useful for educational and short films. The library that has one probably does not need the other, and the first choice would be *Film Review Index.*

While more than an index to reviews, *Film Literature Index* thoroughly covers major reviews found in more than 200 periodicals, including (unlike other services) reviews in commercial and professional journals directed to nonschool audiences. However, its real importance is the timely index it provides to articles on films. There are more than 1000 subject headings, and material is listed under screenwriters, directors, performers, and so on. Libraries that do not need (or cannot afford) the quarterly issues may subscribe to an annual cumulation.

Film Bibliographies and Lists

Educational Film Locator. New York: R. R. Bowker Company [to be published].

Educators Guide to Free Films. Randolph, Wis.: Educators Progress Service. Annual.

Feature Films on 8mm and 16mm and Videotapes. New York: R. R. Bowker, 1978.

Kowalski, Rosemary. *Women and Film*. Metuchen, N.J.: Scarecrow Press, 1976.

NICEM (National Information Center for Educational Media). *Index to 16mm Educational Films*. Los Angeles: University of Southern California. Biennial.

NICEM. *Index to 8mm Motion Cartridges*. Los Angeles: University of Southern California. Biennial.

U.S. Library of Congress. *Films and Other Materials for Projection*. Washington, D.C.: Government Printing Office, since 1953. Quarterly.

There is no single bibliographical tool for films. A few years ago this presented problems enough, but real difficulty arose with production of more and more films. Like books, films multiply in alarming quantity.

Worldwide nontheatrical film production between 1915 and 1977, not including films produced for television, totaled 500,900. Total nontheatrical production in 1977 in the United States alone was 15,390, which represents a 4 percent increase over the previous year's production. NICEM's 16mm title entries numbered 108,356 in the first quarter of 1976. As of April 1978, Library of Congress MARC film data base tapes contain 43,521 records, of which 20,636 are 16mm film. OCLC's member input of film records stood at 43,112 in March 1978, with library of Congress MARC film tapes on hand waiting to be loaded, which will double the size of that file.[29]

Cureton points out that:

A conservative estimate of the educational and short film features available in 16mm at the present time might be made at approximately 75,000. This figure does not include the many feature or entertainment films which have also been reduced to the 16mm format for home and library use.[30]

[29] Ruth F. Rains, "Bibliographic Control of Media: One Step Closer," *Library Trends*, Summer 1978, p. 90. Rains gives various sources for these figures.
[30] Op. cit., p. 96.

Some bibliographies begin to indicate the vast number of films. Films and similar media (videorecordings, filmstrips, slides, and transparencies) cataloged by the Library of Congress are included in the basic *Films and Other Materials*. While not a union catalog, it is often used in connection with the *National Union Catalog*. It gives full catalog card information not only on feature films but on all educational motion pictures released in the United States and Canada cataloged or recataloged on L.C. printed cards.

The next most useful place for a partially complete listing of 16mm and 8mm motion pictures is the NICEM indexes. There are some 130,000 entries (about 22,000 for 8mm), each with full bibliographic information and often a content note. Arrangement is alphabetical by title, although there is a useful subject listing as well. The list is nonselective. Films are listed for every age group, from preschool through college, and each has an age–grade-level indicator. Both sets have a useful section on how to use the index and a directory of producers and distributors, which is helpful for ordering.

Lacking a national union catalog, films will be able to be traced as to location, if only in part, through the *Educational Film Locator*, which will represent holdings of the some 50 academic film libraries who are members of CUFC (Consortium of University Film Centers). Arrangement is to be alphabetical by title, with subject, utilization, and grade-level indexes. Of the 40,000 16mm titles listed, locations will be given for each, and there is to be full information on how films may be rented from CUFC members. The Locator remains in the planning stage as of early 1979, and while the compilers still hold out promise for publication, librarians must wait and see.[31]

A similar work, often updated, is Jim Limbacher's *Feature Films on 8mm and 16mm and Videotape*. Here the librarian will find about 20,000 titles available from some 190 film companies and distributors. Full information is given as to availability for rental and sale. There is an index to directors and to film serials. The list is of feature films and includes documentaries, experimental works, and even animated cartoons. The sixth edition (1979) has added 1500 video-cassette entries and includes a section on film reference books. Limbacher updates the listings at regular intervals in a section of *Sightlines*.

The *Educators Guide to Free Films* follows the pattern of others in this series. Each annual issue includes about 5000 annotated films, arranged by broad subject. All necessary information is given about loan period, distributor, running time, and so forth. Most of the films are instructional, ranging from health and history to science.

One example of a subject bibliography is *Women and Film*. It is subdivided into four areas: women as filmmakers, women performers, images

---

[31] For a history of CUFC and background on the Locator see Rains, op. cit. A list of members of CUFC will be found in *Educational Media Yearbook, 1978*, pp. 33–36. News on the elusive Locator will be found at the head of this annual listing; interested librarians might look there for developments.

of women in film, and women critics and columnists. Here the focus is on books, not on films. This type of listing is useful for the librarian trying to build a program around a subject area (the books will lead to films that may be rented or leased) and tie in a film shown to a particular book or books (which will be of added interest to the viewer and reader).

Leads on other bibliographies and books about film may be found in the review journals discussed earlier or in (1) the *Film Literature Index*, which gives a running account of new titles, and (2) the *American Reference Book Annual* (Littleton, Colo.: Libraries Unlimited, since 1970), which critically annotates the basic American books on film each year. There is a separate section dedicated exclusively to film titles, and this is one of the best retrospective check lists available.

Another basic, often updated bibliography is the standard Educational Film Library Association (EFLA) *Film Library Administration: Selected Bibliography* (New York: EFLA, 1977). This covers a wide spectrum and includes a listing of periodicals and books.

There are countless lists of films, most of them without criticism. Dozens of these are listed and annotated in Rufsvold's *Guides to Educational Media*; as new ones appear they are reviewed in most of the reviewing magazines. Numerous dealer catalogs offer a subject index, no matter how crude, to films.

SELECT LISTS

Films for Children: A Selected List, 4th ed. New York: New York Library Association, 1977.

Notable Children's Films. Chicago: American Library Association, since 1973. Annual.

"The Core Film Collection: 500 Titles Selected by the FLIC Board for a Medium Sized Public Library." *Library Trends*, Summer 1978, pp. 67–79.

Selected Films for Young Adults. Chicago: American Library Association, 1978.

AAAS Science Film Catalog. New York: R. R. Bowker, 1975.

Rehrauer, George. *The Short Film*. New York: Macmillan, 1975.

Parolato, S. J. *Superfilms: An International Guide to Award-Winning Educational Films*. Metuchen, N.J.: Scarecrow Press, 1976.

There are no completely satisfactory selected lists of films, particularly adult titles. Librarians must rely upon their own judgment and what can be found in a few carefully chosen lists.

Films for Children, put out by the New York Library Association, is suitable for libraries serving children in any part of the country. It has gone through several editions and represents the effort of people working closely with film and children. The 200 or so titles are carefully annotated and represent the best available for the age group.

"Notable Children's Films" is a select list of titles that follows much the same pattern as the notable book list. This is selected by children's librarians and appears in several places, but always in *Booklist*.

The American Library Association's service divisions often compile select lists of films. An example is the "Selected Films for Young Adults," which consists of a dozen or so annotated films the committee thinks superior in quality. Similar to "Notable Children's Films," it is an annual listing of some 26 16mm titles. The annotated list appears widely after it is selected in early spring, but is always found in *Booklist*.

The Short Film is a critical listing of 500 short films (no longer than 60 minutes) addressed to a wide audience, from children to adults. The annotated titles are drawn from recommendations found in one or more standard books or periodicals. Most of the films are from the 1960s, and the book is arranged alphabetically by title with a broad subject index. There is also a list of distributors. While somewhat dated, the list remains one of the best currently available and is a good beginning point for any film collection.

Another approach to films for a wide audience, *Superfilms* lacks annotations but does list about 1500 award-winning productions. For each title, information is given as to who awarded the prize and the audience level. There is a subject index of about 100 categories. Emphasis is on short educational films, although a few are almost feature-length.

The Film Library Information Council (FLIC) *Film Library Quarterly* provides one of the best general 16mm film lists for libraries. Although the 500 titles are limited to educational films for medium-sized public libraries, the list is applicable for larger public, academic, and high school institutions. The compilation places emphasis on general-interest titles, avoids both highly specialized works and purely curriculum-oriented films. The listing is alphabetical by title and gives color, length, and distributor information. There are no annotations or other data, so the librarian should also consult the distributor catalogs.

Many of the review media feature annotated bibliographies and lists of films in given subject areas. These are most useful for topics too new or too controversial to make the standard lists. For example, a solid approach to the women's movement will be found in Catherine Egan's "From Kitchen to Camera: Feminism and the Family Film" (*Sightlines*, Spring 1978, pp. 9–14). The running commentary concludes with an alphabetical listing of the 16mm films discussed, with information on running time, date, and distributor. This is representative of the better listings that appear throughout the year in the major review magazines.

One of the more useful subject listings of films for librarians trained in the humanities is the listing of some 5600 science films in the uncritical annotated *AAAS Science Film Catalog* (junior high through adult). Full information is given for each film. After the main 300-page section there is a brief (55-page) section on films suitable only for elementary grades. Within the sections films are arranged by Dewey classification, and there are several indexes. Compiled under the direction of the American Association for the Advancement of Science, the catalog includes several related areas; social sciences are heavily represented. It is updated by the organization's *Science Books and Films*.

Rufsvold's *Guides to Educational Media* lists and annotates numerous select lists in various subject areas and is an excellent place to begin a search. Many librarians will find useful *Alternatives: A Filmography, American Issues Forum Film List, Films on Death and Dying, Film Reviews in Psychiatry*, and *A Filmography of Films about Movies and Movie Making*.

Television

Surveying television in public libraries, one observer believes that by early 1977 "the number of libraries committing time, money and effort to any and all aspects of video was small, probably no more than 400 to 500."[32] This seems small when measured against 9000 or so public libraries, but substantial in view of the fact that only about 600 public libraries have book funds larger than $50,000.

Use by Type of Library

Library involvement with television is at one or several levels:[33]

1. The most familiar is the selection and circulation of prerecorded video cassettes, tapes, and disks; the situation is much like the selection and the lending of other materials in the library, particularly films and records.

The major problem for libraries is failure of the industry to standardize either the equipment or the video recordings. Equipment rapidly becomes obsolete or (as in the case of video players) is still in the high-cost experimental stage. The tapes, cassettes, and disks are in a complete state of flux, and the librarian purchases any one type at his or her own risk.

Add to all of this the real problem of the lack of players for videotapes in homes and the reason for less than wild enthusiasm for television in public libraries is understandable. (School and academic libraries have tended to absorb television as a teaching device.)

2. In school and academic libraries the media center coordinates the use of video for classroom instruction. This is sometimes called "remote access" audio and video, which may mean everything from supervising use of individual tapes by students to arranging for day- or semester-long series of video programs to augment the instructional program. Material used may include prerecorded tapes but is just as likely to utilize tapes made by the media center.

[32] Seth Goldstein, *Video in Libraries* (White Plains, N.Y.: Knowledge Industry Publications, 1977). Goldstein believes budget plays no particular part in whether television is available or not, but this is questionable, at least where there is a meaningful program. For an updated overview of television and libraries see Deidre Boyle's "Video in Public Library Service . . . ," *Film Library Quarterly*, no. 3 (1978), pp. 27–36.

[33] Few of the guidelines give space to television, although they always detail standards for school libraries. *Media Programs: District and School* has several entries and includes quantitative measurements, although grouped together with film.

Television instruction brings even the most remote or poorest area some of the world's greatest teachers through the screen. At the adult level it is conceivable that, given proper television programs (along with some printed aids), it would be possible to do much college work with the aid of television.[34]

(3.) In public and academic libraries, the librarian becomes involved with the creation and production of local public-interest programs, usually for public-access cable television, a natural extension of the library as a public information center. Also, the library will transmit programs prepared elsewhere.

The obvious problem with the library producing television (as with operating a radio station) is that it must have material not readily available on other channels. This may mean beaming of prerecorded material not otherwise seen in the area, but more likely (to avoid copyright problems and overlap with educational television stations) reliance will be on limited original broadcasting.

One survey found that many libraries produce their own tapes.[35] This may be done at numerous levels, although it can become part of the teaching process, with video as an art form; this is often reported on in various articles in *Film Library Quarterly*. Or the tapes may be part of practical training, as in the New Orleans Public Library, where participants in one program are given an opportunity to learn how to become announcers—and to see their own victories and errors by means of television tape.

(4.) In England, Prestel was introduced in the late 1970s. This is an extension of reference service that enables people to call up necessary information via the television set. Actually, the television is no more than a transmission screen for thousands of pages of information, any one of which can be requested by the user. Such topics as stock prices, sports results, train and plane times, and similar data are included. This is not television in the accepted sense today, although anyone with access to cable television will immediately recognize the element that systematically gives news and weather, although without any stimulus from the viewer.

Evaluation

The evaluative measures applicable to films may be applied to television—particularly video cassettes, which are little more than another form of film. The real differences come in how the video is employed and the equipment required.

[34] The television university is the object of an experiment at the Univeristy of Mid-America which offers courses to students who otherwise could not attend a campus. For a summary of activities and problems, see Gene Maeroff, "TV is Rarely Used as an Instructional Tool," *The New York Times*, November 2, 1977, p. 71.

[35] Carol Emmens, "Video Use Today," *Sightlines*, Winter 1977–1978, p. 5. See also Patrick C. Boyden, "Audio Production and Services in Academic Libraries," *Catholic Library World*, November 1978, pp. 162–165.

This is not to say that evaluative techniques for judging the intrinsic qualities of television tapes are exactly the same as for film, particularly when one considers commercial programs, but most television used in libraries is of an educational nature. The film guidelines are therefore adequate for the moment.

Format and Equipment

As with films, there are two basic types of prerecorded video program. The first is the feature, found on the national networks and sometimes on educational systems. The second is the educational program, usually produced by schools, National Educational Television, and private producers.

Most libraries now involved with video are closely allied to the educational approach, and few have much to offer in the way of feature films. The educational videotapes or cassettes are normally available with teaching guides for use in the classroom.

The past six or seven years have seen a quiet revolution in film and video, with the latter challenging the longtime role of the traditional 16mm film. This is primarily a battle of equipment, not content, as the content for both the film and the tape or cassette may be the same.

The advantages of the television cassette or tape over 16mm film are summarized by Carol Emmens:

Whatever the format, virtually everyone predicts that video will grow in importance. Video is easily indexed for viewing short segments or for retrieval; it is easily advanced, rewound, and frozen. Production of tapes is relatively easy. For the immediate future, video will co-exist with film, though one large university media center plans to "phase out 16mm film and develop video capability."[36]

Other advantages of the video format: (1) Video equipment is more flexible and easier to operate. For example, the Sony portapak system allows inexpensive, small-format video for almost anyone. (2) Prerecorded video tapes are less expensive than standard 16mm films—sometimes as much as 50 to 75 percent less. (3) Videotapes are easier to check and maintain as well as likely to have a much longer life than the average film. (4) Not only is the production of original tapes easy, but it is a simple matter to duplicate tapes or duplicate films onto tape.[37]

The disadvantages of video in the late 1970s:

1. Video equipment is more expensive than the average film projector, although with mass production this cost differential is likely to be eliminated.

---

[36] Ibid., p. 7. See also a dated although still-valid argument for video in John Chittock's "Future Playback . . . ," *Sight and Sound*, Spring 1976, pp. 46–49.

[37] Technically simple, that is—but there are the usual problems of copyright. For an explanation of practices and demands of film distributors made on a library that wants to duplicate films on videotape, see Jerome K. Miller, "Licenses to Videotape Films," *Library Trends*, Summer 1978, pp. 101–105.

2. There are considerably fewer videotapes and cassettes available than 16mm or even 8mm film, with choice therefore limited.[38]

A good summary of the future of television equipment was made by a critic:

We're standing on the verge of gettin' it on with home video, and as soon as record companies, music publishers and hardware manufacturers can figure out how to divide up the money to be made, we the consumers will be faced with a vast new horizon of home entertainment options. Video cassette recorder systems (now sold in 2-hour Betamax and 4-hour VHS formats) can, of course, record off your television and play pre-recorded cassettes, but those cassettes—of concerts, movies, etc.—retail from $50–80 now. And the VCR itself hovers around $800 to $1,000 retail.

Video disc recorders, however, will probably be available sometime next year [1979] and they do some different things. The disc is vinyl, looks like a phonograph record, is pressed like one, and is strictly pre-recorded. But the machine will cost as little as $400, and the discs will sell for about $12. Sound quality is vastly better than even audio records, and, unlike video cassettes, a stereo videodisc will be playable through a home stereo (there is even talk of using this "super" disc for strictly audio recordings). A movie on video disc will be able to carry a bilingual soundtrack, since the disc is in stereo.[39]

When this happens there is going to be a considerable change in library handling of films as well as video cassettes and related items. Meanwhile, most librarians are simply waiting before they invest what are now impressive sums in equipment that may become quickly outdated.

Why Television?

The basic justification for the use of television in the library is much the same as for other nonprint media. Television is a major form of communication, familiar to many Americans who may never read a book or periodical. If used properly, it can serve the nonprint-oriented public. It also serves people who read and simply want another means of approaching information or recreation.

But questions remain about the real role of television in libraries. It may be no accident that in a recent survey of public libraries, "the great majority . . . perhaps two-thirds of the total, either did not respond to our survey or indicated they had no plans whatsoever to introduce video."[40]

[38] This is not likely to be a lasting problem. In 1978, for example, Allied Artists announced it would put 500 feature films (from *Cabaret* to *The Man Who Would Be King*) on video cassettes and sell them for $50 each. There are now types of book clubs for video cassettes and tapes, such as the Video Club of America (Industrial Park, Farmington Hills, Mich. 48024), which makes feature films available on cassettes and tapes.

[39] *Soho Weekly News*, October 12, 1978, p. 56. Youth-culture magazines and newspapers often have articles on the use of television and its development. See, for example, almost any issue of *Rolling Stone* and "Home Video Disk Unit Offered," *The New York Times*, December 14, 1978, p. D4.

[40] Goldstein, op. cit., p. 3.

Here it is important to make distinctions. When videotapes, cassettes, or disks and players become more common, there is reason to suspect libraries will purchase the recordings as they do film and music records today. The technology may even replace the 16mm and 8mm films in libraries. Less likely to happen, if for no other reason than lack of funds, is any deep commitment to television production, particularly beyond the immediate school or library facility.

Few would argue the viability and value of videotapes and cassettes devoted to education and instruction, but there is an argument as to what place, if any, television should occupy in the schools and the public libraries. Beyond the question of cost is a deeper one regarding the role of the library and, in the case of children and young people, the effects of television on children.[41] The debate is too involved for consideration here, although it is one librarians must constantly keep in mind, particularly when applying for funds for other than purely educational video.

BOOKS AND TELEVISION

The antagonism between television fans and readers is primarily one of misunderstanding and bias. The avid reader may be almost equally interested in television. One study, for example, found that "Book readers spend almost as much time watching television (15 hours per week) as do non-book readers."[42] Nonreaders are more likely to turn to television than readers, of course, if only to fill in time not spent on reading or other activities. However, these nonreaders are *not* the ones normally using a library; they are a different audience. Library users want books, but they just as likely will want access to television.

The point is not to match format against format but to consider content, skill of presentation, style, and such matters—which should be equally high in both. It is the content, not the form, that should be evaluated.

A nice distinction between television and reading was drawn by a writer for *The New Yorker*'s "Talk of the Town." It is worth quoting at length because it draws the proper kinds of distinction.

Television is the *public* medium par excellence. Beaming its news, as it now does, over the whole earth, it gathers the earth's people into a single audience. Not a global village but a global amphitheatre is what television creates. . . .

Print offers little in the way of communal experience with a world audience; by contrast with television, it is a private medium. Many people may read what is printed, but they do so at their leisure, when and where they wish. Each reader

[41] A good summary of this situation is Joanne R. Cantor, "Research on Television's Effects on Children," *Phaedrus*, Spring 1978, pp. 9–13, which includes a good bibliography. See also the more general rationale for television in Deidre Boyle's "The Library, Television, and the Unconscious Mind," *Wilson Library Bulletin*, May 1978, pp. 696–702.

[42] "Who Reads Books and Why," *Publishers Weekly*, November 6, 1978, p. 16. This conclusion is debatable, at least in actual number of hours the average reader watches television.

is alone. Isn't this why it is an invasion of privacy to read over someone's shoulder? . . . Print can whisper confidentially to the reader; television is always addressing a crowd. But if only television can provide the horizontal dimension of a world community, only print can provide the vertical dimension—the dimension of time. Television vanishes into thin air, but newspapers endure. In a sense, what happens on television occurs in the present alone, whereas what happens in print goes on happening indefinitely. Print is the medium of continuity—the medium of history. . . . The *Times* is said to be the country's newspaper of record; it would be absurd to speak of a television station of record. Television may have become our eyes and ears and our public meeting place, but print continues to be our memory.[43]

Ordering

Outlets for film and recordings often sell videotapes and equipment. Procedures for ordering are much the same as for films or recordings. And as with films, the best source for information on videotapes and cassettes is the catalog of the dealer or distributor. For example, Electronic Arts Intermix is one of the major U.S. distributors of independent video efforts and regularly updates its catalog. Addresses may be found in the NICEM indexes, the *International Television Almanac*, and in the more general *Audiovisual Market Place*.

The *International Television Almanac* (New York: Quigley, since 1956; annual) is primarily prepared for commercial television but is a good source of directory information on performers, producers, feature releases, and stations thoughout the world. It is an excellent reference aid when trying to find addresses and data on commercial television. Usually the sources for film and hardware recording may be used for television equipment.

Video equipment is evaluated by EPIE and the American Library Association's *Library Technology Reports*. Check, too, *Consumer Reports* and the standard film and record magazines, which often feature television equipment. Decisions regarding equipment depend entirely upon the services provided by the library, and many of the same rules apply here as for film equipment.

General Television Aids

Gordon, George N., and Irving Falk. *Videocassette Technology in American Education.* Englewood Cliffs, N.J.: Educational Technology Publications, 1972.
Video and Cable Guidelines for Librarians. Chicago: American Library Association, 1977.

[43] October 7, 1978, p. 27.

Kenney, Brigitte. "Cable Television for Libraries," *Drexel Library Quarterly*, January-April 1973.
North American Film and Video Directory. New York: R. R. Bowker, since 1977. Irregular.

There is no text or guide for television in libraries equivalent to George Rehrauer's *Film User's Handbook*. Most background material must be picked up among the books listed here and, of course, from frequent periodical articles on the subject of television and libraries.

The *Video and Cable Guidelines for Librarians* offers a nontechnical overview of the subject. Prepared by and for librarians, it covers such topics as video for library service, programming, hardware, sources for programming, and the like. It has a check list of information sources and a useful bibliography.

Edited by Brigitte Kenney and Roberto Esteves, the *Guidelines* may be supplemented by the special issue of the *Drexel Library Quarterly* devoted to uses of television in libraries. Its nearly 200 pages can serve as a textbook, and most of the articles still are applicable.

Valuable and also by Kenney and Esteves is *Video and Cable Communications* (Chicago: American Library Association, 1975). The previously mentioned guidelines developed from this initial report, but it remains useful for some information not found in the guidelines.

Within the American Library Association there are several committees and groups concerned with television. The major one is the Video and Cable Communications Section of the Library and Information Technology Association, but there is also the Video Committee of the American Association of School Librarians.

A check of *Library Literature* shows that numerous library periodicals are devoting special issues to television; see, for example, *Wisconsin Library Bulletin* for July-August 1978, which has short articles on how television actually, not theoretically, operates in Wisconsin.

The *North American Film and Video Directory* lists college, public, and special libraries and media centers that have collections of videotapes available for loan, rental, or on-site viewing.

While dated, the Gordon text on video-cassette technology is useful for an overview of possible television uses in various educational situations, from school media centers to adult education. The author indicates reasonable expectations for constructive use of television, and there are good references.

Librarians looking for more information, including bibliographies, should contact the Cable Television Information Center (2100 M. St. N.W., Washington, D.C. 20036). While this organization is primarily concerned with local government, it does have publications (and will give advice) on the more general use of television. Another good contact is Alternate Media Center (144 Bleecker St., New York, N.Y. 10012), which has several publications in this area and offers consulting services.

VIDEO REVIEWS

Cablelibraries. Box 566, Ridgefield, Conn.: Tepfer Publishing Co., since 1973. Bimonthly.

Cablelibraries is approved by the American Library Association and serves as an official publication for video-inclined librarians. The eight-page newsletter informs readers of meetings, personalities, reports, and the like. While there are no video reviews as such, there are often descriptive (sometimes even critical) notes on catalogs, books, and similar material.

Several of the media reviews, such as *Previews*, include references to video that are sure to increase. *Booklist* is one of the few book-oriented reviews that regularly includes a section on video cassettes. However, since many films are now being distributed in cassette form, it will be necessary to see if the film is (like recordings) available in both the traditional and new form. In this respect video is reviewed vis-à-vis the film reviews.

No indexes cover review of television tapes and cassettes exclusively, but *Media Review Digest, Film Review Index,* and *Film Literature Index* report on television and do include citations to reviews of film, cassettes, and tapes.

Video Bibliographies and Lists

National Information Center for Educational Media. *Index to Educational Video Tapes.* Los Angeles: University of Southern California, since 1967. Biennial.
Chicorel's Index to Video Tapes and Cassettes. New York: Chicorel Library Publishing Corporation, since 1978. Irregular.
Catalogue of Programs on Videocassette. Washington, D.C.: Public Television Library.
The Video Bluebook. White Plains, N.Y.: Knowledge Industry Publications, 1975.

As of early 1979 there is no single satisfactory list or bibliography of videotapes or cassettes—in fact, no single source for even locating video recordings. The closest one can come is two far-from-satisfactory approaches.

The NICEM index includes more than 15,000 entries, listed alphabetically and indexed by subject, limited to tapes and cassettes of interest almost exclusively to elementary and secondary schools. Some tapes are of value to universities and to adults, but the preponderance of listings are educational and for younger people. With new editions and new advances in the technology of video this balance is likely to change more in favor of older viewers.

The *Chicorel's Index to Video Tapes* offers fewer entries but does include more titles suitable for the academic and the public library. There are about

4000 videotapes and cassettes, arranged by title with a limited subject approach (about 150 headings). Annotations, taken from the producer-distributor catalogs, are in no way critical. The brief bibliographic information includes producer, distributor, release date, specifications, sale-rental data, and age level. The index leaves out many distributors and it is somewhat dated, although it does include some material not found in the NICEM index.[44]

The Library of Congress catalog *Films and Other Materials* includes some video programs, although not all. However, as the production of video cassettes or records increases it is expected that most eventually will find their way to the Library of Congress listing.

Public television offers several hundred programs and series on video cassettes through its catalog. These cover all grade levels, most interests, and range from the purely educational to entertainment and feature films. The catalog is often updated and can be used in conjunction with others of this type, such as those issued by the Audiovidual Center of Indiana University at Bloomington, one of the largest centers for video.

The *Video Bluebook* is a listing, by subject, of some 5000 videotapes. Most of the material is directed to business, government, and industry and is not of interest to the general public. Full information is given for each title, including its preview availability. This listing should be useful in public and academic libraries. The publisher is planning a revised edition.

SELECT LISTS

As of this writing there were no specific lists of selected video cassettes. There are, however, selections in the *Core Media Collection for Secondary Schools* and *The Elementary School Library Collection*, and select lists appear from time to time in such basic media reviewing sources as *Previews* and *Booklist*.

[44] For a short critical no-buy advice review see Deidre Boyle, "Media Minded," *American Libraries*, June 1978, pp. 393–394.

13
From Filmstrip to Realia

I̤N ADDITION TO recordings, films, and television, the average library has other nonprint forms, with relative importance depending primarily on the goals and audience of the library. No matter what type or size of library, the user is likely to find at least a representative collection of most of the nonprint materials discussed in this chapter.

Filmstrips

The filmstrip is usually a wound section of 35mm film that delivers a significant single-frame message to the viewer about a particular subject.[1] An ideal medium for instruction, it is less likely to be used for entertainment.

Filmstrip has distinct advantages, particularly in the learning situation: (1) It is easy to control, and the equipment needed is both inexpensive and simple to operate. (2) Since the filmstrip is in one piece, it is easier to check for damage and easy to manage. A series of slides may perform the same function, but there is always danger the slides will get out of order or one or more be lost. (Conversely, slides permit easy addition and deletion of material for changing sequence of presentation.) (3) The single greatest benefit is that the user can pace the single frames to his own needs. One may speed through a presentation or take an afternoon for it.

Another advantage to the filmstrip is quantity. There is a wide diversification and amount of illustrative material available in this form.

Today the majority of filmstrips are tied to sound; most come with cassettes or disks, which may be automatic or manual. The annual "Best

---

[1] There are several formats, but 35mm is the most prevalent. There are both single-frame and double-frame strips, but less than 1 percent of filmstrips are double—something that should be checked when ordering; most equipment will not take the double type. Other formats include 16mm and the 8mm or super-8mm film, normally in a cartridge. While not precisely a filmstrip (it moves at a given rate of speed and probably has sound), 8mm is often used in place of the filmstrip.

Filmstrips and Slides of the Year" for 1978, in *Previews* (April 1978, pp. 2–6) featured 54 filmstrips, and almost all included the cassette or disk for sound. The automatic are what the name suggests, while the manual allow the user to turn to the next frame at will. There is an audible cue for the viewer to move the strip forward.

The sound filmstrip, thanks to its convenience and relative low cost, has replaced 16mm films as the prime contender for the largest share of the audiovisual educational materials market. Part of the reason is that many filmstrips are now spinoffs of the first-place multimedia kits, no longer dependent upon the kit itself. Also, the automatic cassette makes the operation of the filmstrip more interesting, certainly easier than the manual system.

TRANSPARENCIES

Closely associated with filmstrips, transparencies are in a sense single-frame filmstrips. However, as single sheets (often sold in sets), they normally are used separately. (They also offer the advantage of projection in normal light.)

Overhead transparencies are used primarily in school and academic libraries and, to a lesser extent, in special libraries. They are graphic or printed works transposed to a 10-by-11-inch transparency that requires a special projector for showing.

Transparencies may be purchased from commercial firms or produced in the library. They cover every conceivable subject and range in interest from preschool through adult.

USE BY TYPE OF LIBRARY

Filmstrips are identified primarily with the school, academic, and special library and are not likely to be present in many small to medium-sized public libraries. The filmstrip, public librarians reason, "is a useful classroom teaching device, but inappropriate for public library collections and programs."[2] But there is hardly a consensus. Many small and medium-sized public libraries do purchase filmstrips. They argue that—compared to other media —the expense is low, the equipment simple to operate, and the wide subject areas ideal for both adults and children. Perhaps this is the true picture, for few will deny that as the public library develops in size and the audience served, it is likely to consider filmstrips.

Precise figures for filmstrips and transparencies are given for school libraries; the guidelines call for 500 to 2000 filmstrips, or one to four items per user as the minimum requirements for a base collection in a school with 500 or fewer users. Transparencies are put together with slides, with a call

[2] Elizabeth Futas, *Library Acquisition Policies and Procedures* (Phoenix, Ariz.: Oryx Press, 1977), p. 337.

for 2000 to 6000 items, or four to 12 items per user.[3] In addition there are quantitative guidelines for equipment.

In the academic library, filmstrip is suited for independent study, particularly when there is adequate viewing and listening equipment. More important, it is a primary instructional device, often used in the classroom. Unlike the typical school media center, however, the academic library is likely to hold only a fraction of the total filmstrips. They are usually found in various departments and sections—as well as in the audiovisual center, if one exists. A particular stronghold of filmstrip is the curriculum library of the school of education, a library that may or may not be a part of the central library system. Ideally, there will be central control of selection, acquisition, and cataloging. In reality, there are almost as many approaches to all these factors as there are universities and colleges.[4]

EVALUATION

Filmstrips are evaluated in most of the standard media reviewing sources, such as *Previews*, but there is no single source devoted exclusively to them. The necessity for the librarian to judge filmstrips, either alone or with the assistance of others, preferably subject experts, is stronger here than with other types of nonprint materials.

The rules concerning content, audience, scope, and purpose are as applicable here as for any medium. One must also ask if the filmstrip is the appropriate medium for the message. Beyond that are more technical questions of format:

1. The strip should be in logical order with some verbal or visual signal to indicate when to turn to the next frame. A written text or verbal guide should be in syncronization with the strip.

2. Do the filmstrip's transitional frames add anything, or are they there simply to fill time and space?

3. Are the frames in focus, clear, and—if in color—are the colors true? Does the focus retain clarity from frame to frame?

4. Can captions be read clearly and at a reasonable distance? Is vocabulary level and caption length suitable? If there is sound, is the voice pleasing and clear? Are captions and voice integrated with the picture?

The quality of filmstrips has improved considerably during the past decade. In 1974 a critic pointed out that the majority of filmstrips lacked both intelligence and visual imagination.[5] Today the situation is much better, and

[3] *Media Programs: District and School* (Chicago: American Library Association, 1975), p. 73.

[4] See, for example, Dennis Fields and Tony Schultztenberg, "Filmstrips," in Pearce S. Grove (ed.), *Nonprint Media in Academic Libraries* (Chicago: American Library Association, 1975), pp. 134–147.

[5] Ethel Heins, "Literature Bedeviled: A Searching Look at Filmstrips," *Horn Book*, June 1974, pp. 306–313.

"the bulk of this format is no longer poor to mediocre."[6] Perhaps the summary that does most to outline what one should expect in a good filmstrip precedes the *Booklist* "Notable Children's Filmstrips of 1977":

[Filmstrips] should exhibit venturesome creativity and, in exemplary ways, reflect and encourage children's interest. They make effective use of special techniques and are aesthetically and technically well done with clear and appropriate use of visuals and (if any) voices, music, language and sound effects, together creating a unified whole.[7]

5. Is the filmstrip timely, and the level of presentation imaginative (many filmstrips are pedestrian beyond description) and relevant for the particular situation?

EQUIPMENT

The average filmstrip projector is inexpensive, easy to operate, and presents few real problems—at least in theory. Just to make sure (this is true for all equipment), ask for advice from a librarian who has had the equipment in operation.

Another consideration, equally true for slide projectors, is of sound. If records or cassettes are to be used in conjunction with the filmstrip, be sure combination equipment is easy to obtain, will fit the space, and can be used both individually and with groups.

Purchases should be made only after applying the rules suggested for film equipment and checking such basic consumer reports as EPIE and the American Library Association's *Library Technology Reports.*

ORDERING

Dealers of filmstrips are to be found in many of the sources that handle film (see pages 277–278). Distributors are also listed in the NICEM index as well as the *Audiovisual Market Place.* Another somewhat dated list will be found in *The Filmstrip Collection.*

GENERAL AIDS

There are no satisfactory general aids or guides to filmstrips. *The Filmstrip Collection* (Salem, Ohio: Dale Shaffer, 1972) is a privately produced 25-page mimeographed guide that covers most aspects of the subject. Lacking any book on filmstrips, this is a useful substitute. The lengthy list of producers and distributors of filmstrips is particularly helpful.

[6] *Previews,* April 1978, p. 2.
[7] *Booklist,* October 1, 1978, p. 311.

REVIEWS

Filmstrips and some transparencies are reviewed regularly in *Previews* and on occasion in *Booklist*, as well as in the standard film periodicals. The reviews are indexed in *Media Review Digest*, which covers reviews in many other periodicals. Another useful guide is *Film Review Index*, which indexes filmstrips by title and by subject and indicates where they have been reviewed.

Particularly useful is the annual choice of filmstrips and slides in *Previews* and the "Notable Children's Filmstrips" that appears in the October issue of *Booklist*. Both lists are ideal buying guides for libraries with limited budgets.

FILMSTRIP BIBLIOGRAPHIES AND LISTS

NICEM. National Information Center for Educational Media. *Index to 35mm Filmstrips*. Los Angeles: University of Southern California. Biannual.

NICEM. *Index to Educational Overhead Transparencies*. Los Angeles: University of Southern California. Biannual.

Educators Guide to Free Filmstrips. Randolph, Wis.: Educators Progress Service. Annual.

The NICEM index covers about 75,000 filmstrips. As in the other indexes the strips are arranged alphabetically with full data about each, preceded by a subject breakdown by title. The filmstrips are for all ages, although there is more emphasis on material for grade and secondary schools than for adults. Closely related to this service is the NICEM *Index to 8mm Motion Cartridges*, another way of saying filmloop.

The NICEM *Index to Educational Overhead Transparencies* has over 60,000 entries for all grade levels and the Library of Congress *Films and Other Materials* includes filmstrips as well as transparencies and slides.

The annual *Educators Guide to Free Filmstrips* arranges the material under 18 to 20 subject headings and generally follows the pattern of other lists in this series. Slides and transparencies are included as well. Full bibliographic information is given for each entry and there is a helpful introduction on the use of filmstrips.

Slides

Slides have much in common with filmstrips but have distinct advantages: (1) They can be shuffled about for a new approach to a subject. (2) If one slide becomes dated or destroyed it can be replaced. (3) In certain subject areas, such as art, slides are preferable because they are more readily available than filmstrips.

Slides are to be found in almost every public, school, academic, and special library. Each tends to handle them differently, and in academic libraries there is rarely centralized control. So closely is the slide tied to the lecture that in larger universities they may be selected, organized, and stored in various departments and sections. School libraries with media centers control the slides, although even here it is not unusual for a teacher to have a private collection.

As noted, the guidelines for school media centers call for 2000 to 6000 slides and transparencies, with no distinction between the two.[8] Standards for academic and public libraries are more general.

EVALUATION

There are a few commonsense rules about evaluating slides. After determination that the subject matter is suitable for the audience there is the technical matter of how faithful the slide is to the original object. This is particularly important for art reproductions; they are never quite right and can vary drastically, which leads Freitag and Irvine to warn that libraries should always order slides on approval: "Many factors cause variations in color reproductions, necessitating the examination of each slide to determine its suitability for the study of art and some of the life sciences."[9]

In the evaluation of filmstrips, most of the criteria for slides apply.

EQUIPMENT

Standard, relatively inexpensive equipment for showing slides is available in almost any photography store, including some projectors that can handle either filmstrips or slides. Unless the library is going to use slides daily, the number of the projectors needed should be gauged realistically.

Slides may be stored in various ways, but carousels that attach to the projectors are favored. (Be sure the trays are compatible with several types of projector.)

One consideration is mobility. In some schools and academic libraries the projectors are fastened to a showing area (even an individual carrel). When this is the case, at least one or two mobile units are needed.

The screen or other viewing surface is another important factor. And, if the projector is to be used in groups, there should be provision for remote operation.

Slide equipment is evaluated in several sources, ranging from *Consumer Reports* to the ALA *Library Technology Reports* to EPIE.

Equipment costs are relatively low, as are prices of ready-made slides, which accounts for a sometimes alarmingly large collection. "Slide libraries can double or triple within a few years with a relatively small expenditure.

[8] *Media Programs*, pp. 73–74.
[9] Wolfgang M. Freitag and Betty Jo Irvine, "Slides," Grove, op. cit., p. 115.

. . . It is not uncommon to find a collection to which ten thousand slides are being added annually. What is often neglected, however, is the cost involved in efficiently organizing and maintaining these visual resources."[10] There is a vast number of sources for slides; almost all of the world's major museums offer them, as do many commercial firms listed in such guides as *Audiovisual Market Place* and *Picture Sources.*

The Slide Buyer's Guide (Kansas City, Mo.: College Art Association of America, since 1972; annual) is primarily a list of commercial slide sources (and some museums) and the best of the guides. It also includes some valuable basic advice on slide collections and includes an extensive subject index.

As Freitag and Irvine point out, whenever possible the library should try the museum before going to the commercial producer; museums usually charge less than commercial firms and their slides are often quite superior in quality. A useful aid is the *Handlist of Museum Sources for Slides and Photographs*, often updated, available from the University of California Art Department at Santa Barbara, California.

Many librarians, working alone or with instructors or photography experts, produce slides for the library collection. A process outside the scope of this book, it is an important one for librarians. Normally the slides are produced in conjunction with tapes as instructional aids—at all levels, from elementary school through graduate study. For a detailed bibliography of books and articles on slide-tape presentations see the Hardesty guide.[11]

GENERAL AIDS

Irvine, Betty Jo. *Slide Libraries: A Guide for Academic Institutions and Museums.* Littleton, Colo.: Libraries Unlimited, 1974.

Freudenthal, Juan. *The Slide as a Communication Tool*, 2nd ed. Boston: Simmons College, 1974.

Slide Libraries is a basic text on the subject, although applicable to larger libraries. The author covers most of the aspects of slides of interest to librarians, and the text may be used to advantage by those in all types of situations. There are many lists, including a directory of sources, producers, and the like.

The Freudenthal volume, a bibliography, may be of more value to the researcher than to the librarian. Even so, it offers numerous sources concerning slides and is the best bibliography of its type now available. For a fast overview bibliographic approach to what is available for slide librarians

[10] Ibid., p. 104.

[11] For a brief discussion of production, see ibid., pp. 115–120. See also C. F. Orgren's "Production of Slide-Tape Programs," *Unabashed Librarian*, Summer 1975, pp. 25–28. This short, easy-to-follow article should be a first step for anyone considering developing a slide show. The best book on the subject is Larry L. Hardesty, *Use of Slide/Tape Presentation in Academic Libraries* (New York: Norton, 1978).

see Freudenthal's "The Slide as a Communication Tool" in *School Media Quarterly*, Winter 1974, pp. 109–115. Now a bit dated, but probably the single best article available on the subject.

REVIEWS

Slides are covered from time to time in the basic media review sources (*Previews, Booklist*, etc.). There are also art magazines that regularly review material of interest to libraries, such as *Umbrella* (P.O. Box 3692, Glendale, Calif. 91201; since 1978. Bimonthly). *Picturescope* (see page 303) often has material on slides; the Fall 1977 issue has a bibliography on "The Organization of Slides" (pp. 158–166) that is updated about every three years. See also the Irvine *Slide Libraries* for more suggestions.

SLIDE BIBIOGRAPHIES AND LISTS

NICEM (National Information Center for Education Media). *Index to Educational Slides.* Los Angeles: University of Southern California. Biannual.
Arts of the United States. New York: McGraw-Hill, 1960.
Text-Fiche Series. Chicago: University of Chicago Press.

The NICEM index to slides lists more than 28,000 slides, the majority of which are fine-art slides for audiences of all ages. The others are commercial or governmental slides to be used in the classroom.

The NICEM index does not include slides from major art museums; for these one must turn to other sources. Many of the museums, such as the Metropolitan Museum of Art and the National Gallery in London, issue their own catalogs. The best way to keep up with new slides in the field is to follow reviews in *Previews, Booklist*, and other standard sources as well as in art magazines.

Slides are listed in the *Educators Guide to Free Filmstrips*. There are about 220 sets available on loan, and several include scripts and other accompanying aids.

Arts of the United States is a listing of 4000 works of American art on color slides. The catalog is arranged by subject, with each subject preceded by a brief essay. Complete bibliographic information is given for each slide as well as a black-and-white reproduction of each, and there is a complete artist, title, and subject index. Almost all these slides are still available and the date of the publication (1960) rarely interferes with use.

Using microform technology, the Text-Fiche series issued by the University of Chicago Press is really another version of the slide applied to art.[12] Microfiche is used as the medium for reproductions from some of the world's largest art museums. The format is familiar to microform users: a 4-by-6-inch

---

[12] Advertisements point out that this makes it possible to reproduce art at much less than the cost of a printed version; one example is the American Prints collection from the Baltimore Museum of Art—44 pages of text, one color fiche of 81 pictures for $9.95.

card with about 84 reproductions on each card. The cards are accompanied by a text. Thanks to a new development, the color reproductions are superior to most slides. The drawback is that a microfiche reader must be available, and, of course, the card cannot be projected for more than individual use.

An English firm, Somerset House, combines formats in many of its series, such as *European Literary Periodicals* (a collection of 28 twentieth-century serials, including some on the art of the book). Here the library is offered several of the periodicals on microfilm and color slides. In other series the library may buy color microfiche similar to the Text-Fiche series.

The Picture Collection

A librarian speaks of a picture collection at two or three distinctive levels. The first and most common is pictures in a vertical file. The library may also have a small collection of reproductions. Beyond that is the special library with detailed photographs and other pictures employed in science, technology, or business. Finally, and least common, is a museum-quality collection of photographs and prints. This section is concerned with only the first level.

As with the other graphic media, pictures may be represented in a library solely by books, particularly art books and illustrated children's works. However, most libraries do have varying sizes of vertical-file collections in which, under suitable subject headings, one will find filed the much-called-for pictures of horses, personalities, and whatever else is popular.

Beyond the books and vertical files stand the picture sources, which may be used more often to answer a reference query than to acquire pictures for the library. No matter how they are used, they are of importance in most libraries.

Where the picture collection is more than books or a vertical file, one is likely to find: (1) In public libraries, a group of framed prints for loan, or a specialized group of pictures and photographs that illustrate the history and development of the community. (2) In academic libraries, the picture collection may be closely associated with the art department and not even a physical part of the library—situation that may also be the case with at least part of the slide collection. (3) In school media centers, the pictures are most likely to be centralized in the center and made available upon request to users.

Although addressed to conditions in academic libraries, one observer's comments are applicable to other types:

It does not appear that [picture] collections will . . . constitute more than a modest segment of the average college library's holding. It would appear that large collections will . . . be maintained primarily in museums. . . . [Few librarians] have available the skills to produce such materials, relying primarily on commercially available materials.[13]

[13] H. Joanne Harrar, "Photographs, Pictures and Prints," in Grove, op. cit., pp. 183–184.

EVALUATION

What must be considered first is the audience likely to use the picture, followed closely by such considerations as (1) space available for the pictures (vertical file, walls, shelves); (2) methods of cataloging or otherwise retrieving pictures: (3) duplication between the pictures and what can be easily found in books or periodicals; and (4) time available to the librarian adequately to select, organize, and keep a picture collection up to date.

One need not be too careful about the standards of reproduction when the pictures cost nothing; when, for example, they are taken from a discarded magazine. Where cost is a factor (as in sometimes expensive reproductions of paintings), many of the rules used to judge slides apply. Quality of color, faithfulness to the original work (in reproduction techniques and relative size), the overall image clarity, and the like must be considered.

GENERAL AIDS

Muehsam, Gerd. *Guide to Basic Information Sources in the Visual Arts.* Santa Barbara, Calif.: Jeffrey Norton/ABC Clio, 1978.
Picture Sources, 3rd ed. New York: Special Libraries Association, 1975.
Hill, Donna. *The Picture File.* Syracuse, N.Y.: Gaylord, 1978.

Compiled by the Special Libraries Association's Picture Division, *Picture Sources* is the basic directory. It lists more than 800 collections of prints, slides, and photographs in American and Canadian libraries and private collections. Material is arranged in 15 categories. Indexes help the user find specific types of pictures. It is a particularly well-organized and sophisticated guide that gives clear, concise information for each source listed. The guide is primarily for the location of pictures for use by commercial firms and lists several private companies (such as The Bettmann Archive)[14] that specialize in providing pictures, but it includes basic information of value to any library.

The Special Libraries Association has a division concerned solely with pictures and photographs, which publishes a useful quarterly called *Picturescope*. This newsletter is filled with tips on how to find pictures and often includes notes about new bibliographic aids in the field.

A good basic guide to pictures is Donna Hill's *The Picture File*, a practical manual that considers sources of pictures, selection aids, equipment, and the like. (About half the book consists of suggested subject headings that may

---

[14] "Drawing Upon His Vast Resources . . ." (*Publishers Weekly*, August 21, 1978, p. 33) says of Bettmann, one of the best-known commercial sources of pictures in the United States: "The Bettmann Archive is familiar as the source of illustrations, photographs, graphics amassed by Bettmann over more than 40 years. Some 3-million pictures comprise the collection, and those have been supplemented by still more millions from the Underwood & Underwood Photo Collection. Bettmann had plenty to choose from."

be of limited use to anyone except the small to medium-size school or public library.) Hill, who has had many years experience as a picture-collection librarian, gives the basic information needed either to begin or to modify a collection. While the manual is primarily for schools, it can be used in the development of almost any type of basic picture collection.

The *Guide to Basic Information Sources in the Visual Arts* is a handbook intended for art students, but in the process of discussing basic reference works in art it gives many hints of use to librarians. For example, there are individual chapters on prints and photography and a useful bibliography. This is a discursive approach, and while the author discusses many titles, it is not meant to be as exhaustive as the basic bibliography in the field: Mary Chamberlin's *Guide to Art Reference Books* (Chicago: American Library Association, 1959), which is being revised.

D. L. Foster's *Prints in the Public Library* (Metuchen, N.J.: Scarecrow Press, 1973) is a thorough discussion with a good explanation of basic selection tools. The appendix includes a list of dealers.

PICTURE BIBLIOGRAPHIES, LISTS, AND INDEXES

National Geographic Index 1947–1969 (plus supplements). Washington: National Geographic Society.
Illustration Index, 3rd ed. Metuchen, N.J.: Scarecrow Press, 1973.
Monro, Isabel. *Index to Reproduction of American Paintings* (plus supplement). Bronx, N.Y.: The H. W. Wilson Company, 1948, 1964.

Among numerous indexes to illustrations in books and magazines, typical and much-used is *Illustration Index*, which covers the contents of some 15 magazines and as many books (including *American Heritage, Ebony,* and *Sports Illustrated*) and is frequently updated. Arrangement is by subject; since most libraries have the material indexed, this provides a handy way of getting at sometimes hard-to-find pictures. Other useful indexes of this type include Jessie Ellis, *The Index to Illustrations* (Boston: Faxon, 1967), which covers illustrations in a selected group of books and magazines; and Patricia Havlice's *Art in Time* and Jane Clapp's *Art in Life, 1936–1956* (plus another volume for 1957–1963)—both published by Scarecrow Press.

Most of the H. W. Wilson indexes indicate whether or not pictures, illustrations, and portraits accompany articles. The same company's *Art Index* will lead the researcher to both articles and reproductions.[15]

The Monro index located reproductions of paintings in 500 books and more than 300 exhibition catalogs, and the supplement adds another 400 titles. While this is more of a reference aid than a selection aid, it can be used in acquisition. Most of the books identify the museum or institution in which the original painting is held. The library then can write the museum and inquire if reproductions or slides are available for the needed work.

[15] D. J. Patten, "The Art Index: An Index to Illustrations of Works of Art," *Picturescope*, Autumn 1971, pp. 145–156. How to use the index to locate pictures.

One of the best sources for the widest number of pictures likely to appeal to adults and young people is the *National Geographic Magazine*. Most libraries have numerous issues, even complete runs of this national institution. Thanks to a basic index and supplements, retrieval of pictures is quite easy— usually by subject. A supplementary guide is *Handy Key to Your National Geographics* (East Aurora, N.Y.: C. S. Underhill), which has been published about every two years since 1954 and offers about 4500 approaches by subject to pictures in the magazine.

ART REPRODUCTIONS

Collections of art reproductions have become popular in public and school libraries, and often the former will lend them to patrons for use in the home. In purchasing reproductions the library should seek the finest ones possible (those that come closest to repeating the color, size, and graphic clarity of the original). This is not always easy, particularly since truly fine reproductions are extremely expensive—and many distributors and publishers market terrible reproductions at somewhat the same prices.

How is one to judge the accuracy of the reproduction? Unless you are familiar with the original, or have ready access to it or superb reproductions, the comparison can only be relative. The source of the picture may be the best evaluative guide; there are reputable dealers who handle only the best. Their names are best secured from a local museum or through the experience of other librarians.

The librarian should be careful about buying packages of reproductions. As one experienced librarian points out:

One inhibiting factor in the development of framed art collections is the unattractiveness of the instant collections of old master reproductions offered by library supply dealers. Spray coated with lacquer and sturdily framed, these are certainly durable, but they tend to be stale and sentimental in theme and have a definite commercial look.

High quality reproductions of works by established artists, in which the color fidelity and paper quality are the best available, form a good base for a public library collection when framed in a manner appropriate to the picture.[16]

There are several sources for quality reproductions. Two of the best known are listed below. The UNESCO catalog includes nearly 1400 reproductions of paintings that can be purchased from various sources, and a companion volume covers the period 1960 to 1969. *Fine Reproductions* is limited to some 1500 works available from the New York Graphic Society.

---

[16] Sue Radel, "A Circulating Framed Art Collection in Public Libraries," *Connecticut Libraries*, no. 3 (1977), pp. 20–25. Concludes with a list of some sources of quality reproductions.

ART REPRODUCTION LISTS

UNESCO. *Catalogue of Reproduction of Paintings prior to 1860.* New York: Unipub, 1972.

New York Graphic Society. *Fine Reproductions of Old and Modern Masters,* various editions. Greenwich, Conn.: New York Graphic Society.

Maps and Globes

Virtually all libraries have a selection of atlases (or access to maps in an encyclopedia), guidebooks and works associated with geography, travel, history, and business.[17] Beyond the familiar atlas one is likely to find other geographic materials: (1) Globes will be found particularly in school libraries or media centers. If not in the library itself, globes are located in geography or related departments. (2) Individual maps are more likely to be part of large map collections than found in the average library. (The exception, of course, will be the maps in the vertical file or the reference-desk maps covering the local community or region.) (3) Wall maps are to be found in related departments, but in school media centers there are usually special wall maps for display purposes in the school or individual classrooms. (4) There are likely to be "substitutes"—maps on slides, transparencies, and the like. (5) Finally, there will be different types of maps, atlases, and the like that cover not only the globe, but also the stars and the planets, special periods of history, and so on.

EVALUATION

The first consideration, unless you are in charge of a highly specialized large map collection, is how the maps are likely to be used by the faculty, students, or general public. Audience is a major factor, possibly even more so than with some other media, because user need will dictate both the number and the type of maps purchased. For example, in the typical public or academic library the map collection (except in the reference section) is not likely to be large because there is little call for such material that cannot be met through normal channels. Conversely, the Library of Congress, the British Museum, or the Harvard Library will have somewhat different criteria for selection—with an emphasis on completeness in many areas.

For most libraries acquisition is limited to approved atlases, some individual maps and globes, and possibly kits to be employed in geography lessons. Purchase is made through large map publishers such as Rand McNally or

---

[17] For a description of various collections, see Mary Galneder and Alberta Koerner, "Maps and Map Collections," in Grove, op. cit., pp. 148–170.

Hammond. Except for special map-library requirements, criteria for the selection of other media are applicable.[18]

MAP SOURCES

As the single largest map publisher, the United States government has a map for almost every need—from a chart of a local bay or river to the whole of Mars. These are listed (at least those available from the U.S. Geological Survey) in John Andriot's *Guide to U.S. Government Maps* (McLean, Va.: Documents Index, 1975, 2 vols.). Additional maps may be located in the *Monthly Catalog of United States Government Publications.*[19]

Local maps may be purchased, or often simply obtained at no charge, from a number of sources. Within the city the chamber of commerce is a likely beginning, as is the city planning office. At the state level the librarian should first inquire about availability of maps from the state library.

Globes and related equipment are handled by numerous jobbers, many listed in the media guides.

There are numerous bibliographies, several by the Library of Congress. The *Books in Print* approach is found in *International Maps and Atlases in Print* (2nd ed.; New York: R. R. Bowker, 1976), which lists 8000 maps and atlases from more than 700 publishers. One should not forget the maps to be found in the *National Geographic*, listed and indexed in the *National Geographic Index.*

The best source for ongoing information on maps is the *Bulletin of the Special Libraries Association, Geography and Map Division.*

Kits, Models, and Games

Kits are the most popular nonprint item in many elementary and secondary libraries, although rarely found in public or academic libraries.[20] There is no totally satisfactory definition of the term, but it usually is a combination of many elements (from nonprint to print). The typical education kit is directed to elementary and secondary school students, usually concentrates on a given subject or part of a subject area, and is a common feature in numerous classrooms. Librarians tend to classify as kits anything that will not neatly fit into another nonprint category. A kit can be anything that "works," that "sells," and meets the criteria of a useful educational tool.

[18] Katz, *Introduction to Reference Work* (3rd ed.; New York: McGraw-Hill, 1978), pp. 304–310, lists evaluative tests for maps and atlases.

[19] A more selective list will be found in the regularly published *Selected U.S. Government Publications.*

[20] See *Marketing, Selection and Acquisition of Materials for School Media Programs* (Chicago: RTSD Office, American Library Association, 1977). Close behind in popularity, according to this study, are filmstrips, cassette tapes, models, 8mm film, sound loops and transparencies, and reel-to-reel tapes.

Whatever the definition, kits are regularly reviewed in several of the education magazines and *Booklist* and are indexed in *Media Review Digest*. They are also listed in standard directories such as *Index to Instructional Media Catalogs*.

MODELS

A model is a replica of a real object, and aside from the familiar airplane, boat, and railroad models serves primarily to illustrate and support teaching. One may view the representative model with an eye to accuracy—in fact, the impact of an impressive model is in the microscopic details. Some models are the same size as the original; others are vast enlargements of the original —for example, models of sections of the human nervous system.

Various self-descriptive terms—cutaways, cross sections, dioramas (three-dimensional scenes with a background)—are applied to models. The librarian, particularly one in a school library, should be familiar with (1) the basic types and their advantages and disadvantages, (2) the needs of the teachers for models in classroom use, and (3) reputable sources of supply, which are listed in such basic directories as *Index to Instructional Media Catalogs*.

GAMES AND SIMULATIONS

Games certainly are familiar to every reader, as are simulations to those who have played "war games" on sometimes involved playing boards.[21] Their use is fairly well limited to school libraries as an extension of the classroom. They may be purchased from reputable dealers listed in *Educators' Purchasing Guide* and *Index to Instructional Media Catalogs* and other directories, always after consultation with the teachers who will be using them in the classroom.

The basic, although dated, guide to games is Jean Belch's *Contemporary Games* (Detroit: Gale Research Company, 1973, 1974). This two-volume set includes an annotated bibliography about specific games and their uses (in the second volume) and lists some 900 games in the first volume. The listing gives vital information, from age level to the names of designers. The bibliography is an excellent source of further information about game sources. For a more current list of sources see the "Games, Toys, Play, Simulation" section of "Mediagraphy: Print and Nonprint Resources" in the latest edition of *Educational Media Yearbook* (New York: R. R. Bowker). The 1978 edition lists more than a dozen other sources, from *Serious Games* (New York: Viking, 1970) to *Thinking Games* (Ottawa: Ontario Institute for Studies in Education, 1975).

---

[21] Simulation is used by most librarians as synonymous with games, although an expensive, large-scale simulation (as for learning how to drive a car, or even learning how to fly by night in a dummy cockpit) is definitely more than a game. Simulation (such as practice in the library reference interview or role-playing) is also a method of teaching that may or may not require formal materials from the library.

These materials may be checked in *Media Review Digest*, where they may be listed under a variety of subject headings, including "manipulative materials." From time to time *Booklist* and some of the educational magazines have lists of games (see issues of *Previews*, for one). Several magazines concerned with simulations (*Simulation and Games*, for instance) are listed and annotated in Katz, *Magazines for Libraries* (3rd ed.; New York: R. R. Bowker, 1978).

Realia

Realia—"real things"—can be just about anything from plant specimens to playing cards to relics to live animals. Realia were the horror of museum directors for years; all too often community benefactors proudly presented to museums (and sometimes to local libraries) bits of realia that ranged from stuffed skunks to elk heads to dioramas of sometimes moth-eaten birds. Things are a bit more orderly today, and realia are fairly well confined to natural history museums and school libraries.[22]

If one gives a broader definition to realia, it may include such things as tools and high-fidelity equipment as well as film projectors and microform readers. Where this definition is understood, the public library very well may take an active interest in the materials. (Some librarians include in realia almost anything from games to filmstrips.)

Commercial firms that sell realia, usually in kit form, to school media centers may be located in standard directories. These kits usually are well planned, containing materials that will add to students' understanding of, say, various uses of woodpulp or what might be found along a stretch of local beach. Museums are other good sources. For example, the American Museum of Natural History in New York issues lists of replicas of fossils and animals.

In both tactile and visual aspects, good realia are important for the educational experience. They can, however, be a headache for librarians, who must not only select them, but must also find a way to store, classify, and circulate them. Little wonder, then, that many librarians prefer to "forget" realia, assign them to the province of classroom teachers, or, at best, quickly arrange them in static exhibits that merely fill space and gather dust.

One way to avoid the problem is to limit purchase to basic realia for classroom use and then prepare a file of places in the community (museums, other schools and larger libraries, individual collections, etc.) where realia may be seen and examined when there is a specific need. This requires a bit of field work by the librarian, who should closely examine the realia shown before including them in the file.

---

[22] Some public libraries deal with realia insofar as they supply tools, from sewing machines to strobe lights, to the public. See J. Eisner, "A Full Service Library," *Unabashed Librarian*, Winter 1974, pp. 6–7. Realia is a subject in the *ALA Yearbook* (Chicago: American Library Association, since 1976) and the article offers a brief overview of current developments.

Evaluation of realia depends, of course, on what one declares to be realia. A good beginning is suggested in the January 1, 1977, issue of *Booklist* (pp. 671–674) and subsequent issues. Here a committee of the American Library Association gives a rationale, criteria for selection, and an annotated list of some realia that may help the beginner understand what the term means.

Part Four

SELECTION AND CENSORSHIP

14
Censorship

Two kinds of people appear comfortable with the problems of censorship: the dedicated censor and the dedicated civil libertarian. Each group makes convincing arguments for its cases, attracts followers as well as foes, and rarely has any self-doubts. Most others, including the majority of librarians, find a discussion of censorship tumultuous, requiring as much self-knowledge as emotional control. It is a debate without winners, and the faster the arguments go the faster the nonconclusions arrive.

Consider the classic question: Is selection censorship? Is censorship little more than a euphemism for selection? The censor may answer "yes," but anyone who takes issue with censorship is forced to make distinctions that are not likely to be logical to the censor. Still, the problem must be faced, if only to insure the ability of the librarian to ward off the censor's more persistent dialectic.

Selection Is Not Censorship

The problem is a matter of a logical equation. The censor rejects. The selector rejects. Therefore, they are one and the same. There have been some fancy efforts to defeat this equation, or at least point out it is not entirely logical.[1]

The censor makes a career of rejection. The selector does reject, but makes a career of acquisition. Not only is this a practical difference, it is a major difference in attitude. One may say, with some conviction, that the censor approaches materials with a negative viewpoint (what can be found that makes this item unworthy of a place in the library?). The selector is positive, is seeking the qualities that make the item acceptable.

The selector is aware of the multifaceted nature of evaluation, particularly

Basic difference ATTITUDE
censor – negative
selector – positive

[1] Still the most useful article on this subject is Lester Asheim, "Not Censorship but Selection," *Wilson Library Bulletin*, September 1953.

of the fact that an item must be judged on two counts: (1) its intrinsic quality or lack thereof and (2) its likely contribution to the community served by the library. The censor, aware only of what makes an item unacceptable, has certain key words, phrases, and opinions that trigger a thumbs-down decision.

Selection is a complex, intellectual affair. Censorship tends to be simplified and rather emotional. However—and this is important—it is a gross error to think of censors as merely fools or cranks. Many have standards quite as high as the civil libertarian's; many are as intellectually able to make judgments.

Possibly the most crucial attitude that separates censor from selector is the censor's denial of the right of individual choice. The selector gives the individual every opportunity to be heard, to influence selection. In fact, a good part of selection is awareness of what the community wants, even when those wants may be foreign to the desires and interests of the librarian.

The dictionary clearly distinguishes between the two poles and in so doing indicates certain aspects of both censorship and selection. A censor is "one who supervises conduct and morals, as an official who examines publications or films for objectionable matter, who deletes material considered harmful to the interests of [an] organization.[2] Selection is to choose for "special value or excellence"[3] and is synonymous with such terms as "discriminating" in taste and "choice." Synonyms for censor include "excise," "delete," "cut out," "purge," "purify," and "restrict." Educated society, by implication, would prefer selection to censorship, informed choice to arbitrary restriction. There is something censorious in being a censor.

Further differences between the two is the matter of certainty. The censor is inclined to think another synonym for censorship is infallibility; the selecting librarian is the first to admit a lack of it.

Censors know what the community should not read, view, or hear and are willing to enforce that judgment on the community by refusing its members access to the materials. Selectors think they know what the community needs and wants and are willing to test that judgment on the community by not buying certain materials. A major however: the selector, unlike the censor, is willing to admit error, willing to be shown that the rejected item should indeed be purchased.

For example, the librarian may reject Victoria Holt's novel *My Enemy the Queen* on the grounds it is intrinsically poor and there is no one in the community interested in reading the book. When the title is requested by two or three people and reaches the best-seller list, then the librarian should admit to a mistake and buy or otherwise obtain the title (possibly by rental). The censor may reject the same title (although this is unlikely) for too-explicit sex scenes. Public pressure, coupled with the best-seller list, will

---

[2] *Webster's New Collegiate Dictionary* (Springfield, Mass.: G & C Merriam Company, 1973), p. 180.

[3] Ibid., p. 1047.

mean nothing. The scenes are still in the book, and no matter how many millions want to read it, it is not to be in the library.

The library should take as its principle that it is the neutral carrier of information, entertainment, and culture. Material should be evaluated on the standards repeatedly enumerated in this book. No title should be excluded solely because of its content, nor should the librarian, no matter how well-intentioned, attempt to block purchase of materials solely because they carry objectionable viewpoints.

This lets the user determine what to censor or not to censor. Self-censorship is the only acceptable form of censorship, but it cannot exist if material is precensored by the librarian.

Barbara Cartland and Victoria Holt are two of the ten authors whose works have been banned from Copenhagen's 20 municipal libraries as not up to the standards of Danish readers. My informant Alan Moray Williams tells me that the other "unwanted" writers include Harold Robbins, Frank G. Slaughter and Holland's Hans Martin. The ban means that none of their books will be bought by the chief Copenhagen library which supplies the others. Existing copies will be discarded.[4]

The censor's extremes have been a source of lamentably true anecdotes, but too many librarians have not been far behind.

The Law

If there is no totally satisfactory way of isolating censorship from selection, what of the law? The law, after all, must surely deal with the problem. Unfortunately, however, the law is of little assistance. Freedom of expression is guaranteed by the First and the Fourteenth Amendments, but beyond this generality there is a broad area of interpretation. One may argue that the censor's affable assurance that he or she knows what is best for the community is in violation of the Constitution, at least when attempting to enforce her or his will on that community. Not so, say many local courts.

And the law itself gives little guidance. Interpretation of national legal decisions is broad, but material must be judged as it affects a normal human adult, not a deviant or a child. Library material must be evaluated on the whole, not in part (a word or a picture or a single scene), and cannot be considered out of order if it has redeeming social significance or artistic merit. To be deemed pornographic a book has to be "utterly without" any social value.

This was the situation until 1973, when the Supreme Court did a turn-around, modified the necessity of proving the book was "utterly without" social significance, and—more important—declared that guidelines should be established by the local community. Now each community can develop its own definition of what is to be censored or not censored.

[4]*The Sunday Times* (London), June 4, 1978, p. 35.

The stress on local community standards, reaffirmed by Supreme Court action in 1977, has drastically changed the obscenity laws in the United States. By April 1977 all 50 states had introduced, and 25 had passed, laws designed for obscenity control under the 1973 and 1977 Supreme Court decisions. Similar laws, at this writing, are pending or being acted upon in 22 states. Furthermore, many state school governing bodies adopted guidelines of a similar type for the local schools. In late 1976, for example, the New York State Board of Regents suggested that "each local school district should develop a materials selection policy that would reflect the thinking of the district."[5]

The use of local community standards, according to its library opponents, threatens the national accessibility of communicative materials through both commercial and noncommercial means, and thus a threat to each citizen's full exercise of the rights guaranteed by the First and Fourteenth Amendments.[6]

Some of the difficulty has been resolved by 1978 legal rulings which give the state primary right over local communities in determining "community standards." Still, this is far from clear for all areas.

The problem for librarians is that, depending on the community or state, the definition of obscenity may be different, and a book acceptable in one community may not be so in another. As a result many librarians are reasonably certain to omit materials that under any interpretation may be declared obscene.

Typical of confusion over law and censor is the Plainview, Texas, situation where the public librarian purchased six titles on sex and marriage, including three best sellers—Alex Comfort's *More Joy of Sex*, *The Redbook Report on Female Sexuality*, and the feminist handbook *Our Bodies, Ourselves*. The books were purchased, according to the librarian, at the request of some users who, if they did not know the titles, at least expressed an interest in the subject matter. After some confusion and discussion the library board stated a policy that would place the books on an "adult only" restricted-access shelf. The librarian objected—and, as one reporter put it, the librarian is not likely to be rehired.

Many think this may be Judy Smith's last year as librarian, because a few powerful people are asking the same question that [a user] asked last fall: "How did these books get into our library in the first place?"[7]

Throughout the whole affair, the city council and the courts, typically, stayed clear of the controversy. The issue was (or will be) decided in public meetings by citizens and the librarian. So, while laws do exist to protect the library from gross cases of censorship, in general the average censorship

---

[5] *The New York Times*, October 30, 1976, p. 27.

[6] National Commission on Libraries Resolution, in *College and Research Libraries News*, December 1977, p. 332.

[7] "Deviate Sex in Plainview," *Texas Monthly*, August 1978, p. 70.

case never gets to court, is decided outside the law by public opinion—or at least by that part of the public interested and vocal enough to participate.

L. B. Woods found the expressed reasons behind censorship efforts in libraries ranked as follows: Obscenity, 15.7 percent of the objections; related to this: sex and nudity, 12.9 percent, language, 12.7 percent, morality, 3.3 percent. Second in importance: political, 13.4 percent; followed by racism, 8.6 percent (divided between both pro and antiracism attacks), and religion, 5.9 percent (both pro and antireligious). Violence was far down the list, only 1 percent. Objections that were less than 3 percent of the causes for censorship include drugs, war, abortion, bias or inaccuracy, and poor quality.[8]

The Case for Censorship

Why is there so much interest in these topics by censors? First a general answer. In every case censors justify themselves with numerous familiar arguments.

1. Censorship is necessary to protect society and the individual from immorality, violence, political subversion, and other evils that threaten the citizen and the social fabric of the country. For example, consider why pornography must be banned:

a. Pornography coarsens life: the downtown areas of many cities are spotted with porno bookstores and movie houses that turn the neighborhood into a miniature slum of bad taste.

b. Pornography causes a breakdown in morals, the family, and hence society.

c. Pornography hastens unacceptable behavior: the reading of book X or seeing movie Y will encourage the reader or the viewer to be promiscuous.

d. Pornography trivializes life, and sex in particular.

e. Pornography is an exploitation and brutalization of women and, to a lesser extent, men.

If one accepts any of these arguments as fact, there is little reason to debate the necessity of censoring pornography.

Consider, too, violence. Violence on television should be censored because if only one in a hundred television viewers should be influenced to commit a crime of violence by watching television, it would add up to many thousands of cases. To censor television violence is simply to save lives.

2. Censorship is required when social opinion lacks force. Where a community has neither the laws nor the will to do anything about the corruption of that community (say the X-rated movie houses that destroy a downtown area), it is the duty of the censor to take action.

3. Censorship is only another way of protecting minorities from the

---

[8] "For Sex: See Librarian," *Library Journal*, September 1, 1978, p. 1566.

abuse of the majority. Racism, sexism, and other isms in books, magazine articles, and television shows should be censored because each works toward the destruction of the human dignity of individuals.

Finally, censorship is only the recognition that freedom does not necessarily give the individual the right to act wrongly. There are laws to protect the community from the bad driver and the murderer. There should be laws to protect the community from the equally harmful media.

In summary, four factors are often considered as prompting the censor to action: (1) Family values are challenged, particularly at the sexual, moral, and recreational level. (2) Political stability is threatened because the publishing of something or the free expression of an idea may bring down the government. (3) Religiously proscribed practices such as abortion and birth control will become unrestricted. (4) Minorities are seen to challenge the family, political, and religious structure.[9] Actually, all of these tend to flow together in the thinking of the assertive believer in censorship.

Turning attention to the library, the censor may misunderstand the role of the library in society, at least from the point of view of the librarian:

[The censor] may fail to see that the library fulfills its obligations to the community it serves by providing materials presenting all points of view, and that it is not the function of the library to screen materals according to arbitrary standards of acceptability. The censor may think that it is the role of the library to support certain values or causes, which are of course his values and his causes. . . . The censor may not understand that his request that certain works be labeled or restricted would, if fulfilled, lead to an abridgement of the rights of other library users.[10]

There are numerous other points to be made for censorship, but for a moment let us examine the other side. Why are so many people, including the American Library Association, directly opposed to censorship?

The Case Against Censorship

The primary argument against censorship is logically practical: in a democratic state it simply is inoperative. The classic example is the effort to censor drink by coercion. Prohibition did not work. The local and national laws against certain forms of pornography in the years before the 1960s failed because anyone with any knowledge of books could readily locate any banned title, as he or she could get a drink during Prohibition.

This is not to dismiss censorship as of no danger. It can be a nuisance and has cost librarians their jobs as well as weeks of loss of sleep. Some people have gone to jail, and will continue to be willing to be jailed. Others have spent thousands of dollars defending themselves against censorship. The fact

---

[9] *Intellectual Freedom Manual* (Chicago: American Library Association, 1974), part 4, pp. 21–22.

[10] Ibid., p. 22.

that censorship does not work on any national level has not deterred local censors from full operation.

The more frequent <u>arguments against censorship,</u> which rarely if ever sway the determined censor, should at least help swing the undecided to the side of the librarian:

1. Those who believe in the ultimate responsibility of people to make their own free choices will reject anything that limits those choices. Censorship implies that people cannot judge for themselves, an antidemocratic notion.

2. Censorship is dangerous because most censors are not qualified to rule for others. This is the most telling case against censorship, for no legislative or judicial body has been able to arrive at a plan of action, or even a definition of pornography acceptable to even a majority of people.

If censorship is really to work—and here I urge a rereading of Milton's *Areopagitica*—the censors must begin by cataloguing and proscribing all scandalous works already in print, prohibit the importation of all foreign writings until they have been examined and approved, expurgate those works that are partly useful and excellent and partly pernicious, and require all new materials to be submitted prior to publication. Such arduous tasks require censors of unusual quality and diligence, and very many of them to boot. Where will we find them?

By the very nature of the task they are likely to be, as Milton argued, second- or third-rate minds, "illiterate and illiberal individuals" who refuse their sanction to any work containing views or expressions at all above the level of "the vulgar superstition." Men and women of worth would obviously refuse such an assignment as tedious and unpleasant, and as an immense forfeiture of time and of their own studies. Such censors as we would be likely to get would be a constant affront to serious (for I worry not about scurrilous) writers, and could only do more harm than good.[11]

3. Despite laws and judicial decisions, pornography and other objectionable materials and ideas continue to circulate. Inoperative laws simply hasten disobedience of the law and a breakdown of society.

4. One must decide what is good or evil on one's own, not with the assistance of a censor. Robbing the individual of the right to even make wrong choices, at least at the intellectual level, is a serious moral curb.

5. To bar questionable material from the library, and particularly the school or academic library, is to undercut the purpose of education. Censorship will not deny an individual material that be found at almost any local newsstand, but it will deny the student the right (under guidance) to analyze and evaluate the material—a function fundamental to education. One learns how to cope with evil and wrong-headed ideas by confrontation. The only way to grow emotionally and socially is to test oneself against foreign and sometimes hateful ideas. A student may need guidance, but not censorship.

[11] David Spitz, "The Problem of Pornography," *Dissent*, Spring 1978, p. 206.

Banning fiction of a certain type from the classroom is one of the surest ways to keep students from exercising and expanding their imaginations. Denied the opportunity to learn how to respond to all literature imaginatively—instead of simply accepting it—a student can lose the ability to handle real and potentially damaging events. The tragic outcome is that the myopia which characterizes the zealot's outlook may become reincarnated in the life of the student . . . barred from a literary work because it contains an "objectionable passage."[12]

6. Public judgment will eventually drive out the pornographic, the violent, and the unsavory because the public will not buy the books, read the magazines, watch the television or films. In other words, the classic argument goes, good will be triumphant because the public's taste is good. (Experience, censors might argue, shows differently, but this is hard to prove objectively.)

OBJECTIVE STUDIES

Neither the law nor the researcher is of much assistance in settling the basic debate between the censor and the defender of intellectual freedom. The censor believes reading may do harm to an individual. The defender denies this, or at most says the media are not likely to have any lasting effect on a person. Here the civil libertarian is fond of quoting the famous 1970 *Report of the U.S. Commission on Obscenity and Pornography* (Washington, D.C.: U.S. Government Printing Office).

The report, following a number of commission-sponsored independent research studies, concluded that there is no relation between criminal sex offense, other forms of crime, and juvenile delinquency and the use of pornography. Continued exposure to pornography results in satiation, not further interest. Established patterns of sexual behavior are not likely to be altered by pornography.

However, as more than one authority who tends to agree with the findings has pointed out:

The results must be accepted with more than the usual reservations, since the methodological difficulties of social-psychological research are compounded by the nature of the problem. . . . In addition none of the experimental studies assessed the long-range effects of pornography, and, for obvious reasons, no studies involved children.[13]

Many librarians are cautious about purchasing books, periodicals, or other materials that might be employed by people for violent purposes. For

[12] Jerzy Kozinski, "Against Book Censorship," *Media & Methods*, January 1976, p. 22, an article that resulted from one of Kozinski's books having been banned by a high school.

[13] Murray Hausknecht, "The Problem of Pornography," *Dissent*, Spring 1978, p. 194. For an analysis of the report see a special number of *Journal of Social Issues* (No. 3), 1973. See also *Newsletter on Intellectual Freedom*, September 1974, pp. 109, 135–137, and Victor B. Cline, *Where Do You Draw the Line* (Salt Lake City: Brigham Young University Press, 1974), which includes an essay by Cline on the presidential report.

example, the United States government at one time published in manuals for members of the armed forces detailed instructions on how to make bombs. The manuals have been incorporated into books such as the *Improvised Munitions Handbook*.[14] And the periodical for mercenaries, *Soldier of Fortune*, takes a less than liberal position in its editorial stance.

As with pornography, though, one cannot be objectively sure of the effects of violence on readers or viewers. Nor is there much help to be found in the literature; the Surgeon General's and National Institute of Mental Health reports in the early 1970s found TV violence had no harmful effects on youth. (Critics have pointed out the committee that submitted this report included five representatives from television out of a group of 12, and the television members were able to exclude from the committee anyone of whom they did not approve.)[15]

While the link between violence and reading (or viewing) has yet to be proved, one may have strong personal suspicions and convictions, but these should not interfere with a librarian's selection duties. One might logically object to purchase of the aforementioned magazine or book on arms, but at the same time would the librarian then have to screen all books for potential violence? This might lead to problems. For example, the most common complaint against children's books is not profanity, politics, racism, sexism, or disturbing words, but titles that indicate violence, even of the most modest variety.

At first, I expected to get only complaints on the sex education books or those children's books that more and more dealt frankly with themes of homosexuality, abortion, drugs and sexual awareness that had previously been No. 1 no's. I was surprised at how few of these complaints I received. Instead, I found myself defending "frightening," "disturbing," "menacing" and "violent" picture books. There was "Father Christmas"—the patron felt Santa's use of the word bloody was "very sarcastic" and would ruin a child's simple faith in Mr. Claus. "The Cat Came Back" taught cruelty to animals." "Fee Fi Fo Fum" had the word hell in it. "Let's Play House" was sexist, "Espiomondas" was racist, "I'll Protect You from the Jungle Beasts" condoned violence. "Super Sam and the Salad Garden" which contained only 10 words in its controlled vocabulary somehow managed in those 10 words to encourage lawlessness. The list went on.[16]

Censorship Problems

Some librarians make the error of simplifying the censorship struggle. The good guys are the librarians and the American Library Association, which defends the First Amendment, the right to read, freedom of expression. The

---

[14] Duncan Campbell, "Teaching Terror to the Right," *New Statesman*, June 16, 1978, p. 804. Campbell gives examples from a manual, concluding "It is astonishing that legislation does not prevent the open sale of such a compendium."

[15] H. J. Eysenck and D. K. B. Nias, *Sex, Violence and the Media* (London: Maurice Temple Smith, 1978), unfortunately a tract rather than a persuasive objective study. The authors assert that violence in the media is conducive to violence.

[16] Betty Gibb, "Book Selection . . . ," *BCLA Reporter*, Winter 1978, p. 2.

bad guys are those who take exception to the knowledge and wisdom passed to the librarians from the mountaintop of objectivity and fairness. This conclusion seems to be borne out when one examines what is most often under fire in libraries. Only boobs, or so it seems, could object to many of these titles.

A study of censorship from 1966 through 1975 found that: (1) *Catcher in the Rye* was first on the list, with 41 censorship attempts. As in many cases, a number of objectors admitted they had not read the book but objected on the grounds of the book's reputation for bad language and ideas. Other identified books, often found on lists of objectionable titles, include *Catch-22* (number 5 on the list), *The Grapes of Wrath* (number 6), and *Of Mice and Men* (number 8). (2) Racism and political activists scored high, with *Soul on Ice* coming in second (20 times the attack of censors), followed by third-place *Manchild in the Promised Land* and tenth-place *To Kill a Mockingbird*. (3) Young adult titles that make a point about such things as the horror of drug addiction ranked high: *Go Ask Alice* scored as the fourth most challenged title—"Sex and graphic description of the hippie life style [were] added dimensions in the book."[17]

Turning from school libraries and public libraries to colleges and universities, objectionable items include *Playboy*, *Evergreen Review*, both magazines, and such films as *The Devil and Mrs. Jones*, *Deep Throat*, and *Pink Flamingos*. "Political issues, primarily anti-Vietnam War views, were illustrated by objections to such books as *Why Are We in Vietnam?*"[18]

Books (55 percent) are by far the most popular item to be censored. In order of objection, others include textbooks (13.7 percent), newspapers (8.6 percent), speakers (4.9 percent), periodicals (3.3 percent), films (2.3 percent), and art works (.6 percent).

YES, BUT . . .

Censorship cases are not always clear-cut and not always nicely divided between the good guys and the bad guys. Sometimes they switch sides.

The most devoted civil libertarian sometimes will draw the line at certain subjects, admit a singular lack of ability to discuss reasonably such things as pornography, racism, and sexism. "It's like a Jew trying to discuss *Mein Kampf* or a black trying to discuss the Ku Klux Klan reasonably."[19]

Those who would make exceptions and would ban certain types of sexist or racist titles argue that this is not simply a case of banning verbiage or graphics but of protecting people from an incitement to violence, particularly against minorities and women. It is claimed that pornography "is the

[17] L. B. Woods, "The Most Censored Materials in the U.S.," *Library Journal*, November 1, 1978, p. 2171.

[18] Ibid., p. 2172.

[19] Judy Klemesrud, "Women, Pornography, Free Speech: A Fierce Debate . . . ," *The New York Times*, December 4, 1978, p. D10.

propaganda of sexual terrorism" and that it is protected by men who become civil libertarians "when male privilege is confronted by . . . women."[20]

The "incitement to violence" claim for certain types of material is carried a step forward and sideways by the proposition that they are also filled with misinformation. Part of the selection process is to screen out wrong information where possible, so blatant examples of misinformation about race, sex, and the like should be banned from the library. If one agrees that librarians are competent to make judgments about the accuracy of information, why, it is argued, don't they eliminate material that is patently in error?

The problem becomes complicated when we move to a discussion of attitudes within books. Some of us feel strongly that there should be no sexual relationships outside of marriage. Others of us feel that love, caring, and a sense of responsibility toward the other person are enough. We, and the authors of sex education books, are entitled to our views and we can express them as strongly as we know how. However, we are not entitled to use our views to convey misinformation. In other words, an author may not suppress or distort information to support her or his view of sexual morality.

I am in complete sympathy with the ALA Intellectual Freedom Committee's concern that there are librarians who say, "I don't like the attitudes of this book, therefore its facts are wrong." Librarians who behave that way are not apt to lose any sleep over violating the Library Bill of Rights.[21]

The obvious problem, at least for devoted civil libertarians, is that what one person calls misinformation another may call opinion.

Essentially the dilemma for many librarians, no matter how they feel about censorship, is put by an English critic:

Question: Is censorship always a Bad Thing? Answer: Yes, always. Question: When is censorship a Good Thing? Answer: When it is censorship of what the Socially Committed disapprove of. Question: But if censorship in those circumstances is a Good Thing, how can it be said to be *always* a Bad Thing? Answer: Because a Bad Thing becomes a Good Thing when the Socially Committed approve of it.[22]

Here the "Socially Committed" is the librarian who feels he or she has the right to reject a book because it is sexist, racist, or, in fact, expresses any opinion thought to be antisocial. In other areas, from sex to art, the librarian may be perfectly objective, quite capable of accurately divorcing personal feelings from selection and evaluation. In fact, here the librarian would be the first to defend the freedom of choice. But when it comes to issues, such as a Nazi march in Illinois, the question becomes purely subjective.

[20] Ibid.

[21] Dorothy M. Broderick, "Racism, Sexism, Intellectual Freedom and Youth Librarians," *PLA Bulletin*, November 1976, p. 122.

[22] Bernard Levin, "The Censors Crawling Along Our Bookshelves," *The Times* (London), May 30, 1978, p. 14; continued on May 31, p. 14. A negative reaction against librarians in England who wish to purge the library of books that are racist, sexist, and the like.

The classic modern example is the defense of the National Socialists (Nazis) by the American Civil Liberties Union. The ACLU claimed (and won a case that said) the Nazis had the right to march through a predominantly Jewish community in Illinois. The parent who says the library should not buy a racist title would find it difficult to support the ACLU's action. Yet the ACLU was consistent in its efforts to save the First Amendment, even for the Nazis. At least that is the opinion of the courts, and of this writer, although about 30,000 ACLU members disagreed and canceled their memberships.[23]

The point about opposition to censorship is that one must be consistent. This often can be difficult, particularly when asked to defend the right of people such as the American Nazis to march and to publish. But as soon as exceptions are made a dilemma arises. First Amendment absolutists abhor pornography, racism, sexism, and the like, but all people have the right to read what they wish to read. One either is or is not committed to rights of individuals and cannot make exceptions without diluting the intent of the First Amendment.

Activists, including many feminists, say this is ridiculous, a lack of conviction, certainly a lack of sensibility about where sexism and racism may lead:

I would like to curtail expression of certain kinds of messages that demean and hurt groups of people. Because I am for nonsexist terminology in textbooks and against the media presentation of black men and women as shuffling, illiterate, lazy and inept, or of Jews as crafty and avaricious, I am also against porn movies, television programs, and magazines that portray women—and men—as victims who love their victimization.[24]

Civil libertarians reply that the risk is too great although they too abhor the materials. As Irving Howe puts it:

My response to pornography is not so much to be socially alarmed as imaginatively disheartened. I don't know what damage, if any, it does to society or the future generations. I don't know if it encourages rape or stimulates perversion. I don't know if it threatens the family. But when I walk along 42nd Street in New York City and pass the peep-hole joints, the hard-core movie houses, the shabby bookstores, I find myself growing depressed. Is *this* what humanity, or even a portion of it, has come to in the late years of the 20th century?[25]

And as David Spitz says, "Only salacious individuals are likely to deny that pornography is a serious problem."[26] Pornography is offensive, as are racist and sexist tracts, but they should not be censored.

---

[23] This case ran through the spring and summer of 1978. The executive director of the ACLU is Eryeh Neier, who lost nine relatives in a concentration camp.

[24] Cynthia Fuchs Epstein, "The Problem of Pornography," *Dissent*, Spring 1978, p. 203.

[25] "The Problem of Pornography," *Dissent*, Spring 1978, p. 204. Of course, libraries are not buying these types of materials, but the discussion is applicable philosophically.

[26] Op. cit., p. 205.

CHILDREN'S AND YOUNG PEOPLE'S RIGHTS

Often a line is drawn between what the child and the adult may read. Today everyone, from the ALA to most school organizations, agrees that young people have the right to objective information on sex, drugs, abortion, and the like. It is, however, a right that can be canceled by the parent. The New York State Board of Regents in its book-buying guidelines for schools notes that parents have the right to veto books for their children only, not for the children of others. But what about the child? Doesn't the child have rights that override the decision of the parent?

This is a vital question because where the child has made this decision, the library should have the material available. Also, of course, when parents do not object to what is read by the child the implication is that they are looking to the librarian's selection policy for guidance.

What type of material should be available? Kay E. Vandergrift sums up:

Can the student who wants information on the latest religious or political cults find this in our media centers? For a particular young person it might be just as crucial to find out about the "Moon children" or the "Jesus freaks" or Hare Krishna sect as it is for another to get the phone number of the nearest abortion referral center. And even more critical for some young people is the right to survival information, that is, such things as hard information on welfare, legal rights, medical aid, and suicide prevention. Even those of us who advocate the child's or the adolescent's right to all this information have a great deal of difficulty keeping our own biases from intruding in the selection process and thus limiting access to that information which the child or adolescent does indeed have a right to know.[27]

The argument for acceptance of all viewpoints, no matter how outrageous to the librarian or the majority of the community, applies to all adults. Many say it should not be applicable to children. Why?

Our lack of knowledge about its effect on children combined with the plausibility of arguments that they are at the greater risk . . . than adults favor retaining the present restrictions on children's access to it.[28]

I have thought long and hard and cannot come up with one item of information that I am not willing to see presented to children or young adults. But using that information to advocate limiting the options, opportunities, or life itself to any group of people is unacceptable. . . . When I talk about rejecting a book, it is either a juvenile or a teenage book. I would not limit the books for adults.[29]

Librarians view the rights of children and young people in different ways, although in most selection policy statements the libraries clearly state that

[27] "Are We Selecting for a Generation of Skeptics?," *School Library Journal*, February 1977, p. 42.

[28] Murray Hausknecht, op. cit., p. 197. He is talking about pornography, but the same argument holds for racism and sexism in books.

[29] Dorothy Broderick, op. cit., p. 123.

most collection policies state

✱ "the decision as what a minor may read is the responsibility of his parent or guardian. Selection will not be inhibited by the possibility that books may inadvertently come into the possession of minors."[30]

Who Is the Censor?

The censor concentrates on the library for many reasons. One of the most important is that when a library purchases a book, magazine, or film it is giving it an official sanction, sometimes making a questionable item socially acceptable. The dedicated censor sees this, rightfully, as a danger in that the librarian's sanction is undermining the ground on which the censor stands.

CENSORSHIP TARGETS

All libraries are potentially censorship targets—or perhaps one should say all "good" libraries are potential targets. The library without the least bit of character or controversial material is simply not a library.

In a survey of total number of censorship attempts in the United States by level of library and year, 1966–1975, L. B. Woods found that: (1) High school librarians are most likely to be harassed—386 cases reported. (2) The next most vulnerable type of library is a college or university—221 cases. (3) Public librarians are bothered less frequently—110 cases. (4) Librarians in elementary grades and junior highs have the least difficulty of all, 40 and 77 cases.

most likely targets

Censorship is on the increase. In 1975 there were 563 items censored in libraries, an increase of 47.8 percent over the previous year. (In actual number of cases, 57 were in high schools, 24 in colleges and universities, and 10 in public libraries.)

Censorship is more likely to take place in some states than in others. Washington, D.C., Rhode Island, and Vermont are six, five, and three times above the national average for censorship cases, while South Dakota and Hawaii have had no reported incidents of educational censorship. Overall, the librarian in New England is likely to be in for most trouble, as is a librarian in a heavily populated coastal region (the Southeast and Gulf Coast states excepted).[31]

THE CENSORS

The censors are primarily school administrators and trustees, parents, organized groups—and librarians. There are others. Going through only two

[30] Elizabeth Futas, *Library Acquisition Policies and Procedures* (Phoenix, Ariz.: Oryx Press, 1977), p. 6. Much more, to be sure, can be said about this subject and is likely to be highlighted in 1979 and beyond because of special attention given to children through the United Nation's Year of the Child. For a summary of this year see Frank McManus, "Year of the Child 1979 . . .," *Publishers Weekly*, February 26, 1979, pp. 105–106.

[31] "For Sex: See Librarian," pp. 1562–1566. The study includes public junior and senior high schools, junior colleges, and colleges and universities.

1978 issues of *The Newsletter on Intellectual Freedom* can be revealing.[32] The publication, backed by other reports, shows the following types of censors:

1. School boards Woods found that "Administrators and trustees account for 38.7 percent of all educational censorship attempts."[33] An example is Island Tree, New York, where the school board in 1976 pulled some 60 books off the shelves of the junior and senior high school libraries, subsequently banning nine of them.[34]

Another example: In late 1978 a northern California county school board banned five books by novelist Richard Brautigan (including *Trout Fishing in America*). The reason: the individual board members' moral, social, and political views are opposed to those of the author.[35]

2. Parents A book was ordered removed from the seventh-grade classroom of a Vermont school because a parent complained to a county state's attorney. The complaint concerned *Saturday, the 12th of October* by Norma Fox Meier, a book that concerns girls dealing with their first menstrual periods. (*Newsletter*, March, p. 31.)

Woods makes a point about parents and educational materials. No library is safe in that

the interrelationships of censorship as they affect classroom and library should not be ignored. Many cases that begin with the reading list in a school classroom are transferred to the library when someone checks to see if the "objectionable" item is on library shelves. The librarian who ignores these facts or who thinks he/she will never be affected by a censorship case is naive, to say the least.[36]

School boards and other governing bodies recognize the parent's request that an item not be given to their child should be honored. However, many draw the line at "any parent or group of parents to determine what materials may be used for pupils other than their own children."[37]

3. Concerned citizen groups In a Maryland high school an English teacher assigned such books as *Grendel* by John Gardner and *Tell Me That*

---

[32] Examples are from *The Newsletter on Intellectual Freedom*, January and March 1978; but similar findings appear in almost every issue. For additional cases see Ken Donelson, "Forty Iceberg Tips: The State of Censorship, 1972–1978," *California Librarian*, July 1978, pp. 32–38. Donelson lists and annotates 40 cases that show a wide variety of groups moving in on libraries as censors.

[33] "For Sex: See Librarian," pp. 1565–1566.

[34] *Wilson Library Bulletin*, May 1978, p. 687. At this writing the case has yet to be resolved. Interestingly enough, the students launched a class-action suit protesting the removal of the books, which included titles by Kurt Vonnegut and Bernard Malamud.

[35] "Seymour Lawrence and ACLU Fight Ban on Brautigan Books," *Publishers Weekly*, October 16, 1978, p. 32.

[36] "For Sex: See Librarian," p. 1566.

[37] Statement of New York State Board of Regents, *The New York Times*, October 30, 1976, p. 27.

You Love Me, Junie Moon by Marjorie Kellogg. Some 160 persons, the Concerned Citizens of Middleton Valley, objected to these titles and called for banning all books "containing obscene language or crude vulgarity." The superintendent of schools refused to go along with the request. The books still are in the library. (*Newsletter*, March, p. 39.)

Organizations of so-called concerned citizens may be local, regional, or national. Woods found that "The most notable change in sources of censorship during the decade related to the (number) of organizations that sprang up to fight materials considered objectionable."[38] Among the most active groups: the John Birch Society, PTA, American Legion, NAACP, Concerned Parents Committee, Citizens for Decent Literature, and Constitutional Heritage Club.

The usual procedure of the groups is to issue lists of proscribed books. Individuals are then asked to check libraries to see if any of the titles are on the shelves; where they find the proscribed books, they are instructed to ask the librarian to have them removed.

A legitimate request is to have books added. Some organizations properly complain that librarians fail to represent their point of view. For example, a frequent complaint of the John Birch Society is that such conservative periodicals as *American Opinion* and *The Review of the News* are not found in libraries. They should be, but of interest here is the suggested approach:

Appeal to the Librarian's sense of fairness and professionalism, noting that a Gallup Poll in January shows that 47 percent of Americans now consider themselves Conservative as opposed to 32 percent who think of themselves as "Liberal," yet the libraries virtually ignore the Conservative journals while carrying a full complement of "Liberal" magazines. Observe that all issues of both of our periodicals are available on microfilm from University Microfilm, Ann Arbor, Michigan. Note that *American Opinion* has been published continuously since 1958, and *The Review of the News* since 1965. Offer to drop by with recent issues, or to provide the address so that the library might write for sample copies and subscription information.[39]

5. Religious groups Clergymen from seventeen Richland, Texas, churches in early 1973 wanted to have *The Grapes of Wrath* removed from the school library because it was pornographic. (This is a popular title among all censors, not just religious organizations.)

6. Local police The police are more likely to interfere with bookstores, movies, and plays than with libraries. In Lexington, Kentucky, for example, the police tried to stop the showing of *Oh! Calcutta!* under a local ordinance a judge refused to hold as legal. (*Newsletter*, March, p. 41.)

[38] "For Sex: See Librarian," pp. 1555–1556.

[39] *The John Birch Society Bulletin*, February 1978, p. 25. The Society notes that one basic reason for exclusion of these titles is the fact that *Readers' Guide to Periodical Literature* does not index them; they are absolutely correct.

7. Legislatures and initiatives Decency in Environment Today supported and Washington state voters approved in 1977 a law that permits the padlocking of any establishment found to be a "nuisance"—anyone selling what the group believes to be obscene. (*Newsletter*, January, p. 3.)

8. Local or regional legislators Two members of a Maryland county governing council suggested the county libraries remove *Our Bodies, Ourselves* because it was obscene. No action was taken by the library. (*Newsletter*, January, p. 6.)

The Librarian as Censor

In a censorship battle there can be no neutrality, but many librarians solve the problem by exerting a type of censorship before the fact. They may call it "selection," but they have in fact selected to avoid potential difficulty.

For example, three high school librarians in Iowa, Michigan, and Illinois canceled subscriptions to *Car and Driver* because an article in the magazine attacked the federal 55-mile-an-hour speed limit. One librarian explained the cancellation: "The magazine is not conducive to accomplish our goal of teaching . . . respect for the law."[40] Actually, librarians tend to do more precensoring than taking material off the shelves once it is purchased.

Some librarians feel uncomfortable with the First Amendment, and, given the opportunity, would be happy to abridge it to exclude certain types of materials from the protection of freedom of speech. Librarians of the nineteenth and early twentieth centuries solved the problem neatly by embracing rather than shunning censorship. As Evelyn Geller and others have pointed out, "It is only recently that the word 'censor' became a term of opprobrium."[41]

Here is a teacher and former editor of *American Libraries* on the subject:

We know that in practice many librarians do not support the concepts outlined in the ALA program and its interpretive documents. There is also considerable evidence appearing recently to indicate that librarians do not support and understand the attempts to identify and refine the concepts and concerns embodied in the words "intellectual freedom" on the part of ALA and other state and local library groups. . . . And intellectual freedom is not popular with many except as a possible source of titillation in a conference program. The support for the Freedom to Read Foundation, the Intellectual Freedom Round Table, and sub-

[40] *The Newsletter on Intellectual Freedom*, March 1978, p. 30.

[41] "The Librarian as Censor," *Library Journal*, June 1, 1976, p. 1255. An excellent article on the history of censorship and American libraries. A similar argument for limited censorship in developing countries based upon the early experience of American librarians will be found in Rasu Ramachandran, "The Librarian's Commitment to Intellectual Freedom . . . ," *Libri*, December 1975, pp. 324–331. A broader view is taken by Richard Darling in his thoughtful "Access, Intellectual Freedom, and Libraries," *Library Trends*, Winter 1978, pp. 315–326.

scriptions to the *Newsletter on Intellectual Freedom* run at about ten percent of the ALA membership.[42]

The classic study of the librarian as censor is by Marjorie Fiske: *Book Selection and Censorship: A Study of School and Public Libraries in California* (Berkeley: University of California Press, 1959). The conclusion of this two-year survey (1956–1958) was that the most active censors are librarians, who avoid any possible trouble by not purchasing materials likely to cause difficulties. Nearly two-thirds of those questioned supported this cautious view of selection. Furthermore, 58 percent of the school librarians, 50 percent of the county librarians, and 66 percent of the urban librarians either "habitually" or "sometimes" avoided purchase of controversial or potentially controversial materials.[43]

Subsequent studies and surveys have substantiated the Fiske findings. Charles Busha's *Freedom versus Suppression and Censorship* (Littleton, Colo.: Libraries Unlimited, 1972) was a report of extensive study of Midwestern public librarians (1969–1970). Busha found only 22 percent strongly opposed to censorship; 14 percent were sympathetic toward censorship and 64 percent were neutral, although they tended to favor the American Library Association statements against censorship. He found that as the community increased in size, the attitude against censorship increased as well.

In a survey of Texas librarians, the same story was evident: 28 percent indicated they had practiced self-imposed censorship; 8 percent labeled materials; 15 percent had removed materials voluntarily; 29 percent said they would not risk their jobs in a censorship case.[44]

Then, too, there is truth to an accusation by a librarian often in difficulties over censorship:

People are embarrassed when someone says we have censorship problems. A consensus has been reached: there isn't really any intellectual freedom crisis, there are just crackpots on both sides; nice people don't pay any attention to them.[45]

[42] Gerald R. Shields, "Intellectual Freedom: Justification for Librarianship," *Library Journal*, Spetember 15, 1977, pp. 1823–1824.

[43] A variation on the librarian as censor is suggested by an experienced librarian: "How many librarians have experienced internal censorship problems in their technical services departments—either the material is being processed 'forever' or someone bypasses the selecting public service librarian and tells the director it is unfit for purchase? I've heard enough of these tales in young adult services alone to wonder if anyone would dare to submit replies" (Mary K. Chelton, letter to the Action Exchange, *American Libraries*, October 1978, p. 516). How reviews are employed in checking controversial material is covered in detail in Judith Serebnick, "An Analysis of the Relationship between Book Reviews and the Inclusion of Potentially Controversial Books in Public Libraries," *Collection Building*, vol. 1, no. 2 (1979), pp. 8–53.

[44] Hamilton Monroe, "The Texas Librarian as a Censor," *Texas Library Journal*, Winter 1978, p. 14. The entire issue is devoted to censorship problems.

[45] Gordon McShean, "Nobody Knows the Troubles I've Seen," *American Libraries*, June 1978, p. 321. McShean documents some of his problems with censors in his book *Running a Message Parlor* (Palo Alto, Calif.: Ramparts Press, 1977).

In a self-test, one librarian asks of others:

1. Have you, in re-evaluating your collection, removed a title that you considered racist or sexist?
2. Have you declined to purchase a book because it offended your personal tastes or standards?
3. Have you restricted access to an item because of its controversial nature?
4. Have you removed an item from your collection because of a complaint against it?
5. Have you screened your book acquisitions to avoid the purchase of controversial or potentially controversial books?

An affirmative answer to any of these questions reveals *you* as a censor, one who has violated the principle of intellectual freedom; a principle, moreover, which provides the underpinning for librarianship as a profession.[46]

Fighting Censorship

The arguments about censorship aside, what does the librarian do to prevent censorship problems, or once they arise what practical steps can be taken?

The best defense is a good offense.

Let people in the community know the selection policies of the library. *to prevent* Make a point of widely publicizing the criteria employed in selection. Make clear that those who want to add anything to the library are free to suggest *P.R.* additions. Try to create an atmosphere in which anyone will feel free to discuss selection policies and problems with the librarian. Public relations is advisable on as broad a scale as possible. Make the library a viable part of the community by participating in local affairs and events.

Beyond the obvious, the librarian should have a firm understanding of his or her own views of censorship and selection. If totally opposed to any kind of censorship, be able to argue this position from a point of strength—from knowledge of the practical and philosophical writings on the subject. Read extensively in the literature, and know the position of the censor as well as that of the defender of intellectual liberty.

If the librarian secretly feels the censor is right, the case is likely to be lost before it starts. If the librarian has no real feelings about intellectual freedom and censorship (and therefore is neutral), the case is probably lost. This is hardly to suggest that the strong-minded, well-informed, and equally intellectual librarian always will win, but the odds against winning are considerably higher when the librarian has both an intellectual and an emotional stake in the outcome of the case.

[46] Don Colberg, "Are Librarians Enemies of Intellectual Freedom?," *The Georgian Librarian*, no. 1 (1976), p. 5.

LITERATURE

Newsletter on Intellectual Freedom. Chicago: American Library Association (ALA Intellectual Freedom Committee), since 1952. Bimonthly.
Intellectual Freedom Manual. Chicago: American Library Association, 1974.
Busha, Charles H. (ed.). *An Intellectual Freedom Primer*. Littleton, Colo.: Libraries Unlimited, 1977.
Banned Books. New York: R. R. Bowker, 1978.

These are representative of only the more practical readings available to the librarian in the field of censorship. Some of them, such as those in the *Intellectual Freedom Manual*, are fundamental. While dated, the *Manual* contains the basic documents with which every librarian should be familiar: (1) The Library Bill of Rights and interpretations of the document—Intellectual Freedom Statement; nonremoval of challenged library materials; sexism, racism, and other isms in library materials. (2) The Freedom to Read Statement. (3) The School Library Bill of Rights. (4) Labeling. (5) Policy on confidentiality of library records, and several others. The librarian can update these statements by following the actions of the Intellectual Freedom Committee in the library literature.

Reviews of the statements are a constant concern. During the 1979 American Library Association midwinter meeting the Intellectual Freedom Committee devoted a substantial amount of time to reviewing, editing, and proposing revision of the Library Bill of Rights. (For a discussion and a copy of the proposed changes, see *Library Journal*, March 1, 1979, pp. 565–566.)

The Newsletter on Intellectual Freedom is a 20-to-24-page bimonthly report on: (1) national legislation and legal decisions likely to affect intellectual freedom, libraries, and censorship and (2) a running account of "titles now troublesome" from books to periodicals, television, films, recordings, and other materials. This keeps the reader advised of specific works under the censor's eye and what actions are being taken to protect the library. Much of 2 falls under the separate sections, which include "censorship dateline," "from the bench" (legal decisions), "is it legal?" (news of pending cases), and "success stories" (resolution of censorship cases). Each report ends with an "intellectual freedom bibliography" of articles, reports, and books published over the preceding two or three months. For a retrospective bibliography on censorship, see Maxin McCafferty's *The Right to Know* (London: Aslib, 1976). This includes nearly 700 citations, and while primarily applicable in the United Kingdom, some of the broader issues will be of interest to Americans. Note, too, that the 1972 Busha volume includes an annotated bibliography of censorship for 1950 to 1971.

The Intellectual Freedom Primer is a collection of seven articles on various aspects of censorship. There is a broad introductory essay and an article by the editor, and pieces on danger to freedom in the film, visual arts, and so forth. The work ends with a good piece on aspects of censorship research.

A collection of documents and excerpts from major censorship cases and legal decisions, *Banned Books* is an accurate, up-to-date overview of the subject. It is particularly useful for the long section on the legal status of censorship and includes many other suggested readings.

PRACTICAL STEPS

Once the librarian has both a practical and a theoretical appreciation of the questions of censorship and intellectual freedom, then other steps should be considered. The first, certainly, is the selection policy statement (see Chapter 1).

1. The library should have a written selection policy that clearly states the policy for selection, preferably endorsed by the library's governing body. If nothing else, such a policy helps "disarm crackpot critics; the accusations of local cranks seldom prevail when the library's operations are based on clear-cut and timely written procedures. . . ."[47]

Be as specific as possible, particularly about areas which as a librarian you recognize as likely to cause difficulty in the community. For example, if there is material in the library which you know is offensive to some parts of the community, discuss it in the policy statement and explain why that material has been and will continue to be purchased.

The statement should include the American Library Association pronouncements on censorship from the *Intellectual Freedom Manual* (along with current additions), supplemented with modifications suitable to the particular library. For example:

No materials shall be excluded from the collection because of the race or nationality of the authors, or the political, moral, or religious views expressed therein.

The library does not promote particular beliefs or views, but instead presents quality materials containing opposition views for examination by the public.

Selections will not be made on the basis of anticipated approval or disapproval, but solely on the merits of the work in relation to the building of the collection.[48]

While useful, a written selection policy is hardly a magic shield against censorship. As the editor of *Library Journal* put it:

A book selection policy, no matter how well thought out, cannot fight your battles for you. Policies are general and cannot cover specific titles. No matter how hard a library tries to keep a controversy in the fragile realm of principle and policy, its adversaries keep punching away on the Plain of Specificity. . . . A public response either for or against censorship is more effective than written policies. If you want support for free access to your collections for everyone, regardless of age . . . the labor and thought devoted to developing a written policy would be

---

[47] *Intellectual Freedom Manual* (Chicago: American Library Association, 1974), part 4, p. 4. The use of *crackpot* and *cranks* is questionable.

[48] Elizabeth Futas, op. cit., p. 167, 363, 365.

much more effectively used to establish alliances with groups of all persuasions in the community, and to publicize and provide good, responsive library service.[49]

2. Request the person who objects to an item to discuss the reasons privately with the librarian. Here two points are important: (1) The vast majority of people who make complaints are genuinely concerned and are not crackpots. They deserve respect and attention. (2) A good many people, given the opportunity to discuss a problem with another, solve the problem through the conversation. At a minimum the librarian is able to explain why the item is in the library and why the item should not be removed. During the conversation, the librarian must make every effort to listen—to hear out the person first. Try to be calm and as objective as possible. If the person wishes to interrupt your explanation, let him or her interrupt. Give as much time as necessary. If, and only if, this approach fails, move on to the next step.

3. Request that the person placing the complaint fill out the American Library Association's standard "Request for Reconsideration of Library Materials."[50] This procedure is usually written into the policy statement. For example, a typical wording would be: "Criticism or attempts at censorship of library-owned materials submitted in writing by those related to the [library] will receive a written reply from the librarian quoting the [intellectual freedom] policy. Cases of continued criticism will be referred to the Library Committee for decision."[51] Or simply: "Serious objections to titles owned by the library should be in writing. The library provides a form for such objections."[52]

The standard form asks for bibliographic data about the questioned material, name and address of the person who objects, and a key query: "Do you represent . . . yourself . . . an organization [name] . . . other group [name]." This in itself is often enough to turn back the censor. Beyond these basic queries come the essential ones: "To what in the work do you object (be specific, cite pages)? Did you read the entire work? Are you aware of judgments of this work by literary critics?" and five more as precise questions.

If the complaint actually is filed—and in most cases it is not—the librarian should follow through with steps to insure that the person launching the complaint receives a speedy reply.[53]

It is worth repeating that the written complaint form should not be used until there has been a personal interview with the individual making the complaint. Even people who fill out a form are likely to feel coerced. They may already be angry, and they are likely to attempt revenge by bad-mouthing the library throughout the community.

[49] John Berry, "It's People and Politics, Not Policy," *Library Journal*, February 15, 1977, p. 433.

[50] *Intellectual Freedom Manual*, part 4, p. 12.

[51] Elizabeth Futas, op. cit., p. 167.

[52] Ibid., p. 365.

[53] *Intellectual Freedom Manual*, part 4, pp. 13–14, details steps to take in answering a complaint. See also the aforementioned policy statements.

At any rate, it is of considerable importance that when a complaint form is given an individual he or she be given time to fill it out at home, not forced to do so in the library. Also worth repeating: If the form is filed, it should be treated promptly and with the utmost courtesy.

4. In the silver-lining-to-every-cloud department the ALA backs into some solid advice: "A censorship attempt presents the library with a good opportunity to explain the philosophy of intellectual freedom which underlies library service in the United States."[54] It next suggests that if a would-be censor continues to press the library, the case should be given wide publicity if it appears it can't be settled without difficulty by the librarian and governing board. Inform as many potential allies as possible, and let them turn their collective attention and power on the censor. Allies normally include:

a. The newspapers and radio and television stations, but particularly the first because there is more space available and editors, no matter what their political views, normally take a strong, vocal stand against any threat of censorship. They are morally opposed to it, but, more to the point, censorship is too close to home: today the library, tomorrow the newspaper or radio station. They have a vested interest in keeping the censors in place.[55]

b. Community leaders who support the library and its governing body and who are likely to be convinced that the challenge to the library is a personal challenge to them and their support of the library and librarian.

c. A few select community politicians, especially those whose interests are likely to be in opposition to those of the censor.

d. Religious leaders in the community if they are likely to support the library cause, not the censor.

5. Have a list of names (with numbers and addresses) of those you may turn to for assistance in case of a censorship struggle. This list should be as available as the list for the fire and police departments, and it should be developed over a period of time. Don't wait until the censor strikes before charting the territory of assistance.

6. If in a school situation, call upon the National Council of Teachers of English and its many affiliates. Related groups include the American Association of University Professors—and any organization with a stake in a free and open library.

7. Look for ammunition for inclusion of materials by an occasional visit to local magazine and newspaper stands:

where [censors] can find materials which make the "objectionable passages" in school texts seem ridiculous. The students, whose protection is so earnestly invoked, have free access to these sources. A cursory review of local theaters will turn up films which portray violence and human destruction on a much more

---

[54] *Intellectual Freedom Manual*, part. 4, p. 24.

[55] As do, of course, the major library journals such as *Library Journal, Wilson Library Bulletin,* and *American Libraries,* who should be routinely notified. Their editors may be able to suggest further ways to do combat.

impressive scale than the "objectionable" passages in some school readings. Many a local supermarket offers boudoir confessional accounts in publications of questionable character, lubriciously illustrated, and placed conveniently near the checkouts for casual perusal if not actual purchase.[56]

8. Notify the local, regional, and state officials of the state library association. This organization may have a formal system for dealing with censors, or at least may give the support needed to draw the interest of those who can assist. Associated assistances may come from the state library, faculties of library schools and law schools, and certain specialists in the community who are concerned about censorship.

9. Notify the Office for Intellectual Freedom at the American Library Association in Chicago. They will assist with suggestions of how to handle the situation; if legal aid is needed they will work through the Freedom to Read Foundation (a separate corporation connected to the OIF). The Foundation will give legal advice and aid where it is deemed advisable.[57]

10. Call the American Civil Liberties Union. Not only will the Union give prompt and good advice on what to do in a censorship case, but it may come to the defense of the library. The ACLU has a number of useful booklets that outline steps to take to prevent censorship. Incidentally, librarians would do well to join this organization before the censor strikes.

11. Notify the publisher of the materials. If the challenge is thought to be considerable, the publisher may come to the aid of the librarian. At the very least, the publisher may supply supporting evidence for the questioned work.

Know when to compromise or to quit. Often an intelligent compromise is not a defeat. For example, Ervin J. Gaines, a former chairman of the ALA's Intellectual Freedom Committee and a champion of free access to information, was forced in 1970 to restrict access to alternative newspapers to those under eighteen years of age. He subsequently conceded a loss, but, at the same time, purchased even more such newspapers for adults. In explaining his action, Gaines said frankly: "It is folly to press too rapidly against substantial public fear and hostility. To ignore public opinion is to invite the kind of retaliation that would severely cripple the library's ability to operate."[58]

Economic pressures may be too great for the individual librarian to withstand the threat of the loss of a job. Here only the individual can make

[56] Kozinski, op. cit., p. 24.

[57] There has been some criticism that the legal aid is limited to national issues, not to assistance for local libraries, or that when the aid has been available it has been late or of limited value. See *Wilson Library Bulletin*, May 1978, p. 687, and *Library Journal*, June 1, 1978, pp. 1111–1112, and May 15, 1978, p. 1011. The local librarian cannot count on the foundation for automatic legal assistance, although it may give advice. A fuller explanation of ALA assistance will be found in the *Intellectual Freedom Manual*, in various issues of *Newsletter on Intellectual Freedom* published by the ALA Intellectual Freedom Committee, and in the *ALA Yearbook*.

[58] "Moderation in Minneapolis," *Library Journal*, May 15, 1971, p. 1683.

a decision, not a textbook writer (or anyone else). It is certainly a major consideration today, and one that has to be worked into the equation of fighting or not fighting the censorship battle.

Finally, be sure you understand yourself—why you continue to fight, why you never began the battle, or why you quit.

INDEX